Studies in International Institutional Dynamics

VOLUME 1

The Politics of Trade

The Role of Research in Trade Policy and Negotiation

Edited by

Diana Tussie, *Latin American School of Social Sciences and Latin American Trade Network, Argentina*

BRILL

DORDRECHT • LEIDEN • BOSTON
2009

International Development Research Centre
Ottawa • Cairo • Dakar • Montevideo • Nairobi • New Delhi • Singapore

This book is printed on acid-free paper.

Library of Congress Cataloging-in-Publication Data

The politics of trade : the role of research in trade policy and negotiation / edited by Diana Tussie.
p. cm. — (Studies in international institutional dynamics ; v. 1)
Includes bibliographical references.
ISBN 978-90-04-17278-4 (hardback : alk. paper) 1. International trade—Research. 2. Foreign trade regulation. I. Tussie, Diana.
HF1379.P667 2009
382'.3—dc22

2008044929

ISSN: 1874-2025
ISBN: 978 90 04 17278 4

International Development Research Centre
PO Box 8500, Ottawa, ON K1G 3H9, Canada
www.idrc.ca/info@idrc.ca
ISBN (ebook) 978-1-55250-400-0

CONTENTS

PART THREE

UNDERSTANDING INTERESTS THROUGH RESEARCH

PART FOUR

THE WTO: THE USE OF RESEARCH FOR GLOBAL COALITION FORMATION IN TRADE NEGOTIATIONS

PART FIVE

UNDERSTANDING EPISODES: IS THIS A NEW WORLD OF POST-ACADEMIC RESEARCH?

ACKNOWLEDGMENTS

As always in the case of editing a book one relies on the collegiality and generosity of many people and institutions. Our book does not stray from the norm. Many hands have helped in the conception of the initial project and the step by step preparation of the book. It is by a chain of coincidences that only my name has made it to the cover as sole editor.

Although I can only mention only a few of all the hands that helped I am nonetheless most grateful to all of them. In some cases the debt is such that I feel bound to record it here, and in this respect I should like to start by expressing my sincere thanks to the institution that conceived the initial idea and allowed the authors to come together, the International Development Research Centre (IDRC). Without exception our colleagues at the IDRC have given freely of their time and experience both in the initial steps and the subsequent steering, in particular, Fred Carden, Susan Joekes, Martha Melesse and Andres Rius. Not only have they read drafts but also helped to conceptualise how the methodology meant to be the underpinning of the book could be applied. In this regard, I must recognize a double debt to Fred Carden, who has helped us to understand the complex dynamics of policy influence, the limits of academics as speaking "truth to power" but at the same time, the power of research to improve policy ideas. John Young shared his extensive understanding with generosity and provided constructive critical comments when the original papers were first discussed at a meeting in Buenos Aires in 2006.

The book would not have been possible without the analytical and editorial incisions of Patrick van Zwanenberg, Jorgelina Loza and Pablo Trucco who time and again scrutinised drafts with diligence. Finally, it is high time to recognize the unlimited forbearance of all the authors who dealt with every round of comments in good spirits. I am very conscious of my good fortune in this regard.

Diana Tussie
Buenos Aires
November 2008

CHAPTER ONE

THE POLITICS OF TRADE: THE ROLE OF RESEARCH IN TRADE POLICY AND NEGOTIATIONS

Diana Tussie[1]

Policy makers and academics relate to each other in complex ways. Sometimes they do not relate at all. There have always been those in policy circles who are aloof to the products of research and who go about their business with only some evidence gathering along the way in a mostly do-it-yourself fashion. By the same token there have always been academics quite content in their ivory towers, working in priest-like fashion at their intellectual constructions regardless of the world beyond or the policy implications of their research. In the area of development policy such divorce was never paramount. The idea of development itself was born out of a sense that knowledge could make a difference. Its conceptual apparatus as well as the values, images, and emotions it attracted are bound to the idea of progress and the belief that knowledge would yield advancement. The domain of trade is an area that has lagged behind, but the once-pervasive segregation between policy and research is now fast retreating, as the ideological cleavages and paradigm wars of yesteryear began to subside and trade liberalisation has become enshrined as a development model in itself. Except for a small number of holdouts, virtually every country today is either already a member or seeking to accede to the World Trade Organization (WTO). Most countries are engaged in proliferating bilateral and regional agreements. The complexity of these issues virtually compels policy makers to seek out frames of reference and evidence for their policies. These frames of reference are cognitive maps that describe problems and map out realities; but they also have the power to create and shape realities. Since actors are not automata responding

[1] Research assistance by Jorgelina Loza and Pablo Trucco is gratefully acknowledged. Both were attentive eyes who contributed all along to bring the many strands together.

to structurally determined incentives, their ideas and the process by which they acquire them are extremely significant.

This book deals with two topics that are intertwined throughout. One thread addresses the research and policy interface, itself part of a wider debate on the role of ideas. The other analyses the context of trade liberalisation and how research has mobilised and legitimised change. Policy change involves cognitive maps, the articulation of a vision and of its companion instruments, as well as an understanding of the ways to make them viable. Research creation and deployment are of growing importance in the drawn-out contest of trade negotiations where competing agendas are at stake. After all, trade policy and negotiations are about who gets what and how.

Little attention has been paid to the manner in which research is produced, deployed, and taken up by policy in countries or to the specificity of the realm of trade despite the fact that trade reform has been consecrated as central to development. Moreover, the trade reform debate has largely taken for granted the role of research production, dissemination, and uptake. Most students of trade liberalisation acknowledge that a significant change in the intellectual landscape played a role in the wave of trade reforms that took place in the aftermath of the debt crisis and the collapse of the Soviet Union. However, the difficulty in measuring intangibles in the development of knowledge and research has prevented scholars from testing their influence in the wave of trade reforms of the past 20 years. While hypotheses based on economic crisis, democratisation, and conditional lending by multilateral agencies have been tested, knowledge-based explanations have been marginalised. Thus, this volume offers an analytical framework for the study of the episodes, highlighting the various contextual factors that may play a key part both in defining a trade problem and in influencing the solution. In what ways has research influenced episodes of trade policy change? There may be a growing body of literature on the use of knowledge in a variety of policy fields, but studies on how research has been used in the area of trade policy and negotiations have lagged behind those in some other areas, despite the fact that trade policy making presents many instances where public policy decisions must be made at well-defined points in time and often with more than one country involved, which could allow for comparative assessments.

The choice of *policy change* is key to this work, as it emphasises the capacity of research to modify a status quo and to catalyse the knowledge-based policy discussion to another level. To understand how this uptake occurs is to understand not only how knowledge is generated but also the effects of internal political contexts and external influences on the policy process. Each of the case studies in this book looks at the various contextual factors that play a key part in defining a trade problem and in influencing the solution. In this new era of post-paradigm strife, the telescopic focus has zoomed in to the microscopic view in order to shed light on the actual implementation of policies and concurrent negotiations. Altogether this volume shows the growing relevance of commissioned research by governments and by interest groups that support a particular cause in increasingly contested settings—research not as independent truth, but as instrumental and supportive to policy decisions taken on other grounds, opening a window onto a new camp of post-academic research.

This introduction will not attempt to summarise and assess the wealth of material contained in this book but provides the underpinnings on which the case studies have been constructed (see Chapter 10 by Fred Carden). It proceeds by first reviewing how the trade policy reforms, and indeed the trade policy revolution of the last decade, have been explained, focussing on the missing role of the ideational dimension and how available knowledge and specific actors use windows of opportunity to frame issues and graft agendas. It then fleshes out the questions on the use of knowledge and the research and policy interface that the book addresses. Any discussion of these intertwined processes cannot ignore the ways in which change is related to the production and movement of knowledge. Changes in trade policy are essentially distributive. They produce 'winners' and 'losers', both within and between countries, as well as between the short and long term. In addition, trade negotiations are characterised by reciprocity: if a concession is provided, something must be granted in return. The interests of stakeholders are prominent in any trade negotiation and therefore they have a direct impact on both research production and uptake. Thus, in the context of trade policy and negotiations, research and researchers swim in partisan waters. In practice, trade remains an inherently and overtly political process.[2]

[2] This particular feature of the trade field stands in contrast to findings on the role of research in the field of the Millennium Development Goals (MDGs), which could be understood as a global public good and therefore relatively less vulnerable to the sway of partisan fights (see Ayuk and Marouani 2007).

Part I: Paradigmatic Shifts

Trade Reform and Trade Negotiations

Neoclassical economics and liberal political theory have held that authoritarian governments would be reluctant to embrace trade liberalisation in the presence of a small but uncontested coalition of domestic interest groups that depend on protection for the maintenance of their rents. Yet there is substantive evidence that both democratic and authoritarian regimes have embraced protection to manage tensions that arise from the distributive consequences of international trade (Rodrik 1995). Protection has been common throughout history, and has been more pervasive than is warranted by liberal arguments. But there is little doubt that the massive transition from closed to open economies that swept one country after another into liberalisation in the 1990s gave liberal thought a new lease on life. The trade policy revolution inspired vast theoretical and empirical efforts to explain why so many trade reforms were implemented in such a short time. It was argued that democratisation and liberal trade policies in countries are correlated (Haggard *et al.* 1994; Milner and Kubota 2001; Przeworski 1991; Remmer 1990; Milner *et al.* 2000; Diamond and Plattner 1995; Smith *et al.* 1994).

A cluster of studies looked at the impact of economic crisis and the influence of international financial institutions as the International Monetary Fund (IMF) and the World Bank.[3] The terms under which life-saving loans were granted were not only of financial nature. In many instances changes in trade policy were responses to conditionality, whether in the form of broad structural adjustment loans or the more focussed trade policy loans from the World Bank. These were all debt-led trade openings. Crises opened a window for reform (Drazen and Easterly 2001; Drazen and Grilli 1990; Keeler 1993; Nash and Takacs 1998; Bruno 1993). Simply put, the costs of existing privileges and rents drew the economy to a halt and downfall (Haggard *et al.* 1994). The status quo became unsustainable.

Windows of opportunity are just that: opportunities. They cannot explain why the crises in the 1980s led to trade reforms while previous crises did not. In addition, for the crisis argument to explain trade

[3] The following chapters draw on Niño (2004).

reform by itself, it requires a latent policy alternative such as a first best policy. Unless such a policy exists, how can we anticipate which policy is adopted after the previous one fails? In the absence of a singular policy alternative or a first best option, the crisis hypothesis can only explain policy change, but fails to give any insight about the new policy adopted. The use of knowledge to select the subsequent policy choice raises further questions. The prevailing conventional wisdom recommends, in fact, avoiding the simultaneous implementation of trade reforms and stabilisation programmes aimed at reducing inflation or correcting short-term budget and current account deficits (Papageorgiou *et al.* 1990; Diaz-Alejandro 1975; Corbo and Fischer 1995). Whereas fiscal policies and monetary interventions are standard instruments of stabilisation programmes, trade policy affects resource allocation. If jointly implemented, trade liberalisation undermines price stabilisation by encouraging a policy of depreciation of the domestic currency. Alternatively, stabilisation undermines the sustainability of trade reforms by fostering a strong domestic currency that strengthens the bias against exporting and increases the current account deficit (Edwards 1989). In short, no research has supported the promotion of trade liberalisation reforms in the path to a crisis or in the aftermath of one. If the adoption of trade liberalisation together with stabilisation does not follow from research, then one must assume that the crisis has been an opportunity to push an idea that so far had been in background. Hence a good deal of the explanation lies in the power politics of knowledge rather than in the mere strength of the evidence.

When trade reform was not rolled back but continued unrelenting, regardless of the conditionality push, studies on the weight of policy-based lending then switched to the study of domestic preferences and institutions (see, for example Bates and Krueger 1993; Drazen and Easterly 2001; Edwards 1997; Haggard *et al.* 1994; Jenkins 1999; Krueger 1993; Milner and Kubota 2001; Przeworski 1991; Stallings 1992; Kahler 1992; Dollar and Svensson 1998; Sachs and Warner 1995). Research about how democratic institutions influence trade regimes has grown quite rapidly since then (Laird and Messerlin 1990; Rodrik 1995; Niño 2004; Jordana and Ramió 2002). In general, explanations based on institutions seem to fit situations where political actors hold different views. However, institutions may not provide enough structure to produce a unique equilibrium in certain situations. This is typically the case of uncertain environments, where lack of better knowledge about the effects of policies can lead to multiple policy decisions (Braun and Busch 1999; Goldstein and Keohane 1993). These accounts omit the significance of the power politics intrinsic in trade negotiations and the power politics of knowledge in influencing first the conceptual change and then the instrumental change to a scenario of permanent negotiations. In this context, research can serve as a focal point that allows members of a community to share analyses of the environment, the consequences of policies, and the legitimisation of change.

At the risk of belabouring the point, while policy can contradict prevailing conventional wisdom, the availability of research and ideas does not always produce policy change. There is plenty of evidence of research that only translates into action after being in the public domain for decades. Furthermore, situations where research findings do not translate into policy are just as common as situations where research shared and accepted by a minority becomes actual policies. Paradoxically, this lack of understanding discourages the study of how the construction of research itself influences policy and has relegated ideas-based explanations of trade policy to a subsidiary role. Trade negotiations on a reciprocal basis are driven intensely by knowledge. It is essential to avoid cleavage along simple moral or ideological lines in order to develop viable negotiating positions. Placing demands directly under the aegis of visibly ideological grounds tends to extinguish rather than create political synergy. Negotiations require a continuing series of moves on which some agreement can be developed even between partners of opposing camps. Research can matter, not simply because it can provide the substantive content of a country's demands in a trade negotiation, but also because it can serve as an important legitimising device. There are thus two distinctive, and sometimes mutually exclusive, purposes for research: the first is to shape to a country's negotiating agenda, whereas the second is to build consensus and legitimise the implementation of an agenda that has evolved as a result of several other, often political, forces (see the chapters by Rafael Gomez and Morley Gunderson, Clive George and Colin Kirkpatrick, Paul Mably, and Amrita Narlikar and Diana Tussie on the weight of legitimisation). The distinction between these two purposes of research assumes special relevance in the context of negotiations.

What Role for Ideas and Research?

To some scholars, ideas operate at a normative level by limiting the choices available to actors, while to others ideas operate at the cognitive level by providing new information in uncertain environments. Rational choice approaches to modelling ideas frequently use the former. These models treat ideas in much the same way as institutions that influence choice by constraining the options available to decision makers (Jacobsen 1995). Recent work on ideas as focal points incorporates elements of both approaches. Ideas constrain policy choices and induce unique equilibriums under uncertain environments (Braun and Busch 1999; Goldstein and Keohane 1993).

Peter Hall (1989) suggests that a new system of economic ideas will take hold in a society when there is a clear need for them, as well as a clear and congruent political dimension. He uses the concepts of 'viabilities' (economic, political, and administrative) to explain the reception of Keynesian ideas in the post-war decades. Peter Gourevitch (2005) provides a somewhat different schema. Synthesising the theoretical and empirical literature on the role and power of ideas and drawing on European and North American experience he selects three explanatory factors—which drive change. These are:

- first, the influence of epistemic communities, or key intellectual elites within a particular discipline, in this case economics;
- second, the extent of external pressures from the international community; and
- third, the role of internal political actors—especially those to whom decision makers listen.

In contrast to models of the diffusion of new economic ideas in industrialised countries, Gourevitch's approach emphasises that in some circumstances external pressures need to be considered as an active force (not a mere constraint) and that training in economics needs to be taken into account as a crucial transmission mechanism. Gourevitch develops the second driver—external leverage—under four headings: the U.S. administration, the international financial institutions such as the IMF, multilateral treaties such as the WTO and the North American Free Trade Agreement (NAFTA), and global market actors. Their influence can be considered as part of that of the epistemic community of economists: the leverage arises from their ability to influence economic outcomes through access to research, finance, and markets.

The problem with ideational arguments arises from the fact that the availability of ideas does not alway produce policy change. While institutions may produce regular and predictable patterns of behaviour, there is a perception that ideas only influence political processes under certain circumstances. This situation has led many scholars to view ideas as 'hooks' selectively used by political actors to further their interests (Shepsle 1985; Jacobsen 1995). According to this argument, the problem with ideas-based accounts is not that they do not explain how ideas influence policy, but that they fail to predict when. Prediction is possible if we are able to identify *ex ante* the interests of those who use ideas as hooks. The production of research and the chains of transmission to enable hooking remain unquestioned, treated as the luck rather than the skill of deep-sea fishers.

In short, the third factor—domestic politics—holds the balance and can make a substantial difference. The case studies in this book are set at the level of domestic politics and in-country conditions and look at the interaction between in-country research and globally produced and circulated knowledge. In much mainstream literature, knowledge is conceived as a product travelling freely and that the transfer of knowledge occurs in a political vacuum. From discussions of international best practices to initiatives such as the Global Development Network, research is often packaged as a value-free technical entity that can be delivered untouched as a development solution.[4]

Strands of Research: Is There a Difference between Ideas and Research?

In the context of analysing policy change, Carol Weiss (1979) suggests grouping research into three main categories: research as ideas, research as data, and research as argumentation. Although these are ideal types, the breakdown is useful when examining when and how research contributed to an episode of policy change.

- Research as an idea exists in a diffuse form, and can be equated to the particular beliefs and principles held by a large number of people. As capacities these enable certain kinds of action or 'ways of being in the world'. Ideas can be traced to epistemic communities. This category of research is usually brought to bear when a broad (or conceptual) policy direction is sought: in the realm of trade, the initial turn to trade liberalisation, or the acceptance of a major

[4] For a discussion about the Global Development Network, see Stone (2000).

negotiation that will change the given structure of incentives. Here the research contribution is often over long periods of time.

- Research as data provides answers to the 'real' questions that preoccupy policy makers, such as 'how far should I go in opening'—answers that cannot be deduced form the beliefs and principles. In the realm of trade, such research can play a role to guide the choice of instruments at a certain point in the decision-making process. The product of such research is often put forward in rational, technocratic terms and is aimed at addressing an existing policy problem.
- Research as argumentation emerges when it is employed in advocacy; it is brought to bear to advance a specific cause.

The chapters in this volume cover all three categories (see Table 1–1). For the purposes of this study, we adopt a broad definition of research to encompass any systematic exercise to increase the existing stock of knowledge. In the context of trade, this may include various forms of knowledge generation, such as academic research conducted at universities, policy briefs and papers from research think tanks, critiques by advocacy groups, and consultancy reports, as well as statistical analyses of trade flows conducted by national statistical institutes. Such research may therefore be conducted by a variety of individuals, including academics, policy consultants, researchers in major international financial institutions, advocacy groups and government statisticians.[5] The initiation of a policy tends to be more idea and advocacy intensive. As the policy becomes embedded the need for data takes the lead, and research becomes more demand driven with a short-run dictating the need.

Policy Communities: Does Geography Matter in Trade Negotiations?

Prevailing ideas may be an important determinant of policy choice and persistence. Scholars have offered arguments with respect to the power of broad visions of reality, or epistemes, that provide the assumptions from which policies follow and shape the pattern of politics along time. Peter Haas's work (1992) on the role of international epistemic communities illustrates how the transnational collaboration of 'professionals'

[5] There is a growing literature on the subject of research utilisation involving the International Development Center (IDRC) and the Overseas Development Institute (ODI) as well as the Economic and Social Science Research Council (ESRC) among others.

Table 1–1: Classification of the Episodes

		Type of Policy Change	
		Instrumental Changes	Conceptual Changes
Categories of Research	Research as Ideas		Canada–United States Free Trade Agreement of 1989 (Chapter 2)
			Establishment of the Capital Goods Protocol between Argentina and Brazil (1985–88) (Chapter 4)
			Shift in India's position on trade facilitation from an inward-looking defensive approach to an outward-oriented approach (Chapter 7)
	Research as Data	North American Free Trade Agreement of 1993 (Chapter 2)	
		Common External Tariff of Mercosur (1991–94) (Chapter 4)	
		Most favoured nation tariff reductions (Chapter 6)	
	Research as Argumentation	Hong Kong ministerial of the World Trade Organization in December 2005 (Chapter 3)	Nigeria's adoption of the Common External Tariff of the Economic Community of West African States (Chapter 5)
		Ministerial summit of the Euro-Mediterranean Partnership (Chapter 3)	Egypt–European Union Partnership Agreement (Chapter 6)
		Internal consensus among G33 countries (Chapter 9)	Effective participation in rulemaking in the World Trade Organization (Chapter 8)
		Consensus in the World Trade Organization (Chapter 8)	

Note: The types of influence in this table are drawn from Carden, Neilsen, Smutylo *et al.* (2002).

can shape policy preferences and are applied to problem solving. The term epistemic communities refers to a congregation sharing the same world view (or episteme). It is an international network of professionals with recognised expertise and competence in a particular domain and an authoritative claim to policy-relevant knowledge within that domain or issue area. The professionals in an epistemic community have a shared set of normative and principled beliefs: common casual beliefs, which are derived from the analysis of practices leading or contributing to a central set of problems in their domain and which then serve as the basis for elucidating the multiple linkages between possible policy actions and desired outcomes. They also share notions of validity and a mutual policy enterprise. The policy ideas of epistemic communities generally evolve independently, rather than under the direct influence of government sources of authority, but they are in close contact with policy events. The inclusion of some academics in state policy-making bureaucracies or in the decision-making process further entrenches the influence of the knowledge-based community (see Chapter 6 by Ahmed Farouk Ghoneim). It is the political infiltration of an epistemic community into governing institutions that lays the groundwork for a broader acceptance of the community's beliefs and ideas. The result in turn may be the creation of the proper constructions of reality with respect to a particular issue area as well as mutual expectations and a mutual predictability of intention. Members of international epistemic communities can influence state interests either by directly identifying them for decision makers or by illuminating the salient dimensions of an issue from which the decision makers may then infer their interests. Within this framework, epistemic communities are international sources of policy innovations. Economic and political networking allows them to control the channels by which these innovations diffuse and to become the torchbearers of new ideas, setting standards for some policies and freezing out others as wrongheaded.

The reform of trade policy can be viewed as a process by which intellectual innovations were carried out by domestic and international organisations and were introduced into the policy process to become the basis of new or transformed domestic interests. Likewise, under specified conditions, international politics can be seen as a process by which innovations are diffused to become the basis of new or changed international practices. While the proliferating reforms of the 1990s can be explained by the influence of hegemonic epistemic communities, trade negotiations cannot be explained away under the same rubric. They require more interest-based problem solving and hands-on research. Agenda setting, assessment, and the construction of counter-proposals involve continuous evaluations and filtering to suggest alternative modes of actions. Research is more a servant of policy-in-the-negotiating-mode rather than its master.

Negotiations require the construction of a 'maximum aspiration' position as well as a reserve position, which will be the lowest acceptable outcome. A negotiating strategy includes a comparison of the potential advantages of a negotiated solution with alternatives available away from the negotiating table. The strategy of walking away should be based on sound analysis of the likelihood of securing a better or more acceptable outcome through negotiations. A negotiating party can develop the strength and availability of what is often called a BATNA (best alternative to a negotiated agreement) while conversely introducing evidence into the negotiating process that threatens the attractiveness of other negotiating parties' BATNAs. Clear analyses of BATNAs are important factors in a successful negotiating strategy because they allow for wise decisions on whether to accept a negotiated agreement. As such, BATNAs provide a standard that will prevent a party from accepting terms that are too unfavourable and from rejecting convenient terms. Furthermore, having a good BATNA increases a party's negotiating power and a well-prepared negotiating team will be able to gauge the desire of the other team for an agreement. This will allow for the most effective use of pressure and the most appropriate demands being placed upon the other negotiating team.

In the process of negotiation, analyses and integration of different proposals is required. Here a proposed 'package' is developed that involves each party making a concession in different topics to produce relative satisfaction to all parties. The gap between the interests is breached when each side gives something to the other side and vice versa. This is possible through issue linkages; each party makes concessions in different topics so that the balance produces relative satisfaction. Parties must work to develop potential options for such issue linkages and need to have something to offer each other. Negotiators can enlarge the space of agreement by identifying and discussing a range of alternatives, by improving the quality and quantity of information available to the other parties, and by trying to influence the perception of the other party. Much of trade negotiation involves such integrative bargaining because parties can enlarge the area where their interests overlap by identifying and discussing a range of alternative options and opinions

(Saner 2001; Narlikar 2005; Odell 2006). The purpose of research cannot be understood narrowly as self-serving because the most important function is to justify and explain demands of one group to other groups. Tainted by special interests, it must reach out to others.

Facing the demands of complex and perennially moving agendas, negotiators seek research-based support that is usable for a specific place and space of time. Governments may therefore need the capacity not only to produce their own research but also to critically examine what is produced by authoritative centres, such as the World Bank and other multilateral organisations, which may have been shaped by perspectives that do not reflect national priorities. As demands for such context-specific research arise, networks of communities of specialists capable of producing and providing it emerge and proliferate. The episodes studied in this book show how prevalent these sources of research are in trade negotiations and how intense the chains of transmission from policy to the research community are (see the chapters by Rafael Gomez and Morley Gunderson, Mercedes Botto and Andrea Bianculli, and Kehinde Ajayi and Philip Osafo-Kwaakoy). They emphasise the social and constructive character of research and how it is continuously reproduced and negotiated, and hence always dynamic and provisional.

Research produced by insiders or outsiders that are plugged into the machinery as compared to research produced outside is based on quite different forms of problem conceptualisation. The ways in which research is used in the policy process also differs substantially. The chances of directly influencing the policy regime are greater, but the chances of mutual enlightenment drip by drip are also high. Thus the generation of research advances in a dialogic and evolutionary process that manifests itself in the interpersonal and inter-institutional exchanges of the policy community.

Several analysts argue that policy-making processes can usefully be investigated using notions such as policy community or advocacy coalition (see, for example, Kingdon 1984; Sabatier and Jenkins-Smith 1993). While these two notions differ, they broadly share the view that some specialists, such as academics, consultants, and other researchers, in a particular policy area, will help form a community that is bounded. However, without a focus on the political and institutional context within which research and policy interact, such dynamics may be lacking.

Although international influences are important, they also need the systematic and active engagement of actors within a country to be translated into policy. It is important to distinguish the initial acceptance of a new idea from the embedding of the research in policy (see the chapters by Abhijit Das and Ahmed Farouk Ghoneim on the moment of uptake). To be able to do so, an idea requires what Peter Hall (1989) calls viability. Differences between countries become more evident in this transition than in the generation of research, and the complex role of internal social and political structures and institutions is revealed. As an idea moves from acceptance to being embedded and as a country moves from reform to negotiations, political influences of particular sectional and regional interests come into play, influencing the political potential of research insofar as they imply support for a particular sector (such as export agriculture), social group (such as import competition), or geographical region (such as a regional grouping). It is this political dissonance between general principles and particular influences that often underlies the adoption of—as opposed to the acquiescence to—a policy proposal. In the process of adopting the proposal, considerable degrees of adaptation, translation, and integration take place, and local community of practice comes into play (see Chapter 4 by Mercedes Botto and Andrea Bianculli). Few if any of the authors in this volume consider external leverage to be the overriding determinant of uptake in trade negotiations. Rather, internal political structures respond to and modify the products of knowledge, so that the interaction between external leverage and internal agendas determines how research is played out through a complex and contested process of social decoding, feedback, and redefinition. The third driver identified by Weiss—the forces of internal politics and group interest—becomes more important as the discussion shifts from the issue of policy shifts to trade negotiations.

Trade negotiations occur at two levels (Evans *et al.* 1993). The first refers to the relation between the country authorities and the external partner. The second refers to the in-country negotiations with relevant actors, legislature, business, trade unions. These games occur simultaneously and interact with each other constantly along the process. At the second level, negotiations with domestic interests take place, in order to reflect those point of view at the first level and ensure that the results will be subsequently accepted and ratified. At the second level, all stakeholders that can influence the process or the final ratification are alert, and active, either on the offensive or the defensive. These may range from legislative members to various representatives of civil society. Negotiations require more interest-based, problem-solving, hands-on research, from inside the policy process. In practice trade remains an inherently and overtly political process and, consequently, research uptake is also political. Decision makers will not always defer to the opinion of consultants 'out there' or trust broad-based knowledge as impartial, usable, or applicable.

Research matters, but it is shaped by geography and it needs to respond to demand in order to be effective. Research is not produced nor does it exist in a vacuum. The interaction between the production of research and the policy process make it possible to understand when and why research influences trade negotiations. Research and policies evolve as the product of a cycle in which events lead to new thinking and new policies the consequences of which, in turn, often reveal new problems, thereby giving rise to further developments in thinking and policies. But both thinking and policies are heavily influenced by powerful interest groups, themselves shaped by the consequences of policy.

Scholars have made significant progress in explaining how ideas and research can influence policy decisions (Weiss 1991; Carden 2004; Court *et al.* 2005). However, it remains difficult to pinpoint when policy change is due to influential research and how the trade policy process incorporates and embeds research-based innovations. One way to examine this question is to start with the research and look out to the influence that intervention had on the policy canvas, pinpointing how a body of research is called in when a window of opportunity opens or when interests can be hooked on to it. The case studies in this book have employed a contrasting dynamic, tracking backward from policy to identify research-based influences (see Chapter 10 by Fred Carden). The episode study is a particular approach to a case study, where the episode of policy influence is the starting point for the case study. Thus, this method focusses on a clear policy change and tracks back to assess what impact research had among the variety of issues that led to such policy change.

Part II: Instrumental Change, Operational Research

What Is an Episode of Policy Change?

In order to define an episode of policy change we first need to be clear as to what we mean by policy. We need to know what it is that might be changing before we can decide whether any observed differences constitute an 'episode of change'. Policy is commonly used to refer to many different things but policy can be grouped into two general types.

One classical and relatively straightforward type of policy is primarily defined as a product or object; typically it is the result of a choice (or a series of interrelated choices) to undertake some course of action (or inaction). Expressions of general purpose, specific proposals, decisions, and formal rules all fit within this conception of policy (Minogue 1997). A second, more interaction-based type of policy refers more to the processes of negotiation and influence than to the products of that process. Examples of what constitutes policy in this conception include particular ways of defining problems within organisations, and the range of participants and the diversity of their agendas that are brought to bear on the activities of negotiation and decision making.

Any of these notions can play into defining an episode of policy change. However, some policies are far more readily identifiable as formal and discreet, for example a legislative decision; and changes to this kind of policy—or a lack of change—are relatively easy to recognise. With more interactive conceptions of policy, such as those concerned with negotiations and the inclusion or exclusion of stakeholders, it may be difficult for researchers to distinguish whether any aspects of policy have changed. As Carden explains in Chapter 10, this is partly because such changes are less evident, and also because those changes may be incremental and may well occur over long periods. For example, it is far less clear when gradual shifts in the way policy makers define problems constitute an episode of policy change, unlike when a new piece of legislation or declaration of intent is made. Nonetheless, those more subtle changes may be no less important.

Policy changes may be categorised in a variety of ways, but many commentators distinguish between instrumental change, which refers to relatively small, incremental changes in daily administrative policy issues, and conceptual change, which refers to more gradual shifts in terms of policy makers' awareness and reorientation of their basic perspectives (e.g., Caplan 1979; Weiss 1991; Neilson 2001; Davies *et al.* 2005). This distinction is ideal because, in practice, changes to policies likely lie somewhere on a continuum between instrumental and conceptual. Nevertheless, the differentiation is useful, especially since, as far as the relationship between research and policy is concerned, policy makers use research not only in the more instrumental sense of applying data and information to policy decisions, but also, or even predominantly, as a source of ideas and a means of enlightening or broadening the existing knowledge base over time. This in turn can gradually shift conceptual thinking (and the policies supporting that conceptual thinking).

Compared to instrumental shifts, conceptual policy changes—whether in relation to changes in specific proposals, decisions, or rules, or in relation to the processes of policy definition, negotiation, and influence—are likely to be far less transparent, more subjective in nature. They usually occur over a longer time and are frequently affected by a wider range of factors. For those reasons, conceptual policy changes may not be difficult to recognise although it may be very difficult to establish the influence of any one factor, such as a piece of research. Thus, in examining instances of policy change, or lack of change, instrumental shifts may be easier to research. Conversely, when examining the effects of a piece of research it may be easier to consider only the impact of research on instrumental shifts in policy, perhaps missing the potential contribution to less visible—but perhaps just as significant—conceptual shifts in policy. What windows of opportunity were used and how? Tracking backward from policy to identify (research-based) influences represent a challenge in disaggregating the impacts of multiple influences and multiple research strands (Davies *et al.* 2005). The central purpose is heuristic; it can make influence intelligible but in a way that does not lose the connection to other factors at play.

What Is the Value of Researching the Research/Policy Interface?

The interface or relationship between research and policy change can be examined empirically in a number of different ways. These include, for example, general studies of research institutions and their strategies for influencing policy, studies of policy institutions and their relationships with research providers, or studies of the nature and activities of epistemic networks related to particular policy topics. The approach that has been adopted for this book—of choosing to focus on discreet cases of policy change and asking if and how research has contributed to those changes—has several potential benefits, but also poses a number of potential risks that must be considered in order to draw insights and conclusions (Carden 2004).

One important risk is that this approach may tend to focus on clearly observable, distinct, instances of policy change. As discussed above, the relatively more diffuse effects of research—in particular gradual shifts in conceptual thinking—are difficult to recognise. They may, however, constitute a far more important and significant impact of research, compared to more immediate direct impacts on policy. Even when they are recognisable, such shifts in conceptual thinking take place over a long period and thus may be difficult empirically to investigate. For example, Paul Sabatier and Hank Jenkins-Smith (1993), hold that the process of policy change and the role of policy learning requires a decade or more of observation. Yet how in practice might we explore the likely multiple causes, including research, of a ten-year shift in conceptual thinking on the part of policy makers? The temptation will be to focus on more 'do-able' examples, in the process perhaps missing some interesting aspects of the research-policy relationship. The latter might include, for example, the effects of research, among many other activities, in the inclusion of new issues in policy discussions, e.g., environment into trade policy discussions.

Furthermore, certain kinds of research tend to lend themselves more than other kinds to changes in conceptual thinking. An example here might be research illustrating how greater civil society participation in policy making brings a range of potential benefits to processes of governance (see Chapter 3 by Clive George and Colin Kirkpatrick). The value of these kinds of research, or their potential impact, may not be picked up by methods that focus solely on instrumental policy changes, unless analysis of policy changes is sensitive enough to capture the more diffuse ideas-based changes. Thus one consequence of focussing on episodes of more instrumental instances of policy change may be that 'research as data' is recognised as more influential than 'research as argument' or 'research as advocacy', although the second and third types may be just as influential in policy change, or more so, although less visible.

Another consequence of focussing on clearly observable, discreet cases of policy change is that such an approach may inadvertently provide support to the assumption that the use of research feeds into the policy-making process in a direct, or linear, manner. Linear conceptions of the research-policy relationship tend to be limited to instrumental, relatively short-term changes in policy decisions and to 'research as data' rather than broader more diffuse changes in policy conception. Several commentators have argued, however, that the relationship between research and policy should be seen as more dynamic and complex than in the linear model, with an emphasis on two-way processes between research and policy (e.g., Weiss 1991; Webber 1991; Garrett and Islam 1998;

Neilson 2001; Court *et al.* 2005).[6] Thus various contextual factors may play a key part both in defining the question that a research project tackles and in influencing the impact of that research on policy. In contrast to the lineal model, where underlying the question is 'What can the researcher do to capture the attention of decision makers in order to utilise the results of their research in policy', the two-way-processes perspective assumes a different key question: 'Why are some of the ideas that circulate in the research-policy arenas picked up and acted on, while others are ignored and disappear?' Is demand-driven research most likely to influence policy effectively? The episodes of trade policy change and negotiations included in this volume show the growing relevance of commissioned research both by governments and interest groups in increasingly contested settings designed from the beginning to support a particular cause—research not as independent evidence waiting to be 'hooked', but as instrumental and supportive to policy decisions taken on other grounds. Such a particular way of doing research differs significantly from the traditional academic approach, enjoying an aura of otherworldliness.

Most studies so far have argued that the role for research is stronger in support of a paradigm change than in operationalisation and reinforcement once the winds of change have settled. The studies of instrumental change in this book show that trade negotiations provide a new pull for analytical activities to search, research, enquire, produce evidence, and validate (see Table 1–1). There is a clear demand for research from policy makers (Carden 2007). The primary users of this type of research are those on the front line of policy development, the in-house machinery requiring thorough research for hard-headed negotiations. Building policy in the context of negotiations requires alertness to opportunity and the ability to be present with policy-driven papers. This post-academic fashion has five distinctive features:

- It is a mode of research production for policy endeavours that stands in contrast to two traditions, that of the public intellectual (the 'sniper'

[6] Thus the development of bridges to overcome supply- and demand-side obstacles to those links does not seem to apply comfortably to the specific case of trade policy and reform. Research and policy are significantly more inter-related (see Stone 2002; Stone and Denham 2004).

challenging and contesting perverse decision making) and that of the apolitical objectivity or rigour of 'pure' academic knowledge.

- It is produced and validated in the context of application as a result of the policy process.
- The research agenda is politically embedded and arises from the policy priorities that result from ongoing engagement with decision makers. It is path dependent, i.e., the problem is conceptualised taking into account the rules of the game and the range of politically feasible options at both international and domestic levels (in terms of international negotiations).
- There is greater accountability to relevant stakeholders than to established professional literature or academic review systems. Instead of relying on peer review, post-academic research relies on a wider set of criteria to judge quality, value, and usefulness to the conceptualisation and resolution of a problem. Such forms of quality control and validation mechanism do not give up the quest for technical excellence, but draw on technical evidence for a cause that weighs more than academic or professional validation.
- The product is problem-driven knowledge that is required and used because it is not only technically sound but also socially robust, i.e., it is perceived as legitimate and fair for a given purpose.

This pushes the analyst of the research-policy interface to focus more on the institutional and political context within which research and policy are interacting, rather than just the characteristics of the research itself or the relationships between researchers and policy makers.

Although there are potential risks associated with deciding to focus on episodes of policy change in order to investigate the research-policy relationship there are several potential benefits too. For example, a detailed focus on specific cases of policy change can begin to untangle some of the complexity of the political processes at work in contributing to that instance of change. In practice, multiple and often confounding variables will contribute to instances of policy change, and without careful empirical study it may be extremely difficult to address the question of when, under what circumstances, and how research is influential in the policy process. Alternative research approaches may simply lack the forensic view that such case studies can provide.

For example, close empirical scrutiny of an episode of policy change may allow us to clarify the causal relationship between research and policy change. Thus the different circumstances in which policy makers or interest groups draw on research to support or legitimate a policy decision that has already been or will be made or in which research contributes to causing that change in policy may not be visible except by using a careful case-study approach.

As argued above, a focus on episodes of policy change may restrict attention to the relationship between research as data and observable, discreet, instances of policy change, rather than research as ideas and gradual shifts in conceptual thinking over time. Yet, if analysts take care to include the latter, a case-study approach may be particularly valuable. This is because one of the characteristics of research as ideas, as opposed to research as data, is that, the actual findings of a study will have disappeared and become transformed into a simple 'story' (Weiss 1991). Perhaps the best way to show how such stories affect policy decisions and policy-making processes and to relate such stories to their origins in research is through careful case studies.

A second type of benefit is conceptual self-consciousness: a careful case-study—based approach may help guard against a tendency on the part of protagonists to exaggerate the actual influence of research on policy makers. Since researchers (and funders) everywhere are under considerable pressure to demonstrate the value of their work, for example in terms of policy relevance and influence, they may overstate the impact of their work unless such claims can be carefully examined using a case-study approach. Similarly, policy makers may sometimes find it easier to defend an account of how and why policies changed by reference to rational evidence-based factors rather than as a response to political circumstances and interests. General analyses of institutions, based for example on interviews with protagonists without tying them to specific cases may, by comparison, present an overly rosy picture of the relationship between research and policy.

The Riddle in Trade Episodes

The above discussion on the complex nature of the interaction of research and policy, and how trade policy has been explained so far, indicates several hypotheses that the empirical studies of the research—policy boundary in this volume can illustrate. These hypotheses include the following:

- Conceptual policy changes are opaque, subjective in nature, take place over a long period, and are caused by a wide and interacting range of factors. As a consequence, the empirical relationship between research and conceptual policy change is very difficult to investigate because it is not a linear relationship.

- The relationship between research and policy is more dynamic and complex than generally assumed by linear models. Instead there are two-way processes between research and policy. Thus various contextual factors may play a key part both in defining the question that a research project tackles and in influencing the impact of that research on policy.
- In practice, multiple and sometimes confounding variables contribute to instances of policy change. Without careful empirical study, the question of when, under what circumstances, and how research is influential in the policy process may be extremely difficult to address. An empirical scrutiny of an episode of policy change can clarify the complexity of the causal relationship between research and policy change and address the problem of attribution.
- If research is not the key driver on policy change, there must be other drivers against which research should be compared, which requires additional research. The additionality of research refers to the value added by research to the policy process.

The chapters in this volume provide valuable insights on these issues and hypotheses and assess the role played by research on specific episodes of trade policy change around the world. Thus chapters two and three focus on paradigmatic shifts, looking at the role of research in changing and adapting the mainstream approach to trade by providing evidence on how trade works as well as endowing legitimacy on a major policy change. Specifically, in Chapter 2 Rafael Gomez and Morley Gunderson look at the trade policy change implemented by Canada and examine how research initiatives can be used to win the support of domestic lobbies and how they can serve as legitimising instruments, whereas Clive George and Colin Kirkpatrick in Chapter 3 explore the influence of the sustainability impact assessment programme of the European Commission on EU trade policy and parallel policy measures.

The fourth and fifth chapters consider instrumental changes in countries that have adopted a common external tariff at the regional level and look at the conditions and timing for research uptake. In this regard, in Chapter 4 Mercedes Botto and Andrea Bianculli compare two instances in Argentina's regional integration process and identify the type of knowledge produced, the articulation established with policy makers, and the factors that either promoted or hindered uptake, while in Chapter 5 Philip Osafo Kwaako and Kehinde Ajayi assess the political context of tariff reform for Nigeria's adoption of the common external tariff of the Economic Community of West African States (ECOWAS), as well as the role of various stakeholders in the process. Chapters six and seven examine how interests are fleshed out through research production and draw a contrast between two institutional set-ups. Ahmed Farouk Ghoneim in Chapter 6 analyses how the process of formulating trade policy in Egypt takes up independent ideas in an informal setting, whereas Abhijit Das in Chapter 7 studies the case of trade facilitation in India and the role played by the United Nations Convention on Trade and Development (UNCTAD) where, in contrast, linkages between research, policy, and implementation are significantly more structured in a democratic set-up.

Finally, chapters eight and nine provide the last episodes analysed in this volume and look at how research can be influential in forming coalitions to negotiate in the WTO process. There are ever growing numbers of such coalitions active in the WTO; not only do they show more resilience than anticipated, but also their proposals are characterised by an unprecedented familiarity with technical detail, which suggests that they are backed by substantive research. In particular, these studies assess the cases of the G20—in Chapter 8 by Amrita Narlikar and Diana Tussie—and the G33—in Chapter 9 by Paul Mably—in the WTO, contrasting the centralised research production for the latter with the multiple research sources of the former. In Chapter 10 Fred Carden looks back at each of the contributions through the lens of the episode approach and teases out the consequences of the issues raised. The book closes with a reflection on the other side of the equation and turns to the influence of policy making on the research setting. It examines the conditions under which trade research is produced and the types of products that result in preparation for these battles.

These episode studies have worked with two types of policy change: instrumental change that leads to the opening of windows and the creation of tools that can expand the texture of negotiations to political exigencies, and conceptual change (or normative change) that involves a more radical overthrow of a policy framework.[7] The purpose of

[7] Lindquist (2001) contends that instances of policy changes may be viewed as being routine, incremental, fundamental, or emergent. Routine changes involve minor

research in each episode can be classified, according to the categories used by Weiss, into research as an idea, research as data, and research as argumentation. These typologies and categorisations provide a useful roadmap[8] to present the episodes here and the type of influence in which research made a difference[9] in a systematic and useful fashion, as showed in Table 1–1.[10]

Bibliography

Ayuk, Elias and Mohamed Ali Marouani, eds. 2007. *The Policy Paradox in Africa: Strengthening Links Between Economic Research and Policymaking*. Trenton NJ and Ottawa: Africa World Press and International Development Research Centre.

Bates, Robert H. and Anne O. Krueger, eds. 1993. *Political and Economic Interactions in Economic Policy Reform: Evidence from Eight Countries*. Oxford: Blackwell.

Braun, Dietmar and Andreas Busch, eds. 1999. *Public Policy and Political Ideas*. Cheltenham: Edward Elgar.

Bruno, Michael. 1993. *Crisis, Stabilization, and Economic Reform: Therapy by Consensus*. Oxford: Oxford University Press.

Caplan, Nathan. 1979. 'The Two-Communities Theory and Knowledge Utilization'. *American Behavioral Scientist*, 22(3):459–470.

Carden, Fred, Stephanie Neilson, Terry Smutylo, *et al.* 2002. *IDRC-Supported Research in the Public Policy Process: A Strategic Evaluation of the Influence of Research on Public Policy*. Working paper. International Development Research Centre, Ottawa.

Carden, Fred. 2004. 'Issues in Assessing the Policy Influence of Research'. *International Social Science Journal*, 56(1):135–151.

——. 2007. 'Context Matters'. In E. Ayuk and M.A. Marouani, eds., *The Policy Paradox in Africa: Strengthening Links Between Economic Research and Policymaking*. Trenton NJ and Ottawa: Africa World Press and International Development Research Centre.

Corbo, Vittorio and Stanley Fischer. 1995. 'Structural Adjustment, Stabilization, and Policy Reform: Domestic and International Finance'. In H. Chenery, ed., *Handbook of Development Economics*, 1 edition. Santiago: Pontificia Universidad Católica de Chile, Instituto de Economía.

Court, Julius, Ingie Hovland, and John Young. 2005. 'Research and Policy in International Development: Introduction'. In J. Court, I. Hovland, and J. Young, eds., *Bridging Research and Policy in Development: Evidence and the Change Process*. London: Overseas Development Institute.

Davies, Huw, Sandra Nutley, and Isabel Walter (2005). 'Assessing the Impact of Social Science Research: Conceptual, Methodological, and Practical Issues'. Background

modifications to a programme and often involve limited debate. Incremental changes occur when particular issues are reviewed without a comprehensive overhaul of policy. Fundamental policy changes lead to rethinking of the policy framework. Emergent changes similarly involve a major paradigmatic shift.

[8] The table in Chapter 10 by Carden fleshes out a framework to analyze these relationships between research and policy.

[9] Types of influence as per (Carden *et al.* 2002).

[10] Table 10–1 fleshes out a framework to analyse these relationships between research and policy.

discussion paper for the ESCR Symposium on Assessing the Non-Academic Impact of Research. University of St. Andrews.

Diamond, Larry Jay and Marc F. Plattner. 1995. *Economic Reform and Democracy*. Baltimore: Johns Hopkins University Press.

Diaz-Alejandro, Carlos. 1975. 'Trade Policies and Economic Development'. In P.B. Kenen, ed., *International Trade and Finance: Frontiers for Research*. Cambridge: Cambridge University Press.

Dollar, David and Jakob Svensson. 1998. *What Explains the Success or Failure of Stuctural Adjustment Programs?* World Bank Policy Research Working Paper No. 1938. World Bank, Washington DC.

Drazen, Allen and Vittorio Grilli. 1990. *The Benefits of Crises for Economic Reforms*. NBER Working Paper No. W3527. National Bureau of Economic Research.

Drazen, Allen and William Easterly. 2001. 'Do Crises Induce Reform? Simple Empirical Tests of Conventional Wisdom'. *Economics and politics*, 13(2):129–157.

Edwards, Sebastian. 1989. *Openness, Outward Orientation, Trade Liberalization, and Economic Performance in Developing Countries*. NBER Working Paper No. W2908. National Bureau of Economic Research, Washington DC.

——. 1997. 'Trade, Liberalization Reforms, and the World Bank'. *American Economic Review*, 87(2):43–48.

Evans, Peter B., Harold Karan Jacobson, and Robert D. Putnam, eds. 1993. *Double-Edged Diplomacy: International Bargaining and Domestic Politics*. Berkeley: University of California Press.

Garrett, James L. and Yassir Islam. 1998. *Policy Research and the Policy Process: Do the Twain Ever Meet?* Gatekeeper Series no. 74. International Institute for Environment and Development, London. <www.iied.org/pubs/pdfs/6138IIED.pdf> [Accessed: March 2008].

Goldstein, Judith and Robert O. Keohane, eds. 1993. *Ideas and Foreign Policy: Beliefs, Institutions, and Political Change*. Ithaca: Cornell University Press.

Gourevitch, Peter. 2005. 'Economic Ideas, International Influences, and Domestic Politics: A Comparative Perspective'. In V. Fitzgerald and R. Thorp, eds., *Economic Doctrines in Latin America: Origins, Embedding, and Evolution*. Basingstoke: Palgrave Macmillan.

Haas, Peter. 1992. 'Introduction: Epistemic Communities and International Policy Coordination'. *International Organization*, 46(1):1–35.

Haggard, Stephan, Steven Benjamin Webb, and World Bank. 1994. *Voting for Reform: Democracy, Political Liberalization, and Economic Adjustment*. New York: Oxford University Press.

Hall, Peter A., ed. 1989. *The Political Power of Economic Ideas: Keynesianism Across Nations*. Princeton NJ: Princeton University Press.

Jacobsen, John. 1995. 'Much Ado about Ideas: The Cognitive Factor in Economic Policy'. *World Politics*, 47(2):283–310.

Jenkins, Rob. 1999. *Democratic Politics and Economic Reform in India*. Cambridge: Cambridge University Press.

Jordana, Jacint and Carles Ramió. 2002. *Diseños institucionales y gestión de la política comercial exterior en América Latina*. Institution for the Integration of Latin America and the Caribbean, Buenos Aires.

Kahler, Miles. 1992. 'External Influence, Conditionality, and the Politics of Adjustment'. In S. Haggard and R.R. Kaufman, eds., *The Politics of Economic Adjustment: International Constraints, Distributive Conflicts, and the State*. Princeton NJ: Princeton University Press.

Keeler, John T.S. 1993. 'Opening the Window for Reform: Mandates, Crises, and Extraordinary Policy Making'. *Comparative Political Studies*, 25(4):433–486.

Kingdon, John W. 1984. *Agendas, Alternatives, and Public Policies*. Boston: Little, Brown.

Krueger, Anne O. 1993. *Political Economy of Policy Reform in Developing Countries*. Cambridge: Cambridge University Press.
Laird, Sam and Patrick Messerlin. 1990. 'Institutional Reform for Trade Liberalization'. *World Economy*, 13(2):230–249.
Lindquist, Evert A. 2001. *Discerning Policy Influence: Framework for a Strategic Evaluation of IDRC-Supported Research*. Background paper. International Development Research Centre, Ottawa.
Milner, Helen, Edward Mansfield, and Peter Rosendorff. 2000. 'Free to Trade? Democracies, Autocracies, and International Trade Negotiations'. *American Political Science Review*, 94(2):305–322.
Milner, Helen and Keiko Kubota. 2001. *Why the Rush to Free Trade? Democracy and Trade Policy in the Developing Countries*. Paper prepared for the annual meeting of the American Political Science Association. San Francisco.
Minogue, Martin. 1997. 'Theory and Practice in Public Policy and Administration'. In M.J. Hill, ed., *The Policy Process: A Reader*, 2nd edition. New York: Harvester-Wheatsheaf.
Narlikar, Amrita. 2005. *Bargaining over the Doha Development Agenda: Coalitions in the World Trade Organization*. Working Paper No. 36. Latin American Trade Network.
Nash, John and Wendy Takacs. 1998. *Trade Policy Reform: Lessons and Implications*. World Bank, Washington DC.
Neilson, Stephanie. 2001. *Knowledge Utilization and Public Policy Processes: A Literature Review*. Evaluation Unit, International Development Research Centre, Ottawa.
Niño, Jaime. 2004. *What Determines Trade Regimes and Reforms? The Role of Ideas and Democracy*. Paper presented at the annual meeting of the American Political Science Association. Chicago.
Odell, John S., ed. 2006. *Negotiating Trade: Developing Countries in the WTO and NAFTA*. Cambridge: Cambridge University Press.
Papageorgiou, Demetris, Armeane M. Choksi, and Michael Michaely. 1990. *Liberalizing Foreign Trade in Developing Countries: The Lessons of Experience*. Washington DC: World Bank.
Przeworski, Adam. 1991. *Democracy and the Market: Political and Economic Reforms in Eastern Europe and Latin America*. Cambridge: Cambridge University Press.
Remmer, Karen. 1990. 'Democracy and Economic Crisis: The Latin American Experience'. *World Politics*, 42(3):315–335.
Rius, Andrés. 2003. *The Knowledge Systems Implications of Building Institutions for High-Quality Growth*. Working paper. International Development Research Centre, Ottawa.
Rodrik, Dani. 1995. 'Political Economy of Trade Policy'. In G.M. Grossman and K. Rogoff, eds., *Handbook of International Economics*. New York: Elsevier.
Sabatier, Paul A. and Hank C. Jenkins-Smith, eds. 1993. *Policy Change and Learning: An Advocacy Coalition Approach*. Boulder: Westview Press.
Sachs, Jeffrey and Andrew Warner. 1995. 'Economic Reform and the Process of Global Integration'. *Brookings Papers on Economic Activity*, 26(1995-1):1–118.
Saner, Raymond. 2001. 'WTO versus Regional Trade Agreements'. In R. Saner and I. Maidana, eds., *Trade Negotiation Cases, Analyses, Strategies at Bilateral, Regional, and Multilateral Levels, Bolivia, 2000*. Bolivia: Editorial "Los Amigos del Libro".
Shepsle, Kenneth. 1985. 'A Comment on Derthick and Quirk'. In R.G. Noll, ed., *Regulatory Policy and the Social Sciences*. Berkeley: University of California Press.
Smith, William, Carlos Acuña, and Eduardo Gamarra. 1994. *Democracy, Markets, and Structural Reform in Contemporary Latin America: Argentina, Bolivia, Brazil, Chile, and Mexico*. Transaction Publishers, New Brunswick NJ.
Stallings, Barbara. 1992. 'International influence on Economic Policy: Debt, Stabilization, and Structural Reform'. In S. Haggard and R.R. Kaufman, eds., *The Politics of Economic Adjustment: International Constraints, Distributive Conflicts, and the State*. Princeton NJ: Princeton University Press.

Stone, Diane. 2000. 'Knowledge, Power, and Policy'. In D. Stone, ed., *Banking on Knowledge: The Genesis of the Global Development Network*. London: Routledge.
——. 2002. 'Using Knowledge: The Dilemmas of Bridging Research and Policy'. *Compare*, 32(3):285–296.
Stone, Diane and Andrew Denham, eds. 2004. *Think Tank Traditions: Policy Research and the Politics of Ideas*. Manchester: Manchester University Press.
Webber, David J. 1991. 'The Distribution and Use of Policy Knowledge in the Policy Process'. *Knowledge and Policy*, 4(4):6–36.
Weiss, Carol. 1979. 'The Many Meanings of Research Utilization'. *Public Administration Review*, 39(5):426–431.
——. 1991. 'Policy Research as Advocacy: Pro and Con'. *Knowledge and Policy*, 4(1/2):37–56.

PART ONE

PARADIGMATIC SHIFTS

CHAPTER TWO

CREATION OF VALUES AND PRINCIPLES: CANADA'S EXPERIENCE WITH THE CUSFTA AND NAFTA

Rafael Gomez and Morley Gunderson[1]

The purpose of this chapter is to examine the role of research on trade policy based on Canada's experience with the Canada-U.S. Free Trade Agreement of 1989 (FTA) and its subsequent expansion to include Mexico under the North American Free Trade Agreement (NAFTA) of 1992.

Examining the impact of research on trade agreements is particularly informative in light of the difficulty of conveying the economic arguments in favour of free trade to the general public and the political process. This has long been recognised. In his famous treatise in the late 1880s, Henry George (1886) argued that the greatest obstacle to free trade was in communicating to labour that the long-run benefits in the form of real wage growth and job destruction exceeded the short-term adjustment costs. In their classic article, Wolfgang Stopler and Paul Samuelson (1941, 58) state: 'Second only in political appeal to the argument that tariffs increase employment is the popular notion that the standard of living of the American worker must be protected against the ruinous competition of cheap foreign labour.'

[1] Rafael Gomez is an associate professor at Glendon College, York University, and a lecturer in management at the London School of Economics and Political Science. He is also a research associate of the Centre for Industrial Relations and the Centre for International Studies at the University of Toronto. Morley Gunderson holds the CIBC Chair in Youth Employment at the University of Toronto and is a professor at the Centre for Industrial Relations and the Department of Economics. He is also a research associate of the Institute for Policy Analysis, the Centre for International Studies, and the Institute for Life Course and Aging. Without implicating them for any of the conclusions, the authors are indebted to Michael Baker, Dwayne Benjamin, Jeremy Bulow, Olivier Deschenes, Don Dewees, Cliff Halliwell, Jennifer Hunt, Lisa Lynch, Alan Nymark, Daniel Parent, Craig Riddell, Dan Trefler, Diana Tussie, and Klaus Zimmerman for helpful discussions. We are grateful to all the participants of the FLACSO seminar August 2006 (Buenos Aires) who provided comments at our presentation of an earlier version of this chapter.

The Canadian free trade agreements are excellent examples for illustrating the issue of the role of research because, although the movement to freer trade was described as a 'leap of faith', it was certainly backed by considerable research. As discussed subsequently, that research ranged from policy-oriented discussion pieces to computable general equilibrium models. It included the spectrum of work related to theory, evidence and policy. There was often a strong advocacy component, but not always.

Issues that will be dealt with in this chapter include: Did the research have any impact on the policies of moving toward freer trade? If so, why did the pro free trade research seem to dominate over the research against freer trade? What are the types of research outputs that seem most important in affecting the policy initiatives? Are there key interactions that must occur between the research and various stakeholders? Are there key inputs into the research that facilitate it having an effect on policy? Are there contrasts between the FTA and NAFTA with respect to a differential impact and does this shed light on the issue?

At the outset it should be emphasised that establishing a causal link whereby research affects policy is extremely difficult for a number of reasons (Gunderson 2007). Reverse causality may be present since policy makers who want a policy initiative in place may well foster the research that will support the initiative. This could come in many forms: commissioning background studies from sources known to favour the initiative, designing the terms of reference in ways that will yield supportive results, 'advertising' favourable results while 'burying' unfavourable ones, or reviewing the research with suggestions tilted toward influencing the results or having them presented in a favourable fashion.

Establishing a correlation between academic research and policy outcomes does not imply causality. For causality to be at work, the research results would have to be so powerful as to have an independent impact on policy initiatives.

It is also the case that we may only observe the research results when they confirm the desired policy change. This can give the appearance that the research results positively influenced the policy change, especially as they are 'trotted out' to support the change. Otherwise, they may be buried or counter studies may be commissioned to offset their impact.

Background

The Canada-U.S. Free Trade Agreement was negotiated between 1985 and 1987 and implemented January 1, 1989. It emerged out of an earlier period of nationalistic views and extensive government intervention in the economy during the 1960s and '70s. From the mid 1970s to the 1980s, the Canadian economy (and generally the U.S. and world economies) were in the worst shape since the Great Depression of the 1930s. As outlined by John Chant (2005) both inflation and unemployment were at double-digit levels and productivity and growth were lagging. Factors underlying this poor performance included the increase in oil prices by the Organization of the Oil Producing Countries (OPEC) and attempts to fund both the Vietnam war and the 'Great Society' at the same time in the United States via an expansionary monetary policy.

In Canada, the response generally involved continued extensive government intervention and a nationalistic orientation in a number of fronts. The Anti-Inflation Board was established to administer wage and price controls from 1975 to 1978, and the National Energy Policy was established in 1980 to fix energy prices. The 1980 government budget under Prime Minister Pierre Trudeau promised 'new levels of government intervention to encourage "Canadianization" of the economy, the strategic use of the Foreign Investment Review Agency, tougher rules for assuring government procurement contracts that would favour Canadian firms, and a new State Trading Corporation to help sell the products of smaller Canadian companies to centrally planned economies' (Chant 2005, 14). A high-tech industrial policy was also proposed.

These nationalistic and interventionist policies of the mid 1970s to the early 1980s were generally supported by earlier royal commissions, task forces, and government-commissioned reports that recommended such initiatives. This was the case with the Royal Commission on Dominion-Provincial Relations reporting in 1940 and chaired by N.W. Rowell and Joseph Sirois, the Royal Commission on Canada's Economic Prospects reporting in 1958 and chaired by Walter Gordon, the report of the Task Force on Foreign Ownership and the Structure of Canadian Industry chaired by Mel Watkins in 1968 and Foreign Direct Investment in Canada, the 1972 report by Herb Gray.

In the early 1980s, however, a transformation in political thinking began to occur. The same prime minister who brought the previously mentioned nationalist and interventionist government initiatives, and who promised 'even new levels of government intervention' and who instituted wage and price controls, appeared to have an epiphany guided by Adam Smith's invisible hand. In a memo to his cabinet in 1982, Trudeau stated: 'Personally, I remain convinced that the primary engine of economic development must be a dynamic private sector and that the market place is in most circumstances the best allocator of scarce resources' (Chant 2005, 17). Soon after in that same year, Trudeau appointed Donald Macdonald to chair the Royal Commission on the Economic Union and Development Prospects for Canada (the Macdonald Commission). The main recommendation of that commission was for a free trade agreement with Canada and the United States. In essence, the Canada-U.S. Free Trade Agreement of 1989 was spawned by the Macdonald Commission, which in turn arose out of a transformation of political views away from a nationalist-interventionist strategy and toward a more market-oriented one.

The Macdonald Commission and the Free Trade Recommendation[2]

As indicated, the Macdonald Commission was established in 1982—a time that marked the beginning of a transformation of political thinking within the Trudeau government away from a nationalistic-interventionist strategy and toward a more market-based one. Macdonald himself appears to have undergone a similar transformation. As minister of energy earlier, he was responsible for nationalistic-interventionist policies including the National Oil Policy, the establishment of a state-owned petroleum company, government investment in oil sands that at the time were not commercially viable, and price controls on uranium exports. Later, as minister of finance, he was responsible for the wage-price control programme. In answer to the question of what made him change his viewpoint, he indicates: 'My experience in the private sector after my departure from government made it clear that state-controlled programs had failed to achieve the rates of growth to which we all aspire' (Macdonald 2005, 9). While his practical private-sector experience appears to explain his transformation from supporting a nationalistic-interventionist strategy to a market-based one that would recommend

[2] Much of this discussion is from Morley Gunderson (2007).

the FTA, that recommendation was buttressed by numerous research studies that also endorsed the FTA, as discussed subsequently.

As stated by Macdonald (2005, 7): 'The use of the Royal Commission instrument to develop broad policy responses has now become a pattern in Canada. Rowell-Sirois, Walter Gordon and our Royal Commission, each in its generation provided a perspective on the political economy of Canada, of our place within a changing world, and of policy responses for Canadians to choose.'[3] In that vein, the issue of the impact of research on public policy becomes closely linked to the extent to which research influences the recommendations of such royal commissions.

The Macdonald Commission's Origins and Mandate

The initial impetus for the Macdonald Commission was to recommend the means to foster internal trade within Canada in the hope that this would further a stronger internal economic union. The mandate was soon broadened extensively to involve the appropriate national goals and policies for economic development, and the appropriate institutional and constitutional arrangements to promote the liberty and well-being of individual Canadians and the maintenance of a strong Canadian economy (Royal Commission on the Economic Union and Development Prospects for Canada 1985, 561). While the mandate was broad, its focus was that of adapting to change.

The mandate was broadened because the forum of a royal commission, with its public hearings and research programme, was regarded as desirable for obtaining information on a broader range of policy issues that were beyond the capabilities of the internal civil service to analyse. Furthermore, the arm's-length nature of the relationship between governments and such commissions meant that the government could select the recommendations it wanted. As Macdonald (2005, 2) says, 'if the recommendations were not acceptable to the government, it could disavow them'. This highlights that the link between research and public policy may be buffered through such institutional arrangements as royal commissions and task forces. They may foster research,

[3] In an analysis of the role of research in royal commissions, Jane Jenson (1994) also indicates that earlier royal commissions based their recommendations on public hearings and legal expertise, while the latter ones turned increasingly to research, requiring the support of facts.

but they may also provide a mechanism for cherry-picking the results wanted by the political process—again highlighting the difficulty of establishing a direct causal line between research and public policy. Even in such circumstances, however, the research has an indirect impact if it supports what the political process deems appropriate—in effect, if it provides the cherries to pick.

The research conducted and synthesised by the Macdonald Commission was extensive, amounting to 280 studies done mainly by 300 different academics in 70 volumes in three areas: law and constitutional issues, politics and institutions of government, and economics. Trade was one of seven areas under the economics umbrella, the others being macroeconomics, federalism and the economic union, industrial structure, income distribution and income security, labour markets and labour relations, and economic ideas and social issues. While trade was only one of seven areas within the economics umbrella, and economics was only one of three major areas under analysis, trade was described as its 'signature analysis' and the most immediate impact of the commission was described as giving 'greater legitimacy and momentum to the argument for free trade with the US' (Banting 2004).[4]

In his foreword to each of the research volumes, Macdonald commented on the dearth of research at the time of previous royal commissions: 'Very little was known about the evolution of the Canadian economy. What was known, moreover, had not been extensively analysed by the slender cadre of social scientists of the day.' He further commented on the importance of research for his own commission: 'We enjoyed a substantial advantage over our predecessors: we had a wealth of information. We inherited the work of scholars at universities across Canada and we had the benefit of the work of experts across private research institutes and publicly sponsored organisations.' He also commented, however, on the importance of mechanisms such as royal commissions to link the research to public policy by filling the research gaps and consolidate the existing research: 'Our problem was not a shortage of information; it was to interrelate and integrate—to synthesise—the results of much of the information we already had.' Gregory Inwood (1998, 16) also states that 'from the very start, the

[4] Michael Hart (2005) states that 'the Macdonald commission examined a wide range of issues related to Canada's economic and social circumstances, but its signature analysis concerned Canada's performance as a trading nation'.

Research Directors decided that the studies commissioned would not be intended to produce new, original or ground-breaking research, but rather work which summed up the state of the discipline in which scholars were writing'.

This underscores the importance of having both an existing stock of cumulative research upon which to draw and the capability of having mechanisms to absorb such research and link it to the policy area. Academic research on its own may stay buried in the ivory towers if it is not synthesised and translated into a language understood by policy makers. The incentive systems within the academic environment, however, generally do not reward such consolidation and translation, preferring instead the basic and applied research published in peer-reviewed refereed journals. As such, it requires mechanisms such as royal commissions and task forces or individuals within government departments who can bridge the gap between academic research and public policy.

The research volumes of the Macdonald Commission were of extremely high quality and done by top researchers in Canada.[5] This is certainly the case with the work on trade, coordinated by John Whalley, an internationally recognised and prolific scholar in the area.[6] As Craig Riddell (2005, 53) points out, the policy influence of the Macdonald Commission 'may have flowed from its detailed diagnosis, as well as from the specifics of its recommendations'.

The Sources of Free Trade Support

Support for the FTA of 1992 came not only from the research of the Macdonald Commission reporting in 1985 but also from the economics research community in general—at least from what could be labelled as economists who followed the conventional paradigm.[7] Of course,

[5] The background research studies, for example, were subject to the normal academic peer review process done in refereed journals (Inwood 1998, 16).

[6] As indicated by Hart (1994, 29): 'He [Whalley] had written, edited, or encouraged the production of seven volumes [Vols. 9–14 and 68] of research related to [free trade]. More than any other person on the Commission staff, he ensured that the free trade option gained a full hearing.'

[7] Positive effects on output, income, productivity, growth, employment, and wages were predicted from the computable general equilibrium models outlined in the background studies for the Macdonald Commission by Robert Hamilton and John Whalley (1985), Richard Harris (Harris 1985), and Richard Harris and David Cox (1984). The Harris-Cox modelling, developed earlier, was particularly influential, presented

this reflects the basic principles of economics that outline the benefits of free trade by exploiting comparative advantage and the benefits of specialization.

Positive impacts of the FTA on output, income, employment, and wages were predicted for Canada based on various macroeconomic forecasting models, including the FOCUS-PRISM models discussed by Peter Dungan (1985), in the Informetrica model discussed in Informetrica (1985) and by Carl Sonnen and Mike McCracken (1985), the Economic Council of Canada CANDIDE model (Magun *et al.* 1988), and the model of Ernie Stokes (1989). While the predicted impacts were positive, they were generally small, in part because the tariff reductions were small and phased over a long period of time. As well, macro forecasting models are not suited to capture the important impacts that can emanate from enhanced economies of scale and productivity improvements that can arise from the associated restructuring.

Computable general equilibrium models can capture both the direct effects that emanate from reductions in tariffs and non-tariff barriers to trade, as well as the indirect effects that emanate from industrial restructuring, economies of scale, productivity improvements, reductions in imperfect competition and induced investments. The computable general equilibrium (CGE) models generally confirmed the results of the macro-forecasting models: positive effects on output, income, growth, productivity, employment and wages (Brown and Stern 1987, 1989; Canada. Department of Finance 1988; Cox and Harris 1985, 1986, 1992; Crandall 1987; Harris and Cox 1985).

The case for a bilateral free trade agreement with the U.S. was fostered by a number of other factors of particular importance to Canada (Winham 2005). Other regional trading blocs were forming internationally and Canada was at risk of not gaining access to a large market. As well, Canada's traditional reliance on exporting primary products was tenuous given that the demand for such products was forecast to be in decline and a reallocation to more manufacturing was considered desirable. To obtain the economies of scale necessary to be globally competitive in that area, secure access to the large U.S. market was regarded as necessary. This was especially the case given the possibility of increased protectionism in the U.S., especially in the

to the commissioners in seminars and summarised in the background studies (Inwood 1998, 29).

form of non-tariff barriers to trade—a dire possibility since more than 70% of Canada's trade was with the United States. Also for this reason, a bilateral free trade agreement with the U.S. was preferred especially since further multilateral free trade through the General Agreement on Tariffs and Trade (GATT) was uncertain. While the benefits of free trade were the ostensible rationale for that recommendation, a more subtle rationale also pertained to the fact that freer trade may foster further market-oriented reforms in domestic policy. This is especially the case since Canada is a federal system where provinces have considerable independent decision making in many areas. Free trade may be an effective way for the federal government to induce market-oriented reforms in such a system.

Although formal macro-forecasting and CGE models were prominent in the research agenda of the Macdonald Commission, such models have been criticised in this area, generally on the grounds of unrealistic assumptions and inability to capture all of the subtleties of the adjustment process.[8] But the criticisms have tended not to be of a research nature published in academic journals and providing alternative predictions based on alternative methodologies.[9] This is also the case with many of the nationalist-interventionist arguments advanced in the 1960s and '70s mainly by political scientists and sociologists—arguments that tended to be rejected by the Macdonald Commission and its associated researchers.[10]

Overall, the solid research done or synthesised by prominent economists associated with the commission as well as that done by the research community in general supported the recommendations for the FTA. While strongly suggestive of the impact of research on fostering free trade, this does not establish a causal connection since there is the possibility that cause and effect worked in the other direction. That is, such reputable and prominent economists may have been commissioned to

---

[8] Examples of criticisms include the conference presentations by Ricardo Grinspun (1991) and James Cypher (1992).

[9] In commenting on a symposium on free trade, an internal memo from the Macdonald Commission indicated that the critics of free trade 'spoke forcefully against free trade but were criticized for not providing at least some definition and dimensioning of whatever the alternative was they were recommending' (Inwood 1998, 30).

[10] Inwood (1998, 5) indicates that their arguments 'found public expression in such journals of contemporary opinion as *Canadian Forum*, *Canadian Dimension*, *Our Generation* and *This Magazine*'. These were magazines of contemporary opinion and not research journals.

do the forecasts or to consolidate the existing literature because it was known that they would likely find outcomes favoured by the Macdonald Commission. This does not imply that they may have been 'hired guns' who prostituted themselves and tailored their results to those who 'pay the bills'. Rather, they were prominent economists or groups in the paradigm mould, and the conventional paradigm would predict favourable outcomes from free trade.

Economists Finally Have Their Day in the Sun

This possibility certainly has been suggested. Inwood (1998), for example, indicates that the nationalistic-interventionist emphasis of the 1960s and '70s (dominated by sociologists and political scientists) engendered a backlash in the 1980s (dominated by economists) with their emphasis on free markets, free trade, and a diminished role for the state. As such, he concludes that 'this combined with the traditionally hegemonic position of economics within state-sponsored research programs meant that, in some ways, the recommendations of the Macdonald Commission research were predictable, if not foregone' (7). Inwood further argues that 'the emergence of free trade as an issue within the Commission' was also a foregone conclusion after 'Macdonald's public pronouncement in November of 1984 that he favoured a "leap of faith" into free trade with the United States, a decision that had neither been communicated internally to the researchers, nor been agreed to by the other Commissioners... Thus, the academics had to scramble to produce studies focusing on free trade after Macdonald went public' (14). This criticism seems unfair, however, since the commission itself only reported in 1985 and by then the research studies were completed and certainly the results of the research would have been largely known prior to then. Inwood himself states: 'As the Macdonald Commission research studies began pouring in throughout 1984 and 1985, the Commissioners started to formulate their conclusions' (179; see also Inwood 2005). As discussed subsequently, the case for free trade was also made earlier to the commission by a number of academics involved with it.

The influence of mainstream economists in the policy recommendations of the commission, and especially its signature recommendation for free trade, is exhibited in various ways. Macdonald was reported to have said that he 'found the economics research produced by the Commission useful in clarifying and supporting his convictions regarding free trade. And he credited Smith and his team of economists, particularly the Wonnacotts [Paul and Ron] and John Whalley for this' (Inwood 1998, 21).[11] The prominent political scientist Richard Simeon (1987) indicated that the rigour and the fairly homogenous view of economics made that discipline prominent as a source of policy advice to the commission. More generally, in their analysis of the relationship between social science and politics, Stephen Brooks and Alain Gagnon (1988, 109) conclude that 'there can be little doubt that economists remain pre-eminent among social scientists in their integration with the policy process'. The virtual unanimity of the economists hired by the Macdonald Commission in favour of free trade, and the general support of the economics profession for such an endeavour certainly also helped make the link between research and policy. As indicated by Inwood (1998, 35), 'only one academic could be found to make the anti-free trade case out of the approximately three hundred hired by the Commission'.

The importance of academic research to the commission in general is illustrated by the fact that of the 1014 references cited in the final report, 67% are from the academic literature, 17% from the background research studies of the commission, 10% from briefs formally presented to the commission, and 6% from references to transcripts of the public hearings. Overall, 84% of references relate to research and mainly academic research, since the background studies were generally synthesis of such research; only 16% of the references were to transcripts of the hearings or briefs presented to the commissioners.[12] The academic research dominated not only in references but also in impact because the briefs and public hearings generally involved advocacy positions opposed to free trade. As Inwood (1998, 18) states: 'The Commission chose largely to ignore the briefs and transcripts.' In this case, at least, it appears that solid peer-reviewed academic research trumped advocacy positions not backed by research.

Importance of Champions in Translating and Delivering the Free Trade Message

For academic research to have an influence on public policy, however, it must have champions who can translate the research and advance

[11] Their influential and long-standing support for free trade is illustrated, for example, in Wonnacott and Wonnacott (1967).

[12] These calculations are based on numbers obtained from a content analysis of the final report (Inwood 2005, 181).

it to policy makers. In the case of free trade for the Macdonald Commission, this was done by three academics associated with the commission: John Whalley (economics); Gil Winham (political science), and Jack Quinn (law). Inwood (1998, 29) states that 'together the three of them coordinated an effort over the summer and fall of 1984 to produce a free trade proposal for the Commissioners'. The credibility of their proposal was likely enhanced by the fact that they came from different disciplines.

In addition to those who influence key decision makers in government, it is also important to have champions who will bring the message directly to the public so as to get public support on side. Without such support, it is unlikely that the political process could simply follow the recommendations of the research, no matter how solid and unanimous in its conclusions. This was particularly important for the free trade recommendation, since advocacy groups were publicly condemning the commission report and its recommendation for free trade.[13] Champions did emerge in the form of some high-profile business leaders, a former politician, Macdonald himself, and some academics, notably John Crispo, whom Macdonald (2005, 11) thanked for 'his robust platform technique which ultimately frightened away the union leaders from contested meetings where initially it was they who had brandished the verbal brass knuckles'.

The 'Mulroney' Election Effect

The movement of the research recommendations and those of the Macdonald Commission into an actual free trade agreement was also fostered by the fact that immediately after the commission's report was published in 1985, a new Conservative government headed by Brian Mulroney replaced the formal Liberal government that had started the commission. Perhaps ironically, the Conservative government had made a bilateral free trade agreement a cornerstone of its platform. Once elected, the government moved swiftly to start negotiations, which lasted from 1985 to 1987, culminating in the FTA that was implemented on January 1, 1989.

The research, especially that of the Macdonald Commission, generally agreed that free trade would positively affect output, income,

---

[13] Daniel Drache and Duncan Cameron (1985) produced an early example of the opposition to the recommendation for free trade.

productivity, growth, employment, and wages in Canada. There would, of course, be adjustment costs, especially for workers displaced by imports produced by low-wage labour in foreign countries. In part to alleviate those adjustment consequences, the commission also recommended a universal income security programme (UISP). UISP was a form of guaranteed annual income with a clawback rate of 20% over the normal income tax rate and applied to all income. It was to replace other income support programmes.

Interestingly, that recommendation did not appear to be based on research, at least not based on research done by the Macdonald Commission. As stated by Jonathan Kesselman (2005, 74): 'It was surprising that the Commission opted for a plan of this kind given that only one if its background studies considered this approach at all and recommended that it not be pursued.' That study, however, did indicate that 'the UISP program also would have entailed a large redistribution of incomes, raising questions of its political feasibility' (74). In that vein, the research of the Macdonald Commission appears to have influenced policy in that the research backed free trade and opposed a more universal income support programme, even though only the free trade recommendation was pursued politically. This raises the question of why the commission's recommendations seemed to follow the research in supporting free trade, but did not follow the research when the commission (but not the research) recommended a universal income security programme. Perhaps the commission realized that the UISP was not politically feasible given its costs, but its recommendations in that direction 'took them off the hook' with respect to dealing with the adjustment consequences of free trade.

As Kesselman (2005, 74) states: 'Despite the fact that Canada has not pursued a guaranteed annual income along the lines of the UISP, the Commissions general approach has nevertheless had a significant impact on subsequent policy developments.' He then cites a number of income support programmes that incorporated many of the general features of the UISP.

The Evolution to the North American Free Trade Agreement

Shortly after the implementation of the FTA, Canada found itself negotiating a trilateral agreement to also include Mexico under NAFTA, signed in 1992 and ratified by Canada in 1993. Daniel Trefler (2005,

111) states that 'the year 1993 was a low water mark for the [previous] Canada-U.S. Free Trade Agreement' since Canada was in the depths of a recession and was experiencing extensive job losses, especially in manufacturing. In that vein, it is somewhat surprising that NAFTA could be negotiated under such conditions. There are a number of contrasts between the FTA and NAFTA, however, that have implications for understanding why it was negotiated as well as the potential impact of research on trade policy.

Major Differences in the Period of Debate

While the research of the Macdonald Commission was likely influential in establishing the FTA, or at least facilitated the political process in establishing it, there was no equivalent commission or body of research to recommend NAFTA. The earlier research and recommendations of the Macdonald Commission, as well as the academic research, however, in general would carry forward to such an extended agreement. Thus the academic research was fairly solidly behind freer trade.

Furthermore, the period of time between the FTA of 1989 and NAFTA of 1992 was far too short for the impact of the FTA to be determined, especially because it was to be phased in over 10 years. As well, there was simply too short a period for a systematic research agenda to be put together. Also, as mentioned, the early 1990s was a period of severe recession in Canada so that it would not be possible to disentangle the impact of the FTA from that of the recession that was largely induced by tight monetary and fiscal policy.

Research on the impact of the FTA did not emerge until after NAFTA was negotiated, so that it was not able to influence that policy process. The research generally found that the FTA led to short-run adjustment costs but long-run gains in productivity and output, as predicted by economic theory. Noel Gaston and Daniel Trefler (1994; 1997), for example, estimate that about 10% of the 400 000 jobs lost in Canada between 1989 and 1993 can be attributed to the tariff reductions of the FTA. The vast majority of the losses are attributed to other adjustment pressures such as the recession, high interest rates, a high exchange rate, and technological change. They further emphasise that the job losses would have been mitigated had there been more wage flexibility in Canada. Trefler (2004) further documents the adjustment costs and the long-run productivity benefits from the associated restructuring.

At the time NAFTA was negotiated there was also no research on the controversial social issue of whether it would foster a 'race to the bottom' in terms of social policy initiatives. As indicated subsequently, such research did not appear until the late 1990s. Furthermore, conflicting evidence is found, with the evidence from political scientists suggesting no downward converge and the evidence from economists suggesting some downward convergence, not all of which is regarded as undesirable.

The Lack of Research-Based Channels of Influence

Even if research on the economic and social impacts of the FTA had been available at the time of negotiating NAFTA, it is unlikely that it would have had much of an impact because NAFTA was more of a defensive move—Canada did not want to be left out of such an agreement that otherwise may reallocate U.S. trade from the north to the south. In contrast, the FTA involved a conscious effort by Canada to negotiate a bilateral free trade agreement with the U.S. so as to secure access to that large market and to foster domestic market-oriented reform. As Winham (2005, 104) puts it: 'Unlike the North America Free Trade Agreement (NAFTA) which was a foreign policy in which Canada sought to maintain its interests against initiatives by foreign countries [Mexico], the FTA was at base a domestic policy in which Canada sought especially to regulate its economy.' Such a conscious domestic policy effort would likely require more research support for its political acceptability than would a more defensive foreign policy move.

Another difference between NAFTA and the earlier FTA was that the FTA involved a trading arrangement with another high-wage country, the U.S., while NAFTA involved a trading arrangement to include a low-wage country, Mexico. This raised similar concerns as were occurring in the U.S.—that is, the possibility that low-wage imports from Mexico would displace low-wage labour in the U.S. and Canada, and this would exacerbate the growing wage inequality that was already occurring. Academic research tends to support the notion that freer trade with low-wage countries has contributed to the growing wage inequality in countries such as Canada and the U.S., although the impact of trade is likely smaller than that of skill-biased technological change.[14] Such trade, however, was already occurring from other low-wage countries

---

[14] Reviews of that earlier literature are contained in William Cline (1997), Susan Collins (1998), Robert Feenstra and Gordon Hanson (Feenstra and Hanson 1997), J. David Richardson (1995), Dani Rodrik (1997), and Adrian Wood (1995).

especially in Asia, so Mexico was only regarded as part of an already continuing trend.

The 'Giant Sucking Sound' Debate

A related concern with NAFTA was what a third-party presidential candidate at the time, Ross Perot, termed the 'giant sucking sound'; namely, that the expansion of free trade to a low-wage country such as Mexico would put pressure on wages and for a harmonisation of labour and social policy, and the harmonisation would be downward toward the lowest common denominator—Mexico. That is, with such freer trade and more open capital flows, multinational corporations (MNCs) would be more likely to locate their production in countries with lower labour costs and labour standards, and export into the higher cost countries. Given this credible threat, governments would be under pressure to compete for business investment and the jobs associated with that investment. They would do so in part by being 'open for business' by reducing their laws and regulatory initiatives that otherwise impose costs on business. The polemics in this area were loud and strong, as evidenced by the phrases that were used to describe the phenomenon: race to the bottom, social dumping, harmonisation to the lowest common denominator, regulatory meltdown, ruinous competition, and the rule of the market replacing the rule of law.[15] The polemics, however, were not backed by research. In fact, it was only in the post-NAFTA period that research was conducted on the topic.[16]

In the U.S., NAFTA was also associated with the issue of illegal immigration. The hope was that free trade would be a substitute for labour mobility—in this case, illegal immigration. That is, individuals can move to another country directly by migrating (legally or illegally)

[15] For discussions in the Canadian context see Roy Adams and Lowell Turner (1994), Morley Gunderson (1993), Brian Langille (1996), Ian Robinson (1998), and Gilles Trudeau and Guylaine Vallée (1994).

[16] Various studies published by Keith Banting, George Hoberg, and Richard Simeon (1997) indicate that Canadian policies have tended to converge toward those of the United States in a number of areas, including macroeconomic policy, industrial policy, and environmental policy, as well as individual political rights and judicial protection from the state. With respect to social policy, however, studies by political scientists tend to suggest little or no convergence (Boychuk and Banting 2003; Cameron and Stein 2000, S30; Garrett 1998, 823; McBride and Williams 2001, 302; Simeon *et al.* 1997, 393); studies by economists suggest considerable convergence (Gomez and Gunderson 2002, 2005; Gunderson 1998, 1999).

or they can 'move' indirectly by having their labour embodied in goods and services that are exported to that country.[17] In essence, the receiving country can 'import' labour directly by immigration (legal or illegal), or it can import it indirectly by importing goods and services that embody the labour that otherwise would have moved. This possibility was emphasised by Mexican president Carlos Salinas when he said 'you can take our goods or our people' during the NAFTA negotiations.

In the other direction, trade and mobility can also be complementary. Immigration can foster trade and capital flows as the new immigrants bring ties with their former country in various dimensions, including customers, suppliers, investment opportunities, and sources of finance. Immigrants also encourage the interactions in the other dimensions of integration, through language and networks. Cities such as Toronto, for example, have a comparative advantage in the global marketplace in all of these dimensions given their high concentration of immigrants.

While free trade and freer labour and human capital mobility can be substitutes or complements in theory, the evidence based on research suggests that they are complements in practice.[18] That is, free trade tends to promote labour mobility and migration rather than being a substitute for it. In general, the research suggests that integration in one area can foster deeper integration in other areas.

This complementarity does not have to be the case with each and every dimension of deeper integration. Earlier Canadian tariff barriers and capital restrictions encouraged foreign direct investment (FDI) and ownership in Canada as a way to 'jump the tariff walls'. Free trade and FDI were substitutes, with FDI increasing when free trade was inhibited. Networking through the internet is a form of trade in services whereby 'virtual mobility' can be a substitute for actual mobility.

[17] This is part of the factor price equalization theorem whereby factor prices (e.g., wages) can be equalised across countries through labour migrating from low-wage to high-wage regions. The supply reduction in the low-wage region and the supply influx into the high-wage region reduce wage differentials. But factor prices can also be equalised by trade in goods and services that embody the different types of labour. According to the Heckscher-Ohlin theorem, low-wage countries export labour-intensive goods that embody the low-wage labour inputs with which they are abundantly endowed. This is equivalent to them exporting their low-wage labour through migration (i.e., trade can be a substitute for migration from the low-wage country).

[18] Evidence on the complementarities between immigration, trade, and foreign direct investment (FDI) is given in Steve Globerman (2000), Keith Head and John Ries (1998), and Saskia Sassen (1988).

Free trade may also be a substitute for the brain drain or the loss of human capital through international migration of highly educated personnel. This is of particular concern to Canada because it extensively subsidises higher education through higher taxes while the U.S. has lower taxes, more user charges for education and a more dispersed salary distribution. As such, individuals have an incentive to acquire their subsidised education but then move to the U.S. given the higher pay and lower taxes. The brain drain after the FTA and NAFTA, however, has not been as large as it was earlier in the century, and not as large as may be expected given the large differences in after-tax income and unemployment between Canada and the U.S. (Helliwell 2001).

Canada's Experience with Free Trade Agreements: Did the Research Matter?

Establishing a formal causal link whereby research affects policy is difficult, if not impossible, for a number of reasons, including reverse causality whereby the political process influences the research to support its already predetermined policies. As well, research results may only be apparent when they confirm the desired policy change; otherwise they are 'buried' or there may be counter studies commissioned to offset their impact.

Subject to these caveats, Canada's experience with the FTA and NAFTA suggests that research did have an influence, at least in facilitating the political process to carry out its more market-oriented agenda to include free trade. It is simply impossible to tell whether the research could have killed the political agenda if the research did not support free trade. Certainly, the opposition to free trade was not backed by research. It had a more polemic, nationalist-interventionist orientation. Such an orientation was more favourably regarded in the 1960s and '70s but by the early 1980s was falling out of favour given the adverse economic conditions starting in the mid 1970s—conditions that many would regard as fostered by the interventionist practices.

While the precise impact of research on the FTA is impossible to establish, that agreement was backed by the extensive research of the Macdonald Commission as well as academic research in general. That research was of high quality and done by top academics, and it involved a synthesis of the cumulative academic research to that time. This highlights the importance of having both an existing stock of cumulative research upon which to draw and the capability of having mechanisms for synthesising such research and linking it to policy.

Other ingredients, however, helped in the link between research and policy. The research had champions within the research community itself who brought the free trade message to the commissioners and who often trumpeted it to the general public afterward. The commission made a point of promoting the message to the general public, in part to counteract the opposition that was coming from trade unions and other advocacy groups. As well, the whole free trade agenda was part of a larger movement away from interventionist-nationalist policies and toward a more market-oriented, deregulated economy. The stars were coming into alignment; research was part of that constellation, but just how important is impossible to establish.

The subsequent extension of the FTA to include Mexico under NAFTA did not have an extensive Canadian research component backing it in part because the period between the FTA and the signing of NAFTA was too short for the impact of the FTA to be determined or for a research programme to be mustered. However, research on the economic and social impacts of the FTA did appear after NAFTA was negotiated, and generally showed favourable results in terms of productivity and growth, but with short-run adjustment consequences that could have been mitigated by more wage flexibility. The evidence on the social impact suggested either no downward harmonisation in social policies or downward harmonisation that is not necessarily undesirable. Even if such research would have been available for the NAFTA policy deliberations, it would not likely have played a major role because NAFTA was more of a defensive foreign policy move to ensure that Canada would not be left out of a trade agreement with Mexico and the United States. Furthermore, the legacy of the research of the Macdonald Commission and the academic research in general certainly would carry through. Research did draw attention, however, to other issues and especially the possible impact of NAFTA on labour adjustment and wage polarisation that was also occurring in response to other forces such as skill-biased technological change.

Conclusion

This chapter has suggested that there is a stronger role for research when it is supporting a large paradigm change (e.g., from nationalist intervention to reliance on market forces as was the case in the FTA) than in paradigm reinforcement, like in the subsequent expansion of free trade in the case of NAFTA. Whether this general finding will apply to future bilateral or regional negotiations is an open question. Such future negotiations research is not likely to play as important a role, because there seems a reasonable agreement that additional free trade is likely to lead to short-run adjustment costs in terms of job losses (especially if there is not wage flexibility) but long-run gains in terms of productivity and growth. As such, politics will likely play an important role because political factors are probably to be crucial in determining the feasibility of absorbing short-run costs for long-run gains.

Overall, the Canadian experiences with the FTA and NAFTA suggest that high-quality research was likely an important ingredient in enabling (but not causing) the political process to adopt these free trade agreements. The process was facilitated, however, by other ingredients, including champions who can synthesise and translate the academic research for the political process and the public in general. Research is likely to be neither a necessary nor sufficient condition for policy change, but it can facilitate such change if the other stars are aligned.

References

Adams, Roy, and Lowell Turner. 1994. 'The Social Dimension of Freer Trade.' In Maria Cook, and Harry Katz, eds., *Regional Integration and Industrial Relations in North America*. Ithaca: ILR Press, 82–104.

Banting, Keith. 2004. 'Economic Union and Development Prospects for Canada.' *Canadian Encyclopedia*. <canadianencyclopedia.ca/index.cfm?PgNm=TCE&Params=A1ARTA0002515> [Accessed: December 2007].

Banting, Keith, George Hoberg, and Richard Simeon. 1997. 'Introduction.' In Keith Banting, George Hoberg, and Richard Simeon, eds., *Degrees of Freedom: Canada and the United States in a Changing World*. Montreal and Kingston: McGill-Queen's University Press.

Boychuk, Gerard, and Keith Banting. 2003. 'The Paradox of Convergence: National Versus Sub-National Patterns of Convergence in Canadian and U.S. Income Maintenance Policy.' In Richard Harris, ed., *North American Linkages: Opportunities and Challenges for Canada*. Calgary: University of Calgary Press.

Brooks, Stephen, and Alain Gagnon. 1988. *Social Scientists and Politics in Canada: Between Clerisy and Vanguard*. Kingston: McGill-Queen's University Press.

Brown, Drusilla, and Robert Stern. 1987. 'A Modeling Perspective.' In Robert Stern, Philip Trezise, and John Whalley, eds., *Perspectives on a U.S.-Canadian Free Trade Agreement*. Washington DC: Brookings Institution Press, 155–190.

——. 1989. 'Computable General Equilibrium Estimates of the Gains from U.S.-Canadian Trade Liberalisation.' In David Greenaway, Thomas Hyclak, and Robert Thornton, eds., *Economic Aspects of Regional Trading Arrangements*. London: Harvester Wheatsheaf.

Cameron, Duncan, and Janice Gross Stein. 2000. 'Globalization, Culture, and Society: The State as a Place amidst Shifting Spaces.' *Canadian Public Policy* 26(Supplement): S15–S34.

Canada. Department of Finance. 1988. *Canada-United States Free Trade Agreement: An Economic Assessment.* Ottawa: Canadian Government Publishing Centre.
Chant, John. 2005. 'Macro Stability and Economic Growth: What the Macdonald Commission Said.' In David Laidler, and William Robson, eds., *Prospects for Canada: Progress and Challenges Twenty Years after the Macdonald Commission.* Toronto: C.D. Howe Institute, 13–24.
Cline, William. 1997. *Trade and Wage Inequality*. Washington DC: Institute for International Economics.
Collins, Susan, ed. 1998. *Imports, Exports, and the American Worker*. Washington DC: Brookings Institution Press.
Cox, David, and Richard Harris. 1985. 'Trade Liberalization and industrial Organization: Some Estimates for Canada.' *Journal of Political Economy* 93(1):115–145.
——. 1986. 'A Quantitative Assessment of the Economic Impact on Canada of Sectoral Free Trade with the United States.' *Canadian Journal of Economics* 19(3):377–394.
——. 1992. 'North American Free Trade and Its Implications for Canada: Results from a CGE Model of North American Trade.' *Economy-wide Modeling of the Economic Implications of a Free Trade Agreement with Mexico and a NAFTA with Canada and Mexico.* Washington DC: United States international Trade Commission.
Crandall, Robert. 1987. 'A Sectoral Perspective: Steel.' In Robert Stern, Philip Trezise, and John Whalley, eds., *Perspectives on a U.S.-Canadian Free Trade Agreement.* Washington DC: Brookings Institution Press, 241–243.
Cypher, James. 1992. "Labor Market Implications of the Mexico-U.S. Free Trade Agreement." Paper presented at the Allied Social Science Association meeting, New Orleans, January.
Drache, Daniel, and Duncan Cameron, eds. 1985. *The Other Macdonald Report: The Consensus on Canada's Future that the Macdonald Commission Left Out.* Toronto: Lorimer.
Dungan, Peter. 1985. *The Macroeconomic Impacts of Free Trade with the United States: Lessons from the FOCUS-PRISM Models.* Working Paper DP85-6. Toronto: University of Toronto.
Feenstra, Robert, and Gordon Hanson. 1997. 'Foreign Direct Investment and Relative Wages: Evidence from Mexico's Maquiladoras.' *Journal of International Economics* 42(3–4):371–383.
Garrett, Geoffrey. 1998. *Partisan Politics in a Global Economy*. Cambridge: Cambridge University Press.
Gaston, Noel, and Daniel Trefler. 1994. 'The Role of International Trade and Trade Policy in the Labour Markets of Canada and the United States.' *World Economy* 17(1):45–62.
——. 1997. 'The Labour Market Consequences of the Canada-U.S. Free Trade Agreement.' *Canadian Journal of Economics* 30(1):18–41.
George, Henry. 1886. *Protection or Free Trade: An Examination of the Tariff Question with Especial Regard for the Interests of Labor.* New York: Robert Schalkenbach Foundation, 1980.
Globerman, Steve. 2000. *Trade Liberalisation and the Migration of Skilled Professionals and Managers: The North American Experience.* London: Blackwell Publishing.
Gomez, Rafael, and Morley Gunderson. 2002. 'The Integration of Labour Markets in North America.' In George Hoberg, ed., *Capacity for Choice: Canada in a New North America.* Toronto: University of Toronto, 309–356.
——. 2005. 'Does Economic Integration Lead to Social Policy Convergence? An Analysis of North American Linkages and Social Policy.' In Richard Harris, and Thomas Lemieux, eds., *Social and Labour Market Aspects of North American Linkages.* Calgary: University of Calgary Press, 309–356.
Grinspun, Ricardo. 1991. "Are Economic Models Reliable Policy Tools? Forecasting Canadian Gains from Free Trade." Paper presented at the conference on 'Critical Perspectives on North American Integration', York University, 6–8 December.

Gunderson, Morley. 1993. 'Labour Adjustment Under NAFTA: Canadian Issues.' *North American Outlook* 4(1–2):3–21.
——. 1998. 'Harmonization of Labour Policies under Trade Liberalization.' *Relations industrielles/Industrial Relations* 53(1):24–52.
——. 1999. 'Labour Standards, Income Distribution, and Trade.' *Integration and Trade* 3 (January–February):24–52.
——. 2007. 'How Academic Research Shapes Labor and Social Policy.' *Journal of Labor Research* 28(4):573–590.
Hamilton, Robert, and John Whalley. 1985. 'Geographically Discriminatory Trade Arrangements.' *Review of Economics and Statistics* 57(3):446–455.
Harris, Richard. 1985. 'Jobs and Free Trade.' In David Conklin, and Thomas Courchene, eds., *Canadian Trade at a Crossroads: Options for New International Agreements*. Toronto: Ontario Economic Council 188–203.
Harris, Richard, and David Cox. 1984. *Trade, Industrial Policy, and Canadian Manufacturing*. Toronto: Ontario Economic Council.
——. 1985. 'Summary of a Project on the General Equilibrium Evaluation of Canadian Trade Policy.' In John Whalley, ed., *Canada-United States Free Trade*. Toronto: University of Toronto Press.
Hart, Michael. 1994. *Decision at Midnight: Inside the Canada-U.S. Free-Trade Negotiations*. Vancouver: University of British Columbia Press.
——. 2005. 'International Trade: Tinker or Transform to Re-energize the Canada-U.S. Economic Relationship.' In David Laidler, and William Robson, eds., *Prospects for Canada: Progress and Challenges Twenty Years after the Macdonald Commission*. Toronto: C.D. Howe Institute, 121–133.
Head, Keith, and John Ries. 1998. 'Immigration and Trade Creation: Econometric Evidence from Canada.' *Canadian Journal of Economics* 31(1):47–62.
Helliwell, John. 2001. 'Canada: Life Beyond the Looking Glass.' *Journal of Economic Perspectives* 15(1):107–124.
Informetrica. 1985. *Economic Impacts of Enhanced Trade: National and Provincial Results*. Ottawa: Department of External Affairs.
Inwood, Gregory. 1998. "The Universe Is in Trouble: Please Advise—Social Science Research and Knowledge Utilization in the Research Program of the Macdonald Commission." Paper presented at the annual general meeting of the Canadian Political Science Association, Ottawa, 31 May.
——. 2005. *Continentalizing Canada: The Politics and Legacy of the Macdonald Commission*. Toronto: University of Toronto Press.
Jenson, Jane. 1994. 'Commissioning Ideas: Representation and Royal Commissions.' In Susan Phillips, ed., *How Ottawa Spends 1994–95*. Ottawa: Carleton University Press.
Kesselman, Jonathan. 2005. 'Labour Markets and Social Policy: Impacts of the Macdonald Commission Report.' In David Laidler, and William Robson, eds., *Prospects for Canada: Progress and Challenges Twenty Years after the Macdonald Commission*. Toronto: C.D. Howe Institute, 67–82.
Langille, Brian. 1996. 'General Reflections on the Relationship of Trade and Labor (Or Fair Trade Is free Trade's Destiny).' In Jagdish Bhagwati, and Robert Hudec, eds., *Fair Trade and Harmonization*, vol. 2, Legal Analysis. Cambridge MA: Harvard University Press, 231–266.
Macdonald, Donald. 2005. 'The Commission's Work and Report: A Personal Perspective.' In David Laidler, and William Robson, eds., *Prospects for Canada: Progress and Challenges Twenty Years after the Macdonald Commission*. Toronto: C.D. Howe Institute, 5–12.
Magun, Sunder, Someshwar Rao, Bimal Lodh, Laval Lavallée, and Jonathan Pierce. 1988. *Open Borders: An Assessment of the Canada-U.S. Free Trade Agreement*. Discussion Paper No. 331. Ottawa: Economic Council of Canada.

McBride, Stephen, and Russell Williams. 2001. 'Globalization, the Restructuring of Labour Markets, and Policy Convergence.' *Global Social Policy* 1(3):281–309.
Richardson, J. David. 1995. 'Income Inequality and Trade: How to Think, What to Conclude.' *Journal of Economic Perspectives* 9(3):33–55.
Riddell, W. Craig. 2005. 'Labour Markets and Social Policy: What the Macdonald Commission Said.' In David Laidler, and William Robson, eds., *Prospects for Canada: Progress and Challenges Twenty Years after the Macdonald Commission.* Toronto: C.D. Howe Institute, 53–66.
Robinson, Ian. 1998. 'NAFTA, Social Unionism, and Labour Movement Power in Canada and the United States.' *Relations industrielles/Industrial Relations* 49(4):657–693.
Rodrik, Dani. 1997. *Has Globalization Gone Too Far?* Washington DC: Institute for International Economics.
Royal Commission on the Economic Union and Development Prospects for Canada. 1985. *Report of the Royal Commission on the Economic Union and Development Prospects for Canada.* Donald Macdonald, chair. Ottawa: Minister of Supply and Services Canada.
Sassen, Saskia. 1988. *The Mobility of Labor and Capital: A Study in International Investment and Labor Flow.* Cambridge: Cambridge University Press.
Simeon, Richard. 1987. 'Inside the Macdonald Commission.' *Studies in Political Economy* 22(Spring):167–179.
Simeon, Richard, George Hoberg, and Keith Banting. 1997. 'Globalization, Fragmentation, and the Social Contract.' In Keith Banting, George Hoberg, and Richard Simeon, eds., *Degrees of Freedom: Canada and the United States in a Changing World.* Montreal and Kingston: McGill-Queen's University Press.
Sonnen, Carl, and Mike McCracken. 1985. 'Free Trade: The Economic Case Is Positive.' *Monthly Economic Review* 4(11).
Stokes, Ernie. 1989. 'Macroeconomic Impact of the Canada-U.S. Free Trade Agreement.' *Journal of Policy Modeling* 11(2):225–245.
Stolper, Wolfgang, and Paul Samuelson. 1941. 'Protection and Real Wages.' *Review of Economic Studies* 9(1):58–73.
Trefler, Daniel. 2004. 'The Long and the Short of the Canada-U.S. Trade Agreement.' *American Economic Review* 94(4):870–895.
——. 2005. 'International Trade: 20 Years of Failed Economics and Successful Economies.' In David Laidler, and William Robson, eds., *Prospects for Canada: Progress and Challenges Twenty Years after the Macdonald Commission.* Toronto: C.D. Howe Institute, 111–121.
Trudeau, Gilles, and Guylaine Vallée. 1994. 'Economic Integration and Labour Law and Policy in Canada.' In Maria Cook, and Harry Katz, eds., *Regional Integration and Industrial Relations in North America.* Ithaca: ILR Press, 66–81.
Winham, Gil. 2005. 'International Trade: What the Macdonald Commission Said.' In David Laidler, and William Robson, eds., *Prospects for Canada: Progress and Challenges Twenty Years after the Macdonald Commission.* Toronto: C.D. Howe Institute, 99–110.
Wonnacott, Ronald, and Paul Wonnacott. 1967. *Free Trade between the United States and Canada: The Potential Economic Effects.* Cambridge MA: Harvard University Press.
Wood, Adrian. 1995. 'How Trade Hurt Unskilled Workers.' *Journal of Economic Perspectives* 9(3):57–80.

CHAPTER THREE

CREATION OF PROCESSES: SUSTAINABILITY IMPACT ASSESSMENTS

Clive George and Colin Kirkpatrick[1]

During the 1990s civil society organisations expressed increasing concern over the potentially adverse effects of further trade liberalisation on the environment, on employment levels and wage rates in high income countries, and on the development process in developing countries. Concerns that had arisen on the eve of the 1994 North American Free Trade Agreement (NAFTA) became a major issue for the World Trade Organization (WTO) negotiations in Seattle in 1999. After the failure of the Seattle ministerial meeting, the subsequent agenda for the WTO negotiations at Doha in 2001 adjusted to focus on development, with sustainable development as a key goal. Similar goals have been established for many regional and bilateral negotiations.

In response to civil society concerns, the European Commission (EC) embarked on an ongoing programme of Sustainability Impact Assessments (SIAs) of all its trade negotiations. The programme aims to ensure that policy choices are informed by an assessment of their potential economic, social, and environmental impacts in both the European Union and its trading partners, and that they are consistent with the overarching objective of sustainable development.[2] SIAs have

---

[1] This chapter draws on work undertaken for the European Commission to develop and apply a methodology for assessing the impact on sustainable development of trade negotiations and agreements. It reviews the work of many other organisations involved in the commission's Sustainability Impact Assessment programme, whose contributions are gratefully acknowledged. The authors are also grateful to the referees for their helpful comments on an earlier version of the text. The views and opinions expressed are, however, those of the authors alone.

[2] The EC has produced revised guidelines on how to conduct the required analysis (see EC 2005a; 2006b). The guidelines quote from commission's strategic objectives as follows: 'We should make policy choices that ensure that our various objectives are mutually reinforcing. Actions that promote competitiveness, growth and jobs, as well as economic and social cohesion and a healthy environment reinforce each other. These are essential components of the overarching objective of sustainable development, on which we must deliver' (EC 2005a, 1).

been carried out for both global and regional trade agreements, beginning in 1999 in the preparations for the Seattle WTO ministerial. The process includes extensive consultation and participation with stakeholders and other interested parties, alongside qualitative and quantitative research into the relationships between proposed trade measures and their potential effects.

This chapter examines two policy episodes associated with the EC's SIA programme: the Hong King ministerial meeting of the WTO in December 2005 and the 10th anniversary ministerial summit of the Euro-Mediterranean Partnership held in November 2005. It examines the extent to which the SIA programme has influenced either EU trade policy or the formulation of parallel policy measures. Many difficulties have to be addressed in conducting meaningful assessments and integrating their results into trade policy making, and this chapter reviews the extent to which such difficulties have been overcome, as well as the factors that have been influential in contributing to policy change.

Greater understanding of the likely impacts of a trade agreement may influence policy either by way of a change in a country's negotiating position, and hence in the negotiated agreement, or by influencing parallel policy measures designed to enhance the beneficial effects of the agreement or counter its adverse ones. Parallel policies may include domestic measures in any of the trading partners, or support for the introduction of such measures through development assistance.

The European Union's SIA Programme

Following the Uruguay Round of multilateral trade liberalisation, it became apparent that although some developing countries had experienced significant economic benefits, others had not. Much of the evidence suggested that many of the least developed countries (LDCs), particularly in sub-Saharan Africa, had failed to gain from trade liberalisation and, in some cases, had suffered losses. As well as these disappointing outcomes for the LDCs, higher income developing countries became concerned about adverse effects on their development potential resulting from other aspects of the Uruguay agreements, such as the agreement on Trade-Related Intellectual Property Rights (TRIPS). Similar concerns were expressed by civil society organisations, along with further concerns about social impacts in high income countries and worldwide effects on the environment.

In response to these mounting concerns during the preparations for the Seattle ministerial, the EC initiated a preliminary assessment of the impacts on sustainable development in its trading partners and in Europe of the proposed negotiations. This involved extensive stakeholder consultation in parallel with technical analysis, in order to provide objective information for stakeholder dialogue as well as for the negotiation process. The methodology was developed in early 1999, building on earlier experience in assessing the environmental impacts of trade policy (Commission for Environmental Cooperation 1999; Kirkpatrick *et al.* 1999; see also NAFTA Environmental Review Committee 1992; Organisation for Economic Co-operation and Development 1994; United States Trade Representative 1993). An overview assessment of the Seattle agenda was undertaken prior to the WTO ministerial in November 1999 (Kirkpatrick and Lee 1999). This initial analysis indicated that while an overall economic benefit could be expected, many of the issues that had been raised were genuine cause for concern and would need fuller investigation.

After the failure at Seattle, negotiations were subsequently mandated by the Doha ministerial. The EC launched more detailed assessments of all aspects of the Doha agenda and those regional trade negotiations and agreements to which the EU is a party, following further development and refinement of the SIA methodology (Kirkpatrick and Lee 2002). Some 16 SIAs have been undertaken to date by a range of organisations, as listed in Appendix 3–1.[3]

From the outset the SIA programme has stimulated much debate and criticism associated with civil society concerns over the trade liberalisation agenda (SUSTRA 2003; WWF 2002). Many detailed lessons have been learned and have contributed to ongoing refinement of the SIA methodology and its application (George and Goldsmith 2006; Kirkpatrick and George 2006). Further civil society contributions have maintained the pressure to strengthen the process, to enhance its relevance to decision making and to embed it more fully in the formulation of trade policy (Aprodev *et al.* 2002; Campaign to Reform the World Bank *et al.* 2006; Royal Society for the Protection of Birds and International 2003; Solidar 2005). The EC has held two international

---

[3] All SIA studies have been undertaken by external consultants, on a contracted basis. Assessment reports are listed in the references, and are also available on the Sustainability Impact Assessment Website at <www.sia-trade.org>.

conferences to review experience and further develop the process (EC 2003a; 2006a).

SIAs contribute to the public debate on trade liberalisation and, through that debate, provide objective information to decision makers to enable them to integrate sustainable development more successfully into trade policy. To achieve this, the SIA process has to include extensive consultation and participation with stakeholders and other interested parties alongside its technical analysis of causes and effects. The process gathers different views and evaluates them in the light of available information, to provide objective information that is intended to inform the negotiations and contribute to the design of national and international policy measures to enhance beneficial effects and mitigate potentially adverse ones.

A typical SIA examines all the trade measures under negotiation and their potential impacts on all economic sectors in the affected countries. A broad assessment may be undertaken in a preliminary overview SIA, which identifies those measures and sectors for which more detailed sectoral SIAs are needed. Consultation takes place at key stages of either type of assessment, as summarised in Figure 3–1.

The technical aspects of the assessment follow the vertical sequence in the central box of Figure 3–1, interacting with the horizontal inputs and outputs of the consultation process. The first need in the technical assessment is to evaluate the causal relationships for all aspects of the trade policy agenda. The principal measures currently or previously under discussion in the WTO agenda are the following:

- Agricultural tariffs
- Non-agricultural tariffs
- Trade in services
- Trade facilitation
- Government procurement
- Trade and investment
- Competition policy
- TRIPS
- Technical Barriers to Trade (TBT)
- Sanitary and Phytosanitary (SPS) measures
- Rules of origin
- Subsidies, anti-dumping and countervailing measures
- Trade and environment
- Dispute settlement mechanism

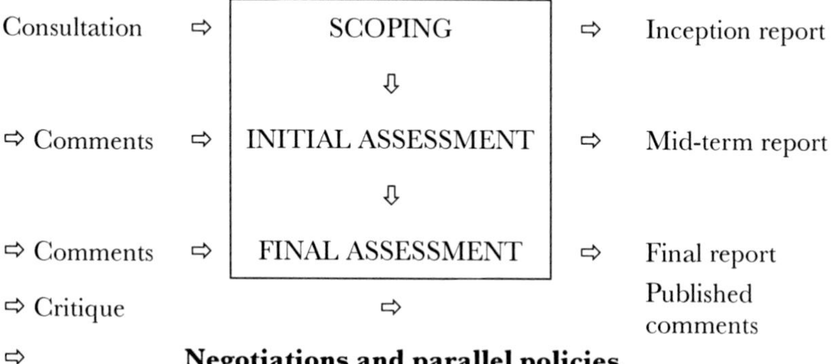

Figure 3–1: Overview of the Sustainability Impact Assessment Process

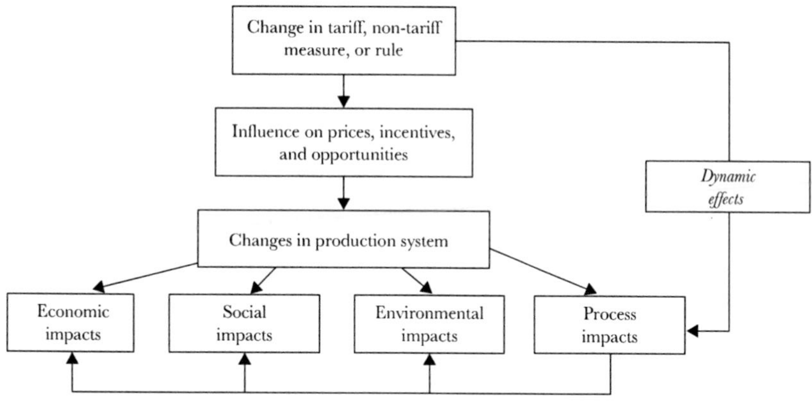

Figure 3–2: Assessment of Impacts

A regional trade agreement may include the equivalents of any or all of these measures.

All of the components of a potential trade agreement have an economic effect, differing between countries, which will in turn have social and environmental effects. Some may also have direct social or environmental effects. The analysis of causal relationships includes, where appropriate, those embedded in economic modelling studies, together with logical analysis of other relationships and empirical evidence from the literature. The process is summarised in Figure 3–2.

For each component of the policy agenda, the central part of the technical analysis begins by identifying the effect of the proposed change on economic incentives and opportunities, in comparison with a baseline of no change to existing agreements. This will cause changes in the production system, differently in different countries, with consequent economic, social, and environmental impacts that may interact with each other. Some impacts may be only temporary, occurring while the system adjusts to the change, while others will continue into the longer term.

Long-term impacts may also arise through the impact of the trade measure on underlying processes of economic development, social transformation, and environmental degradation (or improvement) that are taking place in response to various drivers of change. Any effect that the measure may have on accelerating, decelerating, or otherwise altering any of these processes may have significant long-term impacts on the economic, social, or environmental aspects of sustainable development.

For some components of the policy agenda such as tariff changes, the causal relationships are fairly well understood and may have been incorporated into economic and other models. For others the relationships are less well understood, and empirical evidence of past effects is limited. In such cases much of the analysis consists of evaluating the validity of the various claims made by negotiating parties for and against the proposed measure, alongside stakeholder concerns and further logical analysis of likely causes and effects. The EU's approach to trade impact assessments is not intended to evaluate the impacts of any particular negotiating position or trade policy, but rather to provide information that may contribute to policy development in both the EU and its trading partners. In some of the early studies, attempts were made to evaluate a range of alternative scenarios for a potential trade agreement, but the large number of permutations combined with a relative lack of precision in assessment techniques made this impracticable. Subsequent studies have instead used a single scenario comprising an outer bound for each of the measures under negotiation, from which the likely impacts of any intermediate position can be inferred for each measure.

At the broadest level, sustainable development can be defined in terms of the eight Millennium Development Goals (MDGs) and their 18 targets. Some of the more recent SIAs have therefore assessed the impacts on each target of the MDGs. While this provides important

Table 3–1: First-Tier Indicators or Themes for Sustainability Impact Assessment Methodology

Economic
- Real income
- Fixed capital formation
- Employment

Social
- Poverty
- Health and education
- Equity

Environmental
- Biodiversity
- Environmental quality
- Natural resource stocks

Process
- Adherence to sustainable development principles
- Effectiveness of sustainable development strategies

information, these targets are too general to give a clear indication of many significant impacts. At the regional level a greater degree of precision may be available in an established indicator set. For example, in the SIA of the Euro-Mediterranean Free Trade Area (EMFTA), impacts on each of the 34 priority indicators of the Mediterranean Strategy for Sustainable Development were assessed. Even here however, many of the indicators are designed to monitor the effects of actions other than trade liberalisation, while many of those that are relevant to trade are too broad to indicate important impacts. The SIA methodology therefore steers the assessments according to nine aggregate indicators or sustainable development themes, and two indicators of sustainable development processes (see Table 3–1).

More specific analysis is guided by an initial scoping exercise based on consultation, a review of causal effects, and the evaluation of stakeholder concerns. More detailed second-tier indicators are developed from the significant impacts identified during the assessment, primarily for the purpose of subsequent monitoring.

The Institutional and Political Context of the SIA Programme

The EC developed its SIA programme in response to public concerns. The idea for extensive public dialogue supported by objective analysis of the issues came from within the EC's Directorate General (DG) for Trade and was supported strongly by trade commissioner Pascal Lamy (2005). Informal discussions in the early stages of the programme indicated that some negotiators welcomed the initiative while others felt that it would add little to negotiating positions and might hamper the negotiating process. Officials in the DGs responsible for environmental and social issues were generally supportive.

Whereas the SIAs for the WTO negotiations and most of the EC's regional trade agreements have been commissioned by DG Trade, the SIA for the Euro-Mediterranean Free Trade Area was commissioned by EuropeAid in association with DG External Relations. The difference is associated with a history of EC programmes in the Mediterranean region contributing to the development of a strong network of environmental and civil society organisations, which were active in calling for an impact assessment of the proposed free trade area. Strong support from DG Environment and other DGs working with civil society in the region led to funds being made available for the SIA, with additional support from the DG Trade officials responsible for the other SIAs.

The initial interest to attend to public concerns presents particular challenges for integration into decision making. In assessing impacts in other countries as well as in the EU, the approach aims to be objective and impartial. However, the EU's trade policy is by definition partial, favouring the EU's interests and working toward an agreement with other countries through a process of give and take. If an SIA is indeed impartial, there will inevitably be conflicts between its findings and Europe's negotiating position. This tension is reflected in a clear distinction between the impact assessments conducted under the programme (SIA) and those conducted in parallel under EU procedures for the impact assessment of policy proposals (EC 2005a). For all policy decisions made at the EU level, since 2003 the EC has been implementing an impact assessment process for all major initiatives that are presented in the annual policy strategy or in the work programme of the EC (2002). The majority of these impact assessments involve public consultation and provide full public access to assessment reports. This is not, however, the case for trade policy, where the EC's impact assessments are conducted internally and access to the reports is restricted (EC

2007). If the development of a negotiating position were done publicly, it would reveal the hand of the negotiators and weaken their position. Therefore, although the publicly conducted SIA process is intended to inform negotiating positions, it does not define them.

The EC recognised early on in the post-Doha SIA programme that tensions could arise between the SIA and the established process of building negotiating positions and conducting negotiations. The EC did not expect its negotiating positions to be completely different from the results of an SIA, but accepted that there may be inconsistencies. It established a mechanism for resolving them, in which the EC may modify its position if it considers the result to be robust, but otherwise it may not. In view of the high levels of uncertainty in many of the SIA findings, there is considerable scope for rejecting them on these grounds. The EC may publish its response to the SIA findings and recommendations on its website, although its decisions may entail a degree of confidentiality, to avoid undermining the negotiating position.

Sustainable development is a complex concept covering a wide variety of economic, social, and environmental impacts resulting from many interacting activities. Decisions on appropriate balances and trade-offs can only be made by political processes that take account of the differing values and interests of all the stakeholders in each country. Trade negotiations are one of many such processes, undertaken by negotiators whose prime aim is to maximise particular benefits for their own country. Each country's negotiators consult other government departments in order to develop a negotiating position consistent with that country's interpretation of sustainable development. The subsequent negotiations are primarily a process of give and take on specific economic issues, influenced by each country's arguments that its own interpretation of sustainable development is correct, and that where other countries' interpretations differ from it they are incorrect. Instances where an SIA can demonstrate incontrovertibly that one or other interpretation is correct are extremely rare. More commonly the most an SIA can do is tilt the balance of the negotiations toward Europe's position or against it. A change in the outcome may occur directly if EC negotiators consider the assessment to be sufficiently robust to change their negotiating position, or indirectly through any influence that the public dialogue on the SIA findings may have on the negotiations.

Trade negotiations take place in a wider institutional setting in which the WTO is responsible for maintaining the stability of the international trade regime and promoting further liberalisation of trade, while other international bodies are responsible for international agreements on social and environmental issues. WTO committees on trade and environment and trade and development aim to ensure consistency between WTO agreements and these other agreements, but the WTO's own responsibility is limited to the management and promotion of international trade. The aim of multilateral or bilateral/regional trade negotiations is similarly restricted to promoting trade, while remaining consistent with international agreements on social and environmental issues. To the extent that current global development is socially inadequate and environmentally unsustainable, this may be taken as an indication of the relative weakness of international social and environmental institutions compared with those responsible for economic issues. This weakness may limit the extent to which SIAs can contribute to enhancing sustainability within existing international structures and decision-making frameworks. Alongside this, SIAs may offer the potential to contribute to WTO reform and the reform of other trade policy formulation processes, to steer them more strongly toward sustainable development. The remainder of this chapter examines the extent to which SIAs have influenced trade policy making in favour of sustainable development, and the potential for expanding this influence.

The Effectiveness of SIAs in Inducing Policy Change

Any evaluation of the effectiveness of a programme should in principle begin by specifying its objectives. However, evaluation at the level of final objectives is confronted by the problems of attribution. The methodological problems of establishing a counterfactual baseline from which to assess impacts, and the difficulties of attributing changes to the initial policy intervention, have restricted effective evaluation at this level. A further difficulty often arises with a mismatch between the time over which the impacts have their full effect and the period within which the results of the evaluation can influence decision making. For practical reasons, it will often be necessary to conduct the evaluation at preceding stages in the cause–effect chain. Evaluation at the level of outcomes will assess the effect of the initial activity on the intermediate targets. Output evaluation will assess the outputs of the activity being evaluated. Activities-level evaluation focusses on the procedures followed.

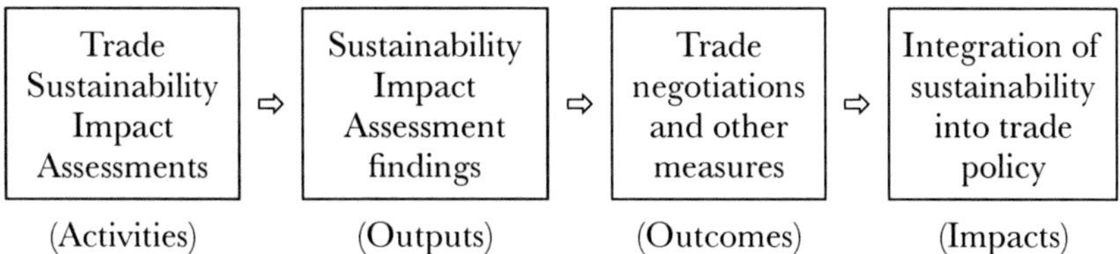

Figure 3–3: Evaluation of Trade Sustainability Impact Assessment

The objectives of the trade SIA programme have been specified by the EC as:

> Sustainability Impact Assessment is a process undertaken before and during a trade negotiation which seeks to identify economic, social and environmental impacts of a trade agreement. The purpose of an SIA is to integrate sustainability into trade policy by informing negotiators of the possible social, environmental and economic consequences of a trade agreement. The idea is to assess how best to define a full package of domestic policies and international initiatives to yield the best possible outcome, not just in terms of liberalisation and economic growth, but also of other components of sustainable development. An SIA should also provide guidelines for the design of possible accompanying policy measures. Such measures may go beyond the field of trade as such, and may have implications for internal policy, capacity building or international regulation. Accompanying measures are intended to maximise the positive impacts of the trade negotiations in question, and to reduce any negative impacts (EC 2005b).

The objective of SIA is therefore to 'integrate sustainability into trade policy', so that the implementation of the negotiated trade measures and accompanying policy measures will contribute to the 'best possible outcome' in terms of sustainable development.[4]

Figure 3–3 illustrates this evaluation chain in the context of the trade SIAs.

The integration of sustainable development into trade policies and accompanying measures was discussed at an international SIA seminar organised by the European Commission in 2003, where participants called for sustainable development to be more firmly established as an overarching aim of trade negotiations (European Commission 2003b). The seminar also sought clarification of the role of SIA in the negotiation process, with many participants worried that SIAs would lead

[4] The core impact indicators used in the SIA methodology are specified in terms of the economic, social, and environmental pillars of sustainable development.

only to accompanying measures to mitigate negative effects of agreements, rather than to modifications in the EU's negotiating position. In responding to these concerns DG Trade (2003, 1, 2) made the following statements:

- 'Sustainable development has to become a central objective in all trade negotiations.'
- 'SIA is an analytical and information tool that should play a key role in attaining this objective.'
- 'DG Trade is committed to SIAs that improve the EU's negotiating positions in the interests of sustainable development. SIAs are not intended to find ways of compensating for the shortcomings of negotiating positions by identifying the need for complementary measures.'

Some indirect evidence on the influence of the SIA studies on the EU's negotiators can be drawn from the position papers published by the EC. For each SIA the EC aims to prepare a paper based on the SIA findings, which defines points of agreement, responds to disagreements, and considers what further action should be implemented. Prior to publication, the position paper is drafted and discussed with member states at the trade committee—the so-called '133 Committee'. This time-consuming process has been completed only for some of the earlier SIA studies. Typical responses fall into one of five main categories:

- specific new action is proposed;
- possible new action is under consideration;
- more detailed analysis is needed before decisions on action can be taken;
- sufficient action is already being taken;
- the EC disagrees with the SIA findings.

Where the responses fall in the first group, the proposed action has tended to be non-specific, such as raising awareness of EC delegations. This suggests that the SIA studies have had little direct influence on negotiating positions.

This conclusion is consistent with the outcome of the Hong Kong ministerial of the WTO in December 2005. No agreement was reached, other than to continue discussions, which themselves reached an impasse in July 2006. Efforts to revive the process have entailed reducing the extent of trade liberalisation under negotiation to be considerably less ambitious than originally proposed. This outcome is compatible with the findings of the SIA studies, which indicate that in the absence of effective mitigation and enhancement measures the original proposals offer only small gains with potentially large adverse effects. Negotiating positions on the WTO Doha agenda have moved toward less ambitious proposals, not as a direct response to the SIA findings, but because of limited progress in the negotiations.

In the case of the EMFTA there is evidence that the impact of the studies on EU policy making may have been somewhat greater, primarily through the attention received in Parliament. The Euro-Mediterranean Parliamentary Assembly Resolution on Economic and Financial Issues, Social Affairs, and Education (21 November 2005) was formulated 'having regard to the Executive Summary of Phase 2 of the Sustainability Impact Assessment Study of the Euro-Mediterranean Free Trade Area' (Euro-Mediterranean Parliamentary Assembly 2005, 2). In addition, a parliamentary question was tabled in the European Parliament, which required the EC to react to the findings of the SIA.

The SIA for the EMFTA is one of the more recent studies, timed to coincide with the preparations for the 10th anniversary ministerial summit of the Euro-Mediterranean Partnership. Many of the actions agreed at the summit address specific issues that were identified in the preliminary consultation draft of the SIA report, as detailed in the final report (SIA-EMFTA Consortium 2006). This suggests that the SIA might have had some indirect influence on the outcome of negotiations, arising primarily through the public dialogue on findings and its contribution to the influence of civil society groups and parliamentarians in both the EC and its trading partners.

In order to obtain wider evidence of the impact of the SIA studies, a pilot questionnaire survey was undertaken to solicit the views of internal and external stakeholders. The limited number of responses cautions against generalising the results, which are best interpreted as providing an indication of the range and variety of views that a larger and more representative sample might reveal. Responses were received from non-governmental organisations (NGOs), the private sector, and EC trade negotiators and officials, giving both 'outsider' perceptions and 'insider' judgements informed by experience. In the responses to specific questions no statistically significant difference was identified between the responses of insiders and outsiders. However, differences may be gleaned from the specific comments made. Respondents were asked to consider only those SIA studies with which they were familiar.

In relation to outcomes, the survey asked two questions covering the impact of the SIAs on decision making.

> *Question A*. To what extent has SIA strengthened the integration of sustainable development into trade policy decisions?
> *Question B*. What is your overall impression of the extent to which SIA has influenced decision making in each of the following areas: influence on trade agreement; influence on development aid programmes; influence on EU domestic policy; influence on domestic policy in non-EU countries?

For the first question, 59% of responses considered that the impact was low or very low, on a scale from one to five for very low to very high. Only one respondent gave a score of five, for very high impact. The responses for the second question were similar, indicating particularly low influence on trade agreements or on domestic policy in non-EU countries. They indicated somewhat greater influence on EU domestic policy and development aid programmes. For development aid, 31% of respondents reported a medium level of influence, and 6% a high level. For EU domestic policy 30% of responses ranged from medium to very high influence (10% each), but with 70% reporting low or very low influence. Over 80% of respondents thought that the influence on trade agreements or non-EU domestic policy was low or very low.

An indication of respondents' reasons for these estimates was given by their responses to the questions related to activities and outputs. Nearly 70% of respondents thought that the SIA methodology had improved with the more recent studies, and only one thought that it had deteriorated. While 37% considered that the quality of analysis of the potential economic, social, and environmental impacts was poor, 16% thought that it was satisfactory, and 47% considered it to be good or very good. The responses to all the questions on the consultation process were positive overall, with 78% indicating satisfactory or better, and 50% good or very good. The discussion of mitigation and enhancement proposals and recommendations for policy makers was the weakest element. This was considered to be poor or very poor by 52% of respondents, and satisfactory or good by 48%. None thought that it was very good. A further indication of respondents' views on the influence of the SIA programme is given by their detailed comments. These are given in Table 3–2.

Table 3–2: Stakeholder Comments on the Sustainability Impact Assessment Process

On Integrating SIAs into Policy Decisions

The direct impact on decisions is low but as part of a general process of awareness raising and understanding of wider impacts of trade reforms it is a positive contribution. Expectations were too high and the baseline (impact of a trade policy without SIA) too complex. (Trade official)

SIA are an instrument of awareness raising for decision makers. But as they are vague they offer arguments for protectionists as well as for more liberal negotiators. The WTO negotiations on the DDA [Doha Development Agenda] are still in a phase where the interesting part of the SIA (flanking measures to avoid negative impact of liberalisation) has no relevance yet. (Private sector)

Sustainable development issues are either seen as mitigation issues or sidelined if they run counter to liberalisation goals. The concept of sustainable development applied by the [European] Commission has not exercised a change in the core of EU trade politics i.e., trade liberalisation. (Private sector)

Gut instinct strongly suggests that the current situation is very much better than that which would have obtained if the SIA policy and programme had not been devised in the first place. The policy has fostered and facilitated comprehensive, balanced, systematic, and structured attention of predicted impacts in each of the economic, social, and environmental spheres. (Trade official)

The mere fact of including an independent sustainability indicator in SIA contributes to the integration of sustainable development into policy decisions. (Non-governmental organisation)

On Methodology

One major factor in this improvement is the benefits derived from the integration of a much wider and more rigorous consultation procedure within the SIA method. (Trade official)

It is evolving and being refined with experience (at least among the more experienced practitioners). (Expert)

While the quality improved somewhat, the financial resources available for the research, I heard, were diminished, which did not allow to make the SIA more comprehensive in its methodology as required based on the experience of the first years and the comments from NGOs. (Non-governmental organisation)

The EU Commission developed standards in cooperation with the business community and the NGOs. This makes the SIA comparable among each other and provides the same set of minimum information. Furthermore, due to the harmonized procedures (three-phase approach), it is easier for civil society to participate as procedures are predictable and input can be planned properly. (Private sector)

Table 3–2 (*cont.*)

On the Analysis of Economic, Social, and Environmental impacts

Too general and linkages not systematic enough. (Trade official)

Environmental analysis could have considered a wider range of ecological services/assets (e.g., on the basis of the analysis in the United Nations Millennium Ecosystem Assessment). (Non-governmental organisation)

There have been numerous criticisms—particularly in relation to the earlier studies—of the paucity and poor quality of the analysis of social impacts relative to analysis of economic or environmental impacts. (Trade official)

The difficulties are in the inability, with this methodology, to give a holistic overview in terms of broader public benefits, rather than a set of sectoral and regional impacts. (Expert)

Varies from study to study—some WTO [World Trade Organization] studies have been very good, whereas some other regional studies have been poor. (Expert)

Not taking into account the impact of WTO rules on the possibility to fully implementing the mitigating policies (advised in the SIA or that might be taken by a government) is a major problem. (Non-governmental organisation)

Some were just poor quality work, others reflected the fact that the TOR [terms of reference] assume that there is the information available to carry out impact studies to the level of detail required to develop detailed SIA recommendations. (Trade official)

On Consultation

Quite good overall—e.g., round tables in Brussels, but unknown at local level. (Non-governmental organisation)

Comments may be taken into account by the impact assessment consultants but I have no evidence of the [European] Commission services taking any notice at all. (Expert)

Every opportunity is provided and studies are at least redrafted to reflect comments. (Expert)

While information and opportunity for consultation are good and sufficient, the main limitation of the consultation process may lie in the reduced capacity of actors to perform in depth analysis of the information and produce relevant comments/recommendations. The consultation process has not taken into consideration the need to support capacity building of actors, in particular civil society and in particular South civil society, who have the strongest limitations in engaging in complex processes such as trade SIAs. (Non-governmental organisation)

Lower marks for availability for comment as had reports often late or at short notice. (Trade official)

Table 3–2 (*cont.*)

The above rating applies mainly to those mainly international organisations (NGOs, special interests/lobbying groups) that are active in Brussels. It is questionable if these groups necessarily always represent those parts of civil society that are likely to be most affected by trade liberalisation (either positively or negatively). (Private sector)

Good line of communication with consultants and officials in meetings and briefings, all documents are quickly and online available, input from business side is taken into consideration in studies. (Private sector)

On Mitigation, Enhancement, and Recommendations
Discussions are very useful. However, the challenge is to ensure that the M [mitigation] and E [enhancement] measures are later on integrated e.g., into EU-aid programmes at country or regional level, or into formulation of trade-related support (e.g., capacity building). (Private sector)

The mandate to give mitigation and enhancement measures to alleviate adverse impacts of trade liberalisation was adhered to with a few good examples. However...the recommendations were often ignored and not seen as a condition by which liberalisation could take place and be beneficial. (Non-governmental organisation)

Too general and not specific enough to be useful. (Trade official)

Some clear indications are provided where mitigation and enhancement measures would alleviate adverse impacts of trade liberalisation. The problem is that this advice is often ignored in the trade liberalisation process. Furthermore, the mitigation and enhancement measures fail to give specific recommendations how the EU trade position should be changed. (Non-governmental organisation)

Mitigation holds the most interesting potential in my opinion, and there should be more discussion of it. (Expert)

Level of generality is too high to come up with workable proposals and most recommendations either assume or require a range of non-trade interventions that have separate financial and political implications. (Trade official)

The stakeholder survey revealed that more still remains to be done to improve the technical and consultative aspects of impact assessments, but a fairly large majority of respondents considered them to be satisfactory or better in most respects. The principal shortcoming identified for the assessments themselves related to the relevance and specificity of the recommendations for mitigation and enhancement. As identified by one of the trade officials, many of the recommendations require non-trade interventions with separate financial and political implications. These are outside the remit of negotiators, and therefore cannot directly influence the negotiations. Others are fairly general and identify issues that negotiators should take into account, without specifying the details of any agreement they should reach. Since the issues are mainly social or environmental, while negotiators are concerned primarily with particular economic gains and losses, it is not clear how they can respond to this type of advice.

These shortcomings identified in the technical aspects of the SIA are consistent with the more general shortcomings identified by respondents, concerning a lack of integration of the studies into trade negotiations and linked policies. This is related to the institutional and political context in which negotiations are conducted and SIAs are undertaken. As noted above, there are significant tensions between an impact assessment process that evaluates impacts for all trading parties and a decision-making process based on negotiation between those parties. This difficulty is compounded by the introduction of social and environmental issues into negotiations that focus primarily on specific economic gains and losses.

Some of these tensions have been eased with the a new generation of studies. The EC has moved away from a philosophy in which the SIA is undertaken as in independent evaluation toward playing a stronger role itself in leading the assessment, and in defining specific issues for which better information is needed. To this end there is a steering committee for each SIA, whose members include trade negotiators for the relevant sectors and representatives of other departments with responsibilities for environment, social issues, and international development. The process has strengthened the role that SIA can play in helping to coordinate the different interests within the EC. Additionally, the interest generated within the European Parliament has enhanced its role in guiding the EC. As well as informing the negotiations, the SIA studies are intended to induce parallel policy measures in both the EU and its trading partners. Here again the stakeholder survey indicates that the SIA studies have had little influence to date. In general the studies have not revealed major adverse impacts in the EU, and so most of the recommendations for parallel measures relate to domestic policy in developing countries and the support that can be provided through development assistance programmes.

As identified in the survey, it is not expected that the studies will have a major influence on domestic decision making in non-EU countries. No evidence of significant influence has been identified. Stakeholders do not expect major influence partly because of a lack of specificity in the recommendations for mitigation and enhancement, and partly because the studies are neither commissioned by partner country governments nor steered toward the specific interests of their negotiators. In general the prime aims of partner country negotiators are to secure greater access for their exports and to minimise the concessions they have to make. In doing so they aim to obtain a net economic benefit, which the studies generally show will be small. Adverse social or environmental impacts as identified in the studies are the responsibility of other government departments, which have limited influence on the negotiations.

The greatest influence on parallel policy measures is expected to occur through EU technical assistance. For example, the study for the forestry sector in the WTO added greater weight to international action already being taken to strengthen forest governance, although there is no clear evidence that the policy was significantly changed by the SIA findings. Most of the SIA recommendations for technical assistance are uncontroversial, and assist primarily in identifying priorities. The greatest influence is expected for regional trade agreements. The number of countries involved is smaller than for WTO negotiations, allowing a greater degree of specificity in the SIA findings and recommendations. Also, regional trade liberalisation may be conducted within a wider framework of regional cooperation, allowing trade issues to be considered alongside non-trade issues. The stakeholder survey did not reveal any clear evidence of policy change at this stage. However, a new generation of SIAs have made more detailed recommendations for development assistance.

Barriers to Policy Influence and Possible Future Developments

The broad programme is an ambitious effort to strengthen the evidence base of trade policies and steer them toward sustainable development. Success to date has been limited. While there are signs that the programme has led to a heightened awareness of the potential impact of trade negotiations and has influenced decision-making processes within the EU, this has yet to feed through to significant changes in trade policy.

Many of the studies have shown that appropriately designed trade reforms have the potential to make a significant contribution to development, and, with appropriate parallel measures, can do so in an environmentally sustainable manner. It has, however, proved extremely difficult to realise these goals through the existing trade negotiating process. The Doha agenda did not change the multilateral process, only its stated goals. Multilateral trade negotiations are not designed to deliver sustainable development. Their purpose has always been to maximise gains and through a process of give and take, and move toward freer trade. To give real life to the development component, it may be necessary to reform the negotiating process itself.

Typically, the SIA studies show that global impacts on climate change and biodiversity loss are adverse, with many local adverse environmental impacts that are not cancelled out by the beneficial ones, and significant social impacts that include losers as well as gainers in many countries. The losers are often the most vulnerable groups. Trade negotiators, individually and collectively, are not responsible for these issues. They are given little specific information on how they should handle them, if at all, even when relevant information is made available. Their prime aim is to achieve market access gains, within the constraints placed by the government's overall policy. They are not responsible for delivering the MDGs, nor do they have the competence to do so. They operate instead on the broad assumption that trade liberalisation, in any form, will help to deliver these goals, and that adverse impacts will be countered through the expected economic gains. This assumption is not borne out by the SIA studies. The current impasse in multilateral trade negotiations, and corresponding difficulties at the regional and bilateral level, may be taken as both an opportunity and an incentive for governments to re-evaluate the role of trade in contributing to wider goals and to adapt the policy-making process accordingly.

The SIA techniques may be able to contribute in two ways. First, although the findings of the multi-country studies have tended to be insufficiently specific to influence policy in developing countries, they have highlighted areas of concern that may be studied in more depth using similar methods by each country individually. The United Nations Environment Programme (UNEP) is undertaking a programme to build capacity in developing countries to undertake integrated impact assessments of this nature, with the support of the EC. An expansion of such assistance may be particularly beneficial for countries that do not have the capacity to support their negotiators with detailed assessments of the impacts of other countries' proposals, or of their own proposals. However, while this would assist developing country negotiators in some respects, it would not remove the problem that the negotiations revolve primarily around the interests of key economic actors in each country, with little attention paid to social and environmental issues, even when information is available.

To help address this fundamental disconnect in the trade negotiation process, transparent multi-country SIA studies as undertaken for the EC might make a larger contribution if undertaken on behalf of the wider international community, rather than being commissioned by one of the main negotiating parties. Such studies might for example be commissioned jointly by a group of international bodies (such as UNEP, the United Nations Development Programme [UNDP], the International Labour Organization [ILO], the World Health Organization [WHO], the United Nations Industrial Development Organization [UNIDO], and the United Nations Conference on Trade and Development [UNCTAD]), with a joint steering committee similar to those introduced by the EC, and with the WTO and other international bodies such as the World Bank and the International Monetary Fund (IMF) invited to participate as observers. The findings of such studies would have no mandate to influence the WTO negotiations directly. However, they may carry sufficient weight and credibility in the public arena to influence negotiations indirectly. Similar initiatives may also be taken at the regional level. In the Mediterranean region, for example, the EU and its partner countries have adopted the overarching Barcelona process for regional cooperation and development. This pursues a wide range of development objectives, among which the creation of a free trade area is just one component. In parallel they have developed a Mediterranean Strategy for Sustainable Development. Further refinement of the sustainable development strategy, and its adoption as the defining strategy of the Barcelona process, would allow trade policy to be made subordinate to sustainable development, and steered more strongly toward sustainable development goals. A similar approach might be taken for other regional agreements.

Conclusions

The EU's programme of ISAs of global and regional trade agreements has presented many challenges. These relate to consultation at the regional or global level, the technical aspects of assessing impacts whose origins lie in complex economic effects, and potential conflicts with local, regional, and global decision-making processes. In all these areas approaches have been developed that move some way toward addressing the issues, but many challenges remain. Many of the studies have shown that the benefits that have traditionally been expected from the static efficiency gains of trade liberalisation are small, and that many of the significant impacts occur through long-term dynamic processes. The analysis of these longer term effects and their interactions with other policy areas is expected to be a key area for future developments in trade impact assessment.

In respect of the two specific policy episodes examined, the influence of the SIA programme has been limited. At the regional level of the EMFTA there are indications that the SIA findings may have had some influence on the negotiations, via representations from civil society organisations and from parliamentarians in the EU and partner countries, rather than through any observable change in Europe's negotiating position. At the multilateral level of the WTO Doha agenda negotiating positions have moved toward less ambitious proposals, because of limited progress in the negotiations rather than in response to the SIA findings.

This limited influence is associated with potential conflicts that have been identified between the impact assessment process and the decision-making process. While some of these have been satisfactorily resolved, attention needs to be paid to the decision-making process itself in order to better address the most significant regional and global issues that have been identified in the assessments. Most trade agreements have adopted sustainable development as a goal, but the bodies that negotiate them are not responsible for sustainable development, do not have the competence to define what sustainable development means, and are not subject to the requirements of any other authority except as provided through international environmental law and other mechanisms of regional and global governance. This chapter has identified steps that might be taken to address these limitations at both global and regional levels, which might help to make trade policy more readily steerable toward sustainable development goals.

Finally, the trade impact assessment techniques that have been developed for use by high income countries may prove to be highly appropriate for helping to strengthen trade policy in developing ones. For single country studies the decision-making processes are more straightforward, impacts can be studied in more detail, and recommendations can be made more specific. The integrated assessment of economic, social, and environmental effects, by each country for its own purposes, may be particularly influential in helping developing countries to formulate their trade policy more effectively, and to play a stronger role in international trade negotiations.

References

Aprodev, Begegnungszentrum für Aktive Gewaltlosigkeit, Berne Declaration, Campagna per la Riforma della Banka Mondiale, Centre for International Environmental Law, Center for Environmental Public Advocacy, Eurostep, Fern, Friends of the Earth Europe, Green Alternative, ICDA, International Confederation of Free Trade Unions, KULU Women and Development, Solidar, Solidaridad International, Weltladen-Dachverband, Women in Development Europe, Weltladen-Dachverband, Werkgroep Globalisering, World Development Movement, and WWF European Policy Office. 2002. *Joint NGO statement on Sustainability Impact Assessments of EU Trade Policy.* July. Brussels. <trade.ec.europa.eu/doclib/html/122192.htm> [Accessed: January 2008].

Campaign to Reform the World Bank, Friends of the Earth Europe, Greenpeace International, and Women in Development Europe. 2006. *Learning Lessons from Sustainability Impact Assessments: The Responsibility of the European Union to Exclude Natural Resources—Forestry, Fisheries, and Minerals—from the WTO NAMA Negotiations.* 21–22 March. Brussels. <www.foeeurope.org/publications/2006/NGO_Statement_natural_resources_SIAs_March06.pdf> [Accessed: January 2008].

Commission for Environmental Cooperation. 1999. *Analytic Framework for Assessing the Environmental Effects of the North American Free Trade Agreement.* Montreal: Commission for Environmental Cooperation. <www.cec.org/programs_projects/trade_environ_econ/pdfs/frmwrk-e.pdf> [Accessed: January 2008].

Euro-Mediterranean Parliamentary Assembly. 2005. *Resolution of the Euro-Mediterranean Parliamentary Assembly on Economic and Financial Issues, Social Affairs, and Education.* 21 November. Rabat. <libr.sejm.gov.pl/oide/empa/2_rabat_en.pdf> [Accessed: January 2008].

European Commission. 2002. *Communication from the Commission on Impact Assessment.* COM(2002) 276 final, 5 June. Brussels. <eur-lex.europa.eu/LexUriServ/LexUriServ.do?uri=CELEX:52002DC0276:EN:NOT> [Accessed: January 2008].

——. 2003a. 'SIA of Trade Agreements: Making Trade Sustainable?' Brussels. <ec.europa.eu/comm/trade/issues/global/sia/seminar.htm> [Accessed: January 2008].

——. 2003b. *SIA of Trade Agreements: Making Trade Sustainable?* Proceedings of the DG Trade Seminar, 6–7 February. Brussels. <trade.ec.europa.eu/doclib/docs/2006/september/tradoc_130035.11.pdf> [Accessed: January 2008].

——. 2005a. *Impact Assessment Guidelines.* SEC(2005) 791. Brussels. <ec.europa.eu/governance/impact/docs/SEC2005_791_IA%20guidelines_annexes.pdf> [Accessed: January 2008].

——. 2005b. 'Sustainability Impact Assessment: FAQs.' Brussels. <ec.europa.eu/trade/issues/global/sia/faqs.htm> [Accessed: January 2008].

——. 2006a. 'EU Trade SIA Stocktaking Conference: Agenda and Speeches.' Brussels. <ec.europa.eu/trade/issues/global/sia/sem0306_prog.htm> [Accessed: January 2008].

——. 2006b. *Handbook for Trade Sustainability Impact Assessment.* Brussels. <trade.ec.europa.eu/doclib/html/127974.htm> [Accessed: January 2008].

——. 2007. 'List of Impact Assessments Planned and Carried Out.' Brussels. <ec.europa.eu/governance/impact/practice_en.htm> [Accessed: January 2008].

——. Directorate General Trade. 2003. *Challenges Identified at the Seminar and Replies from the Commission.* Following the DG Trade Seminar, 6–7 February. Brussels. <trade .ec.europa.eu/doclib/html/130036.htm> [Accessed: January 2008].

George, Clive, and Bernice Goldsmith. 2006. 'Impact Assessment of Trade-Related Policies and Agreements: Experience and Challenges.' *Impact Assessment and Project Appraisal* 24(4):254–258.

Kirkpatrick, Colin, and Clive George. 2006. 'Methodological Issues in the Impact Assessment of Trade Policy: Experience from the European Commission's Sustainability Impact Assessment (SIA) Programme.' *Impact Assessment and Project Appraisal* 24(4):325–334.

Kirkpatrick, Colin, and Norman Lee. 1999. *WTO New Round: Sustainability Impact Assessment Study, Phase Two Report.* Institute for Development Policy and Management and Environmental Impact Assessment Centre, University of Manchester. <www.sia-trade .org/wto/Phase2/frontpage2.htm> [Accessed: January 2008].

——. 2002. *Further Development of the Methodology for a Sustainability Impact Assessment of Proposed WTO Negotiations.* Institute for Development Policy and Management and Environmental Impact Assessment Centre, University of Manchester. <www.sia-gcc .org/gcc/download/new_method_april_2002_civil.pdf> [Accessed: January 2008].

Kirkpatrick, Colin, Norman Lee, and Oliver Morrissey. 1999. *WTO New Round: Sustainability Impact Assessment Study, Phase One Report.* Institute for Development Policy and Management and Environmental Impact Assessment Centre, University of Manchester, and Centre for Research on Economic Development and International Trade, University of Nottingham. <www.sia-trade.org/wto/Phase1/frontpage1.htm> [Accessed: January 2008].

Lamy, Pascal. 2005. *Trade Can Be a Friend, and Not a Foe, of Conservation.* Speech at the WTO Symposium on Trade and Sustainable Development, 10–11 October. Geneva: World Trade Organization. <www.wto.org/english/news_e/sppl_e/sppl07_e.htm> [Accessed: January 2008].

NAFTA Environmental Review Committee (Canada). 1992. *North American Free Trade Agreement: Canadian Environmental Review.* October. Ottawa: Government of Canada.

Organisation for Economic Co-operation and Development. 1994. *Methodologies for Environmental and Trade Reviews.* OCDE/GD(94)103. Paris: Organisation for Economic Co-operation and Development. <www.olis.oecd.org/olis/1994doc.nsf/linkto/ocde-gd(94)103> [Accessed: January 2008].

Royal Society for the Protection of Birds, and Birdlife International. 2003. *Trade and Environment: Sustainable Development (and Sustainability Impact Assessments).* Sandy, Bedfordshire, and Cambridge. <www.birdlife.org/action/change/trade/sdsia.pdf> [Accessed: January 2008].

SIA-EMFTA Consortium. 2006. *Sustainability Impacts of the Euro-Mediterranean Free Trade Agreement: Final Report on Phase 2 of the SIA-EMFTA Project.* Impact Assessment Research Centre, University of Manchester. <www.sia-trade.org/emfta/en/Reports/Phase2FinalreportMar06.pdf> [Accessed: January 2008].

Solidar. 2005. *Trade for Decent Work, Decent Life: Assessment before Agreement.* Statement for the 6th World Trade Organization ministerial, Hong Kong.

SUSTRA. 2003. *Sustainability Impact Assessment: Policy Brief Paper.* Based on the SUSTRA seminar on "Sustainability Impact Assessment, 26–27 April 2003, Center for Philosophy of Law (CPDR), Université catholique de Louvain, Louvain-la-Neuve. Montellier. <www.agro-montpellier.fr/sustra/publications/policy_briefs/policy-brief-sia-eng.pdf> [Accessed: January 2008].

United States Trade Representative. 1993. *The NAFTA: Report on Environmental Issues.* Washington DC: Office of the United States Trade Representative.

WWF. 2002. *Changing the Balance of Trade: A Seminar on Sustainability Assessments of EU Trade Policy.* 9-10 July. Brussels. <www.panda.org/downloads/policy/july2002 balancedtradeproceedings_mt0n.doc> [Accessed: January 2008].

Appendix 3–1: European Union Sustainability Impact Assessments

Sustainability Impact Assessments before 1999

Initial development of SIA methodology (Kirkpatrick *et al.* 1999)
- Overview SIA (IARC)

World Trade Organization's Doha Development Agenda

Further development of SIA methodology (Kirkpatrick and Lee 2002)
- Preliminary Overview SIA (IARC consortium)
- Sector studies
  - Agriculture: Major food crops (Stockholm Environment Institute)
  - Non-agricultural market access: Textiles and clothing, non-ferrous metals, pharmaceuticals (Overseas Development Institute/IARC)
  - Competition policy (British Institute of International and Comparative Law/World Trade Institute/IARC)
  - Environmental services (Cordah/Westlake/IARC)
  - Distribution services (International Trade and Services Policy/IARC)
  - Forests (Savcor Indufor/IARC)
  - Agriculture: General (Overseas Development Institute/IARC)
  - Fisheries (Natural Resources Institute/IARC)
- Final Overview SIA (IARC)

Regional Sustainable Impact Assessments

- European Union–Gulf Cooperation Council (PriceWaterhouseCoopers)
- European Union–African, Caribbean, and Pacific countries (PriceWaterhouse Coopers)
  - overview SIA
  - sector/sub-region SIAs
- European Union–Chile (Planistat)
- European Union–Mercosur
  - overview SIA (Planistat)
  - sector/sub-region SIAs (Impact Assessment Research Centre consortium, in progress)
- Euro-Mediterranean Free Trade Area (SIA-EMFTA consortium/IARC)
  - overview SIA

Sector/Sub-regional Sustainable Impact Assessments

- In progress

Note: IARC = Impact Assessment Research Council, University of Manchester; EMFTA = Euro-Mediterranean Free Trade Area; SIA = Sustainability Impact Assessment.

PART TWO

INSTRUMENTAL CHANGE, OPERATIONAL RESEARCH

CHAPTER FOUR

THE CASE OF ARGENTINE RESEARCH IN BUILDING REGIONAL INTEGRATION

Mercedes Botto and Andrea Carla Bianculli

By the mid 1980s, the Argentine government had launched a process of trade liberalisation that would not be reversed in the future. This decision was framed within the political guidelines—conditionalities—demanded by the World Bank in order to release the loans the country needed to manage its foreign debt difficulties. However, within these broad guidelines, Argentina, as was the case with borrowing countries in general, still had ample freedom of action in terms of both strategic and contingency decisions, as when deciding to opt for either a unilateral liberalisation process or a negotiated one, when privileging a project involving deep integration or mere trade initiatives, or when choosing to establish bilateral agreements with border or with northern countries. In sum, options were not limited.

The novelty and complexity of each of these definitions opened a window of opportunity for the influence of knowledge and academic research. Through their participation in the decisional process, academics could bridge the gap in terms of the uncertainty posed by these new challenges and make a contribution to prevent or avoid the unwanted costs of the reforms, such as those brought about by trade liberalisation.

Political and academic literature has strongly debated the impact of ideas on the decisional process since the early days after the Second World War. Two paradigms have emerged. While the first approach argues that social researchers play a crucial role in the rationalisation of the decision-making process, the second one, which assumes a rather sceptical vision of this relationship, portrays the decisional process as chaotic and decisions as being the result of mutual adjustments among the different actors and arenas. Using this second paradigm, this chapter claims that researchers are only one of the agents involved in the decision-making process, endowed with a specific type of knowledge—namely, scientific knowledge—and their influence depends on their rivalry or connection with the knowledge of other local actors.

The chapter thus evaluates to what extent social research has influenced the trade policy-making process since the re-establishment of democracy in Argentina in 1983, highlighting the factors that promoted the impact of such studies on trade policy. Hence, this research emphasises those least-known or least-publicised aspects of the trade policy by focussing on the processes, actors, and capabilities that have had an impact on decision making.

Building on the current debate about the nexus between knowledge and politics, this chapter analyses two processes of influence. The first, which can be characterised as a successful case, refers to the establishment of the capital goods protocol (CGP) signed with Brazil during the initial period of tariff preferences negotiation (1985 to 1988) and part of the Programme of Economic Cooperation and Integration (Programa de Integración Comercial y Económica [PICE]). The second episode, by contrast, is portrayed as a failed case: the negotiation of the common external tariff (CET) between 1991 and 1994, where, in spite of the technical complexity of the issue at stake, research and knowledge did not have a prominent role in the decision-making process.

Apart from focussing on these two policy episodes and inquiring about how research has contributed to their actual implementation, this analysis is intended to identify the type of knowledge produced, the articulation established with policy makers, and the factors that either promoted or hindered its use in the policy process. The information and data presented are based on secondary sources and the analysis of 18 interviews conducted with policy makers and researchers in the field of foreign trade, representing both private and public research centres, and who were directly involved in the process under the administration of either Raúl Alfonsín (1983–89) or Carlos Menem (1989–99), or both.

This chapter is structured in four parts. The first identifies the contributions to the literature in terms of the conceptual and methodological definitions. The second and third sections delve into the analysis of both episodes of policy change and focus on the research-policy relationship. The fourth section offers a comparative assessment of the field research and an initial impact evaluation. Finally, the conclusion presents the main lessons derived from both cases.

Literature Review and Concept Definition

Interest in the role of ideas and academics in the decision-making process is not new, and the impact of ideas on the decision-making process has been strongly debated in the political and academic literature since the post-war period. Two main paradigms can be identified regarding the role of social researchers—taken as knowledge producers—in the public decision-making processes (Brunner and Sunkel 1993).

The first of these paradigms, the engineering model of information use, which is part of the policy-making theory developed during the 1950s in the United States, promotes a favourable attitude toward social and political engineering. Its main argument is that researchers play a fundamental role because they provide the necessary knowledge and instruments for the rationalisation of the decision-making and coordination processes. In other words, they provide the empirical evidence that clarifies doubts and reduces the uncertainty brought about by policy reform. Four phases are identified, on the assumption that the decisional process is linear and incremental. In each of these phases, one main actor is responsible and stamps its own activity specificities and particular characteristics on the process.

While this first approach argues that social researchers play a key role in the rationalisation of the decision-making process, the second paradigm assumes a rather sceptical vision and characterises the decisional process as mainly chaotic. From this perspective, decisions are the result of mutual adjustments among different players and the diverse arenas where they interact. Within this 'building blocks' game, researchers are just another player, endowed with a very specific type of knowledge—namely, scientific knowledge—and their influence depends on their interaction with the knowledge of other local actors.

The engineering model of information use, which argues that the produced information fits into the decision to be made, has thus been superseded by an approach based on the idea that there are multiple decision-making arenas and that various actors are involved in this game, endowed with only partial information and local knowledge. These actors include social researchers and academics, whose knowledge—based on scientific rules—is only one of the many competing sources of information. However, arguments are put forward in the sense that only in exceptional cases does empirical research produce a direct, instrumental, and clearly identifiable impact on the decision-making process. On the contrary, in most cases, the decisional process is diffuse and lacks a concrete order of stages; in fact, routine governs. Hence, if research and information do have an impact, it is only indirect. This is what has been called 'the enlightenment function of research' (Weiss 1977), which illustrates the idea that knowledge gained by means of research provides a diffuse enlightenment function and broadens the existing knowledge base of policy makers. As long as it offers an understanding and interpretation of the data and the situation that are critical to the policy decision, research may lead to a gradual shift in concepts and paradigms. In other words, Carol Weiss's (1979) enlightenment model highlights the role of research as clarifying, accelerating, and legitimising changes in conceptual thinking and, therefore, in policies.

When social research influences the decisional process, this is because it is just another knowledge or area of expertise. Moreover, this influence takes place in decision-making arenas already informed by other kinds of previous local knowledge—i.e., partial information, anecdotes, and accumulated experiences and practices, among others—used by the wide range of players involved in the process as soon as they implement their own strategies. Within this context, social scientific knowledge can have some limited influence on the decision-making process only by establishing competition with previously provided local knowledge and information. In most cases, the influence of research may lead to the construction of a framework consisting of empirical generalisations and ideas that can then be absorbed by policy makers in a rather unconscious manner.

The second research paradigm appears to be more realistic than the first. Based on the idea that knowledge and academia diversify rapidly, it argues that it is difficult to identify 'social researchers' as a clear and homogeneous social and professional group. Their specificity is not given by their belonging to a particular institution such as university. Instead, it is their experience and technical knowledge on certain issues that determine their specific character (Restier-Melleray 1990, 546).

In terms of the scope of this research, three concepts require a more precise definition: academia, policy change, and research influence.

Certainly, academia may be an elusive concept. The analysis in this chapter, with its focus on the influence of local academia on trade policy decisions, will revolve around the production—knowledge—of local academia, rather than on the ideas and findings produced by epistemic communities as defined by Peter Haas (1992). Academia operates as an actor, whose peculiarity is the production of knowledge according to rules, evidence, and positive—empirical—and scientific criteria, based on measuring and contrasting.

The general working definition here is based on a broad characterisation of academia, rather than on the idea that academia belongs or is confined to a specific ambit or production place, such as university. Clearly, this type of knowledge is currently quite dispersed across diverse circles, and academics are increasingly being appointed as service providers by other actors and institutions. Thus, in order to apprehend the concept of academia, the main changes in terms of its area of action and activities must be made explicit. As far as the area of action is concerned, and in the context of trade policies, academics can now be found within think tanks and as consultants and experts in the broader social and political community: ministries of the economy and foreign affairs and different public agencies, parliament, business sectors, domestic and international non-governmental organisations (NGOs), as well as international organisations, among others. In terms of their activities, the traditional characterisation of social research seems inadequate in the face of the new challenges imposed by policy making today. In this sense, Robert Reich's (1991) concept of 'symbolic-analytical services' turns out to be of great utility, given that it includes a whole set of activities regarding the identification, solution, and arbitration of material problems and disputes by means of the manipulation of knowledge.

In sum, a vast amount of academia revolves around the notion of 'actorness', both in the private field and in the public field. However, within the realm of academic and scientific research, the information and knowledge that are produced to influence on public policies is of concern here.[1] The focus is on policy-oriented intellectual and academic production. This leads to a second key concept in the analysis.

Policy change refers to the particular ambit or context where the impact of academic research is actually measured. Here the analysis will rely mainly on the categorisation put forward by different authors who distinguish between instrumental and conceptual changes in policy (Caplan 1979; Chudnovsky and Erber 1999; Davies *et al.* 2005; Neilson 2001; Weiss 1991). Building on this literature, the impact of academic research may be either instrumental or conceptual.[2] Instrumental changes are brought about by small and incremental transformations in policy issues and practices. Clearly associated with micro-level decisions, these changes are limited to the day-to-day policy issues and are

[1] See the concept of post-academic research in the introduction of this volume.

[2] To learn more on the difference between instrumental and conceptual policy changes, please see the introduction of this volume.

mainly concerned with 'bureaucratic management and efficiency rather than substantive policy issues' (Caplan 1979, 462). On the contrary, conceptual changes lead to more gradual shifts in terms of policy makers' knowledge and understanding of certain issues, and are related to macro-level decisions involving key policy matters.

Nevertheless, this distinction must be understood as an ideal type because reality is often far more complex and changes to policies may fall somewhere on this spectrum (Tussie 2006). Moreover, in most cases, the impact of research and information on the policy process is indirect. Here, the diffuse enlightenment function of research turns out to be of interest in order to overcome the idea that policy makers only resort to research and academia in an instrumental manner—to apply data, statistics, and facts to their policy decisions—and to highlight that knowledge or research utilisation is built on a gradual shift in conceptual thinking over time. Nevertheless, this broad double categorisation offers an appealing departure for the examination of both episodes of policy change.

Assuming that research is only one of the many competing sources of information policy makers can make use of, and one of the various factors that affect the final policy decision (Garrett and Islam 1998; Tussie 2006), this chapter argues that the availability of research and ideas does not translate directly into policy change. In other words, the research-policy link is not direct, and ideas only influence policy decisions under certain circumstances. In order to capture those circumstances, it is important to understand how the production of research and the policy process interact in a particular context. Specifically, policy influence is defined here as the result of a process where three conditions must be present: the availability of research or the 'production of knowledge', its articulation with the stakeholders and mainly with decision makers, and, finally, the political will of decision makers to make use of it.

Building on the current debate regarding the nexus between research and policy making, and the factors that contribute to this relationship, this chapter analyses two episodes of policy change within the Mercado Común del Sur (Mercosur) and the integration process initially launched by Argentina and Brazil: the CGP, signed within the PICE in 1987, and the CET established in 1994. The selection of these cases is based on the importance of both decisions within the broader process of trade liberalisation initiated by Argentina in the mid 1980s. While the CGP stands out as the first step toward liberalised trade between

Argentina and Brazil—although that liberalisation remains a negotiated and highly controlled opening intended to constitute an agreement of economic complementarity—the negotiation of the CET implies a crucial move toward the establishment of the customs union within Mercosur. In addition, the CET constitutes a fundamental decision. On the one hand, it worked as a lock-in device, limiting the governments' autonomy in terms of their domestic trade policies. On the other hand, it complemented internal trade liberalisation while, at the same time, moved toward reducing Mercosur external barriers. Furthermore, both decisions were taken by two different governments: whereas the first democratic government led by Alfonsín signed the PICE, the CET was established by the following administration, headed by Menem.

The next two sections explore the research-policy relationship regarding the design and implementation of the CGP and the CET, taking into account three conditions: the existence of research, its articulation with policy makers, and the political will or at least the possibility of putting this research into practice or the possibility of its utilisation. Based on the assumption that the research-policy relationship is neither linear nor automatic, and that it entails a highly complex and dynamic two-way process (Tussie 2006), these case studies focus on two particular instances of policy change to deepen the understanding of the dynamics of the political process and assess the importance of the different factors that have contributed to these instances of policy change.

A First Move toward Trade Liberalisation: Alfonsín and the Capital Goods Protocol (1987–89)

In the mid 1980s, and after having implemented an inward-oriented development model for more than 50 years, Argentina began slowly but steadily to open its economy to international trade through the promotion of multiple strategies that combined unilateral opening and trade negotiations both at the regional and multilateral levels.

During the initial phase of the first democratic government led by Alfonsín, strict austerity and market-liberalising measures were resisted. In time, this resistance would be superseded by a different vision. In 1985, the newly designated Ministry of Economy, led by Juan Sourrouille, launched the Plan Austral, an economic programme that called for restructuring public companies and liberalising trade. Nevertheless, the decisive and final implementation of trade liberalisation as a unilateral policy started only in 1988. Two factors explain this. The first refers to the so-called Canitrot Reform, and the second to the relationship between Argentina and the International Monetary Fund (IMF) and the World Bank, which would play a more definitive role in shaping the reform policy in Argentina, particularly in terms of trade policy, public sector reform, and privatisation. Moreover, the discussions with the World Bank gave the economic team and policy makers a solid argument to convince the private sector of the need to move toward trade liberalisation and to overcome their opposition.

It is in this context that the PICE was established in 1986. Together with the Integration, Cooperation, and Development Treaty of 1988—both signed by the presidents of Argentina and Brazil, Raúl Alfonsín and José Sarney—these two agreements can be seen as the bedrock of the future Mercosur agreement. Based on gradual mechanisms that would be implemented in successive stages, allowing thus for adjustments, the PICE was intended to promote intra-industry trade between Argentina and Brazil and the overall expansion of bilateral trade, without inducing inter-industry specialisation. Sectoralism was a key principle of this initiative. The PICE entailed the negotiation of sectoral agreements to stimulate bilateral trade on the grounds of complementarity and political symmetry, to foster changes in the efficiency of production in key economic sectors through the expansion of bilateral investment flows, and to promote cooperation in areas of critical importance for joint economic development.

Academic Research

The initiative to sign a programme of strategic cooperation and commercial integration was basically of a political nature.

When newly elected president Alfonsín asked both Dante Caputo, the minister of foreign affairs, and Oscar Romero, the undersecretary of international economic relations, to develop an integration project with Brazil, his aim was to put an end to the traditional hypothesis of conflict cultivated between both countries over time. Certainly, regional integration initiatives were not new, but this bilateral initiative was intended to go beyond previous experiences. Apart from the idea of overcoming this old conflict hypothesis, three elements appear to have converged in the mid 1980s to produce a major change in the political and economic environment. In the first place, the processes of political transition and return to democratic rule, with institutional reorganisation in Argentina (1983) and Brazil (1985), created new incentives to redress the bilateral relations. Second, the macroeconomic and regulatory crisis of Argentina and Brazil clearly showed that the development model based on high protection and state intervention was already exhausted. Third, in an international context marked by the expansion of the forces of globalisation and the deepening of the multilateral system, regionalism initiatives appeared to be useful instruments for avoiding marginalisation and, at the same time, enhancing their voice in the international arena. In sum, this initial plan sought mutual economic cooperation as a means to improve bilateral relationships, foster economic growth in the region, and promote a new positioning of the two countries in the international arena. In terms of the type of decision at stake, it is clear that the agreement between Alfonsín and Sarney implied a paradigm change.[3]

During this first commercial integration initiative, the debt crisis of 1982 played a key role: it promoted closeness between the governments of Argentina and Brazil. Even if the debt crisis and the international financial institutions—the IMF and the World Bank—clearly demanded the initiation of a process of trade liberalisation and the reform of the highly distorted tariff systems, the government opted for a process of deep integration, which, in terms of trade liberalisation, entailed a minimum and negotiated opening with Brazil. The aim was to privilege the development of a productive project.

According to the main actors involved in the process, this option was inspired by the European experience, which appeared as a successful case of regional integration, and by the lessons derived from the failure of previous integration experiences, such as the Latin America Integration Association (LAIA). This is clearly expressed by Carlos Bruno, undersecretary of economic integration, who argued that 'if we try to develop a model of multilateral integration—such as that of LAIA—we will just develop the minimum common denominator of what we can build together... if—on the contrary—we choose those countries we consider to be the most dynamic ones—Argentina and Brazil—and we attempt to design a model of integration based on certain sectors of their economies, we will develop a model with a great degree of

[3] Interview with former undersecretary of integration and Mercosur, Ministry of Foreign Affairs.

internal dynamism, and this is the key difference in terms of the traditional model' (cited in Campbell 1999, 74).

Both the origin and evolution of this first approach to an integration project with Brazil were surrounded by worries mainly over the damages brought by the association in Argentina given the existing structural asymmetries between the new partners, derived from Brazil's long process of sustained industrialisation during the 1960s and '70s. In order to face these fears, the process would be guided by the idea of gradual integration, through selective and joint projects, advancing at different speeds. Thus it was expected to promote industrial and trade complementarity within each of the sectors, minimising the negative effects on both economies and inducing specialisation in certain lines of production (Lavagna 2001). In terms of the negotiation procedures, the consensus was to adopt a selective scheme, by means of 'positive lists' that specified where commitments were made, rather than making broad commitments and listing exceptions. In addition, an integration process based on gradual schedules and flexible negotiation mechanisms was initiated.

Within this model of deep integration, the capital goods sector was chosen as the 'star' of the PICE.[4] Given the economic situation of the mid 1980s and the existing structural asymmetries between the economies of both Argentina and Brazil, this sector presented some comparative advantages, just as the European Coal and Steel Community—where those sectors producing basic inputs—represented the first major step toward integration in Europe. In the first place, the capital goods sector was the most dynamic sector of global industry and trade. Second, it could have a multiplying effect throughout the productive

[4] The basic components of the PICE included 24 sectoral protocols, signed between 1985 and 1990, which specified the customs categories to which the agreement was to be progressively applied. Initially, there were only 12 protocols. Ten covered economic sectors, such as capital goods, food, wheat, and the iron, steel, and auto industries. The other two had to do with the nuclear industry and aeronautics cooperation. While seven protocols sought to boost bilateral trade in specific sectors—capital goods, wheat, iron and steel, automotive industry, food industry—two more general protocols were intended to promote trade expansion and the complementarity of the food supply. In 1988, there would be 22 protocols in all, and in 1989, there would finally be 24, including issues regarding trade and trade-facilitating measures, scientific and technological development, and infrastructure development, among others. Annexes to each protocol established the list of specific items subject to tariff reduction. All 24 protocols were targeted to expand trade, encourage bilateral investment flows, foster cooperation in areas such as nuclear energy and biotechnology, and facilitate transportation.

structure. Third, it employed a highly qualified labour force. In addition, both countries had a high deficit in this sector, especially Brazil, which at the time was compelled to import from third countries. For Argentina, this represented a unique opportunity because these sectoral agreements would entail the initiation of a process of rapid industrialisation, after the deindustrialisation led by the economic plan headed by former minister of economy José Martínez de Hoz (1976–81). In sum, within these national and regional contexts, the capital goods sector was considered strategic because, in the long term, imports of capital goods would prompt an increase on the productivity of the economy, expanding exports, and fostering growth.

From an intellectual point of view and in terms of the debate that led to the liberalisation process of capital goods and the elimination of non-tariff barriers, the Economic Commission for Latin America and the Caribbean (ECLAC) provided a key report, which was the basis for the PICE.[5] Two main reasons account for this.[6] In the first place, and given that most of the members of the economic team had been trained at ECLAC, they shared many of the assumptions and paradigmatic guidelines promoted by this regional organisation. In the second place, and especially regarding the country office in Buenos Aires, ECLAC's experts had undertaken industrial policy as an important area of research.

The private sector was also involved in the design of the macro proposal, but it did not present any concrete written document on the final text of the CGP. Business participation was induced by the government as a way of preventing conflicts and technical difficulties within both administrations. The summoning was immediate after Argentina and Brazil gave the first step toward regional integration, by the end of 1985.

Indeed, at the presidential meeting that took place in Foz de Iguazú in November 1985, Argentina and Brazil agreed to establish a high-level bilateral commission. Composed of government and private sector

[5] ECLAC was established in 1948 as one of the five regional commissions of the United Nations. Aimed at contributing to the economic development of the region, reinforcing economic relationships among the countries, and promoting social development as well, it had a leading role during the 1960s and '70s, when the region experienced a profound and diverse move toward regionalism. This trend was mainly influenced by ECLAC's philosophy and the ideas of its first secretary general, the economist Raúl Prebisch.

[6] Interview with Chief of the Office in Buenos Aires, ECLAC.

representatives, this commission was intended to discuss and launch the bilateral integration process. Oscar Romero recalls that this decision was based on the fact that 'the integration process design and the design of the concrete solidarity scheme between both countries, should not be developed at the grey desk of a bureaucrat or political official; instead this should result from the participation of real actors or economic agents. Both presidents decided to include the most representative private agents, businessmen and business groups from both countries, so that they would not protect the apples, the rice or the meat, but instead would be the individuals capable of helping in the design of the bilateral relationship that we so much needed' (Campbell 1999, 65).

Once the CGP had been signed, governments embarked in the difficult task of compiling the positive lists of the products and items to be liberalised. This implementation phase involved the direct participation of an external expert, especially appointed by the Argentine government, given the lack of technical knowledge and expertise in this particular area. Only a reduced number of companies, from some highly concentrated sectors and oligopolies (namely, the iron and steel industry and the petrochemical industry), counted with this extremely specialised information and expertise since they had also been part of the negotiations carried out for both the Latin America Free Trade Association (LAFTA) and LAIA. However, these sectors were not included in the agreement.[7]

Daniel Chudnovsky, an academic with no previous experience in public administration, was then appointed for the implementation of the CGP. Chudnovsky's designation was intended to fulfil two crucial goals, apart from drawing up numbers and comparative statistics regarding the situation of the capital goods sector in Argentina and its potential complementarity with Brazil: to advise policy makers during the negotiations and to persuade producers in the machine tools industries about the feasibility of a productive complementarity agreement with Brazil.[8] Persuading business groups was not an easy assignment since the positive lists prompted serious fears among Argentine manufacturers, who were concerned by the larger size and greater competitiveness of Brazilian producers (Chudnovsky and Erber 1999). In fact, it demanded an active

---

[7] Interview with researcher, Centre for International Economics (Centro de Economía Internacional [CEI]) at the Ministry of Foreign Affairs.

[8] Interview with former director, Centre for Research on Transformation (Centro de Investigaciones para la Transformación [CENIT]).

role and effort to put across these groups the differences between this new integration scheme and the unilateral liberalisation implemented during the 1970s, which had had a terrible and devastating impact on these industries.

With funding provided by the World Bank, the project developed by Chudnovsky entailed the elaboration of positive lists of those items and products that Argentina would offer Brazil during the final round of negotiations. These products would be marketed with a zero tariff and would be free of any non-tariff barriers by January 1987, after the entry into force of the CGP. The final composition of these positive or common lists was determined by the participation of different domestic manufacturers and the acceptance or refusal of each partner's proposal.

Research-Policy Articulation

As already mentioned, both the idea of promoting a closer relationship with Brazil and the actual first negotiations were articulated inside the Ministry of Foreign Affairs. During this initial stage, negotiations and discussions were mainly political in nature, and handled by the Ministry of Foreign Affairs. Capitalising on the presidential political discourse and mandate, which urged close ties with Brazil and the removal of the old conflict hypothesis from the bilateral relation, policy makers within this ministry—namely, Oscar Romero and Carlos Bruno, undersecretary of international economic relations and undersecretary of economic integration, respectively—decided to promote a trade agreement between both countries. When asked about the initiation of this process, one of the academic respondents commented that public officials 'got together as if they were spies organising a command attack, away from the noise; the idea was so awkward that they could not get together in a meeting room as it happens today...the whole process remained as highly informal. During this first stage, the Ministry of Economy knew nothing about this project; it was mainly focussed on the debt and inflation problems.'

However, in 1985, during the definition of the final design and concrete implementation of the initiative, the Ministry of Economy was assigned the whole responsibility for it. Two reasons explain this decision: the articulation with the private sector and the technical issues at stake. Indeed, Chudnovsky, the secretary of industry, and his political counterpart, Jorge Campbell, the undersecretary of foreign trade, launched a round of meetings with different sectoral chambers, especially with the Association of Metal Industrialists of the Argentine Republic (Asociación de Industriales Metalúrgicos de la República Argentina [ADIMRA]), and different individual industries.

Subsequently, the Ministry of Economy would increasingly take the lead in the initiative. Nevertheless, this new situation did not create mistrust in the Ministry of Foreign Affairs, and did not give way to a duplication of efforts. In fact, Juan Sourrouille and Dante Caputo, the heads of both ministries respectively, were deeply involved in the process. They worked on the project on a team basis, and shared the same vision and idea regarding the integration process with Brazil.[9] This personal connection would also be strengthened by the interministerial coordination achieved after the parliamentary elections of 1985, which reinforced President Alfonsín's leadership in Argentina. In turn, this would lead to the incorporation of an important number of officials and technical experts in the Secretary of Industry and Foreign Trade (Secretaría de Industria y Comercio Exterior [SICE]), who were deeply committed to the integration process with Brazil. This project was regarded as a possible main motor of the trade liberalisation scheme, or even as a means of positive adjustment. In sum, by the end of 1985, an interministerial taskforce was already in place. It relied on direct access to the highest political officials and policy makers, and its main objective was to promote the technical issues on the negotiating agenda. This taskforce was assisted and complemented by the private sector, which was acting in the shadows and was led by the so-called 'captains of industry'.[10] Nevertheless, this idyllic relationship would not last long, coming to an end in 1987 when Roberto Lavagna and his team left the SICE and were replaced by Beatriz Nofal, after the defeat of the Radical Party in the 1987 legislative elections.

---

[9] Interview with former undersecretary of international relations and president, CENIT.

[10] At the same time, although showing greater confidentiality, an informal working and advice group was created with these so-called captains of industry in order to gather their political endorsement to the initiatives. Later on, this same group would form part of the mixed commission. The 'captains of industry' was the name given to the economic groups that grew as state suppliers, and which, as detailed by Jorge Campbell (1999, 110), included the following business representatives: Jorge Haieck (SOCMA), Eduardo Braun (ASTARSA), Ricardo Zinn (SEVEL), Guillermo Livio Kühl (SAAB—Scania), Jaime Núñez (BAGLEY), Vittorio Orsi (SADE), Miguel Roig (Bunge y Born), Carlos Bulgheroni (BRIDAS), Carlos Tramutola (Propulsora), Alberto Hojman (BGH), and Sebastian Bagó (Laboratorios Bagó).

Based on the suggestions and proposals presented by the different chambers and industrial sectors, Chudnovsky elaborated the final positive lists on national capital goods. In those cases where consensus could not be achieved among two or more chambers producing the same product or item, the government would directly eliminate it from the final common lists, given that there were no adequate instruments to perform a technical evaluation of the competitive situation of the different products, thus revealing the government's lack of capability to avoid conflictive situations (Chudnovsky *et al.* 1987). This would result in a quite different dynamic from the one originally proclaimed in the PICE: the promotion of intra-industry restructuring and specialisation. On the contrary, the common lists that had been agreed upon at the national level would only allow for the promotion of trade in terms of the lines of production in which each country had already specialised, and did not include or affect those sub-sectors or activities that showed greater reticence about this market opening.

Utilisation in Decisions

The list elaborated by the SICE was part of the negotiation with Brazil. The agreement—the Protocol on Goods—entered into force at the beginning of 1987. The original list of 224 items was subsequently enlarged as the years passed by means of successive rounds of negotiations and following the same initial dynamic. The sectors included in the voluntary tariff reduction referred to most electric and non-electric equipment and machinery and their components and pieces, together with automobile components. Electrical equipments and parts and transport vehicles were excluded from the common lists and were subject to a separate sectoral negotiation (Porta and Fontanals 1989).

Negotiations on wheat and food supply—Protocols Two and Three—were as successful as the previous one. Given that Protocol Two was intended to promote a balanced exchange for Argentina and to make up for existing asymmetries, it established annual commitments for the purchase of this product by Brazil and other technical issues—such as the price calculation, ports, and schedules for loading. Protocol Three was different because it was not intended to promote trade liberalisation or the elaboration of lists; instead, it defined a common list of fruits, vegetables, and dairy products to be mutually provided in case of undersupply.

The remaining protocols—the steel and iron industry, the automotive and food sectors—faced numerous difficulties in their implementation and had a relatively small commercial impact during this first phase of the integration process. In this sense, for example, the steel and iron agreement had only a limited scope, leaving aside the main products. The automotive protocol, on the contrary, was successively postponed since there was no agreement regarding the small print. Actually, according to those who were directly involved in the negotiations, a vital element was missing: the support of the private actors involved in the process: 'Opening the final sectors without ensuring the previous liberalisation of the intermediate sectors and/or the elimination of the subsidies granted to sheet entailed higher costs for the Argentine manufacturer, who was thus obliged to buy sheet at a higher price than the one paid by his competitor, the Brazilian manufacturer, and consequently his production was not competitive.'[11] A similar evaluation was provided for the automotive sector: 'The automotive sector offered several advantages to be liberalised first: in the first place, consensus building within the sector was easy to achieve since only five companies comprised 90 percent of the total market; and, secondly, the sector allowed for a specialisation criterion. We proposed this scheme to Brazil, but companies would only accept it in 1991, when Mercosur ensured universal, automatic, and linear reductions.'[12]

Out of the six protocols dealing with production integration, the CGP was the only one to promote liberalisation, generating in turn quite important results in terms of the broader integration project. The implementation of this agreement led to a large increase in trade: between 1986 and 1990, regional trade in those products included in Protocol One grew from U$S16.7 to U$S 95.5 million, which accounted for a notable 472 percent growth. These benefits were even greater for Argentina than for Brazil. While trade in capital goods represented just 50 percent of Brazil's total exports, in the case of Argentina this stood at 80 percent. In qualitative terms, this increase also benefited Argentina through the diversification of the export supply.

Nevertheless, this was a short-term process of limited scope. Different analyses emphasise that even if the CGP led to increased productivity

---

[11] Interview with an academic, Universidad Nacional de Quilmes.

[12] Interview with former undersecretary of international relations and president, CENIT.

and a better use of installed capacity in both countries, there were neither significant investments nor important transformations in the structure of the national supply. Difficulties in the availability and conditions of credit for acquiring capital goods and the lack of credibility of the regional approach hindered the decision making of Argentine producers in the medium term. In addition, the increase in bilateral trade—by 40 percent between 1985 and 1988—was circumscribed to specific sectors, particularly capital goods and wheat, products of relative high importance in macroeconomic terms. Most of the relevant productive sectors had only a marginal or symbolic participation in the impact of the integration initiative. Moreover, they did not seem to be interested in assuming a more active role in the near future. These sectors included the steel and iron industry, different branches of the food industry, and the automotive complex.

Acceleration of the Liberalisation Programme: Menem and the Common External Tariff (1991–95)

Born in a context of industrial promotion and protection, where states led in economic functioning, the PICE constituted a cautious approach to regional trade liberalisation and integration. This first phase of integration (1986–89) was marked by sectoral negotiations on trade instruments. However, after an initial period of intra-regional liberalisation and rapid trade growth, the exchange of concessions slowed down and trade flows reached a plateau. This sector-by-sector integration was then replaced by a universal approach to regional trade liberalisation after the signing of the Acta de Buenos Aires (1990), which accelerated the integration process and anticipated that the common market would come into effect in December 1994.

The Acta de Buenos Aires was signed by the newly elected presidents Fernando Collor de Melo (Brazil) and Carlos Menem (Argentina). The latter continued the trade liberalisation process initiated by the previous administration, and even if there was a rapid move toward market reform, trade liberalisation was kept in a secondary and discreet place. The economic team established a policy aimed at reducing tariffs, progressively applied, although mainly stemming from the requirements and demands of both the IMF and the World Bank. Subsequently, this was accelerated and deepened with the implementation of a new economic plan headed by Domingo Cavallo.[13] The government later adopted a series of measures intended to promote exports and reduce the manufacturing costs through the reduction and elimination of different taxes and the establishment of credit facilities and measures aimed at stimulating exports.

In this line and in terms of the regional integration process already established with Brazil, the Acta de Buenos Aires implied a key transformation by adopting an approach to trade liberalisation based on an automatic, linear, and universal mechanism of tariff elimination within the zone (Lavagna 2001). Shortly afterward, negotiations began giving way to the Treaty of Asunción in 1991 and extending these commitments to Paraguay and Uruguay. Mercosur was finally born.

Four mechanisms were included in the founding treaty to move toward a common market. In first place was the trade liberalisation programme that would lead to the establishment of a zero-tariff area by 31 December 1994. Second, as of 1 January 1995, a CET and a common commercial policy with a third country or groupings of countries would be established. A third mechanism referred to the coordination of macroeconomic and sector policies: foreign trade, agriculture, industry, fiscal, monetary, foreign exchange, capitals, services, customs, transport, and communications, among others. Finally, sector agreements were established to deepen and speed up the liberalisation of intra-regional trade flows (Bouzos *et al.* 2002).

The trade liberalisation programme started in 1991 and, in spite of some delay in the original plan, the bloc finally achieved free trade among the member countries by 1999, when the CET finally started to rule. The adoption of the CET entailed the commitment to a long-term political project with Brazil, which in turn allowed for better integration into the multilateral trade arena. Both the Argentine and Brazilian ministries of foreign affairs strictly opposed any formal weakening of the CET since this was an effective policy tool for opening up the economy to the rest of the world, and it was crucial for the countries to negotiate as a bloc the incorporation of Mercosur into free trade agreements both within the Americas and with the European Union.

---

[13] After being at the Fundación Mediterránea think tank, Domingo Cavallo served as minister of foreign affairs (1989–91) and was instrumental in the realignment of Argentina with the United States.

During those years, regionalism and regional integration appeared to be effective in facilitating an entrance into a much more developed multilateral trading system. However, once again, two options were then on the agenda: the creation of either a free trade zone or a customs union. The first option was clearly promoted by the Ministry of Economy on the basis that a free trade zone would allow for more manoeuvres in the negotiation of the foreign trade policy—a vision shared as well by certain business think tanks such as Fundación Mediterránea and Centro de Estudios Macroeconómicos de Argentina (CEMA). The other option was the establishment of a customs union, an idea promoted mainly by public universities and the ECLAC.

Academic Research

In operative terms, the definition of the CET would compel the member states to subordinate their trade policies toward third countries to a common policy settled within the bloc. This was an extremely complex assignment given the structural asymmetries among the partners, which were reflected in their divergent tariff systems. Those countries with less diversified productive structures—such as Paraguay and Uruguay—objected the idea of granting tariff preferences to the larger partners, while Argentina and Brazil showed differences in terms of the most competitive sectors, an element that added more complexity to the process as well as to the possibility of building consensus (Giorgi 2003).

Mercosur governments appointed the design of the CET to the Common Market Group (Grupo Mercado Común [GMC]). Within this, the Sub-Group 10 (Subgrupos de Trabajo [SGT])—which dealt with issues related to macroeconomic policy coordination—would be in charge of examining and analysing the CET. During the first two years, national delegations focussed on the exchange of their own harmonised national systems of nomenclature and the elaboration of consensual rules and basic criteria for the creation of the CET. Given the existing diversity among the national tariff systems, consensus was easily achieved for the establishment of an escalated external tariff system, including at least three positions. However, difficulties emerged in terms of the tariff level attributed to each sector. In order to overcome these important differences, it was agreed to carry out the negotiation on the basis of the different proposals taken to the negotiating table. These were to be presented by May 1992.

Faced with this schedule, national governments required several studies and analyses that obligated a critical participation of academics. The elaboration of these proposals entailed big challenges for the governments in terms of the complexity of the issue: each country had diverse nomenclatures and tariff systems, and there were no comparative statistical analyses. In addition to this basic survey, the evaluation of the different possible scenarios and their expected impact on each domestic productive sector was another necessary task.

At the regional level, similar surveys were carried out. In 1993, the GMC appointed Honorio Kume, an expert from the Instituto de Pesquisa Econômica Aplicada (IPEA), a research centre associated with the Brazilian government. With funding provided by the EU and the Inter-American Development Bank (IADB), Kume was designated to perform a survey and to assist national governments in the meetings of the GMC, where he turned out to be an active participant.

In Argentina, the need to come up with a proposal gave way to a proliferation and overlapping of studies and the appointment of different working groups. In all, three special studies were particularly important, as described below.

The first group was composed of technical experts from the Ministry of Economy, who were to fulfil certain tasks regarding Mercosur, and academics from the Department of Economics at the Universidad de Buenos Aires (UBA). The tasks were divided between the two groups: the academics focussed on the development of the parameters—since there was a perceived need for this information during the negotiations—and the coordination of the different activities within this joint group, and the technical experts worked on a comparative study and elaborated diverse statistical measures given that these data were of great utility for the negotiations.[14] The experts group was coordinated and financed with the ministry's budget and its main objective was to collect all the existing information about the tariff positions in the four member countries in order to build a comparative matrix. This survey was guided by the demands and specific requirements of the officials of this public agency, who were also part of different working groups within Mercosur. In addition, these technical experts produced several proposals and reports that were submitted to the negotiators.

---

[14] Interview with Argentine GMC negotiator.

The second survey was appointed by the Ministry of Economy. With funding provided by loans from the United Nations Development Programme (UNDP), a group of academics were selected on a personal basis. The remuneration of these appointed experts tripled those of the ministry officials who were responsible for the negotiation process, a situation that was thus regarded with suspicion. This consultancy group relied heavily on the information that they already had as well as on a matrix based on outdated data. Moreover, the directives and parameters of the research were settled by the Ministry of Economy and did not necessarily respond to the needs of the actual negotiators.

Finally, the Ministry of Foreign Affairs developed some documents and reports on its own. Julio Berlinski, an economist from Universidad Torcuato Di Tella (UTDT), was appointed for this survey. He was an external advisor and a specialist in tariffs who had already had some experience working for previous administrations on various tariff issues. He was asked to define the criteria for the CET. Unlike public experts from the Ministry of Foreign Affairs, Berlinski had a global vision of the whole situation that enabled him to develop a more comprehensive analysis, different from that of a public expert who had taken the Argentina tariff system and made consultations with the private sector on the basis of the demands put forward by Brazil.[15]

Most of the private sector did not provide inputs into the CET negotiating process because they perceived the customs union would not be actually implemented. In fact, 'most of the chambers and sectors in general did not participate; neither did they come to know about it. What is commonly being said, that business actors came to know about this project through the newspaper, is quite true. We [the negotiators] did not receive any proposals from the business sectors. Therefore, as we had no proposals, we had no instructions either; we worked in a very theoretical manner—our job was mainly based upon calculations done at the desk. We analysed how far we could go in terms of the productive chain and its maximization, and we struggled for this as much as we could.'[16]

Only two research reports were produced by the private sector. The Chamber of the Chemical and Petrochemical Industries (Cámara de la Industria Química y Petroquímica [CIQyP]) produced a paper of an

---

[15] Interview with a CEI researcher.
[16] Interview with Argentine GMC negotiator.

operative nature intended to contribute to the survey and harmonisation process of the regional tariffs. This agreement was presented both to national governments and Mercosur institutions. As soon as the initiative was launched, chamber members reacted immediately: they decided to anticipate to the governments and presented a sectoral proposal. This was expressed by one CIQyP leader, who recalled that only the petrochemical sector would elaborate a proposal regarding a future nomenclator: 'We held meetings during four months; every 15 days, 20 people per country got together. Moreover, this nomenclator is still valid today since it has barely undergone any changes. Governments signed it... We were the only sector that carried out such a task, but in fact we were the only ones that would need to do so since the steel and iron sector includes 14 chapters of the nomenclator while the chemical sector includes 2.849 tariff lines, and stands for 30 percent of the total number of lines... We finished this report... and then said that that would be the tariff system to be applied; because it had been said that it would be proportional to the added value. So we determined what the added value should be and proposed our own tariff scale. We ended up presenting a proposal, which was also a joint proposal—only with Brazil, for the time being—from 2 to 16. The government accepted it and made a slight modification: from 2 to 14, but they did respect the escalated scheme.'

The second case refers to the study published by Fundación de Investigaciones Económicas Latinoamericanas ([FIEL] 1993), whose pro-market philosophy had become well known with the publication of *El comercio administrado de los '90: Argentina y sus socios*. This book argued that the best possible negotiating scenario for Argentina would be a free trade agreement with the United States, rather than a deep integration process with Brazil. Written between 1992 and 1993, it was based on a research project financed by an American foundation.[17]

Research-Policy Articulation

Most of the documents and studies detailed above were the result of either an appointment or a special request made by the governments to those academics involved in the in-house think tanks. The articulation between policy makers and researchers seemed therefore guaranteed.

[17] Interview with a senior economist, FIEL.

However, things turned out to be more complicated. In the first place, only one of these different reports got to the Argentine negotiators in due time and proper form. This was the report elaborated by the experts and academics of the Ministry of Economy and the UBA. Unlike the others, this study was the result of teamwork, and certainly fulfilled the demands and requirements of the negotiators. Moreover, negotiators were also actively involved in its creation. In turn, these meant that the working group could have access not only to information but also to the instructions of the negotiating group.

Another group of studies, including the reports by Kume and Berlinksi, was also produced in proper form and in response to the demands and urgencies specified by the negotiators. These studies were intended to fulfil the same demand: the identification of the criteria to harmonise the nomenclatures of the countries in order to attain a common denominator. In the case of Kume, the report arrived too late for the Argentine negotiators: 'By the time Kume had finished this study... the decision-making process was already over. The delay was terrible... We did have a close relationship with him; in fact, he attended the meetings held between the four governments, and was a keen supporter of Mercosur; he provided negotiators with regular reports. Nevertheless, the final document could not be taken as input for the final policy decision since it arrived once this had already been agreed on. I then took it to the library, and I think the report turned out to be useful to me, but only later on.'[18] In addition, the usefulness of Kume's report was only relative, at least regarding the elaboration of the positions of the national negotiators, since it focussed mainly on the distributive struggle in which each country would try its best to assure the survival of the most sensitive sectors: 'These surveys and reports were helpful not for making decisions, but rather in terms of the advice they provided governments, for instance, during the CET negotiations, which entailed settling a common tariff for over 9,000 positions for the more than 90 chapters of the nomenclator... Some reports were elaborated, and then we analysed which products could be raised or lowered... In addition, when we had to negotiate within the SGT on trade issues, we really needed to know what they were asking for, but at the same time we had to move toward the dismantling of the tariff barriers, so we needed to be informed of what we should ask for, what we should

[18] Interview with Argentine GMC negotiator.

not demand, where we could push further, where we could yield our positions, and what problems could then come up.'[19]

In the case of Berlinski's report, its utility was limited to providing arguments to the negotiators of the Ministry of Foreign Affairs given that the technical issue was still centralised at the Ministry of Economy. Berlinksi did not have the chance to work directly with the negotiators, who had the latest and most accurate information. Instead, his study was only a laboratory experiment. Another challenge was the lack of continuity in time, which limited its utility to an exclusive issue of political legitimacy, as indicated by one interviewee: 'I think negotiations are a process, along which papers are irrelevant. Papers and documents can provide ideas and advice, but the consultant should somehow participate along this whole negotiating process. However, this is never the case, or at least this was not my experience. I may be partly guilty for this since I find politicians boring. I believe that they are not interested in showing all what they know to us [the academics]. Assuring continuity is what really matters. But in real terms, nobody is interested in establishing a certain amount of tariffs because this is a quite complicated task, so a particular case is just taken, and in the end, it turns out to be useless.'[20]

The other studies and reports, together with the consultancy jobs that were appointed by the government between 1991 and 1994, were not intended to contribute to the definition of the CET, but to promote the public debate in favour of a process of deep integration with Brazil. The initiative came from the Ministry of Foreign Affairs, and mainly from Alieto Guadagni, who relied on international research centres, think tanks, and financing provided by the UNDP and the IADB either to appoint or to put ministerial positions out to tender.[21] Different research centres, representing a wide variety of ideological assumptions, were chosen, according to their expertise in the different negotiating issues: CEMA, FIEL, UTDT, and Facultad Latinoamericana de Ciencias Sociales (FLACSO-Argentina). There was thus a clear division of labour: '[Osvaldo] Schenone, from Fundación Mediterránea, was appointed to work on the establishment of a regional market of capital goods;

[19] Interview with researcher, Centro de Estudios para el Cambio Estructural (CECE).

[20] Interview with academic, UTDT.

[21] Guadagni was undersecretary of international relations, Ministry of Foreign Affairs (1991–96), and secretary of industry, Ministry of Economy (1996–98).

academics from FIEL were asked to analyse labour asymmetries and the tariff system of public services, while ECLAC specialists would have to focus on issues of macroeconomic coordination.'[22]

Guadagni intended to summon political will to promote Mercosur and constitute a solid critique in terms of the confrontation he had with the Ministry of Economy, now headed by Cavallo. This was expressed by one of the public officials involved in the process, as follows: 'There was certain inertia—especially in terms of the proposed opening within Mercosur—in some sectors of the Ministry of Foreign Affairs, who were suspicious of Brazil and clearly preferred an agreement with the U.S. What we did was to take the agreement signed by Alfonsín and Sarney and extend it. There were conflicts, and quite important ones (within the Cabinet itself), that were never made public. I would now like to tell you an anecdote. Before the ratification of the Treaty of Ouro Preto, [Fernando Henrique] Cardoso—who had just been elected president of Brazil—made his first official visit to Argentina. During this visit, a meeting was organized in Olivos [presidential residence]. The minister of economy, who was also late for this bilateral meeting, proposed an integration arrangement different from that of Mercosur. Those present made no comments on this proposal until the following meeting, where Cardoso was told that such a scheme was not valid at all.'[23]

Cavallo was not interested in deepening Mercosur. Instead he leaned toward the establishment of a free trade zone with Brazil. The underlying reason for this was that the entrance of Argentina into a customs union would diminish autonomy in the handling of the trade policy given that the final aim was to establish a common tariff. In turn, this limitation would also affect the external trade policy, which, in the context of the economic plan known as the Convertibility Plan launched in 1991, was the only economic field where policy could be implemented. On the other hand, Cavallo's increasing power over national politics, which was based on the initial success of the Convertibility Plan, turned out to be a positive signal for private sectors, revealing that the Treaty of Ouro Preto was not mature enough and would most likely not be signed.

[22] Interview with former national director of industry, Ministry of Economy.

[23] Interview with former undersecretary of international relations, Ministry of Foreign Affairs.

Utilisation in Decisions

With regard to the analysis of the various research studies and the different channels opened to promote the knowledge–policy makers articulation, it is clear that in terms of technical applicability, the studies that offered the greatest utility were the ones performed by the experts and academics from the Ministry of Economy and the UBA. This team, unlike the others, relied on an interesting virtue: its capacity to respond to the demands and requirements of the national negotiators in the regional arena in due time and proper form.

However, these reports were based on the technical conception of the experts and economists who did not have access to the medium- and long-term priorities established by those politically responsible for the negotiation process. Consequently they were dismissed when the need to make a political decision was finally imposed at the domestic level, mainly as a result of increasing Brazilian pressures.

Indeed, Argentina and Brazil had different and opposing positions in terms of the agricultural, capital goods, and computer and telecommunications sectors, which were certainly difficult to solve.[24] Moreover, negotiations came to a halt when Cavallo decided to promote a closer relationship with the United States and revealed his intention of boosting a free trade agreement with it. Thus the position of the Argentine negotiators and experts within the GMC became blurred. By the mid 1993, it was evident that the schedule settled by the Treaty of Asunción regarding the establishment of the CET—by 1 January 1995—could not be fulfilled. Even if the process of harmonisation had already reached 95 percent of the whole tariff universe, there were still crucial debates to be solved. It was in this context that Brazil decided to assume the leadership in the debate both in political and operative terms.

---

[24] In terms of the agriculture sector, Brazil intended to establish low nominal rates, an idea that Argentina refused since it feared that the establishment of lower tariffs for products such as powder milk, wheat, meat, or rice would hinder the entrance of Argentine products to the Brazilian market when competing with the subsidised prices of third countries. In the case of capital goods, Argentina wanted to place this sector in one of the lowest levels of protection since this would allow upgrading equipment and processing and product technologies through the acquisition of less expensive equipment and technology in the international market. However, Brazil rejected the proposal. Furthermore, and as far as computer and telecommunications goods were concerned, Brazil was determined to establish high tariffs, remaining thus as the exclusive supplier in the region (Giorgi 2003).

In political terms, Brazil held meetings with the highest ranked officials of the Argentine government and explicitly rejected the latter's proposal to call off the establishment of a customs union and limit integration to a free trade area. Moreover, Brazil posed a serious threat: the removal of Argentina's preferential access to the Brazilian market, especially for wheat and cars, the only sectors where exports were then growing. With this in mind, and given that the United States no longer seemed interested in the idea of signing a free trade agreement, Argentine president Carlos Menem declared his firm decision to fulfil the commitments previously assumed in Asunción and create a customs union within Mercosur.

At the operative level, Brazil managed to impose its own tariff scheme because there was no major resistance from Paraguay and Uruguay. The CET was 'escalated'—meaning that tariffs increased with the added value of the products, with higher rates for finished goods—and the average tariff was settled at between 0 and 20 percent, protecting those industrial sectors in which Brazil was the only regional provider. Nevertheless, this tariff structure included some flexibility as shown by the four lists of exceptions included in the Ouro Preto Protocol. In exchange for the signature of this protocol, Argentina obtained what was called the Régimen de Adecuación Final a la Unión Aduanera (Final Adjustment Regime to the Customs Union [RAFUA]), which established an extra time period—a unique and maximum closing date of four years—granted to specific sectors for conducting a reform that would allow them to become competitive and survive in the new context: they could keep the national tariffs within the intra-zone trade, but these would have to disappear gradually and automatically by 1999.[25]

The domestic distribution of these exceptions did not rely on the knowledge and research works already performed, but on the traditional lobby practices deployed by the private sector. Fearing that the launch of the CET would lead to the disappearance of some business sectors or the loss of the acquired preferences during the previous intra-Mercosur liberalisation phase, private lobbies now demanded protection from the national government. The only business sectors to become

[25] Thus, while first list of exceptions included those products already under the RAFUA, the second one comprised the national lists of specific exceptions to the customs union. Both the third and fourth lists were sectoral lists including capital goods and computer and telecommunications goods, where Brazil, under the request of Argentina, committed itself to the reduction of rates before 2006.

involved in this process were those that knew this dynamic because of previous negotiations or those that represented the most powerful economic sectors, given either their veto power—as in the case of the iron and steel and automotive sectors—or lobby power—as in the case of the textiles, sugar, and paper sectors.[26]

Impact Evaluation: An Initial Comparative Analysis

The following section compares both episodes of policy change. With regard to the agenda-setting process, they share a similar paradigm, which is clearly based on the idea promoted by international financial institutions—especially the World Bank—that portray trade liberalisation policies undertaken as a change of paradigm as being the unique possible solution to financial and economic crisis, and to growth problems as well. Promoted by the global epistemic community, this vision found support at the domestic level: the economic and political elites were deeply convinced of the need of reform. However, the strategies designed and implemented by the first two democratic governments—the Radical administration led by Alfonsín and the other, led by Menem from the Peronist Party—would show important differences.

The administration headed by Raúl Alfonsín followed the reform path proposed by the World Bank, but only partially. This government's innovation was evident in the promotion of a trade liberalisation process based on bilateral negotiations and tariff preferences, precisely when at the global level unilateral liberalisation was actively promoted in order to deepen multilateralism. Thus the negotiations initiated with Brazil would be structured around a set of sectoral agreements, which followed a clear logic of productive complementarity. On the contrary, the following administration strictly followed the structural adjustment programme more explicitly involved with deregulation, privatisation, and trade liberalisation, including tariff reduction and the elimination of subsidies. These actions formed the Washington consensus, proclaimed by the international financial institutions—namely, the World Bank

[26] Argentina included 221 products under this regime, basically those regarding the steel and iron sectors, footwear, and paper, all of which still continue to be exempted. The textile sector constitutes a paradoxical case: apart from including this sector in the RAFUA and creating a special committee aimed at elaborating a proposal for an intra-zone regulatory policy, the member states agreed on exempting it from the customs union as well.

and the IMF. Nevertheless, in following these policy recommendations regarding an unrestricted opening of the economy at all levels—unilateral, regional, and multilateral—there was still room to manoeuvre and, in the case of Argentina, this opening was carried out with a foreign exchange rate that evolved increasingly eroding competitiveness. At the regional level, the logic of the integration process with Brazil changed dramatically. Negotiations with Brazil, and with Paraguay and Uruguay in order to create Mercosur, were aimed only at attaining a free trade zone and a zero tariff within five years. The proposal of creating a customs union would be brought about by the larger partners of Argentina and Brazil, which clearly needed to establish a lock-in mechanism for the trade liberalisation already achieved and to resist the pressures of protectionist sectors interested in reversing the process.

The question that arises is whether this similarity led to a similar paradigm in terms of the nexus between research and policy making, as shown by the three conditions already mentioned: research, articulation, and utilisation.

When analysing the academic research that influenced the design of these strategies, both experiences exhibit large similarities. In both cases, governments were faced with new challenges, and they also lacked the basic expertise and information required to implement the required transformations effectively. Governments resorted to academic knowledge in order to gather further information and data regarding the policy change and its instrumentation. Thus regional and global epistemic communities had a key role in defining the main content of the final decisions involved in both instances, although there were essential differences in terms of ideas: those of the ECLAC vis-à-vis those of the World Bank.

As far as the CGP is concerned, the academia played a leading role in two different stages of the process. During the definition phase, when the strategy aimed at promoting sectoral integration was defined and designed, previous knowledge provided by decision makers outside the political parties, in both the ministries of economy and foreign affairs, was fundamental. Later on, the government appointed an academic as an ad hoc working group for the implementation of the strategy, basically to collect essential statistical data on the sectors under negotiation and to produce the final lists the Argentine government would present to its partner.

On the contrary, during the negotiation of the CET, academic research was restricted to designing the instrument. Even when the

Treaty of Asunción made no reference to the CET or the sectoral policies that should be coordinated between the partners, the governments' decision left little margin to manoeuvre. In fact, the trade liberalisation process had already been established and this was already out of the agenda under discussion. Thus the only window of opportunity for the participation of academia was given by the design and definition of the final instrument to be implemented: the CET. Nevertheless, in this case, academic research was more vast in terms of the studies, reports, and documents produced. Academics appointed either by the government or by private actors, devoted themselves to two different kinds of research. A first included technical reports, produced by public officials and in-house technicians, or by specialists appointed by the government, who were to collect the basic statistical data needed to construct the tariff nomenclature and to define the tariff levels. In addition, some business sectors, such as the CIQyP, advanced with the production of their own reports. The second kind of documents and studies, focussed mainly on the argumentation and legitimisation of the national positions before the public opinion, proposed different and more convenient negotiating scenarios for Argentina. These documents and studies were required by the government and carried out by private think tanks using international funding.

Differences emerge in terms of the articulation between researchers and policy makers. The CGP was the result of the joint work of researchers and policy makers, who shared and intertwined different types of knowledge and made political decisions. The final list including the capital goods industries and sectors to be liberalised could thus easily be implemented regarding both the technical aspects and the political support at stake. In addition, this group managed to present its final report before the deadline established by Argentina and Brazil. In the case of the CET, research results were finally communicated once the negotiations were over, and in a language that was not only inaccessible to negotiators but also of slight utility. Most of these documents and studies had been commissioned from academics who had no liaison with the negotiators and therefore ignored their day-to-day requirements. Only one of the reports was an exception to the rule: the document prepared by the negotiators within the different SGTs, relying on the technical and professional assistance provided by the UBA academics. This turned out to be extremely technical research, where the negotiators defined their needs and requirements while academics concentrated on collecting statistical data. Nevertheless, unlike the negotiation of the PICE, those in charge of this report did not receive the necessary social and political support in order to use the data and information that had been collected.

Finally, the last of the conditions that can determine the influence of academic knowledge on the decision-making process is the political will of the decision makers and their determination to make use of it. There are very sharp contrasts in this respect between both episodes. In terms of the CGP, the final list compiled by the appointed researcher was the unique element that the Argentine government took to the negotiating table with Brazil. Sectoral accords would thus advance only in those industries or sectors where there was reliable information regarding the benefits of integration, while those sectors where there was no empirical evidence and where consensus building among the stakeholders did not work were removed from the final list. During the final negotiation of the CET, the policy recommendations were put forward through the empirical analyses that had been previously developed but were not taken to the discussions with Brazil. Certainly, this turned out to be a rather atypical negotiation, whose results were determined by the timing and pressure exercised by the main commercial partner—Brazil—given the lack of both definition and interagency coordination on the part of Argentina. Out of the three proposals that were specifically commissioned at the national level, the only one that finally exercised some influence in the bilateral negotiations was the joint document prepared by the chambers of the chemical and petrochemical industries of Argentina and Brazil; it was then presented to both national governments and to the regional authorities as well. Mercosur authorities accepted the inclusion of such document in the final agreement, with only some slight modifications.

Having compared both episodes in terms of the production of academic knowledge, its articulation within the decision-making process, and its use, this analysis now delves into the factors that promoted the production of knowledge in both cases and its articulation and use in the case of the CGP and of the CET proposal by the chemical and petrochemical sector.

The academic research was strongly boosted by the lack of experience of decision makers in the new problematic issues and questions, along with scarcity of the information needed to respond to them. This was precisely the case in terms of the paradigmatic change within the development model experienced in Argentina since the mid 1980s. This issue was new not only for public officials but also for the private sector involved in decision making. It should be noted that these were the first steps promoted by a democratic government after years of military dictatorship. Even in the case of previous trade liberalisation processes—for example, the negotiation of tariff preferences within LAIA during the 1970s—the military coup would then disarticulate these networks by breaking the constitutional order and replacing public officials and cabinets. The only sectors that were involved in this learning process were those related to the most concentrated sectors of the economy and that also experienced a large economic growth during the military regime—such as the steel and iron industry, or the automotive and petrochemical sectors. However, these were not involved in the formulation or implementation of the CGP, which was confined to smaller sectors and industries. In fact, an element that accounts for the influence of academics vis-à-vis other actors involved in the decisional process refers to the relative poor capacity or ability of the latter to respond or produce alternative strategies; this compares the influence of academics within the decision-making process, which was greater than those of other sectors also involved in the process. Indeed, the capital goods industry is not a concentrated sector in Argentina. Unlike other sectors showing great political leverage—such as the aforementioned industries—it is highly disarticulated and does not have a strong and clear labour organisation. This allowed the executive branch to design and implement the sectoral opening without consulting with the actors involved.

Later on, the CET negotiations would make this knowledge demand even more pressing given the lack of interministerial coordination and the different approaches to integration promoted by the ministries of economy and foreign affairs. While the latter promoted a deep integration scheme with Brazil, the former pushed for the establishment of a free trade area with the United States and other developed countries. In order to legitimate their own positions, each ministry and its public officials in charge would appoint the elaboration of research works and surveys in an ad hoc manner. In turn, this knowledge demand would be extended to business actors, such as the chemical and petrochemical sector, which assessed the need for elaborating its own sectoral proposal. From 1991 to 1993, the struggle between both ministries facilitated the proliferation of different studies and reports, although it did not promote the joint and effective work of academics and negotiators in the implementation phase. Unlike previous experiences in trade policy formulation in Argentina, most of the private sector was not involved in the elaboration of the CET, which in turn allowed for this to be the result of technical studies based on empirical evidence, at least in terms of the Argentine negotiating team. However, the absence of a clear leadership and coordination among ministries and public agencies also accounted for the lack of utilisation of the research results by policy makers during the implementation phase.

In the analysis of the second dimension, that of articulation, these three successful cases—the CGP and the CET proposal presented by the public officials within the Ministry of Economy, and the document elaborated by the private sector as represented by the CIQyP—clearly demonstrate that the ex ante articulation between decision makers and academics constitutes a key factor to guarantee that the information produced will be presented in due time and form.

Finally, both the CGP experience and the CIQyP proposal show that the use of knowledge depends on two conditions: interagency coordination and a common and unified vision, as well as the inclusion of non-governmental sectors, basically private actors. The policy-research articulation was possible in both cases because the proposed solutions left uncovered, for different reasons, deep distributive struggles between the sectors involved: in the first case, because the CGP was based on positive lists and, in the second experience, because losers and winners had been previously decided upon within the sector itself.

The comparative analysis on the nature of the policy-research relationship in both episodes of policy change brings to the forefront three initial conclusions. First, in temporal terms, the relative weight and incidence of the academia diminished as the novelty of the issue wore off and negotiating experience accumulated both in the public and private sectors. In effect, although academic knowledge was the only source in the elaboration of the CGP, 10 years later other types of knowledge and information were added to the negotiations of the CET, which were provided not only by the Ministry of Economy but also by think tanks and different productive sectors. Second, in both cases, academic contributions to the decisional processes played a legitimising role. The final aim of the research-policy relationship established was to justify the government's negotiation position and discourse. Finally, and regarding the issues at stake, the incidence of academic knowledge had more possibilities of achieving success—use—in those areas where the distributional impact of the policies were almost inexistent—voice—or where those sectors whose interests would be seriously damaged by the implementation of a specific policy did not have veto power—exit.[27] In the opposite case, the voice of academia and the role played by studies based on empirical evidence were neutralised by sectoral lobbies, which relied either on their traditional veto power or on technical expertise to defend their sectoral interests. This contrast became evident during the negotiation of the CET. While the project of establishing a customs union remained an ideal rather than a concrete policy, experts and academics worked in isolation. However, when the political will to promote a customs union was clearly defined, the strength and influence of private lobbies would obscure all empirical evidence. Table 4–1 offers a synthesis of these main findings.

Final Considerations

The empirical evidence presented along this chapter refers to two episodes of policy change in the process of trade liberalisation launched by Argentina in which there was an important production of local knowledge. The first episode (1986–89) was a process of gradual change, when trade liberalisation would be promoted through a strategy of selective sectoral and productive integration with Brazil. The second episode (1991–95) refers to the liberalisation and integration process initiated among the Southern Cone countries—Argentina, Brazil, Paraguay, and Uruguay—that led to the establishment of a common market: Mercosur.

Both processes also differ in terms of the type of policy change. While the CGP can be categorised as a failed case of conceptual change—intended to promote gradual shifts in policy makers' knowledge and understanding of liberalisation through regional integration—the CET negotiations, on the contrary, can be defined as a process of incremental change, where transformations were brought about by means of micro-level decisions. In contrast, the negotiation of the PICE and the CGP involved a macro-level decision, where policy makers rejected the World Bank's proposal, which suggested unilateral and universal deregulation and used local knowledge to design an alternative—regional and partial—way for trade liberalisation.

---

[27] The concepts of voice and exit are being used in terms of A.O. Hirschman (1970; 1976).

Table 4–1: A Comparative Glance at the Common Goods Protocol and the Common External Tariff

	Capital Goods Protocol (1986–89)	Common External Tariff (1991–95)
Context	Trade liberalisation as part of the structural adjustment programme	Trade liberalisation as a key pillar of the structural reform programme
External Inspiration	European experience and the expertise of the Economic Commission for Latin America and the Caribbean in capital goods sector	Structural reforms promoted by World Bank and International Monetary Fund
Local Knowledge Production (Type of Evidence)	Basic data on capital goods sector and opportunities for industrial complementarity between countries	Impact scenarios analysis (deep integration or free trade agreements) and technical tools for the implementation of common external tariff (as regional basic data)
Knowledge-Policy Articulation	Academic experts hired by Ministry of Economy	Papers commissioned from think tanks; technical studies done within the Ministry of Economy
Policy Use	Evidence used to define technical tools and to inform small private sectors on the windows of opportunity	Impact scenario analyses used by the ministries of economy and foreign affairs to legitimate and persuade (competing and overlapping views on the integration model to be pursued)

Even if both episodes are consecutive and took place within the framework of the structural reforms promoted by the World Bank in Argentina since 1987, each case opens up different windows of opportunity for the academic research. In both cases, the utility of that research in the policy process showed important variations not only in terms of concrete use but also in terms of the exact moment when the research was applied and thus in terms of its impact on policy.

In the first case, research provided ideas, exposed previous experience, and offered the data needed to define the scope of the sectoral integration process, the definition of the strategy, and the final mechanisms and instruments for its implementation. However, local knowledge was not the result of research programmes developed as needed; in fact, it was the 'personal capital' of the academics who joined the working team of public officials and decision makers who would then be in charge of putting that research into practice. The ideas provided by foreign epistemic communities were also part of this process; in this case, these ideas were drawn from the personal experience of these academics who had been part of the ECLAC during the 1960s and '70s, which contrasted sharply with the hegemonic ideas of the World Bank.

On the contrary, in the second episode, academic research offered important inputs for implementing the liberalisation process. In this case, research was abundant and provided by different actors, and it was also intended to fulfil various objectives. The technicians and experts from the Ministry of Economy would collect and systematise the necessary data for the final definition of the CET within the ongoing regional negotiations, but a second group of studies was commissioned by the ministries of economy and foreign affairs. Several external consultants, coming from different universities and think tanks, were then appointed to support the opposing ideological positions held by each of these ministries on whether to deepen the integration process with Brazil. Several regional organisations, such as the IADB, were also part of this ideological debate. In addition, business chambers with regional presence, such as the CIQyP, also provided important knowledge of the conditions and requirements of their sector in the new regional scenario. However, in these different cases, with the only exception of the technicians, research was intended to provide justification for the ideological positions held or to give way to certain lobbies.

Both episodes contrast sharply in terms of the impact local knowledge on the decision-making process. Also, both the PICE and the CGP can be characterised as a successful articulation process, promoted mainly by the government, which intended to build an alternative strategy to the one proposed by the World Bank. This allowed the government finally to be able to articulate a sectoral integration scheme. However, in both cases results would be weak given the strong opposition coming from the most concentrated private groups. In other words, even if there was a strong liaison during the academic research phase, this could not be utilised as sectoral interests would prevail over research evidence.

In the case of the CET, on the contrary, academic research, even if larger in number, had no impact on the decision-making process because the final decision regarding the CET was determined by the external pressures coming from Brazil, the hegemon within MERCOSUR. Brazil's strength relied not only on its economic pre-eminence but also on the internal divisions and rivalries within Menem's administration in Argentina. The only exception was then given by the private sector, which lobbied at the regional and national levels and finally achieved the required protection mechanism to assure its competitiveness in foreign markets.

By providing a comparative analysis of two different episodes of policy change, this chapter has highlighted the idea of influence as a complex process where the impact of knowledge on decisions can assume various forms and scope. Moreover, it is clear that the mere existence of knowledge regarding a certain issue does not constitute a necessary condition for its efficacy. In fact, the articulation between the different stakeholders and the political will to make use of it by the decision makers constitutes a key element. In this sense, expectations of academic incidence on trade policy should be cautious. Unlike other issues, trade policy is still strongly determined by two types of actors: external and private domestic actors.

References

Bouzos, Roberto, Pedro da Motta Veiga, and Ramón Torrent. 2002. *In-Depth Analysis of MERCOSUR Integration, Its Prospects, and the Effects.* Report presented to the Commission of the European Communities, Observatory of Globalization, November. Barcelona.

Brunner, Jose Joaquin, and Guillermo Sunkel. 1993. *Conocimiento, sociedad y politica.* Santiago de Chile: FLACSO-Chile.

Campbell, Jorge, ed. 1999. *Mercosur. Entre la realidad y la utopía.* Buenos Aires: CEI-Editorial Nuevo Hacer, Grupo Editor Latinoamericano.

Caplan, Nathan. 1979. 'The Two-Communities Theory and Knowledge Utilization.' *American Behavioral Scientist* 22(3):459–470.

Chudnovsky, Daniel, and Fabio Erber. 1999. 'MERCOSUR's Impact on the Development of the Machine Tools Sector.' *Integration and Trade* 7/8. <www.iadb.org/intal/aplicaciones/uploads/publicaciones/i_INTAL_IYT_7-8_1999_Chudnovsky-Erber.Pdf> [Accessed: March 2008].

Chudnovsky, Daniel, Masafumi Nagao, and Staffan Jacobsson. 1987. *Bienes de Capital y Tecnología en el Tercer Mundo.* Buenos Aires: Centro Editor de América Latina.

Davies, Huw, Sandra Nutley, and Isabel Walter. 2005. "Assessing the Impact of Social Science Research: Conceptual, Methodological, and Practical Issues." Background discussion paper for the ESCR Symposium on Assessing the Non-Academic Impact of Research, University of St. Andrews, 12–13 May.

Fundación de Investigaciones Económicas Latinoamericanos. 1993. *El comercio administrado de los '90: Argentina y sus socios*. Buenos Aires: Editorial Manantial.

Garrett, James L., and Yassir Islam. 1998. *Policy Research and the Policy Process: Do the Twain Ever Meet?* Gatekeeper Series no. 74. London: International Institute for Environment and Development. <www.iied.org/pubs/pdfs/6138IIED.pdf> [Accessed: March 2008].

Giorgi, Débora. 2003. *Mercosur. El Arancel externo común. Propuestas para su reforma*. Paper commissioned by the Ministry of Foreign Affairs, Argentina.

Haas, Peter. 1992. 'Introduction: Epistemic Communities and International Policy Coordination.' *International Organization* 46(1):1–35.

Hirschman, Albert O. 1970. *Exit, Voice, and Loyalty: Responses to Decline in Firms, Organizations, and States*. Cambridge MA: Harvard University Press.

——. 1976. 'Some Uses of the Exit-Voice Approach: Discussion.' *American Economic Review* 66(2):386–389.

Lavagna, Roberto. 2001. 'Los desafíos del Mercosur.' In Daniel Chudnovsky, and J.M. Fanelli, eds., *El disafío de integrarse para crecer: balance y perspectivas del Mercosur en su primera década*. Buenos Aires: Signo XXI de Argentina Editores.

Neilson, Stephanie. 2001. *Knowledge Utilization and Public Policy Processes: A Literature Review*. Ottawa: Evaluation Unit, International Development Research Centre.

Porta, Fernando, and Jorge Fontanals. 1989. 'La integratión intraindustrial: el caso del Acuerdo Argentino Brasileño en el sector de bienes de capital.' *Integracíon Latinoamericana* 152:14–15.

Reich, Robert. 1991. *The Work of Nations: Preparing Ourselves for Twenty-First Century Capitalism*. London: Simon and Schuster.

Restier-Melleray, Christiane. 1990. 'Experts et expertise scientifique: le cas de la France.' *Revue française de sciences politiques* 40(4):546–585.

Tussie, Diana. 2006. *Understanding the Use of Research in Trade Policy*. Document prepared after "The Use of Research in Trade Policy: Workshop to Understand the Contributions from Episodic Studies. Buenos Aires.

Weiss, Carol. 1977. 'Research for Policy's Sake: The Enlightenment Function of Social Research.' *Policy Analysis* 3(4):531–545.

——. 1979. 'The Many Meanings of Research Utilization.' *Public Administration Review* 39(5):426–431.

——. 1991. 'Policy Research as Advocacy: Pro and Con.' *Knowledge and Policy* 4(1/2):37–56.

CHAPTER FIVE

THE ADOPTION OF THE COMMON EXTERNAL TARIFF IN NIGERIA

Kehinde Ajayi[1] and Philip Osafo-Kwaako

The links between research and policy have been the subject of recent investigations in the literature on development policy. Although the research-policy linkage was previously viewed as a linear process (with research being directly translated into policy), there is now widespread evidence that various other social and institutional factors may intervene in the policy-making process. In most developing countries, policy formulation occurs in a contested field, where political agents, private sector lobbies, civil society institutions, donor agencies, and researchers all seek to influence outcomes. This chapter analyses a particular instance of trade policy reform in Nigeria and assesses the role played by research outputs in the policy-making process.

In October 2005, Nigeria joined other members of the Economic Community of West African States (ECOWAS) in adopting a common external tariff (CET). ECOWAS comprises 15 member states, eight of which belong to a separate regional grouping—the West African Economic and Monetary Union (WAEMU)—composed primarily of states in francophone West Africa. For ECOWAS members not part of the WAEMU, the adoption of the CET was necessary to support the goal of deep economic integration throughout the West Africa. The CET is intended to serve as the most-favoured nation (MFN) tariff that ECOWAS member states can apply to third countries and also to non-preferential products traded within the ECOWAS region. It proposes a four-band tariff structured as follows: 0 percent (for products with social significance, such as medicines), 5 percent (for necessities and raw materials), 10 percent (for intermediate goods), and 20 percent (for finished consumer goods). This chapter examines Nigeria's adoption

[1] With grateful acknowledgement of support from a Fulbright Fellowship and the Department of Economics at the University of Ibadan.

of the CET and assesses the role played by research outputs in this instance of trade policy reform.

Although ECOWAS countries initially agreed to liberalise intra-regional trade by 2000, progress was slow. Nigeria's participation in tariff harmonisation was, however, important in advancing any regional integration efforts: Nigeria accounts for about half of total gross domestic product (GDP) of the ECOWAS region, with an economy that ranks second (in GDP terms) only to South Africa in sub-Saharan Africa (World Bank 2006). Consequently, Nigeria's 2005 adoption of the CET marked an important milestone in the process of deepening economic integration in the region and provided an interesting episode of policy change for investigation.

The primary area of investigation for this chapter was to understand the production of knowledge on trade policy issues and the channels through which such knowledge was disseminated to influence the policy-making community during the process of CET adoption. It was important to assess the nature of research input (theoretical versus applied), the authors of the research exercise (academics or consultants; local versus foreign), and how the research was finally utilised in recipient government departments or agencies. The methodology employed direct interviews with academics as well as policy makers in Nigeria, which provided a broad understanding of the nature of research utilisation in trade policy formulation. The investigation also assessed the political context of tariff reform as well as the role of various other stakeholders in the process. In this regard, it adopted a 'tracer study' approach, in which an episode of policy change was reviewed and the web of interacting factors (including research) that caused the policy reform subsequently examined (Court *et al.* 2005).

The broad conclusion of this chapter is that research played a rather limited role in influencing the CET adoption process. Some CET studies were used directly by an elite policy-making group, and also indirectly influenced the activities of other government bureaucrats. However, there was weak research utilisation during this particular instance of policy reform, and the chapter concludes with a number of suggestions for strengthening the research-policy linkages in Nigeria. The remainder of this chapter is structured as follows: the second section outlines the context of trade policy formulation in Nigeria, focussing on the role played by major domestic stakeholders; the third section surveys the evidence available to policy makers from various sources throughout the process of reform; the fourth section briefly evaluates the policy networks and links between the research and policy communities that provided channels for knowledge uptake; the fifth section synthesises the information presented in preceding sections to construct an account of Nigeria's adoption of the CET and the role played by research in this process; and the sixth section summarises the investigation's main findings.

The Context of Trade Policy Formulation

In order to investigate the role of research in trade policy formulation, it is important to review the existing context in which trade policies are developed in Nigeria and the web of factors that shape the trade policy environment. Various actors and institutional structures interact in the process of trade policy formulation. A history of weak institutional capacity in Nigeria's public administration has significantly weakened the scope for effective trade policy making, resulting in the adoption of *ad hoc* trade policy measures, often supported by vested interest groups with close links to the ruling state elite. Adoption of the CET therefore provided an opportunity for Nigeria's Tariff Technical Committee to streamline the country's external tariffs and to ensure that the tariff regime was simplified, transparent, and predictable.

The 1999 Nigerian Constitution provides for a presidential system of government composed of an executive, a legislature, and a judiciary, with three tiers of government (at the federal, state, and local government levels). The president, vice-president, and appointed ministers constitute the Federal Executive Council, which is chaired by the president. In general, the council is responsible for the formulation and implementation of policies and programmes for the federation. The legislative arm of the federal government is composed of the bicameral National Assembly, with an upper house (the Senate) and a lower house (the House of Representatives). New policies and bills are designed and proposed by the executive branch of government with the assistance of the formal civil service bureaucracy. Ratification of policies, including international treaties, is, however, conducted by the National Assembly.

Regarding trade policy, the actual negotiation and formulation of policy are conducted by the Federal Ministry of Commerce, with support from the Federal Ministry of Finance, the Federal Ministry of Cooperation and Integration in Africa, and the National Planning

Commission (NPC). The ministry of finance oversees the setting and administration of taxes and duties, whereas the NPC ensures compatibility of new trade treaties with existing national development plans. In addition, the Nigerian government utilises a broad range of trade policy measures and instruments, including a duty drawback scheme, export credits, and export processing zone policies. Effective coordination of the various trade-related agencies rests with the Trade Policy Advisory Council, which is convened by the ministry of commerce.[2]

To facilitate dialogue with other stakeholders, the ministry of commerce also convenes the National Focal Point on Multilateral Trading Matters, which provides a forum for consultation and dialogue on trade issues with other non-state actors. Private sector business coalitions remain the dominant non-state stakeholders in Nigeria's trade policy environment, with an increasing participation from civil society and a somewhat limited presence of the academic and research communities. The minister of finance also chairs the Tariff Technical Committee, which oversees issues related to tariff revisions. The Tariff Technical Committee is composed of various stakeholders drawn from government as well as other private sector institutions. Figure 1 summarises the formal process of trade policy formulation that is to be expected.

In practice, the formulation of trade policy occurs differently. Following decades of poor economic management under military rule, Nigeria's public administration capacity had been significantly weakened. The capacity of the civil service to generate and implement evidence-based policies deteriorated, resulting in the adoption of *ad hoc* measures as instituted by a ruling political elite and other vested interest groups with strong political ties. For trade policy, the result was the development of a policy environment and tariff regime that was largely unpredictable, complex, and opaque.

The organised private sector (OPS) serves as the major coalition in influencing the national trade policies. The OPS includes various private sector institutions such as the Manufacturers Association of

[2] Among members of the Trade Policy Advisory Council are institutions such as the Nigerian Customs Service, the Nigeria Port Authority, the Nigerian Export Promotion Council, the Nigerian Export and Import Bank, the Nigeria Export Processing Zones Authority, the Nigerian Investment Promotion Council, the Nigeria Tourism Development Council, the Nigeria Bureau for Public Enterprises, the Nigerian National Petroleum Council, the National Food and Drug Administration and Control, and the Standards Organization of Nigeria.

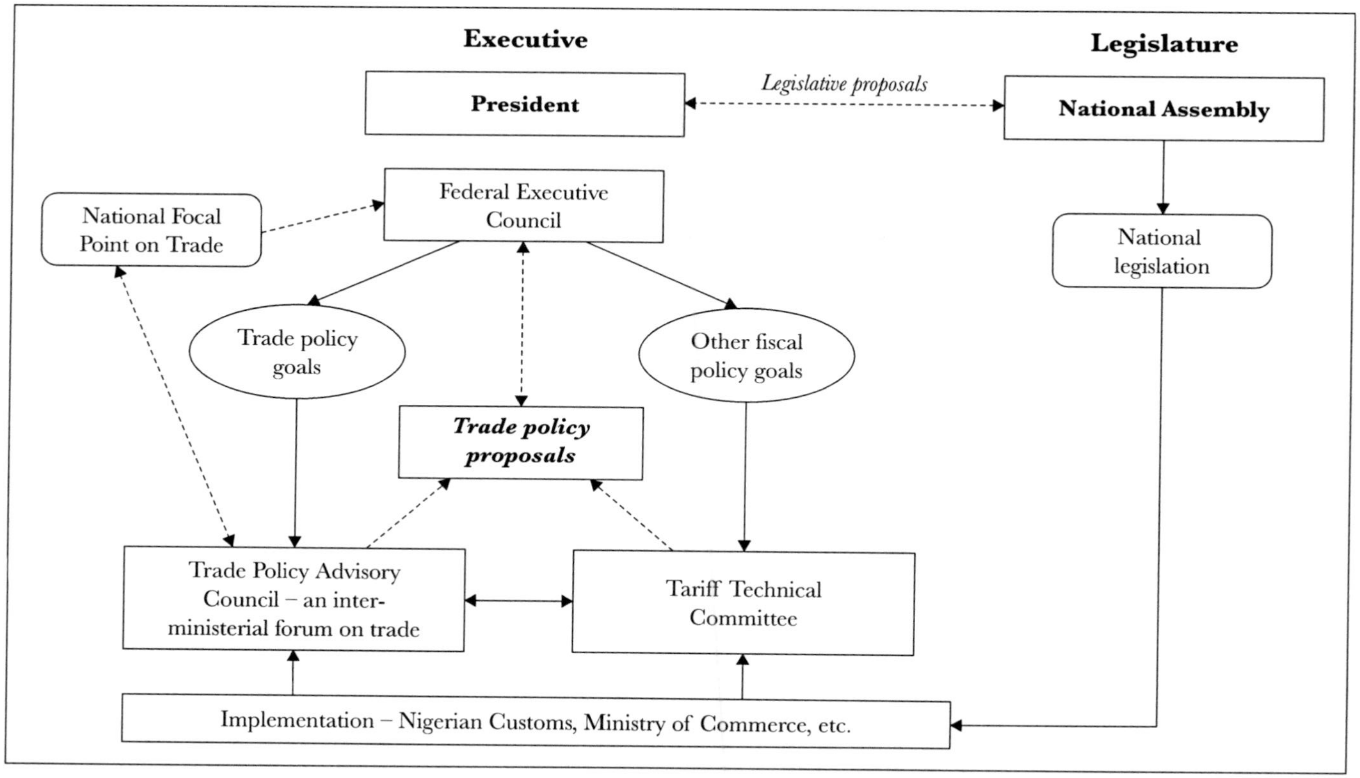

Source: Tim Ruffer, Val Imber, and Jibrin Ibrahim (2004).

Figure 1: The Formal Trade Policy-Making Process in Nigeria

Nigeria (MAN), the National Association of the Chambers of Commerce, Industry, Mines, and Agriculture (NACCIMA), the National Association of Small Scale Industrialists (NASSI), the Association of Nigerian Exporters, and banking institutions and other professional associations. The views of the OPS are often articulated in various fora, particularly through public workshops as well as in the local news media. Other civil society institutions such as non-governmental organisations (NGOs), faith-based institutions, and consumer advocacy groups as well as the Nigerian Labour Congress (NLC) are only recently emerging as contributors to the trade policy dialogue in Nigeria.

Although defending different constituencies, both the OPS and civil society tend to coalesce around common positions opposed to trade liberalisation. Recently, various domestic civil society organisations including the OPS have formed a coalition, termed the Nigerian Trade Network (NTN), to engage the government in dialogue on trade policy issues. The OPS remains the more vocal stakeholder and is often interested in defending commercial interests of its constituents by extensive lobbying of various government offices and the presidency. For the private sector, there remains an entrenched interest in ensuring extended periods of high tariffs to protect their private manufacturing and commercial interests. Civil society institutions, in contrast, aim at serving as advocates for ordinary Nigerians, particularly the majority of the poor in both urban and rural areas. Civil society institutions tend to support similar restrictive trade regimes, owing to a deep-rooted mistrust of neo-liberal policies, which are often viewed as being imposed on Nigeria by international financial institutions.

In a sense, the utilisation of political authority to support clientelist networks reflects Nicolas van de Walle's (2001) theoretical description of the African state as often being 'neo-patrimonial'. Although a neo-patrimonial state may have features of a Weberian rational-legal system (for example, with a modern bureaucracy, a formal legal system, and a distinction between the private and public spheres), this formal structure is often weak in practice. In many instances state institutions are undermined by patrimonial practices where officeholders utilise public resources for private ends and political authority frequently supports clientelist networks. Where there is a large state intervention in the economy, or where there is weak resistance from non-state actors, such patron-client networks serve as important avenues through which patronage and favours are provided, using instruments such as import licences and the granting of quotas. In such a restrictive trade environment, clientelist networks create avenues for rent-seeking behaviour.[3] To the extent that the state elite utilises political authority to provide patronage, there is a tendency for policy formulation to become centralised and driven by vested interest groups, with only limited consultation from other stakeholders.

But this is not to argue that non-state actors, such as civil society, the OPS, or researchers have no influence in the policy process. Such non-state actors do influence the policy environment, albeit in a limited capacity. As argued by Robert H. Bates (1998), among others, policy formulation may also be viewed as the outcome of bargaining processes involving various interest groups. From this pluralist viewpoint, policy formulation is assumed to maximise the welfare of various competing interest groups. Occasionally, such stakeholder groups may lobby the government to obtain special trade concessions or duty exemptions.

In assessing the role played by research in the process of trade policy formulation, it is important to bear both theoretical approaches in mind—the neo-patrimonial view as well as one predicated on interest group behaviour. The scope of research impact differs in each of the models above. Research may be disregarded in a neo-patrimonial framework, but it may also have an impact in an environment where policy is formulated by competing interest groups. In this regard, evidence may be required to support some proposed policy programs. This is particularly important in the evolving trade policy environment in Nigeria, with the state adopting a liberalised and more open trading regime. In a more open trading framework, the autonomy of the state to impose *ad hoc* trade measures is limited. This creates a complex policy environment for trade formulation, which is influenced by interest group politics but also retains elements of a clientelist political system.

Evidence

Various forms of research evidence, ranging from the specific to the general, were available during the CET adoption process in Nigeria. In the review of the available reports conducted for this chapter, it was observed that most policy makers were often unaware of the majority of these studies. This section reviews three major components of such

[3] See, for example, Jeffrey Herbst (1993).

evidence: first, a pool of impact assessment studies generated by various stakeholders to assess the welfare implications of Nigeria's adoption of the CET; second, reviews of Nigeria's trade policies by both local and foreign analysts; and third, the broad international country case studies analysing the costs and benefits of trade liberalisation. The first category of CET impact assessment studies tended to be demand-driven and highly specific. In contrast, trade policy reviews focussed on Nigeria's broader experience in the global trading system and were conducted periodically by institutions such as the World Bank and the World Trade Organization (WTO). The third category of general evidence on trade liberalisation and growth was based largely on experiences from a variety of countries.

Table 1 summarises some of the major studies conducted and their major findings. It also identifies the authors of specific reports, institutions financing the report preparation, and the report's intended audience or beneficiaries. The actual extent of research uptake was, however, determined by the existence of links between the research and policy communities, as well as the degree of legitimacy that various studies possessed. This subject of links and legitimacy is discussed in the next section.

Links: Influence and Legitimacy

Research utilisation theories and empirical evidence point to a lack of interaction between researchers and policy makers as a major reason for poor knowledge uptake. Nathan Caplan (1979) notes that research utilisation is not solely about improving the quantity, but rather improving the quality of links, particularly in cases of 'meta-level' decisions that require the synthesis of various information sources. Strong links create opportunities for researchers to disseminate their research effectively and such connections may similarly improve the quality of research itself.[4]

To understand the nature of trade policy making in Nigeria, it is important to examine who are seen as experts in this field, and how these

---

[4] For example, researchers working on a decentralised livestock services project in Indonesia found that 'when people had faith that the research they produced would be well received, and somebody would respond to it, they would gather good quality information and articulate it well' (Crewe and Young 2002, 17).

Table 1: Summary of Available Research Evidence

Title	Author	Produced for	Funded by	Comments
Category 1: CET Impact Assessment Studies				
A Study of Basic Aspects of a Common External Tariff for ECOWAS	Aninat (1982)	ECOWAS	UNCTAD/ UNDP	RECOMMENDATIONS – Collectively define the structure of an ECOWAS common external tariff through a consultative negotiation process based on stated national interests.
Effects of Tariff and Exchange Rates on the Manufacturing Sector and the Balance of Payments in Nigeria 'Comprehensive Review of Nigeria Customs and Excise Duties'	Consortium of local consultants, namely Skoup & Company, Enterprise Consulting Group, Kuji Intercontinental Agencies, and Adegbite & Company, 2001 to 2003	Federal Ministry of Finance	Federal Ministry of Finance	FINDINGS: Low collection efficiency of customs officials, estimated loss of over $200 million in uncollected tariff revenue in 2001 alone. With the adoption of the CET, estimated revenue losses of 2.9% to 6.9% of government revenue ($195 million to $500 million) depending on accompanying measures. Deterioration of trade balance by 3.5% of GDP. A decline in effective rate of protection from about 82% to 34%. RECOMMENDATIONS – Phased implementation of WAEMU CET over five years, with six bands of 0, 5%, 10%, 20%, 30%, and 50%). – Various complementary policies needed including: nominal depreciation; institutional reform of related regulatory agencies, especially Nigeria Customs Service; reduction in use of tariff waivers, exemptions, and concessions; and improvement in the business climate.
Study of the Implications of the Common External Tariff and Integration in ECOWAS	Adjovi, Beye, Awassi, Smith (2002)	ECOWAS	European Commission	FINDINGS: Estimated revenue losses of $10 million to $1 billion (N1.4 billion to N140 billion), depending on whether commodity-specific or aggregate price elasticities were used. RECOMMENDATION: – Adoption of the WAEMU CET.

Table 1 (*cont.*)

Title	Author	Produced for	Funded by	Comments
Potential Impacts of Extension of UEMOA Tariffs to all ECOWAS Member States: A Case Study of Impacts on Revenue and Trade Balance in Nigeria	Agu, Oji, and Soludo (2003)	ECOWAS ministerial meeting on CET	African Institute for Applied Economics	FINDINGS: Revenue losses of 2.9% to 8.8% of government revenue (N27 billion to N80 billion). Balance of payment decrease of 3% to 6% GDP. RECOMMENDATIONS: – Build 'credible constituencies' by increasing stakeholder consultation to support the CET. – Gather additional empirical evidence to inform policy debate
Estimates of the Impact of a Common External Tariff of the Nigerian Manufacturing Sector: Some Simulation Results Based on Firm-Level Data (Working Paper)	Marchat and Rajhi (2004)	World Bank	World Bank	FINDINGS: Estimated an average of 56% decline in effective rate of protection. Decreases in employment, wages, and profits of about 3% to 4%; 12.3% decrease in output prices; 0.5% decrease in production. RECOMMENDATIONS: – Proposed three-year period for adoption of WAEMU CET. – Accompanying measures such as the use of degressive protection tax, cyclical/ seasonal tax). – Attention to macroeconomic context (particularly exchange rate policies), infrastructure, access to credit, participation of unions/manufacturing associations.
Impact of Proposed New Tariff Regime on the Revenue of the Federal Government of Nigeria: Summary of Findings	Adegbite (2005)	Federal Ministry of Finance	Federal Ministry of Finance	FINDINGS: Revenue losses as low as 2.9% of current revenue, which could be further reduced by increases in collection efficiency (efficiency rate was 38% between 1996≠2001). RECOMMENDATIONS: – Adopt WAEMU CET. – Strengthen revenue collection mechanisms. – Minimise level of informal (unreported) trade.

Table 1 (*cont.*)

Title	Author	Produced for	Funded by	Comments
ECOWAS Common External Tariff (ECOTrade) Recommendations Regarding Changes in Tariff Rates	USAID (2005)	ECOWAS	USAID	RECOMMENDATIONS: – Adopt WAEMU CET allowing for 'Type A' (transitional) exceptions and 'Type B' (permanently desirable) exceptions to be negotiated to revise the ECOWAS CET, with all exceptions resolved by 31 December 2007. – Safeguard tax. – Reclassify certain goods.
End of (Textile) Industry? A Critical Study of the Collapse of Textile Industry in Nigeria and the Implications for Employment and Poverty Eradication	Aremu (2005)	NLC, National Union of Textile and Garment Workers	Friedrich Ebert Stiftung	RECOMMENDATIONS: – 10-year textile ban, a reconsideration of CET (e.g., 10% duty on yarn, an intermediate good will 'kill' the local spinning industry), and an additional 'import safeguard levy' for the short run.
Impact of Common External Tariff and Economic Partnership Agreements on Agriculture in Nigeria	Achike, Agu, and Oduh (2005)	Oxfam GB	Oxfam GB	FINDINGS: High protection coincides with high turnover and growth for key commodities (rice, cassava and sorghum). Decrease in tariffs would lead to decline in agricultural sector. Potential benefits include access to enlarged markets, policy credibility and lock-in, learning ground and practice for further trade integration, and access to cheaper imports of raw materials and capital goods from international markets. RECOMMENDATIONS: – Proceed with adoption of the CET but carefully consider adoption of EPA. – Improve infrastructure. – Facilitate access to agricultural inputs. – Provide a backstop for agricultural prices. – Increase stakeholder consultation.

Table 1 (*cont.*)

Title	Author	Produced for	Funded by	Comments
Category 2: Reviews of Trade Policy in Nigeria				
Nigeria: Trade Policy Review	WTO (1998; 2005)	WTO members	WTO	Provided a general review of Nigeria's trade policies and trade-related institutions.
A Gender and Poverty Audit of Nigeria's Trade Policy	NTN (2005)	NTN and other civil society bodies	NTN	Surveyed perceptions of the poor of the impact of trade reforms on poverty reduction. Argued that although trade policy had been used more for revenue generation than economic development, tariff revenues at Nigerian ports had been low because of inefficient collection.
Improving the Performance of the Nigerian Manufacturing Sub-Sector after Adjustment: Selected issues and proposal	Akinlo (1995)	Nigerian Journal of Economic and Social Sciences	—	Concludes that trade liberalisation generally had a negative effect on the manufacturing sector.
Trade Liberalization in Nigeria, 1970–93: Episodes, Credibility, and Impact	Ajakaiye and Soyibo (1999)	Book chapter	—	Employed regression analyses techniques; concluded that trade liberalisation had no significant effect on real GDP and only one instance of liberalisation (1970–76) increased real imports.
Import Prohibition as a Trade Policy Instrument: The Nigerian Experience	Bankole, Ogunkola, and Oyejide (2005)	Book chapter	—	Reviewed impact of import prohibitions in Nigeria's trade regime.
An Assessment of Nigeria's Import Prohibitions Policy	Ruffer (2004)	DFID	DFID	Reviewed the use of import prohibitions in Nigeria's trade policy.
The Political Economy of Trade Policy in Nigeria	Rugger, Imber, and Ibrahim (2004)	DFID	DFID	Surveyed the formulation and implementation of trade policy in Nigeria.

Table 1 (*cont.*)

Title	Author	Produced for	Funded by	Comments
Category 3: Broader Literature on Trade Liberalisation and Growth				
Economic Reform and the Process of Global Integration	Sachs and Warner (1995)	Academic paper	—	Suggested that, in the 1970s and 1980s, developing countries with open economies grew by 4.5% each year whereas closed economies grew by 0.7% and were characterised by high import tariffs, high non-tariff barriers, a socialist economic system, a state monopoly on important exports, or a big gap between official and black market exchange rates.
Trade, Growth and Poverty, Policy Research	Dollar and Kraay (2001)	World Bank working paper	—	Used cross-country data to distinguish between globalisers and non-globalisers, based on rate of growth of trade to GDP ratio and compared growth rates. Found globalisers tend to grow three times faster. Most globalisers also had the most open trading regimes, pointing to the importance of tariff liberalisation for growth.
Trade Policy and Economic Growth: A Skeptic's Guide to Cross-National Literature	Rodriguez and Rodrik (1999)	Academic paper	—	Questioned the accuracy of 'openness' or 'globaliser' measures, the basis for determining causality, and econometric methods used in cross-country regressions.
Selective Industrial and Trade Policies in Developing Countries: Theoretical and Empirical Issues	Lall (2000)	Academic paper	—	Discussed the use of selective trade and industrial policies by many developing countries, notably the East Asian tigers.

Notes: CET = common external tariff, DFID = United Kingdom Department for International Development, ECOWAS = Economic Community of West African States, EPA = economic partnership agreement, GDP = gross domestic product, NLC = Nigerian Labour Congress, NTN = Nigerian Trade Network, UNCTAD = United Nations Conference on Trade and Development, UNDP = United Nations Development Programme, WAEMU = West African Economic and Monetary Union, WTO = World Trade Organization.

experts establish legitimising relationships. Such experts may exist as individuals, or as part of a broader community (an 'advocacy coalition') in which members share a set of common beliefs. Individuals with such influence operate as 'policy entrepreneurs', and may assume various forms such as *connectors*, who serve as 'networkers' to transfer knowledge to key policy makers, *mavens*, who are 'information specialists' and who gather information and then educate others, and *salespeople*, who use their charisma and persuasive power to gain exclusive audiences and acquire positions of trust (Crewe and Young 2002, 14).

In order to achieve influence, however, research must be seen as legitimate. Knowledge producers in Nigeria use various strategies to establish their legitimacy in trade policy debates. Information and research from international institutions often carry an inherent sense of legitimacy—partly for historical reasons, and partly because such institutions are viewed as having access to extensive technical and financial resources in conducting their research. Government sources similarly bear legitimacy in the provision of data. In contrast, local non-state actors (including local researchers) must cultivate links and establish the legitimacy of their work over a period of time. The following section examines the influence and legitimacy of government information sources, the local research community, lobbyists, international organisations, and domestic policy entrepreneurs.

Government Information Sources

In response to the question of on whom they rely for research input, Nigerian government officials frequently cited public institutions (such as the Central Bank of Nigeria, the Federal Office of Statistics, and the National Planning Commission) as a primary source of their information. Experiential knowledge from senior civil servants was also identified as a common source of information for trade policy formulation. In these cases, knowledge was used to guide minor or incremental policy changes. Public information sources became less legitimate in cases that required conceptual or macro-level utilisation of research. For more complex studies, government officials often outsourced projects to external research consultants. Nigeria's institutional policy-making framework has a central organ for economic analysis within the National Planning Commission, namely the Nigerian Institute of Social and Economic Research (NISER). However, the institute's research influence has recently waned and the institute made no substantial contribution to the deliberations about Nigeria's adoption of the CET. Moreover, although most federal ministries also have in-house research departments, the weak capacity and poor resources of these departments suggest that they make only nominal contributions to actual policy research.

Local Research Community

At the individual level, most members of Nigeria's local research community appear to have only minor levels of influence. However, there are selected groupings or epistemic communities that have significantly engaged in trade policy debates.[5] The African Institute for Applied Economics (AIAE) and the Trade Policy Research and Training Programme (TPRTP) are two such institutions, both located in Nigeria, that have become associated with a specific ideology over time and now play a prominent role in that country's trade policy. The TPRTP is a network of trade economists based in the Department of Economics at the University of Ibadan, and tends to hold a neo-liberal view on trade policy. One interview respondent described members as 'espousing generic dictums on trade'. In contrast, the AIAE is viewed as adopting a rather structuralist approach to development and trade policy issues, employing more applied research methodologies compared to the mainstream neoclassical techniques of TPRTP researchers.

Both the AIAE and the TPRTP have participated in Nigeria's trade policy-making process. The AIAE contributed to the *Comprehensive Review of Nigeria's Tariff Regime*, which the ministry of finance (2003) commissioned prior to adoption of the CET, and the AIAE has been involved in formulating major national policies including the 2002 trade policy and the National Economic Empowerment and Development Strategy (NEEDS). The TPRTP has similarly participated in various national conferences and contributed to the preparation of national negotiation positions in multilateral fora, such as during the 2005 WTO Hong Kong

[5] Theories on knowledge utilization note that researchers can garner significant influence when they constitute a technical elite or 'epistemic community' with access to privileged information and close links to policy-makers. (Sutton, 1999; and Crewe and Young, 2002). Epistemic communities often develop when objective research institutions evolve into politicized 'discourse coalitions' that eventually shape the direction of policy, as was the case with organizations such as the Brookings Institution and Heritage Foundation in the United States (Sutton, 1999).

meeting and the ongoing economic partnership agreements between the European Union and the Africa, Caribbean, and Pacific (ACP) countries. In addition, the TPRTP publishes the *African Journal of Economic Policy*, an academic periodical that often contains articles relating to trade policy.[6] Although the TPRTP and the AIAE have actively participated in Nigeria's trade policy formulation, their geographical distance from federal government officials in Abuja somewhat limits their ability to influence policy making continuously.

Lobbyists

As noted earlier, Nigeria's policy arena is characterised by a significant presence of lobbyists who support various vested interests. Major business associations in Nigeria have merged into the OPS, and each association has some degree of in-house research capacity with a research division that usually consists of two or three employees. Internal research is primarily based on data gathered at quarterly meetings at which member firms and field offices present report updates. Occasional surveys of member firms supplement these basic statistics. Associations contract out more intensive studies to local consultants, usually with project-based funding from NGOs or donor agencies.

NGOs and business associations in Nigeria sometimes work jointly as advocacy coalitions. Two such examples are the National Association of Nigerian Traders (NANTS) and the NTN, with both institutions sharing a common anti-liberalisation viewpoint. The NANTS is an alliance of more than 5,300 corporate and individual members and is rapidly gaining influence in domestic trade policy discussions. For example, it is recognised by the European Commission as the representative non-state actor for negotiationg economic partnership agreements (EPAs). The NTN was also recently conceived as advocacy platform for civil society organisations and the OPS on trade and investment issues, and its main membership comprises the MAN, the NACCIMA, the NASSI, the NLC, and the NANTS. This advocacy coalition offers a united front on trade issues to promote pro-poor policies. It benefits from the

[6] Academic journals and professional networks serve as another means for researchers to establish credibility, by disseminating scholarship through a legitimising avenue. Another leading periodical that covers trade policy issues is the *Nigeria Journal of Economic and Social Studies*, published by Nigerian Economic Society.

legitimacy of having the impact of a united voice, access to external funding, and close proximity to the policy community.[7]

Unlike the numerous OPS groups, the NLC represents the main voice of the national labour movement. The NLC's research resources have somewhat more of an academic basis compared with other OPS groups.[8] Members of both the NLC and the OPS have past relationships with the Nigerian government having served on various government advisory committees. However, the NLC sees itself as lacking economic weight of OPS groups: one NLC respondent characterised interactions with the government as being frequently 'antagonistic' compared to the 'symbiotic relationship' between politicians and industrialists.

Finally, the Nigeria Economic Summit Group (NESG), which organises an annual meeting to discuss Nigeria's economic problems, represents a coalition for economic development led by the private sector. The group's membership is by invitation only and includes representatives from academia, multinational corporations, and the local industrial elite, which has strengthened the NESG's legitimacy over time. In many ways, it has already achieved its objective of ensuring dialogue on economic issues between the public and the private sectors. For example, the NESG's views were incorporated in drafting stages of Nigeria's 2002 trade policy. Moreover, the annual Nigeria Economic Summit serves as a regular means for reinforcing the group's relationship with policy makers and preserving its prominent role in the policy debate. In contrast to other OPS groups, the NESG was not opposed to Nigeria's adoption of a CET. Indeed, industrialists at the 2002 summit called for the harmonisation of tariffs on capital goods and raw materials to the CET adopted by the WAEMU members (Agu *et al.* 2003).

---

[7] Both the NTN and the NANTS are based in Abuja, which gives them close proximity to policy makers. Although the NLC is also headquartered in Abuja, the MAN, the NASSI, and the NACCIMA are based in Lagos, maintaining a limited presence in Abuja through liaison offices. The media also has limited involvement in trade policy. In terms of funding, the NANTS and the NTN receive most of their funding from member dues and international NGOs, namely Oxfam, the Heinrich Boell Foundation, and the Friedrich Ebert Stiftung.

[8] The NLC's Labour Centre for Social and Economic Research is headed by a trade economist and currently hosts a visiting scholar.

International Organisations

Generally, many development institutions recognised that Nigeria's trade policy in particular is politically sensitive and adopted an indirect approach to influence it by focussing on general reforms and broader economic policy rather than specific trade issues. The literature on research utilisation in development policy emphasises the need for international or external actors to create appropriate relationships with local communities. On the one hand it can be relatively easy for external actors to forge legitimising links with government actors if they establish themselves to be 'internationally reputable consultants' with impartial views (Crewe and Young 2002, 15). However, the donor-recipient relationship presents some challenges, such as scepticism from recipients about whether the ultimate goal of such research supports the donor's self-interest. In response to these concerns, international researchers must be conscious of their approach. Indeed, one expatriate survey respondent described his objective as being a 'trusted policy advisor' by offering informed suggestions but being cautious not to interfere.

The international community's focus on indirect approaches to influence Nigeria's trade policy targets capacity building, funding, and technical support for both government and civil society agents. International NGOs have established significant links with local advocacy groups such as the NTN and the NANTS to support research initiatives. Agencies such as Oxfam have aimed to strengthen research uptake and the quality of policy debate by supporting these advocacy coalitions. Similarly, the Friedrich Ebert Stiftung funded a collection of essays on Nigeria and the neo-liberal world system as part of a capacity-building workshop for members of the National Assembly. The essays were published as an edited volume in November 2005. In some cases, bilateral donors have tended to work with national institutions. The EC has funded some ECOWAS studies, whereas the United States Agency for International Development (USAID) developed a project to assist ECOWAS countries in adopting a CET. Similarly, the United Kingdom's Department for International Development (DFID) commissioned several trade-related studies and has provided funding for various technical advisors supporting government policy making (including trade policy issues). Although externally funded research is often conducted by international consultants, international teams occasionally collaborate with local researchers or subcontract projects.

Policy Entrepreneurs

Institutional links in Nigeria's policy environment are reinforced by the movement of individuals between various groups, such as private sector actors engaging in advocacy, civil servants taking up employment in civil society organisations and development agencies, and academics moving into business activities. Additionally, membership of some organisations tends to be cross-cutting. As mentioned earlier, for example, the NESG includes academics as well as local business operators and foreign company representatives. Furthermore, individuals may belong to several groups concurrently. For example, some academics have established civil society organisations, and some national assembly representatives are former academics with businesses ties.[9]

In the midst of these complex interconnections, three individuals may be identified as policy entrepreneurs, to use the terms adopted by Crewe and Young (2002, 14), with keen insights to critical aspects of Nigeria's trade policy scene. Ademola Oyejide of the TPRTP is a maven who passes on relevant information through conferences and research publication, and is a major contributor to Nigeria's trade policy documents. Ken Ukaoha, the president of the NANTS, is an information specialist who has made great efforts to acquire contemporary knowledge on trade issues and educate others through a weekly column in a local newspaper, advocacy programmes, and via the NTN. Finally, Charles Soludo, founder of AIAE, is a salesman of policy research prior to his recent appointment as governor of the Central Bank of Nigeria.

Adoption of the ECOWAS Common External Tariff

Thus far, this assessment has provided a broad outline of the policy environment and available evidence prior to Nigeria's adoption of the ECOWAS CET. In this section, the foregoing discussion is synthesised to identify the various factors that resulted in Nigeria's commitment to reform its tariff policies and adopt the CET. Identifying the major drivers of influence for the policy change is a valuable exercise, as it enables an assessment of the role played by research along each of

[9] For example, Ademola Ariyo, a professor in the Department of Economics at University of Ibadan, established the Centre for Public-Private Cooperation, an NGO that advocates for civil society participation in policy making.

the channels identified. A convergence of three major factors catalysed Nigeria's eventual adoption of the CET: the commitment to reform by the economic management team of President Olusegun Obasanjo, the activities of bureaucrats in the Nigerian civil service, and the political commitment of the Obasanjo government to deepening regional integration in West Africa. These three factors coalesced at an opportune moment, mutually reinforcing each other, and ultimately resulting in the adoption of the CET. Each of these factors is discussed further below, and, subsequently, the influence of research, operating along each of these channels, is examined.

Reform Objectives of the Obasanjo Economic Management Team

At the inauguration of his second term in office in 2003, Obasanjo made a commitment to economic reform aimed at improving the country's economic growth, reducing dependence on the oil sector, generating employment, and increasing investments in the economy. This commitment was operationalised by the appointment of an economic team, chaired by the minister of finance—a former senior official from the World Bank. The economic team was essentially a team of technocrats: a few ministers from key economic sectors and heads of other relevant government agencies (such as the offices for debt management and privatisation). Most of the team members had considerable international experience.

An ambitious reform programme was outlined by the reform team, aimed at ensuring macroeconomic stability, improving efficiency of public expenditure management, tackling corruption, and improving the domestic investment climate.[10] With regard to reform of the tariff regime, the economic team argued that tariff liberalisation was needed to address the anti-export bias of the previous tariff schedule, to reduce incentives for smuggling (due to Nigeria's uncompetitive duty rates), and, finally, to reduce duty rates for capital goods and raw materials in order to encourage the integration of Nigeria's private sector into global value chains (International Monetary Fund [IMF] 2005). Adoption of the ECOWAS CET provided an appropriate means of addressing these

---

[10] See International Monetary Fund ([IMF] 2005) for further discussion on Nigeria's economic reforms under the IMF Policy Support Instrument (2005–2007).

concerns, reducing the country's average unweighted tariff rates from about 30 percent to below 20 percent (IMF 2005) (BOF, 2006).

Activities of Government Bureaucrats

In addition, government bureaucrats, conducting routine administrative functions within the civil service, supported and facilitated the objective of trade policy reform. There was concerted progress made on reform by the economic team and the government stated its policies on trade reform (NPC, 2004). However, a review of the trade policy would not have been achieved without the broader support of government bureaucrats. This is an important concern as previous attempts at reform programmes had sometimes stalled owing to weak implementation capacity or lack of support from the civil service.[11] Indeed, delays in Nigeria's adoption of external agreements (such as WTO legislation) and inadequate participation in regional trade negotiations may be partly attributed to the weak and under-resourced capacity of trade-related departments. However, in the implementation of the ECOWAS CET, relevant government offices showed great commitment in achieving a timely revision of the tariff schedule. There were probably two main reasons for this broad support for tariff revision.

The first reason, largely procedural, emerged from the Nigerian Customs Service (NCS). Senior officials at the NCS noted that the legal basis of the previous Customs, Excise Tariff Decree No 4 (March 1995) had expired—and since 2001, *ad hoc* revisions had been made annually. In addition, the customs service noted that it was important for Nigeria to reconcile its tariff classifications with the current coding nomenclature set out by the World Customs Organization (WCO), which was operational for 2002–06. It was envisaged that Nigeria's timely adoption of the CET (in mid 2005) would permit some experience with use of the existing WCO nomenclature prior to the adoption of the revised schedule in 2007.

The second reason for support resulted from a perceived benefit from tariff liberalisation and regional economic integration, as well as the need to show Nigeria's commitment to regional economic

[11] See, for example, *Business Day* newspaper of 18 May 2006 where delays in port and customs reforms have been reported and attributed partly to inertia from civil service workers.

programmes. In this regard, research played a role in shaping discussions of government bureaucrats, both during informal exchanges as well as at organised committee meetings.[12] Some impact assessment studies had been reviewed by members of the tariff technical committee, and officials at the ministry of commerce and the NPC also indirectly utilised results from such studies during various national seminars and conferences. Although no specific research reports were cited, there was a perceived benefit of tariff liberalisation as public officials frequently compared Nigeria's weak non-oil export performance with other emerging economies such as Malaysia, Brazil, and China. It was often argued that Nigeria's non-oil exports performance could be improved by reducing duties on capital goods, raw materials, and intermediate products. Moreover, Nigeria could also improve its integration into the world economy by participating in global production value chains, for example, by importing machine parts or completely knocked-down components from China and exporting finished products to regional and international markets.[13]

The Politics of Regional Integration

A final factor driving adoption of the CET in Nigeria was the broad political backing for the ECOWAS regional integration project offered by Obasanjo. Throughout his tenure in office, Obasanjo was identified as an elder statesman, not only in Nigeria, but also in most of Africa (Economic Intelligence Unit 2006). The president's statesmanship was strengthened by his support for conflict resolution and democratic processes in other African states. Furthermore, Obasanjo showed a genuine commitment to deeper pan-African integration, serving as a firm supporter of the New Partnership for Africa's Development (NEPAD) (Economic Intelligence Unit 2006). Shortly after assuming office in 1999, the Obasanjo administration established a new government department, the Federal Ministry of Cooperation and Integration in Africa, to address these concerns. Nigeria's adoption of the CET was therefore significantly driven by a political motive of presenting the country's support of the pan-African goals presented in initiatives such as NEPAD. In past instances, Nigeria's participation in ECOWAS

---

[12] See, for example, Nigeria's Ministry of Commerce (2006).
[13] Again, see Ministry of Commerce (2006).

negotiations had been limited (Olympio 2006). For Nigerian trade negotiators, adoption of the ECOWAS CET provided an opportunity to provide concrete support to the regional economic programme.[14] Given Nigeria's limited trade with ECOWAS countries, it is likely that steady political support for the reform programme ensured its successful implementation. Clearly, without such political support, the work of technocrats and bureaucrats as discussed above may not have been implemented.

Discerning the Influence of Research

To understand the influence of research, it is important to outline the model of the policy process identified here. An interactive model of the policy process, complemented by international policy transfer, typifies the CET adoption process in Nigeria (Dolowitz and Marsh 1996; Grindle and Thomas 1991). The interactive model focusses on the role of policy elites tasked with the actual implementation of policy changes (Grindle and Thomas 1990). The model presents the policy process in a political economy framework, where various actors, likely to benefit or lose from a policy change, seek to influence the final outcomes of implementation. Although maintaining a rationalist framework, the interactive model acknowledges the policy process and the broader political context needed for policy reform. In addition, the policy transfer model contends that policy ideas developed in a given geographical location may be transferred, and applied, in other geographical locations with the assistance of agents such as international organisations or researchers (Dolowitz and Marsh 1996).

In line with the interactive model, a central role was played by a policy elite—the economic team—in implementing Nigeria's tariff reform, with political support from the presidency. In addition, the role of international policy transfer of ideas and practices on tariff liberalisation was important in influencing key decision makers in the economic team. Given an interactive and international policy transfer model of the policy process, research can be seen to have influenced the

---

[14] As ECOWAS member states were also in the process of negotiating EPAs with the EU, Nigeria's adoption of the CET (which involved unilateral tariff liberalisation) indicated the country's commitment to deepen trade in the sub-region and its pursuit of tariff liberalisation. Nigeria's specific position on EPAs is currently unknown.

adoption process in two main ways: first, via a direct, but limited process, in which research inputs were used for direct problem solving by policy elites on the economic team and also by government bureaucrats, and, second, via a more diffuse process of enlightenment, in which research ideas gradually influenced the concepts that shape policy discussions. Each of these factors is discussed further below.

Problem-Solving Approaches. Some direct evidence—in the form of CET impact assessment studies—was utilised by members of the reform team as well as government bureaucrats to assess the potential impact of a tariff reform. Technocrats in the economic team embraced tariff reform, not only because it was viewed as important in supporting growth, but also as a means to simplify the tariff structure and reduce instances of rent-seeking practices.[15] Research played an important role in influencing the trade policy decisions of the economic reform team. Their knowledge of cross-country research, acquired from prior professional experiences, influenced the team members and reinforced their commitment to simplifying and liberalising Nigeria's tariff regime. Research was largely based on case studies and other country experiences often including commonly used comparator countries such as Indonesia and Malaysia. The limited research buttressed the decision, providing some analytical credibility and support for the decision.[16] As an example, the use of simple average and weighted average tariff rates became an important index for the level of liberalisation and was cited frequently in government reports and memos.[17]

Yet the instrumental utilisation of research was limited as many other government bureaucrats and officials had very little knowledge of the relevant research on the CET (as reviewed in the third section of this chapter). In many conversations with members of the Tariff Technical Committee, it was observed that they were unaware of many of the previous studies that had been conducted. For example, one senior official of the NCS and member of the Tariff Technical Committee, who had played an active role in revising the existing tariff book, was largely unaware of the research evidence (as presented in Table 1).

---

[15] Interview with Ngozi Okonjo-Iweala (former minister of finance, Nigeria), 25 May 2006.

[16] Interview with Bright Okogu (advisor, Federal Ministry of Finance, Nigeria), 26 May 2006.

[17] The tariff rates used were calculated in reports produced by a consortium of local consulting firms, including Skoup & Company, Enterprise Consulting Group, Kuji Intercontinental Agencies, and Adegbite & Company. See Table 1.

Government bureaucrats often relied on methods other than systematic policy research to clarify trade policy issues—namely, verification exercises or consultations with stakeholders. For example, in the debate on the ideal tariff to be placed on tyres to be used for buses and trucks domestic manufacturers (subsidiaries of Dunlop and Michelin) sought protection against foreign imports while importers of rubber tyres argued for tariff reduction.[18] A previous import tariff of 50 percent had been reduced to 20 percent, but importers requested this be lowered further to 10 percent. To address this difficulty, a verification exercise was conducted on the manufacturers' sites. Domestic production was estimated at about 0.5 million tyres per annum, compared with an estimated 10 million automobiles in use in the country. Using this information as the basis of evidence, it was argued that a 20 percent tariff rate was the appropriate middle ground to balance the interest of domestic manufacturers and importers. From the records of meetings, it is clear that such policy decisions were seldom rigorously analysed and often adopted based on the persuasiveness of arguments presented by particularly constituencies. For the CET reform programme, those members of the tariff technical committee interviewed often cited such past investigation as the basis of their background research for tariff amendments and classification rather than any systematic assessment of the evidence as presented in the third section of this chapter.

Enlightenment Approaches. A global discourse on trade liberalisation also percolated into the policy environment in Nigeria, influencing government bureaucrats, decision makers, and other stakeholders. This percolation process was diffuse as it often related to a broad idea of trade policy reform, rather than a specific tariff liberalisation measure (such as the adoption of the CET). This is striking given that popular opinion in Nigeria in the 1980s had opposed adoption of structural adjustment programmes, resulting in only limited neo-liberal reforms such as tariff liberalisation. Similarly, in the 1990s, Nigeria's tariff regime was characterised as being protectionist and complex (WTO, 1998). However, by 2003, Nigeria had embarked on a process of unilateral tariff liberalisation, which was well articulated and defended by government bureaucrats.[19] There was a gradual knowledge creep on

[18] See Ministry of Commerce (2006).

[19] Interview with Felicia Onyeabo, secretary of the Tariff Technical Committee, 25 April 2006.

the welfare benefits of tariff liberalisation, which had influenced local policy officials and stakeholders. Nigerian officials appeared more open to the opportunities and challenges posed by globalisation, and the need for some measure of tariff liberalisation in order to benefit from 'cheaper access to raw materials and also to expose domestic firms to some degree of foreign competition'.[20]

What channels then may have facilitated this process of research percolation? It is probable that the transfer of research ideas to local policy makers occurred via channels such as international trade meetings, as well as workshops and seminars convened locally by government departments, donor agencies, and international institutions. Nigeria's participation in international trade negotiations (e.g., at the WTO, ECOWAS, and within the EU-ACP) often reinforced the importance of trade and the need for further tariff liberalisation. In addition, various workshops and seminars on trade-related issues addressed the topic of tariff reform, particularly when discussing reports such as the WTO Trade Policy Review for Nigeria or the World Bank's Investment Climate Assessment, or in the preparation of national policy documents such as NEEDS.

Conclusions

This chapter has presented an overview of the CET adoption process in Nigeria, identifying the specific role played by research in the process. Considering the broad context of CET adoption reveals a limited utilisation of research in the reform process. This limited use of research occurred in instances where policy elites relied on research reports to provide some analytical support for the tariff reform programme. A gradual percolation of research ideas on tariff liberalisation and trade openness also influenced government bureaucrats and policy elites in Nigeria's economic reform team—as evidenced by a general appreciation of the importance of tariff reform. However, to a large extent, most government bureaucrats who were responsible for the technical tasks of amending and reclassifying tariffs were often unaware of existing research on Nigeria's adoption of the CET.

[20] Interview with Esther Oyero, chair of the Tariff Technical Committee, 26 April 2006.

The lack of adequate utilisation of research in this particular instance of policy change, in a sense, reflects the complexity and politicisation of the policy process in developing countries such as Nigeria. Trade policy is inherently a contentious issue, and this so not only in developing countries.[21] The process may be more politicised in developing countries owing to the nature of the domestic political economy as well as a history of neo-patrimonial clientelism in government departments that limits the use of evidence-based policies. As an example, it is important to note that despite having officially adopted the CET, Nigeria is conducting a review of its CET tariff schedule to examine the few cases where tariff revision may be needed. This revision process has been driven largely by influential stakeholders who presented cases for consideration either via the presidency or directly to government bureaucrats.[22] Research was considered to be of secondary concern in this process and, if needed, to be conducted *ex post*.

The foregoing assessment leads to two recommendations. First, in order to influence policy formulation, domestic researchers in Nigeria must aim at producing credible research and must also adopt effective communication strategies to disseminate their findings. In particular, it may be important for researchers to move beyond their existing academic spheres to engage in debates with other policy advocates such as from civil society or the OPS, and also to build stronger networks with government. Second, domestic government agencies, who should be the primary consumers of policy research, should improve their internal coordination and information sharing in order to increase the utilization of research in formulating evidence-based policies.

References

Achike, Ifeyinwa, Chukwuma Agu, and Moses Oduh. 2005. *Impact of Common External Tariff and Economic Partnership Agreements on Agriculture in Nigeria.* Enugu: African Institute for Applied Economics.

Adegbite, Oyeyemi. 2005. *Impact of Proposed New Tariff Regime on the Revenue of the Federal Government of Nigeria: Summary of Findings.* Report prepared for the Federal Ministry of Finance, Nigeria.

[21] Slow progress of the current WTO Doha round of trade talks, amidst resistance from agricultural lobbies in the EU and the U.S., demonstrates this.

[22] See, for example, Ministry of Commerce (2006).

Adjovi, Epiphane, Basile Awassi, Aboubakrine Beye, and Murray Smith. 2002. *Final Report: Study of the Implications of the Common External Tariff in ECOWAS*. Report prepared for the ECOWAS Secretariat and the European Commission.

Agu, Chukwuma, Okey G. Oji, and Charles C. Soludo. 2003. *Potential Impacts of Extension of UEMOA Tariffs to All ECOWAS Member States: A Case Study of Impacts on Revenue and Trade Balance in Nigeria*. Enugu: African Institute for Applied Economics.

Ajakaiye, Olu, and Adedoyin Soyibo. 1999. "Trade Liberalization in Nigeria, 1970–93: Episodes, Credibility, and Impact." In Ademola Oyejide, Benno Ndulu, and Jan Willem Gunning, eds., *Regional Integration and Trade Liberalization in Sub-Saharan Africa*, vol. 2. London: Macmillan, 147–177.

Akinlo, Enisan. 1995. "Improving the Performance of the Nigerian Manufacturing Subsector after Adjustment: Selected Issues and Proposals." *Nigerian Journal of Economic and Social Sciences* 38(2):91–110.

Aninat del Solar, Augusto. 1982. *A Study of Basic Aspects of a Common External Tariff for ECOWAS*. Geneva: United Nations Conference on Trade and Development.

Aremu, Issa. 2005. *End of (Textile) Industry? A Critical Study of the Collapse of Textile Industry in Nigeria and the Implications for Employment and Poverty Eradication*. Lagos: Friedrich Ebert Stiftung.

Bankole, Abiodun, Olawale Ogunkola, and Ademola Oyejide. 2005. "Import Prohibition as a Trade Policy Instrument: The Nigerian Experience." In Peter Gallagher, Patrick Low, and Andrew Stoler, eds., *Managing the Challenges of WTO Participation*. Geneva: World Trade Organization.

Bates, Robert H. 1998. "The Political Framework of Agricultural Policy Decisions." In Carl Eicher, and John Staats, eds., *International Agricultural Development*. Baltimore: Johns Hopkins University Press, 234–239.

Caplan, Nathan. 1979. "The Two-Communities Theory and Knowledge Utilization." *American Behavioral Scientist* 22(3):459–470.

Court, Julius, Ingie Hovland, and John Young, eds. 2005. *Bridging Research and Policy in Development: Evidence and the Change Process*. London: Overseas Development Institute.

Crewe, Emma, and John Young. 2002. *Bridging Research and Policy: Context, Evidence, and Links*. Working Paper 173. London: Overseas Development Institute. <www.odi.org.uk/Publications/working_papers/wp173.pdf> [Accessed: 14 November 2007].

Dollar, David, and Aart Kraay. 2001. "Trade, Growth, and Poverty." World Bank. <papers.ssrn.com/sol3/papers.cfm?abstract_id=632684> [Accessed: 13 November, 2007].

Dolowitz, David, and David Marsh. 1996. "Who Learns What from Whom: A Review of the Policy Transfer Literature." *Political Studies* 44(2):343–357.

Economic Intelligence Unit. 2006. *Nigeria: Country Forecast*. London: Economist.

Grindle, Merilee, and John W. Thomas. 1990. "After the Decision: Implementing Policy Reforms in Developing Countries." *World Development* 18(8):1163–1181.

——. 1991. *Public Choices and Policy Change: The Political Economy of Reform in Developing Countries*. Baltimore: Johns Hopkins University Press. [Accessed:

Herbst, Jeffrey. 1993. *The Politics of Reform in Ghana, 1982–1991*. Berkeley: University of Califorinia Press. [Accessed:

International Monetary Fund. 2005. *Nigeria: Request for a Two-Year Policy Support Instrument*. IMF Country Report No. 05/432. Washington DC: International Monetary Fund. <www.imf.org/external/pubs/ft/scr/2005/cr05432.pdf> [Accessed: 13 November 2007].

Lall, Sanjaya. 2000. *Selective Industrial and Trade Policies in Developing Countries: Theoretical and Empirical Issues*. Working Paper No. QEHWPS48. Oxford: Queen Elizabeth House, University of Oxford. <ideas.repec.org/p/qeh/qehwps/qehwps48.html> [Accessed: 13 November 2007].

Marchat, Jean Michel, and Taoufik Rajhi. 2004. *Estimates of the Impact of a Common External Tariff on the Nigerian Manufacturing Sector: Some Simulation Results Based on Firm-Level Data*. Working paper. Washington DC: World Bank.

Nigeria. Federal Ministry of Commerce. 2006. *Minutes of Tariff Technical Meeting.* BD.12237/S.403T, 17 October. Abuja: Federal Ministry of Commerce.
Nigeria. Federal Ministry of Finance. 2003. *Comprehensive Review of Nigeria's Customs and Excise Tariffs: Framework Paper and Summary of Reports.* Abuja: Federal Ministry of Finance.
Olympio, John. 2006. *Needs Assessment of the Trade Department of ECOWAS for EPA Negotiations.* Report prepared for the ECOWAS Secretariat.
Rodriguez, Francisco, and Dani Rodrik. 1999. *Trade Policy and Economic Growth: A Skeptic's Guide to Cross-National Evidence.* WBER Working Paper No. 7081. Cambridge MA: National Bureau of Economic Research.
Ruffer, Tim. 2004. *An Assessment of Nigeria's Import Prohibitions Policy.* Study prepared for the United Kingdom Department for International Development. Oxford: Oxford Policy Management.
Ruffer, Tim, Val Imber, and Jibrin Ibrahim. 2004. *The Political Economy of Trade Policy in Nigeria.* Prepared for the Department for International Development (Nigeria), mimeo.
Sachs, Jeffrey, and Andrew Warner. 1995. "Economic Reform and the Process of Global Integration." In George L. Perry, and William C. Brainard, eds., *Brookings Papers on Economic Activity 1995.* Washington DC: Brookings Institution Press, 1–118.
United States Agency for International Development. 2005. *ECOWAS Common External Tariff (ECOTrade) Recommendations Regarding Changes in Tariff Rates.*
van de Walle, Nicolas. 2001. *African Economies and the Politics of Permanent Crisis, 1979–1999.* Cambridge: Cambridge University Press. [Accessed:
World Bank. 2006. *Nigeria: Country Economic Memorandum.* Draft. Washington DC: World Bank.
World Trade Organization. 1998. *Trade Policy Review: Nigeria.* Geneva: World Trade Organization.
——. 2005. *Trade Policy Review: Nigeria.* Geneva: World Trade Organization.

PART THREE

UNDERSTANDING INTERESTS THROUGH RESEARCH

CHAPTER SIX

RESEARCH UPTAKE IN AN INFORMAL SETTING: THE CASE OF EGYPT

Ahmed Farouk Ghoneim[1]

Trade policy in Egypt has experienced several changes in the last five years both in terms of institutional aspects as well as in policy dimensions. At the institutional level, the position of the responsibility for foreign trade has changed, in some cases being assigned to an affiliate or part of a ministry, and in other cases standing as a ministry of its own.[2] Moreover, several laws and regulations have been enacted to deal with export promotion, organising the process of exporting and importing, and so on.

Regarding the policy dimension, Egypt has undertaken several liberalisation steps on all fronts: unilateral, regional, and multilateral. Certainly such changes were not just a matter of political decisions, as they had some sort of economic rationale behind them. This economic reasoning stemmed at least partially from the reservoir of research (domestic and international) whose policy implications have found their way to policy makers. The decade between 1990 and 2000 did not experience the same interest in trade issues as the five years between 2000 and 2005, whether on policy or at institutional levels. Certainly there are many aspects that have affected such change regarding trade policy and its governing institutional setup, among which are the implementation of Uruguay Round commitments, establishment of World Trade Organization (WTO), the proliferation of regional trade agreements (RTAs), which Egypt joined, and certainly the role of research and policy advocacy.

---

[1] Associate Professor of Economics, Faculty of Economics and Political Science, Cairo University. Email address: aghoneim@gmx.de. The author would like to thank Susan Joekes, Dianna Tussie, Dina Mandour, and an anonymous referee for providing comments on earlier versions of this text.

[2] For the purposes of this chapter, the government agency responsible for foreign trade is referred to as the 'ministry', led by a 'minister', regardless of whether it is a department in a larger ministry or a stand-alone ministry.

The focus of this chapter is on the role of research in formulating the Egyptian trade policy. It focuses on two episodes, namely the tariff formulation process and the partnership agreement between Egypt and the European Union. These two case studies represent the two policy changes mentioned by Diana Tussie in Chapter 1, where the first episode represents a form of instrumental policy change (in which there have been several incremental changes over the two periods mentioned above) and the second episode represents a form of conceptual policy change (in which a gradual change has occurred in the trade policy of Egypt). Although such a distinction is not so precise—the first episode sometimes includes elements of conceptual change and the second episode contains signals of instrumental change—the distinction is appropriate in order to be able to identify the different roles played by research in affecting the two types of policy changes; the entanglement of policy changes is indicated when necessary.

Moreover, in addition to the two distinct episodes, this chapter adopts a time dimension, differentiating between two periods, 1990 to 2000 and 2000 to 2005. The main reason for this distinction stems from the importance of trade matters due to the implementation of WTO obligations, which peaked in 2000. During the first period, there were several changes where the issue of foreign trade was managed by several ministries.

This chapter addresses several sets of questions.

- How is trade policy in Egypt designed and formulated: Who are the different stakeholders? Which has the upper hand, the executive or the legislative body? What is the role of different lobbies? What is the role of the different international donors? What is the weight of social and political aspects in designing such policy?
- What is the effect of research on the design and implementation of trade policy in Egypt: Through what kind of channels do research outcomes reach policy makers? What type of research depends on whether the research originated in the domestic context or internationally? Is the type of analysis used in the research empirical or descriptive?
- How does the interaction between researchers and policy makers, as well as other stakeholders take place: is it through advisors to ministers, or through stakeholder pressure backed up by research that serves their interests, or are there other means?

- Is research in the trade policy area driven by supply or demand: in other words, is it that the government or business community demands certain aspects to be studied or is that the research community comes up with policy-oriented research that serves their intellectual interests and then submits to the concerned parties (whether the government, legislative body, or the business community)?
- Does research have a role in changing trade policy? What are the reasons behind the changes, if any, that are revealed in a comparison of the two episodes and two periods under discussion in this chapter? For example, is the importance of the influence of research due to the institutional setup governing foreign trade, or is it the result of political economy effects? Moreover, what are the impacts of the technological advances brought by the wide use of internet in effects of the role of research in formulating trade policy?

Section One describes the two episodes of tariff formulation and the Egypt-EU partnership agreement and explains the methodology adopted and the limitations of the study. Section Two explains what is meant by research in the context of this study. Section Three focusses on the institutional setup that governs trade policy formulation in Egypt by identifying the main stakeholders and their role together with their effectiveness in affecting trade policy. Section Four traces trade policy developments in Egypt over the periods 1990 to 2000 and 2000 to 2005, while focussing on the two episodes. Sections five and six represent the main core of the study where they discuss the role of research in formulating trade policy in Egypt and the channels through which research affects trade policy. The different kinds of research are distinguished and the extent to which each type is credible for policy makers is explained. The chapter then assesses the role of research in formulating trade policy while controlling for other factors that might influence trade policy formulation, including information technology, and identifies different types of research. The chapter concludes by providing some policy prescriptions on how to enhance the role of research in trade policy formulation.

Section One: Definition of the Episodes, the Methodology Adopted, and Limitations

Definition of the Episodes

The two episodes examined in this chapter represent two major distinguished changes in Egypt's trade policy. The first episode deals with tariff formulation (reform and reduction), a relatively incremental process that experienced several changes starting in the 1990s when Egypt began to implement its structural reform program jointly with the World Bank and International Monetary Fund (IMF). The process of tariff reform and reduction has continued since then. This chapter confines its focus to the most favoured nation (MFN) tariff reductions and does not deal with reductions undertaken in the context of RTAs. The MFN tariff reductions might be a result of international commitments with the World Bank or the WTO, or might be due to unilateral actions undertaken by the government of Egypt. This is investigated here through a review of the available research on the topic as well as interviews with prominent trade economists who have written on tariff changes and whether those changes were responding to any type of research or to domestic or external pressures.

The second episode deals with a major policy change, namely Egypt's joining the EU in a partnership agreement. The event is important as negotiations between Egypt and the EU lasted five years, from 1995 to 2000, allowing ample time for interaction between research and policy. The Egypt-EU Partnership Agreement is considered the most important regional initiative that Egypt has undertaken in its history of regional integration. The EU is the major trading partner for Egypt and represents more than 40 percent of Egyptian exports and imports. Moreover, the relatively long period of negotiations allowed research to proliferate; and this case study is rich with examples of interaction between research and policy decisions and of possible evidence of the impact of research on trade policy. This episode is considered to be a conceptual change as it is akin to Egypt's decision to open up to the whole world, implying a dramatic change in trade policy, although this change has been implemented gradually.

The Methodology Applied

A distinction is made between the so-called incident-based measures and outcome-based measures. Following Robert Baldwin (1989), incident-based measures refer mainly to policies adopted and rules and regulations enacted (e.g., initiating a tariff reform), whereas outcome-based measures refer to the result of the policies adopted and rules and regulations enacted in terms of quantitative indicators (e.g., percentage of exports to gross domestic product [GDP], trade openness indicators, etc.). This chapter focusses on the role of research in influencing incident-based measures as it is impossible to assess the role of research in affecting outcome-based measures. However, Baldwin's narrow definition may be extended in order to investigate the impact of research on broadening the policy debate and enriching the discussions on trade policy. Although any spillover effects of the influence of research on policy might not be the main mechanism by which research affects policy, they may indirectly create a policy environment that is affected by research (see Chapter 2). In analysing the impact of research on trade policy formulation, this chapter draws on the framework developed by Maja de Vibe, Ingeborg Hovland, and John Young (2002), as well as a number of interviews and personal communications with senior government officials and prominent Egyptian researchers.

The research here adopts a descriptive institutional type of analysis that includes aspects of political economy. My own privileged first-hand experience with the process of trade policy formulation (having served as advisor to two ministers and consultant to donors, as well as being an academic by profession) allows me draw some lessons from anecdotal evidence and case studies of how research affects trade policy in Egypt. With regard to the two episodes, a comparative approach between the two periods (1990 to 2000 and 2000 to 2005), and sub-periods when relevant, is adopted with a focus on the main factors that have affected the role of research in formulating trade policy in Egypt. The research depends on the existing body of literature in this field, which is relatively scarce and is complemented by personal communications with government officials and research community.

Moreover, the study here analyses different types of research including that undertaken by domestic research institutions, international donors, and governmental entities when available.

Research Analyzed

This chapter adopts a broad definition for the term 'research' to include all academic research in addition to reports (as long as they are not confidential), policy viewpoints, etc. It includes research undertaken by research institutes, think tanks, in-house research by ministries, and aid donors' reports. Hence any document that contains information and knowledge, whether it takes any of the aforementioned shapes, is considered research (for a similar approach see Chapter 9).

Limitations

As mentioned, this chapter focusses on incident-based measures and how research is likely to influence them. It is impossible to measure the impact of research on outcome-based measures. Nevertheless, this chapter identifies the effects of research on existing outcome-based measures on the reformulation of incident-based measures. In other words, it considers the role of research in broadening policy debates and enriching policy discussions.

Another limitation is the inability to explain what prevents the full adoption of the research results in the formulation of policies. Research output reaches policy makers, and they take action based upon it; that action is in the form of either decisions or policies adopted. But it is always the case that the full prescription of research policy recommendations is not adopted by policy makers. Any attempt to explain this phenomenon of filtering or modifying of policy recommendations by policy makers must be based on subjective opinion, since it is almost impossible to trace its effect using objective criteria.

Section Two: What Is Meant by Research

Different types of research affect trade policy. There is the research produced by the ministry itself, and there is the research undertaken outside the ministry, whether by academics or multilateral and bilateral donors or other stakeholders. Below is an overview of the existing types of research available in Egypt. The quantity and quality have always been developing in a positive manner over time.

One type of research is undertaken by the ministry and can be classified into three categories. The first is what the ministry publishes in the form of monthly bulletins or other publications that produce statistical figures without in-depth analysis or any recommendations. This research monitors the developments in trade statistics and is mainly undertaken by the research department affiliated with the ministry. The research department is divided into three sectors, one dealing with marketing and commodity studies, one dealing with balance of payment studies, and one dealing with the information sector. The second category of research refers to publications undertaken by different ministry departments that publish their achievements, which again does not reflect in-depth research. The third category is research undertaken at the minister's request and can be asked for in response to a certain problem or action that requires the minister to answer quickly. This research can be undertaken by the head of an agency affiliated to the ministry or by the staff of the technical office of the minister, or it can be a joint effort between the agencies assigned and the technical office staff. In many cases, this research produces a short, policy-oriented analysis that is not very in-depth and summarises the main policy implications of previous studies. Time and financial constraints often play an impeding role in undertaking rigorous economic analysis that helps trade policy formulation in a strategic sense. Research undertaken by the ministry often takes the shape of an ad hoc, politically pledged study that must be finished in few days to answer a specific question asked for by the minister. However, it should be noted that the proliferation of the so-called technical offices has improved the quality of research. This is mainly the result of several reasons: the quality of the staff of the technical offices, who are non-government officials employed according to the preference of the minister or his or her advisors and who have an academic background and are highly paid; the resources provided to the staff of technical offices in terms of access to computers, internet, and other research facilities, often not available in the same quantity and quality as in other ministry departments; and the policy research mix of the staff, which again is not different from other ministry departments (Ghoneim 2006). The reliance of the ministers of trade on technical offices has increased in the latter time period (2000 to 2005) compared to the former period (1990 to 2000).

Another type of research is that undertaken by research institutes, bilateral and multilateral donors, and other stakeholders such as business associations. It is in most cases policy-oriented research that either reflects the interests of the researchers based on what they perceive to be important issues to be addressed or the interests of donors who have an interest in further investigating a specific topic. Some cases, the number of which has increased dramatically in recent years, are part of the aid projects of both the United States and the EU; the research is undertaken by donors that subcontract it to consultants, both international and domestic, on topics chosen according to the common interest of the ministry and the donors. Hence, as an example, the Americans might be interested in knowing more about problems at Egyptian ports and how to overcome them, which is a concern for the Egyptian government, too; hence a specific research project might be deigned to tackle this issue, financed by the United States Agency for International Development (USAID) and conducted by American and Egyptian consultants. Moreover, think tanks and research institutes may carry out a research project if they receive a demand from the government in general or from the minister specifically to tackle a specific problem. This has happened with the two well-reputed research institutes in Egypt on a number of occasions, namely the Egyptian Center for Economic Studies (ECES) and the Economic Research Forum for Arab Countries, Iran, and Turkey (now called Economic Research Forum, ERF).[3] Appendix 3–1 shows the number of working papers, including the number of trade policy-oriented papers, produced by those two think tanks since their establishment. As the two tables, show the proportion of trade policy-oriented papers has always been significant in the number of publications produced by the two institutes (in some years reaching 50 percent and 30 percent of the total produced), although there has been a decreasing trend in the number of trade policy-oriented paper in recent years, whether as percentage of total publications or in absolute terms.

[3] ECES, established in 1992, is a non-profit, non-governmental think tank. Its mission is to promote economic development in Egypt by conducting and disseminating applied policy research. The aim of this research is to develop viable policy options for Egypt in light of international experience. ECES activities are carried out in the spirit of public interest, and its board members are well-reputed figures from the business community (see <www.eces.org.eg>). Also in 1992, representatives of a number of multilateral organisations and foundations approached a group of regional economists and scholars for the purpose of creating an independent self-sustaining institution that would help improve the quality and increase the quantity of applied policy-oriented economic research on the Arab region, Turkey, and Iran. This initial outreach resulted in the Economic Research Forum for the Arab Countries, Iran, and Turkey (ERF) in June 1993, with assistance from the Arab Fund for Economic and Social Development, the European Commission, the Ford Foundation, the United Nations Development Programme (UNDP), and the World Bank, subsequently followed by the International Development Research Centre (IDRC). ERF is an independent, non-governmental, non-profit organisation that provides a platform for a wide range of views. Its mission is to initiate and fund policy-relevant economic research, to publish and disseminate the results of research activity to scholars, policy makers, and the business community, and to function as a resource base for researchers through its databank and documentation library. ERF does not conduct research itself but, rather, acts as a research network, clearinghouse, and facilitator (see <www.erf.org.eg>).

Section Three: Institutional Setup Governing Trade Policy Formulation in Egypt

During the 1990s and until 2001 trade policy formulation was the responsibility of the Ministerial Economic Committee, which is chaired by the prime minister and includes a number of ministers involved in trade issues such as the minister of planning (now the minister of economic development), the minister of the economy (now the minister of investment), the minister of industry (now merged with the minister of trade), the minister of agriculture, etc. Trade policy was implemented by the ministry in charge (until the late 1990s, the Ministry of Trade and Supply); however, consultations with all ministries that might be affected by a certain trade policy was always taken into consideration.

In 2002, a special law to promote exports (Law 155 for 2002 for export promotion) was enacted, which aimed mainly at consolidating the decisions related to foreign trade in the Ministry of Foreign Trade and Industry (established in 2001, before which foreign trade was handled by different ministries). Hence, the institutional setup shifted from the diversified role of the Ministerial Economic Committee and the lessened ministerial role in charge to a reduced role for the committee and more active role for the minister of foreign trade. Other features of the law include providing an institutional framework governing exports, establishing a fund for promoting exports, and streamlining different institutional jurisdictions governing exports under the umbrella of one ministry (Ministry of Foreign Trade 2003).

As stated by the WTO (1999), informal advice and consultations on trade policy have always been sought from academia and interest groups, including the General Federation of Chambers of Commerce and the Federation of Egyptian Industries, the Egyptian Businessmen's Associations, and other trade associations. There has never been an independent body that reviews the government's trade policy.

Moreover, there are the commodity councils (now called export councils), which are quasi-governmental forums whose members are exporters of a certain set of products and who meet regularly with the minister to discuss policy-related problems affecting their exports. In 2005, there were 17 commodity councils (e.g., textiles, leather products, chemicals, engineering industries). The members of these councils might come from the private or public sector and the minister issues a decree to appoint members. Each council has a secretariat based in the ministry. The role of some export councils has recently included not only tackling the problems that affect their sectors but also formulating strategies that enhance exports of their specific sector. In the process of formulating the export strategy of a certain sector, a huge amount of research is needed and hence politics, reality, and research are blended in a document that reflects the needs of this specific sector.

The Federation of Egyptian Industries is a quasi-governmental body that protects the interests of different industries. Fifteen industrial chambers are affiliated to the federation. Of all the non-governmental organisations (NGOs) in Egypt, it has the most influence on trade policy formulation. The head of the federation and a percentage of the board members of each chamber is appointed by the Minister of Trade and Industry, with the rest elected by the members of each chamber. The federation is always represented in official meetings that deal with trade and its arguments are often well respected and taken into consideration. The federation has a special committee on foreign trade policies, which includes among its members independent experts, business community representatives, and representatives of different chambers. The committee's role is to express the opinion of the federation on whatever trade policy is conducted or proposed by the government.

The process of trade policy formulation, by its nature, is relatively complex and thus almost all ministries have a say in whatever policy is undertaken, depending on whether such policy affects a particular ministry's interests. For example, the Ministry of Health is extensively consulted in setting health measures regarding different products, and the Ministry of Agriculture is heavily involved in the process of importing cotton. The Ministry of Foreign Affairs has always been represented whenever RTA negotiations with another country or negotiations within the context of the WTO are taking place. Indeed, there is always friction between the Ministry of Foreign Affairs and the Ministry of Trade over which should lead such negotiations, although the extent of cooperation or friction has varied depending on the ministers in charge.

Business associations, at least the big ones, have always been consulted whenever a change in trade policy is initiated by the government. However, there is minor evidence of the influential role they play in formulating the trade policy. On the contrary, business associations have always claimed that their opinions are not being considered (a situation that started to change in 2005). The Chamber of Commerce has never played a significant role in the formulation of Egypt's foreign trade policy, although it is deeply engaged in the formulation of domestic trade policy.

The institutional setup that governs trade policy in Egypt is complex; however, the major leader has always been the Ministry of Foreign Trade. The extent of consultations with other stakeholders has varied over time, as has its effectiveness. Despite the fact that there exist several institutional channels (committees, meetings, etc.) that ensure the representation of different stakeholders, it has been never clear how the actual process of formulating trade policy takes place. The role of big businesses and business leaders with strong political influence has always been evident in the formulation of trade policy, but the process was never transparent.

Finally, the role of the Parliament in formulating and monitoring Egypt's foreign trade policy has been insignificant where it has been confined merely to the ratification of whatever foreign trade agreement the government concludes. The renegotiation of a certain agreement is not allowed by the constitution, and blocking the ratification has never happened. Parliament's role in monitoring the implementation of trade policy has almost been non-existent.

A comparison of the two periods (1990 to 2000) and (2000 to 2005) reveals that trade policy formulation was more of a consultation process between different ministries before 2001, whereas since then the role of the minister of foreign trade has controlled the process. Moreover, the consultations with other stakeholders as NGOs and business associations have been relatively more involved in the second period, although the effectiveness of such consultations has always been questioned. The process of trade policy formulation has experienced a better institutional structure in the second period compared to the first; nevertheless, the effectiveness of such a structured institutional setup in the form of committees and meetings with different stakeholders is different for each type of trade policy adopted. For example, consultations in some cases were highly effective whereas in other cases a non-transparent mechanism has been adopted that undermined the institutional setup of the consultations.

It might be the case that the institutional setup played a role in how research affects policy. When the responsibility of trade decisions is shared among a number of ministers, the need for supportive research to back up a certain decision might be less urgent than would be the case when the responsibility falls on one minister. In this case, the minister in charge might need research to support his decisions. The benefit of research in political terms is likely to be less if the decision is shared by a number of ministers. Moreover, when the portfolio of the minister handling foreign trade diversifies to include other issues such as industry or domestic trade, there is reduced need and time spent asking for research than if the portfolio is restricted to foreign trade. Thus, the political weight of research declines as the portfolio expands. The combination of a culture more welcome to research in the second period with the regular interaction among policy makers and academics, together with the nature of the institutional setup governing trade policy, has created a more conducive environment for the interaction between research and policy, especially in the 2001–2005 period where the foreign trade ministry was established on its own.

With regard to the institutional setup of these two episodes, in the first one—related to tariff formulation—at the top there is a committee for tariffs that consists of a number of ministers and is chaired by the minister of finance. Below this committee is one of senior government officials from different ministries including the Ministry of Finance, the Ministry of Foreign Trade, and others. Any proposal (submitted by business) related to tariff change is submitted to the Ministry of Finance, specifically to the committee chaired by the Minister of Finance, which eventually passes it to the committee of officials. Moreover, any political decision to reform tariffs has to be passed to those two committees to initiate such reform. For the negotiations of the Egypt-EU Partnership Agreement, in 1995 headed a team of negotiators was formed by an ambassador from the Ministry of Foreign Affairs. The team held 491 hearings with different domestic stakeholders and 278 individuals who participated in the negotiations in different periods and meetings. The structure of the negotiating team was not rigid but was flexible depending on the needs of the negotiations, although the head of the negotiating team remained the same throughout the whole period of negotiations.

Section Four: Overview of Trade Policy Developments in Egypt between 1990 and 2005 with Special Focus on the Two Episodes

General Overview of Egypt's Foreign Trade Policy Status

Egypt has never been a major player in the world economy in terms of trade, with the exception of long staple cotton where it has a large market share. Its share of total world exports as well as imports remains around 0.1% (WTO 2007). Its services trade performance has always been better than its merchandise trade performance. For example, Egypt is listed among the world's 40 largest exporters of commercial services, but it has never appeared on the list of merchandise goods. The reason behind such a relatively advanced position for services compared to merchandise is the revenue from the Suez Canal, which is listed as transport exports and tourism. Hence Egypt enjoys a current account surplus and a chronic deficit in its merchandise balance of trade.

First Episode: Tariff Formulation

Egyptian trade policy experienced magnificent changes between 1990 and 2005 (Ghoneim and El-Mikawy 2003). The changes were all in the direction of liberalisation, with few exceptions where some backtracking on such liberal moves was evident. For example, the non-weighted average tariff rate declined from 42 percent in 1991 to 27 percent in 1999 (from 31 percent to 21 percent if tariff peaks on alcoholic beverages are excluded) and further to 20% in 2004 (WTO 2005). The first wave of tariff cuts between 1991 and 1999 was largely a result of the Economic Reform and Structural Adjustment Programme (ERSAP) that Egypt adopted jointly with the World Bank and the IMF starting in 1991 (WTO 1999; see also Table 3–1). The tariff cuts implemented in 2004 were a unilateral initiative of the government of Egypt. That the first episode under discussion represents an instrumental change is evident here where tariff reductions and reforms have been spread over a long time. A large array of non-tariff barriers was removed between 1991 and 1999 as part of the trade policy reform package adopted within the ERSAP. Moreover, as a result of the Uruguay Round, Egypt bound more than 98 percent of its tariffs, compared to an average of 73 percent for developing countries. With regard to the backtracking on trade liberalisation, in 1998 some 12 percent of the tariff lines had applied rates that exceeded their bound levels (WTO 1999).

A number of reforms have been undertaken, including the reduction of tariff bands from 27 to 6 bands in 2004 (Helmy 2005). Other institutional and policy reforms related to customs reform have been taking place, although at a slower pace of implementation, mainly for political and social reasons.

In general it can be argued that in the first period (1990 to 2000) most of the tariff changes were a result of international pressures coming from Egypt's commitments to the World Bank or the WTO. In the second period (2000 to 2005) the tariff changes came as a result of completing international commitments and national initiatives as part

Table 3–1: Developments in Tariff Rates in Egypt (1986–2005)

Year	Maximum tariff rate	Comments	Simple average tariff	Coefficient of variation of tariff rates	Share of lines with international tariff peaks	Share of lines with specific tariffs
1986	160%					
1991	100%					
1993	80%	Short list of exceptions				
1994	70%	Short list of exceptions				
1995	Not available	Not available	38.6	165	72.8	1.2
1996–1997	55%, then 50%	Short list of exceptions				
1998	40%	Short list of exceptions	26.8	127	52	9.5
2005	40%	Short list of exceptions	19.3	148	26	

Source: WTO (1999; 2005).

of larger economic reform package and especially of an expansionary fiscal policy to lift the Egyptian economy out of its recession. The role of research in this episode is investigated in the next two sections.

Second Episode: The Egypt-European Union Partnership Agreement

Egypt's trade relations with the EU date back to the 1970s, when the two countries signed the General Cooperation Agreement that guaranteed duty-free access of Egyptian industrial exports (with few exceptions) to the EU, without granting any kind of reciprocal treatment for EU exports to Egypt. The framework governing trade relations between Egypt and the EU started to change dramatically after the announcement of the Euro-Mediterranean Partnership (the Barcelona process) in 1995. A new regime began to govern the EU regional trade policies toward South Mediterranean countries, including Egypt. This new relationship was based on mutual duty-free access for industrial products and encompassed additional political, cultural, and social dimensions. Moreover, the Egypt-EU Partnership Agreement, which is the byproduct of the Barcelona process, includes a new scheme for abolishing tariffs on the Egyptian side over a relatively long time span of 12 years (with the exception of automobiles, whose liberalisation extends beyond 12 years). The agreement to enter into a partnership agreement, and especially into a free trade area with the EU, represents a drastic move for Egypt as the EU is its largest trading partner in both exports and imports (representing a conceptual change). Hence, since the announcement of the Barcelona declaration in 1995, Egypt has experienced a huge debate over the partnership agreement. The debate was not about whether to join the EU in a partnership agreement or not, but about the terms and conditions of tariff abolishment, agricultural quotas, etc.

The partnership agreement represents a distinguished episode (in the context of conceptual policy change) that is rich in interactions among the different stakeholders in the trade policy arena and is considered a specific case study, with a clear beginning and end. In the episode of the reduction and reform of tariffs (instrumental policy change), the case is rather loose, with much vagueness regarding the stakeholders behind it, the interactions among different stakeholders, and between the stakeholders and the policy makers. The next two sections investigate whether research has played a role in shaping trade policy.

Section Five: Role of Research in Formulating Trade Policy

As explained in Section Two, there are different types of research that affect trade policy. There is the research produced by the ministry itself and there is the research undertaken outside the ministry, whether by academics or by multilateral and bilateral donors or other stakeholders.

The effect of research on policy making in Egypt is not confined to ministers or their advisors reading studies and adopting some of the recommendations therein. There exist other mechanisms by which research influences trade policy formulation, whether through ministers attending conferences or by ministries hiring academics as advisors, a case that shows how research can be diffused throughout the process of trade policy formulation, although indirectly. The minister of foreign trade who served from 2001 to 2004 came from an academic background and had two advisors with academic backgrounds, and his successor has a deputy who also comes from academic background. This link is often overlooked when assessing how research affects trade policy formulation.

Did Research Influence Trade Policy Formulation?

Researching the first episode included interviewing a number of authors who have written on tariff reform at different times. These interviews showed that research did not affect directly trade policy (see Kheir El-Dinn and El-Dersh 1992; Refaat 1999, 2003). According to Hanaa Kheir El-Din and Amal Refaat, their research was undertaken to assess an existing situation, and when they provided critiques or policy evaluations, there was a time lag in implementing the resulting policy change and several issues they had referred to were ignored.[4] For example, the continuing existence of high tariffs on specific items (tariff peaks) and the persistence of high effective rates of protection in several sectors were never explained by policy makers and have been dealt with very slowly in different tariff reform programmes. However, the existence of tariff lines exceeding the bound WTO rates that appeared in WTO's trade policy reviews of Egypt (WTO 1999; 2005) have been dealt with partially by policy makers with no clear indication that such changes happened as a result of research published by WTO. In this episode, research deals with incident-based measures that provide some kind of criticism on the prevailing tariff structure and the loopholes of the system in place. The research usually suggests some sort of policy reforms to reduce tariff escalation or the effective rate of protection or tariff peaks, besides the reform of customs-related measures. In most cases, the issues of tariffs and customs reform, both in Egypt and other countries, are highly politically sensitive, and hence it is difficult to predict that research would likely influence such reforms in a direct, linear manner. The research in this a situation is more likely to provide policy makers, among other consumers of the research, with public awareness of the negative implications of the skewed system of tariffs in general.

Other studies undertaken by international organisations and bilateral donors, together with those written by domestic academics, might be used as evidence of the distorted and high tariff rates that used to be applied by the government. However, it is almost impossible to identify whether the published studies were used to exert pressure on policy makers. It can be safely argued that tariff reductions and reforms have adopted some of the suggestions and recommendations of such studies

[4] Interviews with Hanaa Kheir El-Din and Amal Refaat.

although in an incomplete form. The research produced by the ministry itself is by nature biased and hence not likely to influence policy making. As argued above, the ministry's research unit has been used to produce trends in exports, imports, etc., whereas the role of the technical staff has been geared to responding to the minister's requests and summarising what has been produced by other studies. Hence, it is unlikely that the in-house research has positively affected the policy-making process. The change of the institutional setup to allow more input from different stakeholders and especially the business community in the second period (2000 to 2005) could have played a role in transmitting research findings to policy makers. This is an important issue especially because the second period coincided with the rise of a new segment of the business community that is export oriented and has always been pressing the government for tariff reduction on its inputs. The research findings helped to enrich the dialogue between the business community and policy makers. Moreover, the issue of consumers' interests started to gain more importance in the second period, when high tariffs sometimes worked against such interests and thus policy makers used research findings to protect consumer interests whenever it was necessary to unblock the position of some lobbies.

To analyse the second episode, the head of the negotiating team that negotiated the partnership agreement was interviewed.[5] He revealed interesting insights on the role of research in formulating trade policy. He reported that research undertaken in relation to the partnership agreement was, in many cases, heavily politicised, signalling the loss of credibility. He pointed out that researchers even in some international organisations changed the models they apply or the data they use to reach certain results that can help policy makers by backing up their arguments. As a result he learned it was most important to differentiate between 'good' and 'bad' research. His ability to draw this distinction improved over time and benefited from consultation with different stakeholders. Furthermore, he declared that he learned a lot from the research and that his negotiating positions were affected by the research produced by both local think tanks and international organisations. The role of research in affecting trade policy in this episode profited

[5] Interview with Ambassador Gamal Bayoumi, the head of the Egypt-EU Partnership Agreement negotiating team. The international organisations and the research undertaken are not identified for confidentiality reasons.

from an environment conducive to the interaction between research and policy referred to earlier. In fact, policy makers needed research in order to start the public debate on this issue. In other words, it can be argued that research was driven by supply as well as by demand in this area, compared to the first episode in which research was mainly oriented toward supply. The only demand-driven aspect of the first episode was the investigation of the impact of tariff cuts on the government revenue.

Hence, the influence of research on trade policy formulation differs according to time and issue investigated. In the second period (2000 to 2005) and the second half of the first period (1995 to 2000), research seems to have been relatively more influential in affecting trade policy formulation than in the first half of the first period. This might be due to the creation of a more conducive environment for research, the proliferation of research by outside the ministry, better interaction among policy makers and researchers, and advancements in information technology that facilitated the dissemination of research. If the influence of research is distinguished by episodes, research can be seen to have had relatively more influence in the second episode (Egypt-EU Partnership Agreement) than in the first episode (tariff reductions). The reasons behind the different impacts of research on trade policy formulation are tackled in Section Six.

Section Six: Assessment of the Role of Research in the Formulation of Trade Policy

Assessing the role of research in formulating trade policy is a daunting task. Many variables affect the formulation of trade policy, research being just one of them; hence to be able to disentangle the effects of research in the formulation of trade policy from the effects of other variables is most difficult (see Chapter 8 for a similar argument). In addition, the technological advances (in terms of internet), changes in institutional setup, and administrative developments (in terms of the proliferation of technical offices) might affect the assessment in comparing the two periods and the two episodes under discussion here. This assessment begins with an analysis of the episodes based on empirical evidence when available, interviews with researchers, government officials, and members of the business community, and my own impression. It then moves from this micro-level analysis to a more general assessment of how research affects policy.

The Two Episodes

The two episodes showed that research has affected policy, although in different forms. The effect of research in the second episode (the Egypt-EU Partnership Agreement) was direct and clear, whereas its impact in the first episode (tariff formulation) was non-linear and suffered from time lags. The differences in the influence of research on trade policy formulation arise from a number of several factors, including the nature of problem investigated, the significance of the policy change, and the institutional setup. In the first episode, policy change was an ongoing process and political lobbies coordinated with policy makers in a relatively non-transparent manner. In the second episode, policy change was a once-for-all change, so there had to be enough time for debate, which thus allowed more time for research to influence policy, and the role of lobbies was evident in a relatively more transparent manner than in the first episode. The nature of the second episode (being limited in time and having a starting and ending point in terms of implementation), combined with the favourable developments on the institutional front, marked a clearer role played by research in affecting policy that fed back in the terms of negotiations adopted by the Egyptian team with the EU. Representing some form of conceptual policy change where policy, business, and research circles are hungry for research and information, research seemed to play an important role in affecting policy. The first episode, representing some form of instrumental policy change where the process has no clear time dimension, is subject to multiple political pressures, and has several social implications, showed that research is handicapped in capturing all such variables in one equation. Nevertheless, the published local research and international reports recommendations seem to have been adopted in a partial manner over the years when tariff reforms (as shown in Table 3–1) seem to have responded to the concerns flagged in different studies, although with a time lag. The effect of whether research is driven by supply or demand seems to affect the speed of adopting some of the research recommendations. The research in the second episode was driven by both demand and supply and hence its outcome was highly circulated and debated, whereas in the first episode it was merely supply driven and hence did not experience high circulation rates.

General Assessment of How Research Influences Trade Policy in the Egyptian Context

Using the framework developed by the Oversees Development Institute Julius Court and John Young (2004) concluded that in the Middle East–North Africa region there is a weak link between research and policy where policy makers often neglect the research findings, and there is a missing link between academics and policy makers. In fact, this finding contradicts with the severe need of research findings expressed by policy makers in the developing countries as stated by Lyn Squire (2002). However, the case of Egypt is slightly different: the link between policy makers and academics has been evident and was significantly strengthened in the second period, compared to the first period (for example, as explained above, by ministers attending academic conferences, acting as discussants for relevant papers, or even participating in workshops). However, the research findings often take time to be implemented by policy makers and in some cases are completely ignored, which is normal as research findings often do not take into consideration the sociopolitical context. Personal contacts between researchers and trade ministers in Egypt have proved to be effective (see Eremenko and Lisenkova 2004 for a similar argument in Ukraine). Most of the research undertaken has focussed on incident-based measures that need to be considered to improve the process of trade policy formulation. In most cases, despite focussing on incident-based measures, research has depended largely on empirical evidence or outcome-based measures, whether comparing trade data for Egypt over a time span or undertaking cross-country analysis.

With regard to research undertaken by the ministry, its impact throughout the two periods (1990 to 2000 and 2000 to 2005) has remained modest to a large extent. Despite access to internet, which increased the flow of information available to the researchers, they did not use it effectively. This is a result of several reasons, including a lack of incentives (since they are government officials who are paid regardless of how well they fulfil their job), a low level of English proficiency, neglect from the ministers, and the gradual substitution of government researchers by technical office staff. Hence the role of the research department did not change much in the two periods in terms of producing statistical data without in-depth analysis. However, the two episodes of tariff formulation and the Egypt-EU Partnership Agreement did not depend on this type of research. Moreover, in 2000 and 2002 the Ministry of Foreign Trade published four booklets on the partnership agreement in Arabic to disseminate information; these were free of charge and circulated in all academic and policy-oriented circles.

Research carried out by different ministry departments was also limited in terms of its effectiveness, as rather than undertake real research those departments simply published their achievements and their roles. With regard to research carried out at the request of the minister, one example relates to Egypt's export promotion strategy, which dates back to 1995, when the Ministry of Supply and Trade provided a 20-year strategy up until 2017 through its export promotion centre (established in 1979). Neither the rates of export growth or sectors targeted in this strategy had any scientific basis for the rates of growth of exports, which ranged between 10 percent annual growth rate for the first five years and reached 16 percent annual increase in the last five years) (see WTO 1999). In 2000, the minister instructed his staff at the technical office to disregard the old export promotion strategy and collaborate with the Foreign Trade Sector affiliated to the ministry to develop a new one. Again, neither the rates of growth nor the sectors targeted had any scientific basis. In 2004 when the newly appointed minister completely ignored both export promotion strategies and asked for yet another new one; the project was assigned to one of the bilateral donors and subcontracted to domestic and international consultants. Neither of the two episodes under discussion in this chapter depended on this type of research.

The amount of research undertaken by the ministry's technical staff in conjunction with affiliated organisations increased dramatically, and its role has been comparatively effective in relation to the other two types of in-house research. This is thanks to the proliferation of technical offices with capable staff proficient in English and with good exposure to the business community and academia. However, as mentioned earlier, the type of research is often constrained by lack of time and is undertaken according to the urgent needs of the minister. There is no research agenda developed at the beginning of each year or any kind of strategic research conducted systematically. Most of the research is done on the minister's demand, as needed, on short notice, and is a collection of existing studies on a particular topic. Such research might have affected the process of policy making; however, because the research is unpublished, its effectiveness cannot be confirmed. Moreover, in many cases this type of research was simply a summary of work conducted elsewhere and hence cannot be considered actual research.

The amount of research produced by international donors increased in both quantity and quality from the first period to the second. This was partly thanks to the comparatively increased importance of trade policy in the second period, as a result of the establishment of the WTO in 1995 and the need to implement its agreements, and partly the result of increased attention to Egypt entering into a partnership agreement with the EU in 2004 as well as to the negotiations with the U.S. to start a free trade area. However, one of the problems of such research is that it remains confidential, as required either by the sponsor or the ministry, so that it is difficult to determine how it affects trade policy formulation. This has negative impact on the dissemination of ideas and on the need to build consensus to support or refute such research outcomes. The interviews conducted for this study showed that this type of research was very evident during the second episode, whereas its impact on trade policy has not been clear. The effect of this type of research was more evident in the second episode than in the first.

The research capacity of other stakeholders, such as the Federation of Egyptian Industries and the business associations, did not improve much over the two time periods. However, in the second a number of businesspeople started to establish their own research units, and hired academics to research particular topics. This was evident in the case of at least two businessmen, who are members of Parliament and need data to support their suggestions in the business community and Parliament.

Finally, think tanks and research institutes have diversified the agendas of both their research and their partners. An effective union of research institutes, donors, business community, and policy makers formed during the second period. In many cases the policy implications in the research studies have been implemented by policy makers, including, for example, the upgrading of international standards, the harmonisation of tariff levels, the cutting of red tape, and other issues related to trade policy that were mentioned in several studies during the second half of the 1990s and were implemented between 2000 and 2005. Domestic think tanks and research institutes have been effective in affecting trade policy, as has been evident in the second episode.

In general, one of the main obstacles that adversely affects the impact of research on the formulation of trade policy is the fact that research often ignores political aspects, the power of lobby groups, public opinion, and the media (for a similar argument, although in a general context, see Ajakaiye 2005 and references therein). Another main obstacle that affects the good marriage between research and trade policy formulation is that research might provide a good analysis of the problem at hand, but often fails to provide a realistic, pragmatic solution to solve such a problem (for a similar argument but in a general context, see Edwards 2004). In many cases, researchers fail to get a sense of the reality, either because they are armchair economists or because they cannot have access to the political economy dimensions of the problem they are researching due to confidentiality or the reluctance of government officials to provide them with the necessary information. Moreover, there has always been this type of love-hate relationship between academics and government officials, which is rooted in the Egyptian culture: they often claim to respect each other but in reality academics claim that government officials are narrow minded and government officials claim that academics live in their own world, which has nothing to do with reality (for a similar argument applied to the Latin American context, see Aninat del Solar and Botto 2006). Furthermore, it is often the case, although this has relatively improved significantly, that research findings are not conducted in a manner digestible to policy makers or the public.

In trying to explain the impact of research on trade policy formulation, at least in shaping incident-based measures, this chapter uses the framework developed by de Vibe, Hovland, and Young (2002) because the Egyptian case fits their argument. De Vibe and her colleagues argue that the following assumptions are invalid: the link between research and policy is a linear one where research influences policy in a one-way process, there is a clear divide between researchers and policy makers, and knowledge is confined to a set of specific findings. The Egyptian case study fits the alternative framework, which they suggest argues that the link between research and policy is complex and dynamic. This framework recognises several stylised facts that appear in the Egyptian context, including the fact that the link between policy and research is shaped by multiple relations and a reservoir of knowledge (as is the case of hiring academics as advisors). It also recognises that 'although research may not have direct influence on specific policies, the production of research may still exert a powerful indirect influence through introducing new terms and shaping the policy discourse' (8): the research that was produced affected the incident-based measures, although not immediately. Certainly the alternative framework fits the second episode more than the first, where the whole Egyptian social, cultural, institutional, and political structure allowed for. According to de Vibe and her colleagues (8), Carol Weiss (1977) 'describes this as a process of "percolation", in which research findings and concepts circulate and are gradually filtered through various policy networks'. Such filtration might take place through the role of advisors with academic backgrounds, the impact of the media in policy advocacy, or the participation of ministers in academic conferences and workshops. The increasing influence of research on trade policy in the second period, compared to the first, was confirmed by a number of interviews with senior government officials and staff members of aid donors'.[6]

Conclusion and Policy Implications

In Egypt, research is not well appreciated in all the forms discussed here. For example, the World Development Report 2005 identified that only 0.2% of gross domestic product (GDP) in Egypt is devoted to research and development (World Bank 2005). However, trade policy has been one of the areas that has benefited significantly from research abundance if compared to other fields. The problem in Egypt might have been a lack of research in the early 1990s, when data were not available, and the international and domestic contexts were not hungry for research, a situation that has changed dramatically since 1995. For Egypt, the main problem in this regard lies in the absence of consistent, sustainable type of institutional setup that bridges research and policy. Many of the conventional problems related to the absence of a strong link between research and policy in developing countries have been explored by Julius Court and John Young (2003) and by Diana Stone, Simon Maxwell, and Michael Keating (2001), who have tackled issues related to the political culture, external influences, the role of lobby groups, and a lack of understanding other political context by researchers—all of which apply to Egypt to a large extent when dealing with role of research in trade policy formulation.

That said, the link between research and policy has improved significantly. However, the strength of the link varies according to the preferences of the individual minister in charge, and it remains evident that

[6] Six interviews were conducted with senior government officials, staff members of donor organisations, and former advisors to ministers of trade.

the selection of evidence provided by this research is based on political and social reasons (for example, in many studies the negative impact of engagement in a specific RTA has been identified, yet the minister proceeded with the negotiations for that agreement). The second episode of the Egypt-EU Partnership Agreement showed that research can be heavily politicised and thus should be dealt with prudently. The first episode of tariff formulation showed that the impact of research on policy might take several years to be considered, and it is not clear what type of channels are used to link research and policy. However, in the end, it seems from research findings and policies implemented that there are several similarities. The differences between the two episodes, whether in terms of being instrumental or conceptual change, time dimension, or change of institutional setup, explain that the role of research in affecting policy cannot be understood without accounting for such aspects. Besides the lack of a sustainable institutional setup that governs the relationship between research and trade policy formulation, lack of transparency explains the limited understanding of why some research findings are well taken as supporting evidence for policy actions while others are not. The distinction between the two episodes emphasised that the role of the demand and supply of research seem to play an influential role on the speed and circulation of the research in policy circles. Whenever the research is driven by demand, the findings—especially if in line with policy makers' intentions—seem to have a high circulation rate and expectedly more influence.

Moreover, the Egyptian experience identified that research affects trade policy in different manners through choosing ministers, deputy ministers, and advisors from the academic community, which has a positive spillover effect on the marriage between research and trade policy formulation, even if undertaken indirectly. Moreover, the tradition of ministers attending the opening sessions and acting as discussants in academic conferences and workshops has indirectly increased the impact of research on trade policy formulation.

To sum up, the influence of research on trade policy formulation has been evident and has gained strength over time, where a number of incident-based measures that have taken place since 2000 were based on research findings. The detection of the exact causality between such research findings and policy implications remains an impossible task (as seen in the first episode of tariff formulation); however, the experience of Egypt shows that research has had a stronger influence on trade policy, even though the channels might be indirect or there might be a time lag. The extent of the influence of research on trade policy formulation differs by time, institutional setup, and the episode investigated. What remains missing in linking research and trade policy formulation is the identification of a sustainable institutional setup that can ensure that such link is not created in an ad hoc manner and that there is a systematic way of undertaking research that is needed by policy makers while ensuring the credibility of research.

References

Ajakaiye, Olu. 2005. "Utilization of Economic Research Findings in Policy Making in Sub-Saharan Africa: Challenges and Opportunities." Paper prepared for 'African Economic Research Institutions and Policy Development: Opportunities and Challenges', Dakar, 28–29 January. <www.idrc.ca/uploads/user-S/11085715181Utilization_Economic_Research_Finding.pdf> [Accessed: January 2008].

Aninat del Solar, Augusto, and Mercedes Botto. 2006. *Trade Negotiations and Policy Design in Latin America: Is There Any Scope for Research Impact?* Bridging Brief Series. Moscow: Global Development Network. <www.eerc.ru/details/download.aspx?file_id=10016> [Accessed: January 2008].

Baldwin, Robert E. 1989. *Measuring Nontariff Trade Policies.* NBER Working Paper No. 2978. National Bureau of Economic Research. <ideas.repec.org/p/nbr/nberwo/2978.html> [Accessed: January 2008].

Court, Julius, and John Young. 2003. *Bridging Research and Policy in Development: Insights from 50 Case Studies.* Workign Paper 213. London: Overseas Development Institute. <www.odi.org.uk/publications/working_papers/wp213.pdf> [Accessed: January 2008].

——. 2004. 'Bridging Research and Policy.' *Forum: Newsletter of the Economic Research Forum* 11(1).

de Vibe, Maja, Ingeborg Hovland, and John Young. 2002. *Bridging Research and Policy: An Annotated Bibliography.* Working Paper 174. London: Overseas Development Institute. <www.odi.org.uk/publications/working_papers/wp174.pdf> [Accessed: January 2008].

Edwards, Meredith. 2004. *Social Science Research and Public Policy: Narrowing the Divide.* Policy Paper No. 2. Canberra: Academy of the Social Sciences in Australia. <www.assa.edu.au/Publications/OP/op22004a.pdf> [Accessed: January 2008].

Egypt. Ministry of Foreign Trade. 2003. *Export Promotion Strategy.* Second year. Cairo.

Eremenko, Igor, and Katerina Lisenkova. 2004. *Financial Sector Reforms in Ukraine: Role of Local Research and Foreign Advisors.* Bridging Brief Series. Moscow: Global Development Network. <www.eerc.ru/details/download.aspx?file_id=10009> [Accessed: January 2008].

Ghoneim, Ahmed Farouk. 2006. 'Law Making for Trade Liberalization and Investment Promotion in Egypt.' In Noha El-Mikawy, ed., *The Imperative of Good Governance: Economic Reform, Political Will, Incentives, and Capacities for Meaningful Participation.* Cairo: Economic Research Forum for the Arab Countries, Iran, and Turkey.

Ghoneim, Ahmed Farouk, and Noha El-Mikawy. 2003. 'Political Economy Aspects of Trade Reform in Egypt.' In Heba Nassar, and Ahmad Ghunaym, eds., *Institutional and Policy Challenges Facing the Egyptian Economy.* Cairo: Center for Economic and Financial Research and Studies.

Helmy, Omneia. 2005. *The Impact of Trade Liberalization on Government Revenues in Egypt.* ECES Working Paper No. 101. Available in Arabic. Cairo: Egyptian Center for

Economic Studies. <www.eces.org.eg/Publications/Index3.asp?l1=4&l2=1&l3=115> [Accessed: April 2007].
Kheir El-Dinn, Hanaa, and Ahmed El-Dersh. 1992. 'Foreign Trade Policy in Egypt: 1986–1991.' In Said El-Naggar, ed., *Foreign and Intra-Regional Trade Policies of Arab Countries*. Kuwait: Arab Monetary Fund.
Refaat, Amal. 1999. *New Trends in Egypt's Trade Policy and Future Challenges.* ECES Working Paper No. 36. Cairo: Egyptian Center for Economic Studies. <www.eces.org.eg/Publications/Index3.asp?l1=4&l2=1&l3=36> [Accessed: April 2007].
——. 2003. *Trade-Induced Protection for Egypt's Manufacturing Sector.* ECES Working Paper No. 85. Cairo: Egyptian Center for Economic Studies. <www.eces.org.eg/Publications/Index3.asp?l1=4&l2=1&l3=98> [Accessed: April 2007].
Squire, Lyn. 2002. "Bridging Research and Policy: An Overview." Paper prepared for ABCDE, Oslo, June. <wbln0018.worldbank.org/eurvp/web.nsf/Pages/Paper+by+Lyn+Squire/$File/SQUIRE.PDF> [Accessed: January 2008].
Stone, Diane, Simon Maxwell, and Michael Keating. 2001. "Bridging Research and Policy." Paper prepared for an international workshop funded by the United Kingdom Department for International Development, Warwick University, 16–17 July. <www.gdnet.org/pdf/Bridging.pdf> [Accessed: January 2008].
Weiss, Carol. 1977. 'Research for Policy's Sake: The Enlightenment Function of Social Research.' *Policy Analysis* 3(4):531–545.
World Bank. 2005. *World Development Report 2005: A Better Investment Climate for Everyone.* Washington DC: World Bank and Oxford University Press. <siteresources.worldbank.org/INTWDR2005/Resources/complete_report.pdf> [Accessed: January 2008].
World Trade Organization. 1999. *Trade Policy Review: Report by the Secretariat.* WT/TPR/S/55. Geneva: World Trade Organization. <docsonline.wto.org:80/DDFDocuments/t/WT/TPR/S55-2.DOC> [Accessed: January 2008].
——. 2005. *Trade Policy Review: Report by Egypt.* WT/TPR/G/150/Rev.1. Geneva: World Trade Organization. <docsonline.wto.org:80/DDFDocuments/t/WT/TPR/S150R1-0.doc> [Accessed: January 2008].
——. 2007. *Statistics Database.* Trade Profile for Egypt, October. <stat.wto.org> [Accessed: January 2008].

Appendix

Working Papers Produced by the Economic Research Forum (1994–2003)

Year	Total number of papers	Papers on trade	Trade papers on Egypt only	Trade papers on Egypt and other countries	Trade papers on other countries
1994	20	5	1	2	2
1995	30	6	1	2	3
1996	40	13	0	6	7
1997	20	6	0	3	3
1998	20	9	0	6	3
1999	40	10	4	3	3
2000	40	16	3	7	6
2001	40	8	1	1	6
2002	40	8	1	2	5
2003	40	4	1	2	1
Total	330	85	12	34	39

Source: Compiled by author.

Working Papers Produced by the Egyptian Center for Economic Studies (1996–2005)

Year	Total number of papers	Papers on trade	Trade papers on Egypt only	Trade papers on Egypt and other countries	Trade papers on other countries
1996	8	4	2	0	2
1997	13	7	6	1	0
1998	13	3	3	0	0
1999	5	2	2	0	0
2000	11	2	0	1	1
2001	16	5	1	1	3
2002	11	2	0	2	0
2003	15	6	2	2	2
2004	8	1	1	0	0
2005	10	3	1	1	1
Total	110	35	18	8	9

Source: Compiled by author.

CHAPTER SEVEN

RESEARCH UPTAKE IN AN INSTITUTIONALIZED SETTING: THE CASE OF TRADE FACILITATION IN INDIA

Abhijit Das

A key challenge for trade negotiators and trade policy makers in formulating a country's negotiating strategy in multilateral and bilateral trade negotiations lies in identifying and reconciling diverse range of interests of stakeholders. To illustrate, lowering the customs duty on raw materials is likely to be supported by industries downstream that would benefit from using cheaper raw materials. However, domestic producers of raw materials would oppose reducing the tariff on these products to avoid losing market share or experiencing price suppression or depression on account of cheaper imports. Thus, the same measure—lowering the customs tariff in this case—would affect different segments of stakeholders differently. This is likely to result in different groups of stakeholders seeking to influence trade policy in different directions, often conflicting with each other.

While the above example of a divergent impact of a reduction in customs tariff on stakeholders can be viewed as being simplistic, there is hardly any subject in international trade negotiations that does not involve a clash of interests in the domestic economy. Before a particular trade policy option can be decided, this issue requires a comprehensive examination so that the various interests involved are properly weighed and a balanced position can be worked out in the best interest of the country as a whole. There may also be a need to weight the short- and long-term interests of the domestic economy. Such a detailed examination of trade issues must be based on economic and social considerations, with a view to the various interests and linkages among different aspects of the economy as well as to overall macroeconomic factors. it calls for serious research and wide consultations with different government bodies, interest groups, and economic operators.

While the crucial role of research in influencing trade policy is universally recognised, few specific instances, particularly in developing countries, can be cited in which research led to changes in trade policy.

Existing literature on the role of research on trade policy changes in the developing world focuses on two aspects: why there exists a need for research by developing countries when a significant amount of such research is being done by the developed world, and whether there have been occasions when research by developing countries has influenced trade policies.

Regarding the first issue, a paper by Arvind Panagariya (1999) highlights the need for research by developing countries in the context of World Trade Organization (WTO) negotiations. The author argues that given the far-reaching implications of the decisions made under the auspices of the WTO, the need for continually conducting research and developing long-term strategies is extremely important. Developed country members of the WTO such as the United States and the European Union take such research very seriously and, by the time they are ready to place a subject on the WTO agenda, have conducted numerous studies on it. Furthermore, according to Panagariya, developed countries also promote research in multilateral organisations on the impact that negotiations would have on developing countries.

Panagariya (1999) points out that developing countries heavily depend on the World Bank for research on WTO-related issues that concern them.[1] He argues that this dependence might be risky because at crucial moments during the negotiations, these institutions promote the notion that the interests of developed and developing countries are in harmony. While this may be true to some extent in matters such as trade liberalisation, when it comes to issues such as the Agreement on Trade-Related Intellectual Property Rights (TRIPS) and the social and environmental clauses in the WTO, the interests of the two sets of countries are in direct conflict. He concludes that it is absolutely essential for developing countries to be able to critically examine the research disseminated by such institutions and also supplement it by research they have themselves conducted.

In a similar vein Mbekeani Kennedy, Taimoon Stewart, and Nguyen Thang (2003) argue that what developing countries lack is not skilled and tenacious negotiators but the capacity to analyse and understand their own interests in trade negotiations. According to them, poor

[1] For example, a US$5 million trust fund was created at the World Bank by the United Kingdom with the principal objective to do research on the implications of the round for developing countries and to help them prepare for the negotiations.

countries suffer a knowledge deficit. Unlike developed countries, they have not developed the aggregations of scholars, interest groups, non-governmental organisations (NGOs), and professional public servants that work to generate the hard facts and policy prescriptions informing policy making. Hence the authors point out that the best and urgent course for developing countries is to correct their knowledge deficit with timely, policy-relevant research. They cite three examples of where research might influence or might have influenced policy.

The first example is that of research by CARICOM, the Caribbean Community and Common Market, into the benefits of cartels in some situations in small economies. According to Mbekeani, Stewart, and Thang (2003), this research might be useful for CARICOM negotiators when they address competition questions at the WTO. They also cite the example of the research being carried out by members of the Southern Africa Development Community (SADC) on the links between trade development and poverty reduction. They point out that armed with the right research, the SADC governments can align their trade policies and negotiating positions with their own development programmes. The final example is of Vietnam, which is in the process of negotiating its accession to the WTO. According to the authors, research by the country has helped this process. On the basis of these three examples, Mbekeani, Stewart, and Thang conclude that if trade liberalisation is to serve the real interests of the poor people in developing countries, the hard facts of those interests will have to be understood more thoroughly and shared more widely, and this is possible only through proper research by the countries concerned.

Debapriya Bhattacharya (2005) also argues that in order to negotiate successfully in the current multilateral trading system it is essential for less developed countries to have, along with good negotiation skills, thoughtful planning and preparation based on good research and analysis. He cites the example of Bangladesh's ability to identify through research the necessity of preference on the movement of service suppliers under mode four of the General Agreement on Trade in Services (GATS). As a result Bangladesh emphasised this issue during the WTO ministerial in Cancun and succeeded in achieving its recognition in the final draft of the ministerial declaration.

On the aspect regarding whether research has actually had an impact on trade policy changes, a paper by Shantayanan Devarajan and Sherman Robinson (2002) discusses how research supported by computable general equilibrium (CGE) modelling affected the way the North American Free Trade Agreement (NAFTA) evolved. From the start of NAFTA negotiations CGE models were used both in the negotiating process and in the political debate over the approval of the final debate. Many single-country, multi-country models and industrial and sectoral studies were developed to analyse the potential effects of NAFTA. The authors highlight how the CGE models played a significant role in raising the concerns of Mexico regarding agricultural liberalisation and increased sensitivity on both the U.S. and Mexican sides, which led to the final NAFTA agreement providing 15 years for implementation of the provisions for agriculture.

An excellent example of how research can influence trade policy is that of the Latin American Trade Network (LATN). Research by the LATN on export promotion policies identified 'margins for manoeuvre' within the agreements signed as part of the Uruguay round of trade negotiations, which have subsequently helped the Latin American countries. An LATN research paper also helped Argentina to resolve the dispute regarding competitive imports from Brazil in the footwear sector.

Yet another paper on how research might have an influence on Argentina's trade policies is an analysis by Valeria Iglesias (2004). The study surveys policy makers in the two main ministries associated with the country's foreign trade decision making and also distinguished senior and semi-senior researchers in the field of foreign trade. The study found that the introduction of the Global Trade Analysis Project (GTAP) approach was an advancement. Iglesias maintained that the influence of research on policy was highest for those policies where the scope for major changes was limited, whereas major trade decisions were fundamentally political decisions taken at the highest level of the executive branch. The study basically found that in Argentina local research has not had much influence on the trade liberalisation process. It puts forth a few factors on how research might be able to influence policy, namely the relevance of the subject in the political agenda, the inclusion of policy proposals, and the use of appropriate methodological approaches as well as objectivity of research.

The Global Development Network (GDN) has been exploring the link between research and policy on the basis of an analysis of case studies. One of the case studies looked at South Africa's Trade and Industrial Policy Secretariat (TIPS), which was set up as a clearing-house for policy-relevant and academically credible research, with the Department of Trade and Industry (DTI) as its main client. It has been argued that although the impact of research by TIPS on policy making is still small, there have been two main areas in which that impact has been felt. The first is in the area of policy formulation. For example, DTI has been under pressure to obtain information on South Africa's trade with different partners as an input into negotiations on potential free trade agreements. It has been argued that TIPS has laboured to respond to this need, using its extensive database on trade. TIPS has also influenced policy deliberations by expanding the frontiers of debate, especially those regarding trade and industrial policy in South Africa. The success of TIPS in influencing policy could be attributed to the fact that it is directly accountable to one government department, as opposed to a broader policy-responsive approach. Another contributing factor is that although research may be commissioned from TIPS at the behest of policy makers, there is no guarantee that it will be effectively used.[2]

Linkages among research, policy, and implementation are very complex in a democracy such as India (Das 2006). Despite the complexities involved, there is substantial evidence to indicate that research undertaken by the India Programme of the United Nations Conference on Trade and Development (UNCTAD) through its 'Strategies and Preparedness for Trade and Globalisation in India' project has been successful in influencing trade policy and the policy-making process. This project is a joint initiative of UNCTAD, the United Kingdom's Department for International Development (DFID), and India's Ministry of Commerce and Industry, and is aimed at trade-related capacity building. It seeks to assist India's trade negotiators in improving their understanding of pro-poor aspects of trade negotiations and is helping to create deep and sustained human and institutional capacity within the stakeholders for analysing issues relating to trade and globalisation. Apart from undertaking trade-related research requested by the Indian government, the project also supports research by its partners on specific issues that have a strong pro-poor impact. In order to inform stakeholders of developments relating to trade negotiations, it organises regular stakeholder consultations, which have become an important mechanism for evaluating different negotiating options and building consensus among stakeholders. The wide dissemination of research and trade-related information in local Indian languages is another

[2] GDN, Policy and Research in South Africa.

important activity undertaken b the project. Overall, it has sought to create linkages among policy makers, stakeholders, and researchers so that pro-poor concerns inform trade policy making. The experience gained by the project is illustrated in the rest of this chapter through specific research initiatives, which provide important lessons on the role and relevance of research in trade policy changes.

The remaining part of this chapter is organised as follows: in the second section it looks at the role of research in significantly influencing India's negotiating position on trade facilitation at the WTO. The third section discusses how research undertaken by the project in the context of free trade negotiations not only was able to influence India's negotiating approach, but also helped introduce important changes in the process of trade policy formulation. In the fourth section the paper examines the research initiative relating to super regional cumulation and seeks to identify reasons why there was no uptake of this research in the policy process. In the last section, based on these three research episodes, the paper attempts to weave a coherent framework of certain dimensions and factors which might determine when research might be able to influence trade policy making. As a word of caution, the framework needs to be tested for further refinement.

Research on the Trade Facilitation Problems of Indian Exporters: Reasons for the Success of Research in Influencing Approaches to Negotiations

As part of the Doha work programme of the WTO, countries are actively engaged in negotiating rules for trade facilitation covering issues such as goods in transit, fees and formalities connected with import and export, and the transparency of trade regulations and appeal procedures. India's position on trade facilitation has shifted significantly from an inward-looking defensive approach to an outward-oriented approach directed toward addressing the problems faced by its exporters in important foreign markets. Research undertaken by the UNCTAD India Programme was crucial in bringing about this shift. This section thus starts by looking at India's approach to trade facilitation negotiations during the initial phase, until about December 2004. Thereafter, the research on the trade facilitation problems of Indian exporters supported by the project is described in brief. Subsequently, this section looks at how the research findings were disseminated among the stakeholders. Based on the feedback from the stakeholders, the recommendations of the research were translated into specific negotiating proposals. This section concludes by looking at this experience from the view of identifying the underlying factors when research can influence and change a country's overall approach to negotiations on an issue.

WTO Trade Facilitation Negotiations: India's Approach in the Initial Phase

At the WTO's Doha ministerial in 2001 and subsequently at the Cancun ministerial in 2003, India strongly opposed initiating negotiations on trade facilitation. India's minister for commerce and industry stated at Cancun that 'multilateral rules, binding in nature, in respect of trade facilitation...would entail high costs for developing countries' (Jaitley 2003). This statement provided the basic underpinning of India's opposition to trade facilitation negotiations, which was consistently articulated at various meetings of WTO's Council for Trade in Goods, the relevant body for discussions on trade facilitation issues until August 2004.

At the Council for Trade in Goods, although India recognised the benefits of trade facilitation, it nonetheless believed that trade facilitation measures were best left to WTO members for autonomous implementation, so as to be in tune with their own needs and priorities.[3] India felt that it was in the developing countries' interests to progress slowly in order to be able to balance cost and benefits of trade facilitation according to their ability and technological and institutional infrastructure. Furthermore, as a number of issues related to trade facilitation in nature but arose from existing agreements remained to be resolved, India was wary of getting into new areas. It maintained that developing countries in particular would require a flexible approach when harmonising their national systems with international guidelines, as opposed to conforming to a set of binding obligations. Progressive trade facilitation and integration would be a better option than one that led to a loss of policy autonomy and caused additional institutional burdens for developing countries. Implementation costs were also a very important factor for consideration.

In short, India's position on trade facilitation negotiations appeared to be characterised by an inward-oriented policy approach with concerns about the loss of policy space and implementation costs arising out of multilateral rules. Its approach also indicated a marked absence of

[3] This paragraph is based mostly on the minutes of the meeting of Council for Trade in Goods held on 12–13 June 2003 (WTO 2003).

viewing trade facilitation negotiations as a vehicle for addressing some of the problems faced by Indian exporters in foreign markets.

Trade Facilitation Problems for Indian Exporters

At the request of the Ministry of Commerce and Industry, the project supported research into identifying trade facilitation problems faced by Indian exporters in selected destination countries. Prior to the research, the Indian government did not have a clear idea of the specific needs and priorities of its exporters in the context of trade facilitation negotiations and no comprehensive information base existed, although certain anecdotal evidence was available.

The research on trade facilitation problems of Indian exporters was undertaken between January and June 2005. It included an extensive literature survey, a primary survey of 278 Indian exporters from a list of selected products and sectors in 13 cities, and a visit to two EU ports for a first-hand observation of trade procedures. Discussions were also held with 22 bodies dealing with export development, 47 trade intermediaries (logistics companies), and small and medium-sized enterprise clusters in different cities. Eleven case studies of actual problems faced by Indian exporters were analysed in detail, drawn from interviews with key players. In order to ensure that the study remained relevant for purposes of WTO negotiations, India's key negotiator on trade facilitation was closely involved with the research. The overall endeavour was intended to lead to a realistic reflection of problems faced by Indian exporters and not merely remain theoretical in orientation and analysis.

The research findings were finalised after obtaining the feedback from the government. Based on the issues identified in the study, it was suggested that negotiating proposals could be made on following issues:

- Uniform application of procedures by sub-national authorities and the use of common minimum standards;
- Adherence to similar procedures for disseminating trade alerts and taking remedial measures or rectifications;
- Introduction of normative tariffs or ceilings for charges levied by private operators providing services for import or export clearances;
- Creation of trade enquiry points at the sector level; and
- Establishment of procedures with internationally approved agencies for confirmatory tests in the case of detention.

The Dissemination and Validation of the Research Results

In order to validate the results of the study on trade facilitation, the main findings of research were disseminated as background material and discussed at great length in a national-level stakeholder consultation organised jointly by the project, the Ministry of Commerce and Industry, and customs authorities. The latter would have the ultimate responsibility of implementing the results of trade facilitation negotiations, which might require changes in domestic infrastructure and related procedures.

A wide cross-section of stakeholders was invited to participate in the consultation, which was held on 18 August 2005. These included representatives from industry, trade, freight forwarders, custom house associations, export promotion bodies, and academia as well as experts connected with this field. This ensured wide dissemination and validation of the findings of the research along with an endorsement of the need for negotiating proposals on certain identified issues. Furthermore, the consultation also sought to weigh the costs that might arise from WTO rules and the benefits likely to accrue to Indian exporters.

During the consultation, the generally held view was that the WTO negotiations on trade facilitation present an opportunity for India to consolidate its ongoing domestic reform programme by accepting certain commitments in areas in which it is already undertaking reforms. The negotiations also provide India an opportunity to align with international best practices. However, caution needs to be exercised to ensure that the commitments made by India are not too onerous to implement, as it has limited human and financial resources. Revenue and security concerns would need to be given foremost consideration by the government before commitments are undertaken. India would need to strike the right balance between a substantial reduction in transaction costs resulting from possible multilateral disciplines on trade facilitation and resource constraints in implementing the disciplines.

The consultation broadly endorsed the issues identified by the study for making suitable negotiating proposals for trade facilitation, thus confirming that the study had focussed on the appropriate problems faced by Indian exporters in foreign markets.

The Translation of the Research Results into Negotiating Proposals

The project's research team worked closely with the Ministry of Commerce and Industry to develop and finalise India's negotiating proposals on issues identified in the research. This ensured that the legal language of the proposals appropriately reflected some possible solutions to the problems faced by the exporters, as identified by the study.

Based on the findings of the study, India made certain negotiating proposals on trade facilitation. The proposals on Article X of the General Agreement on Tariffs and Trade (GATT) regarding rapid alerts, detention, test procedures, and appeal mechanisms are contained in India's statement submitted to the WTO(2006b) on 9 February 2006. The proposals on GATT Article VIII regarding uniform border procedures in members of a customs union are contained in another document submitted by India on 10 February 2006 (WTO 2006a). These proposals were discussed by the WTO's Negotiating Group on Trade Facilitation on 15–16 February 2006.

The Views of WTO Members on the Preparations of India's Proposals

While there is no independent evaluation of the extent to which research on trade facilitation supported by the project influenced India's overall negotiating approach, it is instructive to consider the views expressed by India and other member countries when the negotiating proposals were discussed at the WTO.

In their initial response, many WTO members appreciated India's proposals and the efforts made to identify the needs and priorities of exporters through survey-based research. Many also commended India for the process leading up to the preparation of the proposals through direct interaction and feedback from their exporters, which resulted in a realistic reflection of problems experienced. Some countries stated that the proposals were based as much on reality as on legality. Furthermore, the factual examples derived from the research and presented in the Indian proposals would assist all members to better understand when it would be possible to negotiate beyond the provisions already contained in the GATT. Some members found the proposals to be very comprehensive and concrete. Overall, the views expressed by different WTO members indicated that India had done a lot of homework in consulting its traders. These views pointed to the success of the research not only in directly influencing India's negotiating approach, but also in forming the basis of negotiating proposals.

Subsequent Changes in India's Approach to Trade Facilitation Negotiations

The proposals based on the project's research represent a significant shift in India's overall approach to trade facilitation negotiations. During the initial phase of discussions and negotiations on trade facilitation, India's approach appeared to be marked by concerns over financial, human, and infrastructural deficiencies for the implementation of commitments. However, the research provided technical information to the government for approaching the negotiations from the point of view of its traders' and exporters'—marking a significant shift from its earlier inward-looking approach. In the absence of research undertaken by the project, India's orientation in trade facilitation negotiations would likely have continued to focus on the human and infrastructural costs of implementing new obligations.

The shift in India's approach to addressing the problems of its traders did not go unnoticed by WTO members. In fact, one member specifically welcomed India's approach as reflected in the proposals and stated that 'it was good that India was increasingly approaching the negotiations from the point of view of its traders' and exporters' interests. That was the right spirit in which to approach that exercise'. It may not be an exaggeration to state that in the limited context of trade facilitation negotiations, the research undertaken by the project was crucial in influencing India's negotiating approach.

Reasons for the Success of Research in Influencing India's Approach

Given the significant impact of the research on India's approach to WTO's trade facilitation negotiations, it may be useful to examine the underlying reasons for project's success. At least 11 reasons could be attributed to this.

First, the research on the trade facilitation problems of India's exporters was undertaken specifically at the request of India's Department of Commerce, the agency most likely to use the results of the research in deciding policy changes. Had the research requested by some other agency, there would have been reduced certainty of the results being used by the government.

Second, the research was requested because no comprehensive information existed on the trade facilitation problems of Indian exporters. Thus, an information gap existed within the government for deciding its negotiating approach. This gap was crucial to research results being considered an important input for determining the approach to trade facilitation negotiations. If government already had adequate credible information on exporters' trade facilitation problems, its response to the research would have been less enthusiastic.

Third, the demand for research was in the context of WTO negotiations. During these negotiations, countries typically seek to secure results that balance their offensive and defensive interests. Prior to the research, India's approach to trade facilitation negotiations was overwhelmingly defensive in orientation, with a marked absence of offensive interest. The research provided the trade negotiators with specific information that could be utilised to pursue certain offensive interests and bring an overall balance to India's negotiating approach. Had India already identified certain other offensive interests in trade facilitation, there might have been reduced need for the research in changing India's overall approach to trade facilitation negotiations.

Fourth, the research included a wide variety of stakeholders in different locations throughout the country. Thus, the problems identified were not specific to certain product categories, industry segments, or geographical regions. They were fairly representative of the problems faced by the exporters and could be taken as articulation of the interests of broad-based stakeholders. This representative nature of the study facilitated the acceptance of its results, in addition to enhancing their credibility. If the problems had not been representative of the difficulties faced by exporters across different segments, the research could have been viewed to be driven by narrow lobbies, which would have made it difficult for the government to have confidence in the research findings.

Fifth, the methodology for the research used extensive surveys to identify the problems experienced by Indian exporters. As a result, the problems identified were based on the actual experience of exporters and other stakeholders. Thus these were practical problems borne out of real-life situations and not derived from mere theoretical considerations. As stakeholders were seriously interested in these problems being addressed through trade facilitation negotiations, they actively participated in the research and the subsequent consultation in which the research findings were discussed. If the problems had been identified outside this real-life context, there may not have been adequate interest and pressure from the stakeholders for addressing these issues through WTO negotiations.

Sixth, one of India's key negotiators in trade facilitation was closely involved in the study. This ensured that the problems identified were those that could be addressed in the context of WTO negotiations. If the research had not been adequately guided by an expert knowledgeable on WTO negotiations, it is possible that the problems identified would not have been suitable for being addressed through the negotiations. In such a situation even if the problems identified had been representative and realistic, the research would not have been meaningful the government in modifying its negotiating approach.

Seventh, during the consultation, the research results were discussed in considerable detail and endorsed by a very broad range of stakeholders. The possibility of the research results being contested by different segments of stakeholders was thus reduced and a firm foundation for subsequent policy formulation was provided. This nature of the consultation process would likely result in considerable pressure on the government to take follow-up action based on the recommendations of the research.

Eighth, in order to pursue the offensive agenda arising from the results of the study, government would be required to be adequately prepared to implement commitments that might arise out of eventual obligations under the WTO. Customs authorities, who would be responsible for implementing the eventual obligations, were therefore invited to participate in the consultation. Their presence provided a unique opportunity to expose all concerned to the potential benefits of trade facilitation negotiations, which are otherwise viewed mainly as imposing costs on the government. The strong endorsement of the research results encouraged the customs authorities to take a more balanced view of trade facilitation negotiations, instead of viewing them only from the perspective of defensive interests. A facilitative environment was thus created in which the negotiating proposals based on the research were not blocked by the customs authorities.

Ninth, the research was supported by UNCTAD India Programme, which was viewed as an impartial and honest broker. Furthermore, the organisation that undertook the actual research was selected through an open and transparent process. This process ensured that the research body's technical credibility was not questioned. Research by organisations not considered technically competent would have raised doubts about the credibility of the results, which could reduce the likelihood of their modifying the current policy or negotiating approach.

Tenth, the identification of trade facilitation problems and possible solutions may not have been enough to ensure that the research findings were picked by the government. The UNCTAD India Programme did not stop at disseminating those findings and organising the consultation. It actively assisted the Department of Commerce in drafting the negotiating proposals based on the project's recommendations. This helped in assuring that the negotiating proposals faithfully reflected the concerns of Indian exporters as identified in the study.

Eleventh, in the context of WTO and free trade negotiations, generally speaking there is considerable pressure on the government from law makers and civil society organisations for ensuring transparency in arriving at negotiating positions. The methodology of the project's survey and the subsequent broad-based stakeholder consultation provided the necessary open environment for modifying India's overall approach to trade facilitation negotiations.

Overall, the research on the problems of exporters succeeded in influencing India's approach to trade facilitation negotiations as this was not a one-off activity. The research was of high quality based on realistic reflections of the concerns of stakeholders and was embedded within the entire process of determining India's overall approach to trade facilitation negotiations.

Research to Support India in Free Trade Negotiations: The Role Played by Research-Based Knowledge Inputs in Policy-Making Process

In keeping with increasing world-wide trends toward free trade agreements, since 2002 India has started actively engaging with other countries in negotiating free trade agreements (FTAs). These negotiations call for a careful examination of the competitiveness of domestic production vis-à-vis imports from the free trade partner country so that the reduction or elimination of customs tariffs can be suitably calibrated and phased in. It would be reasonable to expect that a country would base its overall approach in free trade negotiations on detailed research. This section thus looks at how research undertaken by the project in the context of free trade negotiations with country X has introduced significant changes in the internal policy processes of the Department of Commerce.

This section begins with an examination of the relevance of research in trade policy making by first looking at certain problems experienced by India after entering into free trade agreements with Sri Lanka and Nepal. These experiences are important as there might not have been adequate research to back India's negotiating approach in finalising these agreements. Thereafter, the section describes the research undertaken by the project for assisting the Department of Commerce in identifying the list of sensitive products to be kept outside the scope of tariff elimination. Subsequently, it looks at the strategy for communication between researchers and stakeholders. This was crucial to the results of research being clearly understood, as the GTAP approach was being used for the first time in India in the context of trade negotiations. Finally, the role played by research in bringing about systemic improvements in the process of trade policy making is examined.

The Consequences of Basing Trade Policy on Inadequate Research

India's experience of a surge in imports from Sri Lanka and Nepal provides a useful context for examining the relevance of research in the policy-making process in India. Since the 1990s, India has allowed duty-free imports of primary products from Nepal. However, alcoholic beverages, perfumes, cosmetics, cigarettes, and tobacco were excluded from the zero-duty access regime. It is not entirely clear whether the products were chosen for exclusion after any detailed study. However, from 1999 onward Indian industry started complaining about adverse impact of the increased imports of certain products such as acrylic yarn, zinc oxide, copper products, and vanaspati (vegetable fat used as a butter substitute). In order to address the concerns of its domestic industry, in 2000–01 India had to expend considerable resources and diplomatic capital to renegotiate the agreement with Nepal.

Trade between India and Sri Lanka is regulated by India-Sri Lanka Free Trade Agreement (ISFTA), which was signed in December 1998 and went into effect in March 2000. Under this agreement, both countries are committed to the elimination of tariffs in a phased manner. India completed its commitment of reducing its duty to zero in March 2005, except for 429 items appearing on the so-called negative list of excluded items. The selection process for those 429 products is not clear. Certain segments of the Indian domestic industry have raised serious concerns on the adverse impacts of preferential imports from Sri Lanka, which appear in some cases to be well grounded and supported by facts.

As these two examples highlight, inadequate research on the likely impact of tariff concessions on trade, output, and employment can result in trade policy decisions that can be modified only at considerable diplomatic cost. Both these experiences underscore the need for detailed research before entering into FTA commitments. As a result, the Department of Commerce requested the project to undertake detailed research and suggested a list of products that could be kept outside the scope of tariff reduction or elimination in FTA negotiations with country X.

Research on the Possible List of Sensitive Products

At the request of the Department of Commerce, during 2004–05, the project conducted research to assist assisting the Indian government in identifying the segments of the industry that would be vulnerable as a result of the tariff preferences that might be granted to country X under an FTA. This was a major challenge as the government and the industry had limited experience in assessing the impact of FTAs on the basis of economic factors. While the government wished to extend a tariff preference to country X, there was also a need to provide adequate protection to those industry segments that might be adversely affected through reduced employment, reduced unit value realisation, etc., on account of imports from that country. Another issue how to balance the interests of large input manufacturers and those of down-stream users, who were predominantly poor and small-scale producers.

Using the GTAP approach, a widely accepted CGE modelling tool, the project estimated the possible effects of tariff cuts on exports, imports, production, and employment on a broad range of sectors. This was complemented by a detailed six-digit level price-sensitivity analysis for identifying the sensitive list.[4] The findings of the research were widely disseminated and refined after 22 consultative meetings held with 15 industry segments all over India. These consultations assured the quality of research outputs. As a result, the government was provided with technical inputs for preparing its list of sensitive products in FTA negotiations with country X.

While FTA negotiations with this particular country remain in progress and the negotiated list of sensitive products is not in public domain, it is understood that the Department of Commerce has picked

[4] The list of sensitive products was arrived at by comparing the import price from country X with a proxy for domestic price. Products imported at zero duty, raw materials, and products in which India has a revealed comparative advantage or has trade specialisation were removed from the sensitive list. Ample opportunity was provided to stakeholders to comment on the methodology for arriving at the sensitive list and well-argued reasons seeking inclusion or exclusion were given.

up the research undertaken by the project and is relying heavily on it for negotiating the sensitive products.

Communications between Researchers and Stakeholders

As the research on sensitive products undertaken by the project involved the use of sophisticated tools such as the GTAP approach, it was considered necessary to explain the methodology and findings to a broad range of stakeholders that would likely be affected by the FTA between India and country X. Close interaction with the stakeholders was particularly relevant because the GTAP approach was being used for the first time for determining India's trade policy and negotiating approach. Furthermore, as research based on econometric modelling is theoretical in orientation, extensive interactions with the stakeholders were required to validate the research results with their actual experience. Thus the dissemination of the results and the communication with the stakeholders became an integral part of the research project.

Through advertisements in newspapers, stakeholders were invited to participate in meetings organised by the project to discuss the research results based on econometric analysis. In order to ensure that the participation was broadly based, the meetings were held in different parts of India. The research methodology and the research results were conveyed in a format that was easy to comprehend but did not compromise accuracy. This was done prior to each stakeholder meeting.

During the stakeholder consultations, the research methodology and the underlying assumptions were explained in considerable detail. In order to ensure that the results did not diverge significantly from the experience of the stakeholders, participants were encouraged to provide their feedback in a prescribed format. Based on that feedback, certain aspects of the methodology were refined, leading to minor changes in the list of sensitive products. More importantly, the stakeholders were able to clearly see how their feedback was being incorporated into the research, thereby directly influencing its results. This process had the added advantage of blending theoretical research with the trade experience of the stakeholders, resulting in final research findings that closely reflected reality and ensured the high quality of research. Overall, the project was able to demonstrate successfully how the list of sensitive products can be prepared on the basis of economic considerations while balancing conflicting interests and reducing the possibility of influence by the lobbying power of big domestic players.

The Role Played by Research in the Process of Policy Making

Apart from providing the Department of Commerce with a list of sensitive products for India's free trade negotiations with country X, this research has helped to bring about significant institutional changes in the manner and extent of background preparation done by the department and other stakeholders prior to concluding free trade agreements with partner countries. Realising the important role that extensive research can play in assisting the government in deciding its approach in free trade negotiations, the Department of Commerce has now started commissioning detailed research on the likely impacts of entering into FTAs with different countries. In addition, the following important and concrete systemic improvements have emerged, within the government and outside, in the process of trade policy formulation in respect of free trade negotiations:

- The development of a mechanism for identifying the products that would require protection from adverse effects of an FTA between India and country X. This model can be used for undertaking research on the likely effects of other FTAs in which India might be engaged. In fact, the project has successfully applied this model in respect of certain other free trade negotiations.
- The development of a mechanism for resolving conflicts of interest between different stakeholders. To illustrate, downstream users of industrial raw materials would support lowering customs tariffs on these inputs. However, domestic producers of industrial raw materials would oppose such action. Because it allowed for factors such as employment, the fragmented nature of industries, the competitive conditions in different industry segments, the possible impact of tariff reductions on the livelihood of poor segments of the economy, etc., the model used by the project found wide acceptability among diverse segments of stakeholders. The absence of such a mechanism would have disadvantaged the small-scale producers, as this process may otherwise have been driven by lobbyists.
- The need to equip different segments and sectors of Indian industry with appropriate analytical tools for assessing the likely impact of an FTA between India and country X. This enabled the stakeholders to articulate their concerns based on economic considerations, which could be taken into consideration by the Department of Commerce in finalising the list of sensitive products. Different segments of

stakeholders have progressively increased their use of the analytical tools for determining their overall interests and concerns in respect of other FTA engagements of India. Not only has this enabled stakeholders to project and promote their interests more effectively, but it has also provided an assurance to the department that its negotiating position is grounded on a realistic assessment of interests by diverse and representative group of stakeholders.

- The ability to provide the government with technical inputs for explaining to certain industry segments why their request for protection in the context of free trade negotiations was not justified. This enhanced transparency in decision making by the government.

Research on Super Regional Cumulation: Research Not Picked Up by the Policy Makers

In one instance, there is no evidence that the project's research has informed the government's decision-making process. This example provides an opportunity to validate the factors that were identified as key to influencing and changing trade policy. This section therefore starts with a brief explanation of the research undertaken by the project on super regional cumulation in the context of Generalised System of Preferences (GSP) and provides a description of dissemination of results. Thereafter, the key factors for influencing trade policy are examined in the context of GSP research.

Research on Super Regional Cumulation

The beneficiaries of GSP schemes have often been affected by the lack of cumulation, which has resulted in the low utilization of such schemes. The EU's GSP scheme allows for regional cumulation as inputs that are imported into a beneficiary country from other members of that regional group, such as the South Asian Association for Regional Cooperation (SAARC) or the Association of Southeast Asian Nations (ASEAN), and used in the manufacture of products exported to the EU are treated as if they originated in the country of further manufacture. While revising its GSP scheme in 2005, the EU indicated that it would now consider SAARC and ASEAN as one single group for the purposes of cumulating origin in respect of inputs imported from the other region, provided a request from all SAARC and ASEAN countries was received.

In November 2004, the SAARC Committee on Economic Cooperation decided that the association's member states would convey their views on super regional cumulation by February 2005. In order to assist the government in taking an informed decision on this issue, in January and February 2005, the Department of Commerce requested the project to undertake research for assessing the possible impact on India of super regional cumulation of SAARC and ASEAN under the EU's GSP scheme. The project completed the research and submitted the report to the Department of Commerce in May 2005.

According to research undertaken by the project, India would stand to gain if super regional cumulation between ASEAN and SAARC were introduced by the EU. Gains were projected in terms of an increase in total exports to the EU, an increase in exports in sectors of significance to India, a limited adverse impact in terms of a marginal decline in exports to the EU in two sectors, an increase in exports of final goods to the EU, and an increase in total exports to ASEAN. Out of the total increase in India's exports to the EU, almost 25% was contributed by the textile and clothing sector. Furthermore, it was found that gains on account of super regional cumulation may mitigate the adverse impact on India if it is implemented gradually in certain significant sectors.

Although more than one year has elapsed since the research findings were submitted to the Department of Commerce, no feedback has been received. It also appears that little discussion on super regional cumulation has taken place within the SAARC Committee on Economic Cooperation.

Dissemination of Results of Super Regional Cumulation Research

All research undertaken at the request of the Department of Commerce can be disseminated only if the government decides to do so. In the specific case of super regional cumulation, the department has not yet made the results public. Thus the findings remain mostly theoretical, without validation by stakeholders. However, feedback on the findings from other research became available from stakeholders in the textiles and clothing sector. Certain influential stakeholders questioned whether price and customs duty are the most important factors in determining exports in that sector. Consequently, the EU's GSP scheme is practically irrelevant to India's exports in this sector. While no consensus exists on the role that prices and customs duty play in determining India's textile and clothing exports, the views articulated by these significant stakeholders point to a disconnect between the results of the project's theoretical research regarding the significant contribution of India's textiles and clothing sector to increased exports to the EU on account of super regional cumulation on the one hand and, on the other, the practical experience and assessment by certain stakeholders. To this extent, some of the theoretical research findings cannot be said to have been validated and endorsed by a broad range of stakeholders.

Possible Reasons for the Absence of Government Uptake

Several reasons could be ascribed to the absence of government uptake of research on super regional cumulation. Some appear to validate the circumstances suggested above regarding the conditions for research to influence and modify trade policy.

While a strong external stimulus in the form of WTO and free trade negotiations existed in the episodes in which results of research were used to bring about significant policy changes, there is no strong external push that would require the government to take a clear position on the issue of super regional cumulation. Although SAARC countries have decided to discuss super regional cumulation, this issue does not appear to be a matter of priority for them at this juncture. This may, in part, explain why the research on super regional cumulation has so far not been used by the Department of Commerce, although the research was undertaken at its request.

At the operational level, there has been a change of personnel within the Department of Commerce. As a result, the results of the research may not have been conveyed to the key officials within the government. Key decision makers may not have access to the research.

Implementing the results of research would ultimately require not only the SAARC countries but also the ASEAN countries to understand the effects of super regional cumulation and perceive benefits from it. On its own, India may not have the authority to convince other SAARC and ASEAN countries for making a joint request to the EU to implement super regional cumulation. Clearly, the political context in which the research was demanded from the government may not be conducive, or provide the trigger, for uptake of research results for policy formulation.

Although the research on super regional cumulation points to certain benefits for India, as the research has so far not been widely disseminated, some of the stakeholders who might benefit from it are not aware of gains to be made. As a result, there is no pressure on the government from the stakeholders to take action on this issue.

As the research has so far not been widely disseminated, its findings remain based primarily on theoretical considerations. With the exception of textiles and clothing sector, no attempt could be made to validate the findings. Thus it is not certain whether the findings accord closely with the practical experience of exporters and other stakeholders in different sectors. The government may not feel encouraged to take decisions on trade policy options based on such theoretical research.

Based on the limited validation of the research by some stakeholders in textiles and clothing sector, the results do not appear to be endorsed by all segments of this sector. Some of the stakeholders have even gone to the extent of questioning the relevance of GSP for India's exports. In the absence of a general endorsement by the stakeholders who are projected to benefit from super regional cumulation, there may be reduced incentive for the government to follow up on the research.

Synthesising the Experience of the Three Episodes: A Five-Dimensional Framework

In this concluding section, the chapter synthesises the separate strands of lessons learned in the three policy episodes discussed above into a coherent framework to suggest the circumstances when research can succeed in influencing the process of trade policy making and also the trade policy itself. This framework should not be taken as a conclusion, but should be viewed as ideas for further research and testing. Furthermore, the chapter has not looked at how political context issues might mediate between research and trade policy making.

Five different dimensions exist outside the political context, which might determine whether research can influence either the process of trade policy making or the policy itself. These are the problem dimension, the research institution dimension, the research dimension, the communication and outreach dimension, and the user dimension. Each determines the relationship between research and trade policy change. Certain factors within each of these dimensions that might facilitate research on influencing trade policy are discussed below.

The Problem Dimension

The problem dimension seeks to capture the different factors that influence initiating the research, locating the trigger and stimulus for that research, identifying the nature of problem being addressed, and the timing of the research request. Overall, the underlying factors in this dimension provide the context in which demand for research is made.

In the context of trade policy, although the demand for research may be made by the government department responsible for trade negotiations and trade policy formulation, the specific trigger for research may lie elsewhere. Various situations can be envisaged where different set of actors could trigger that demand. For example, an emergent situation for dealing with new issues in the context of international negotiations may create an overwhelming demand, as was the experience in the case of trade facilitation and FTA episodes. Another possibility is a demand by certain segments of stakeholders for research on certain trade-related issues. In still another example, the trigger for research may lie outside the context of trade negotiations, as was the case with the super regional cumulation research.

The effectiveness of a particular trigger in determining the role of research in trade policy formulation depends on two elements. First, what is the extent of the pressure exerted by the trigger on the government for initiating the research? Clearly, the need to take informed decisions through an open and transparent process in the context of bilateral or multilateral trade negotiations can be a powerful trigger for research and its subsequent uptake in policy formulation. Second, what are the possible costs to the government if the pressure created by the trigger is ignored or underplayed? Costs could arise in terms of lost opportunity for seeking concessions in the negotiations or taking positions that do not adequately protect large segments of stakeholders. Unlike the episodes related to FTA and trade facilitation, where uninformed decision making can lead to considerable costs, in the case of super regional cumulation there may be minimal costs if the trigger for research is ignored. In the latter case, pressure exerted by the political context was not adequate to ensure uptake of research results.

The nature of the problem to be addressed may also determine the link between the research and its influence on policy. For example, the need for balancing conflicting interests may motivate the government to request research and to respond to that research. Governments may find it easier to resist pressures from different lobby groups if their decisions can be explained on the basis of technically sound research, as was the case in the FTA episode. As shown in the trade facilitation research, uptake can take place if large segments of stakeholders are affected by the research problem.

Finally, the timing of the request can play a crucial role in determining whether the research influences trade policy. In the two episodes of FTA and trade facilitation, research was requested at a decisive moment in the negotiating process. On the other hand, in the case of the research on super regional cumulation, it would appear that deliberation among the SAARC countries had not yet reached a stage when Indian government would be required to have a formal position on the research problem. This appears to have been a crucial factor for there being no uptake of the research for determining the policy approach.

The Research Institution Dimension

The research institution dimension seeks to capture certain features of the organisation undertaking or supporting the research that could be crucial determinants of whether the research influences trade policy or the policy-making process. The underlying features are important in ensuring credibility of research.

The research organisation can be viewed as a connector between the government and other stakeholders. It must have a track record of adopting a professional approach to research. For the research to be effective in influencing trade policy, the organisation should be viewed by both the government and other stakeholders as being technically competent in the problem area. The manner in which researchers address the stakeholders' queries is important in establishing the technical credentials of the research organisation.

Another factor that helps determines the credibility of research is whether the research organisation is perceived as being trustworthy. A climate of trust among the research organisation, the government, and the other stakeholders may be created if the research organisation adopts an independent non-partisan approach that is not seen as favouring or representing any sector or lobby group. Research funding that does not depend on any particular interest group can be an important factor. The honest broker role of the research organisation becomes crucial when research output is used by the government to mediate between different interest groups and to balance conflicting interests, as was the case in FTA episode.

The Research Dimension

The research dimension is perhaps the most important in determining whether the research will influence trade policy. High-quality, objective, and relevant research produced in a timely manner is important in this context. This dimension subsumes those factors that affect the quality of research output and its timeliness.

Rigour in the research methodology can be a crucial factor in perception of the quality of research. The methodology must lead to a sound analysis of the problem, producing hard data that can form the basis for trade policy change, as was the case in the two successful episodes. While quantitative analysis may generate more persuasive inputs for policy makers, quality control of the methodology and research results provides the necessary assurance that policy formulation is grounded on firm foundation.

The nature of evidence used to support the findings is another crucial factor in determining the quality of research, as perceived by the stakeholders, and its acceptability. Evidence based predominantly on theoretical considerations, as was the case in super regional cumulation episode, reduces the possibility of research being accepted by the stakeholders. On the other hand, evidence that is realistic and based primarily on the actual experience of stakeholders, as was the case in the trade facilitation episode, can enhance the quality of research. Theoretical evidence, which is modified in light of practical experience of stakeholders, as was the case in FTA episode, may result in perception of high-quality research.

Not only should the evidence be realistic, but it must also be representative. Evidence drawn from a wide range of stakeholders in diverse geographical locations, across different segments and from different industry sectors, as was the case in trade facilitation episode, constitutes representative evidence, which in turn improves the possibility or research uptake by the government. Evidence that is endorsed by wide range of stakeholders, as was the case in FTA and trade facilitation episodes, has the power to convince the government to make relevant trade policy changes. Thus the absence of contesting claims from the same segment of stakeholders or sector becomes a crucial determinant of how research is perceived by the stakeholders. On the other hand, a lack of consensus on the evidence, as witnessed in the textiles and clothing sector in the super regional cumulation episode, can raise questions about the quality of research.

New ground-breaking research defining the problem and suggesting an appropriate course of action and concrete solutions, as was the case in trade facilitation episode, can contribute significantly to the overall quality of research. Research results that are relevant to trade negotiations, as was the case with the two successful episodes, increase the possibility of being taken up by the government. Often the distributional effects of bilateral or multilateral obligations may be ignored in the research in favour of providing a global and holistic picture of the economy. In the eyes of the government, this may reduce the appeal of the research as there may be political consequences of trade-adjustment costs. However, research that addresses distributional effects, as in the FTA episode, can be more acceptable to the government.

Academic and research organisations may be tempted to undertake research that meets very high standards but may come at the cost of breaching the deadlines set by the government. If the research has to achieve the objective of influencing trade policy, a balance would need to be struck between the quality of research on the one hand and the need to adhere to timelines on the other. In the case of the project, the research findings were made available in a timely manner to the government, which enabled subsequent uptake for modifying trade policy.

The Communication and Outreach Dimension

The communication and outreach dimension concerns itself with how the research is disseminated to the government and other stakeholders. Research that is more clearly communicated and more easily accessible to stakeholders has a higher possibility of uptake by government than research that may be clearly understood only by academicians.

This dimension also determines how stakeholders interact with the researchers for influencing the final research outcome. An intermediate impact can be felt in negotiating proposals based on the research findings. This dimension may also include how the negotiating proposal is prepared and conveyed to other countries.

For effective communication of results of research, researchers need to understand the policy makers' expectations of the research. One possible way of ensuring that research remains aligned with these expectations is to involve key government functionaries closely in the research, as was done in the two successful episodes.

Research, by its very nature, may not lend itself to be easily understood by the government and stakeholders. In order to communicate, researchers must first reach the relevant stakeholders, done in the project mainly through the mass media. Research methodology and its findings can be disseminated to the stakeholders in the form of easy-to-understand briefs, as was done in the case of trade facilitation episode. Another useful way of communicating the research findings can be through face-to-face open meetings between the researchers and those likely to be affected by its results, as was done in the two successful episodes. These meetings serve at least two purposes. They may be a relatively more efficient method of disseminating results of research and ensuring that the message is clearly understood. They may also serve the purpose of creating a feedback loop, whereby the views of stakeholders can be utilised to validate research findings and further refine the results, if required. Such a feedback loop also gives the stakeholders the perception of influencing the research, builds consensus, and may lead to ownership of results by stakeholder and enhancing its acceptability.

If the research is taken up by the government for the purposes of making negotiating proposals, it may be useful to involve the researchers in the subsequent process of drafting of proposals. This ensures that the results of research and the concerns of stakeholders are reflected in the negotiating proposals, as was done in the case of trade facilitation episode.

The User Dimension

Ultimately, whether the research is taken up depends on the users of the research, namely the government. The user dimension encompasses those factors that are specific to the government and determine the chances of uptake of research.

The continued interest of the government, not only at the stage of requesting the research but also in subsequent stages, can assist in keeping the research relevant and also facilitating a better understanding of the research by the government. This would also help in government assuming ownership of the results, particularly by those departments that may have to implement any new obligations arising from trade negotiations. As demonstrated in the trade facilitation episode, endorsement by customs authorities of the results of research improved the possibility of uptake for influencing trade policy.

The presence of change agents in the government with a willingness to use research results and having the authority to push results into policy action, as seen in the trade facilitation episode, can also be a determining factor in uptake for influencing policy.

Conclusion

According to E.J. Clay and B.B. Schaffer (1984), 'the whole life of policy is a chaos of purposes and accidents. It is not at all a matter of rational implementation of the so-called decisions through selected strategies.' Notwithstanding this view, this chapter attempts to bring some order into this chaos. Based on three policy episodes relating to research on trade facilitation, free trade negotiation, and super regional cumulation, the study has identified five dimensions: the problem dimension, the research institution dimension, the research dimension, the communication and outreach dimension, and the user dimension. These dimensions may determine whether the results of research will be used by the government to influence its trade policy and policy-making procedures. However, the five dimensions would need to be tested further for possible expansion of the list.

References

Bhattacharya, Debapriya. 2005. "Least Developed Countries in Trade Negotiations: Planning Process and Information Needs." *Asia-Pacific Trade and Investment Review* 1(1).

Clay, E.J. and B.B. Schaffer eds. 1984. *Room for Manoeuvre: An Explanation of Public Policy in Agriculture and Rural Development*. London: Heinemann Educational Books.

Das, Tarun. 2006. "The Impact of Research on Policymaking: The Case of Labor Market and External Sector Reforms in India." Bridging Brief Series, Moscow: Global Development Network. <gdn.eerc.ru/Details/PolicyBrief.aspx?id=508> [Accessed: 6 November 2007].

Devarajan, Shantayanan and Sherman Robinson. 2002. "The Influence of Computable General Equilibrium Models on Policy." TMD Discussion Paper No. 98, Washington DC: International Food Policy Research Institute. <www.ifpri.org/divs/tmd/dp/papers/tmdp98.pdf> [Accessed: 7 November 2007].

Iglesias, Valeria. 2004. "The Influence of Research in Foreign Trade Policymaking: The Argentine Case." Paper presented at regional workshop on "The Influence of Research in Foreign Trade Policies: The Case of Argentina, Brazil and Chile," FLACSO, Buenos Aires, 18 November.

Jaitley, Arun. 2003. "Statement by H.E. Mr. Arun Jaitley, Minister of Commerce and Industry and Law and Justice." WT/MIN(03)/ST/7, Cancun, 10 September 2003. Geneva: World Trade Organization.

Mbekeani, Kennedy, Taimoon Stewart and Nguyen Thang. 2003. "Viewpoint: WTO—The Knowledge Deficit in Trade Negotiations." International Development Research Centre. <www.idrc.ca/en/ev-44739-201-1-DO_TOPIC.html> [Accessed: 6 November, 2007].

Author. 1999. "WTO Negotiations: Invest in Research." *Economic Times*, 20 October, <www.bsos.umd.edu/econ/panagariya/apecon/ET/et-05-oct99.htm> [Accessed: 6 November 2007].

World Trade Organization. 2003. "Minutes of the Meeting of the Council for Trade in Goods, 12–13 June 2003." G/C/M/70, 19 August 2003. Geneva: World Trade Organization.

——. 2006a. "Communication from India: Proposal on GATT Article VIII." TN/TF/W/77, 10 February. Geneva: World Trade Organization.

——. 2006b. "Communication from India: Proposals on GATT Article X." TN/TF/W/78, 13 February. Geneva: World Trade Organization.

PART FOUR

THE WTO: THE USE OF RESEARCH FOR GLOBAL COALITION FORMATION IN TRADE NEGOTIATIONS

CHAPTER EIGHT

MULTIPLE ACCESS POINTS: KNOWLEDGE GENERATION FOR THE GROUP OF TWENTY

Amrita Narlikar and Diana Tussie[1]
(with the research assistance of Maria-Victoria Alvarez and Pablo Trucco)

The turbulent disagreements between the North and the South over the main trade rules discussed at the World Trade Organization (WTO) are far from settled. Behind the technicalities much is at stake. Despite the competitiveness of agribusiness in many quarters of the developing world, the European Union and the United States retain 50 percent of world trade in agriculture. 'This was only possible due to huge subsidies in the developed world', as one minister said at a ministerial meeting in 2006.[2] In this long drawn-out contest, developing countries have stepped up their efforts to establish trade rules that can take account of their export interests, which include opening up the agricultural markets of the North to their exports.

There are two particular developments that mark the participation of developing countries in the WTO in recent years. First, developing countries have learned to bargain much more effectively through coalitions. Evidence of this can be found in the ever-growing numbers of such coalitions and their longevity. For instance, the WTO's ministerial conference at Cancun in 2003 catalysed the emergence of at least four new coalitions—the G20, the G33, the Core Group on Singapore Issues, and the Cotton Group—in addition to the activism of others that predated the ministerial, including the African, Caribbean, and Pacific (ACP) Group, the Least Developed Countries (LDC) Group, the Africa Group, and the Like-Minded Group. Several of these remain

---

[1] Both authors thank the G20 negotiators, policy makers, and members of think tanks and research institutes who shared their experiences and views—often under the promise of anonymity—and provided access to key documents (both public and classified). This research could not have been conducted without their time and help.

[2] Kamal Nath, Indian minister of commerce, quoted in in Faizel (2007, 136).

active and continue to bargain collectively in the Doha round. Bargaining based on coalitions provides developing countries both weight and resources (including research) to balance the agenda promoted by developed countries. Second, the quality of the proposals advanced by these countries, in terms of their range and feasibility, has improved significantly, especially when compared against those put forward in the days of the General Agreement on Tariffs and Trade (GATT). These proposals are characterised by an unprecedented familiarity with technical detail, which suggests that they are backed by substantive research. Negotiators participating in such coalitions speak with considerable confidence of the research that underlies their bargaining initiatives; furthermore, at least some diplomats present the task of production and exchange of research as core functions of the coalition itself. Research—in the form of information collection regarding the issue at hand, analysis, and exchange—seems to be taken much more seriously than before.

Unlike many other coalitions of developing countries in the past, which would collapse under duress in the endgame (Glover and Tussie 1993; Narlikar and Odell 2006), the G20 has stood united, albeit with some runaway members tempted away by side payments in bilateral negotiations. The influence of the group is manifest in the fact that its two leading members—Brazil and India—have become members of the 'New Quad'. The group draws on several different sources for its strengths. It enjoys legitimacy as the coalition brings together 60 percent of the world's population. With a group of rising economies as its core—Brazil, China, India, Argentina, and South Africa—it occupies an important place in the international balance of power. Furthermore, it is a group that enjoys technical expertise, evidenced in the rich repertoire of proposals and statements that it has put forward.[3] Indeed, Celso Amorim (2004), Brazil's minister of external relations, attributes the successes of the G20 to 'the Group's ability to translate its members' interests in credible and coherent common negotiating proposals'. References to its collective ability to contribute meaningfully to the dialogue through detailed and well-analysed proposals are also found in G20 statements, such as:

---

[3] For further information on such proposals and statements, see the G20 website at <www.g-20.mre.gov.br>.

> The G-20 is proud to have played an important role. The Group constructively contributed to the process, not only with technically sound, Mandate-oriented proposals, but also with a transparent and inclusive negotiating attitude… (G20 2005d, G20 General Statement, October 2004 Special Session, 71)

Especially in the light of these claims, the G20 provides a useful laboratory for investigating some basic questions about how research functions in trade coalitions. This chapter examines the basis of these 'technically sound, mandate-oriented proposals' that have allowed a group of developing countries to participate effectively in the trade rule-making process at the WTO, itself an episode of major policy change. This episode can be considered a conceptual change that allowed the G20 to become a key player and legitimise the tabling of three proposals for negotiation: a proposal for a tiered formula on market access, a proposal regarding a special safeguard mechanism (SSM), and a proposal for product-specific caps.

In the context of the impact of research on the negotiating positions of coalitions, this chapter thus pursues two lines of inquiry. First, it traces the evidence—in the form of a paper trail (when available) and through interviews—of the extent to which the G20's proposals have been backed by solid research. Second, it examines the specific purpose served by research initiatives (and how they relate to political constraints) by exploring the analyses conducted by G20 countries in preparing for the negotiation process. A close investigation generates some counterintuitive results. The significance and constraints affecting research in terms of the impact on the bargaining process will be specified throughout.

The chapter proceeds in four sections. The first section presents the logic of the argument. The second provides an account of the ways in which the position of the G20 has evolved since inception. The third section examines three cases wherein research seems to have made a difference in the G20 agenda in light of the two sets of hypotheses presented in the first section. The fourth and concluding section recaps the hypotheses, indicating the cases where they are corroborated or rejected, and also discusses the limitations of research as far as certain types of coalitions are concerned.

The Argument

The question driving this chapter is the following: what impact has research initiatives had on trade negotiations? The focus here is specifically on the case of the G20 in agriculture. This is partly because the G20 provides an 'easy' case. Negotiators working within the coalition frequently refer to the importance they attach to conducting and drawing on research to formulate and back their proposals. Furthermore, given how complicated just the negotiation of modalities has already proven, not least because of the technical nature of the subject but also the very high stakes involved, agriculture is the one area where countries could be reasonably expected to invest in gaining technical expertise. Indeed, one would expect that most countries—developed or developing, and alone or in coalitions—would need to rely on research inputs from outside sources (think tanks, research institutes, universities, lobby groups, and non-governmental organisations [NGOs]) to be assisted in the negotiation process. In other words, there is a likelihood that a more pluralistic process of policy making is at work, involving different domestic and transnational actors, whereby governments gather information and develop their negotiating positions in the WTO.

Research can matter, not simply in providing the substantive content of a country's demands in a trade negotiation, but also because it can serve as an important legitimising device.[4] A negotiator demanding a very high level of concessions from the opponent, or refusing to make any concessions to the opponent, is likely to be taken more seriously if there are detailed studies to back up the demands. There are thus two distinctive, and sometimes mutually exclusive, purposes for research: the first is to give a genuine shape to a country's negotiating agenda, whereas the second is to legitimise the agenda that has evolved as a result of several other, often political, forces. The distinction between these two purposes of research assumes special importance in the context of the deadlocked Doha negotiations. The key to the deadlock has been the standoff between the European Union and the United States on one hand and the G20 on the other. Whether the coalition's demands actually represent its bottom line or are meant as posturing and brinkmanship can be determined according to which primary function its research initiatives serve.

---

[4] Also see Chapter 5, which further tests this argument.

The level of research examined here represents a level below the standard where epistemic consensus is usually reached. In the case of trade negotiations today, for instance, most academics and practitioners would agree upon the benefits of multilateral trade liberalisation (in contrast to theories of import-substituting industrialisation that were prevalent in the 1960s). But an epistemic consensus at this level still leaves considerable room for the variety of bargains that could be struck within the considerably more pro-liberal framework, and which would have some very different distributive consequences. Research—conducted by governments, directed and outsourced to research institutions or NGOs, or advanced from the ground-level upward by interest groups and other organisations—provides shape and substance to bargaining. Furthermore, research at this level can be considerably more politicised than a consensus driven by an epistemic community; research at the level of implementing the epistemic consensus is often driven by government for strategic (and far from neutral) purposes.

Two sets of hypotheses are advanced here on how research can be influential in coalition politics.[5] The first deals with the external relations of the coalition, whereas the second focuses on intra-coalition politics.

1. *External Purpose*: Coalitions generate and make use of research to influence negotiating positions of outside parties. There are four working mechanisms whereby coalitions can use research to facilitate their negotiations with outside parties; these are assessed against the case of the G20:

   a) *Production of research*: An influential coalition must have the capacity to generate new, policy-relevant knowledge through commissioning studies and creating working groups to draft standards, codes, model laws, and innovative approaches to complex policy problems.
   b) *Research for agenda setting*: Agenda setting refers to the coalition's capacity to bring previously neglected policy issues to the attention of the organisation, to ensure that these issues will receive serious consideration and to generate significant public exposure.

[5] These hypotheses, developed by the authors of this chapter, are also tested in the chapter by Paul Mably in this volume.

c) *Research to support both integrative and distributive strategies*: Most negotiation analyses have focussed on the uses of research as part of an integrative negotiation strategy, whereby negotiation parties attempt to expand the zone of agreement by uncovering new gains that benefit all parties. However, research can also be used to support distributive strategies. For instance, coalitions can invest in research that attempts to expose the weak alternative to a negotiated agreement of the outside party, or redefine the issue space so as to rule out their least preferred options from the menu of choice available.

d) *Research for legitimisation*: Influential coalitions must also have resources for exchanging and disseminating knowledge within and outside the network through meetings, conferences, publications, workshops, and websites. This is especially important if the coalition hopes to build links with transnational NGOs.

2. *Internal Purpose*: Research can be used—explicitly or covertly—to facilitate consensus building within a coalition and thereby cement its membership. Three working mechanisms offer coalitions a way to generate and apply research to influence internal coalition politics:

a) *Research as a club good to attract members*: At least some of the research that coalitions conduct can be regarded as a club good; if countries do not invest in becoming members, they can be denied the benefit of shared research and representation in WTO meetings. This creates an incentive for countries to become members of the coalition and continue their allegiance to it.

b) *Research to prevent defection*: Larger countries of a coalition can expand the agenda of the coalition to incorporate the concerns of smaller countries. The technical character of WTO negotiations renders any such research assistance by the leading members of the coalitions invaluable for smaller members.

c) *Research to win domestic support*: Research initiatives can be used to win the support of domestic interests that lobby for the negotiating position that a government takes in the WTO. In other words, research serves as a legitimising instrument, albeit this time the target audience is domestic (as opposed to 1[d] where the target audience is international).

From Cancun to Hong Kong: The G20 in Agriculture Negotiations

The G20 arose in the run-up to the Cancun ministerial conference on 11 to 14 September 2003, in response to a joint draft proposal issued by the EU and the U.S. Until that point, export interests in developing countries had remained in the back seat, relying on the push of the U.S. and the Cairns Group to represent their concerns. Nonetheless, countries with a more defensive interest in agriculture had hoped to ride for free on the EU's negotiating position. The joint draft between the two major negotiators, however, made both agricultural importing and exporting countries from the developing world realise that they would have to stand up for themselves to prevent a repetition of the Blair House accord.[6] This accord had reconciled the positions of the EU and U.S. at the end of the Uruguay round, ignoring interests elsewhere. However, in the run-up to Cancun, the South had achieved a commitment from the North expressed in the Doha mandate in November 2001. Paragraph 13 of the declaration stated:

> We commit ourselves to comprehensive negotiations aimed at: substantial improvements in market access, reductions of, with a view to phasing out, all forms of export subsidies; and substantial reductions in trade-distorting domestic support. We agree that special and differential treatment for developing countries shall be an integral part of all elements of the negotiations (...), so as to be operationally effective and to enable developing countries to effectively take account of their development needs, including food security and rural development. We (...) confirm that non-trade concerns will be taken into account in the negotiations as provided for in the Agreement on Agriculture (WTO 2001).

Nevertheless, the U.S. and the EU carried on as usual and developing countries began to get concerned about a sidelining of the development agenda (Delgado and Campolina de O. Soares 2005). After a succession of failures to agree on the modalities for the agricultural negotiations they launched a proposal that merely solved their mutual interests. In the words of the Brazilian foreign minister Celso Amorim, 'the deal between Brussels and Washington constitutes a step backwards, which,

[6] The Blair House accord was negotiated between the EU and the U.S. in 1992. For developing countries, the agreement came to symbolise the collusion between the two agricultural superpowers to reduce the level of ambition on agriculture in the Uruguay round, against the interest of many developing countries, particularly the members of the Cairns Group (see Glover and Tussie 1993; Narlikar and Tussie 2004).

if accepted by the rest of the countries, would result in an incredible sacrifice of the Round' (Amorim 2003/04, 29, quoted in; Delgado and Campolina de O. Soares 2005).

The apprehension triggered the formation of coalitions as well as an explosion of research by developing countries both individually and collectively. Developing countries grouped together to try to define reasonable goals, realistic benchmark periods, and appropriate policy instruments. Up to that point only the developed country negotiators tended to be prepared with clear roadmaps and technically driven policy options. Developing countries generally found it difficult to respond collectively to these negotiating techniques because of the lack of consensus among them beyond broad principled beliefs and long-term desiderata. This lack of clarity on feasible medium-term goals and policy targets had resulted in vulnerability toward divide and rule tactics.

The rise and formation of the G20 occurred in a particular global context. Offensive agricultural interests were on the rise. Several developing countries, especially in Latin America, had benefited from a major structural change that allowed a hike in productivity and the expansion of their competitive agricultural products in global markets. For their part, Asian countries face water-scarcity problems and institutional constraints to give way to a process of concentration of land ownership that might increase their agricultural productivity—hence a new 'green revolution' is unlikely in the short run. Economic growth, urbanisation, and high birth rates, as well as the strengthening of real exchange rates, have increased the propensity to import, boosting the demand for foodstuffs. In this context, India and Brazil as leading regional powers were ready to join forces and pull their weight in WTO negotiations.

In this context, to ensure that their agenda for agricultural reform was not marginalised, India and Brazil drafted a joint proposal, and were also able to get the support of China and Argentina. Nelson Giordano Delgado and Adriano Campolino de O. Soares (2005) state that the construction of the coalition was made possible after Brazil and India were informed by a study that allowed the bringing together of their initially antagonic positions. The study carried out by Brazil showing 'that market access concessions for developing countries would not lead to increased costs for Brazil, so that... [Brazil's] export interest would not be affected,... supporting the position that special attention be given to the pillar of subsidies' (14). This understanding allowed a progressive coming together of defensive concerns with offensive interests, which was to become the cornerstone of coalition building. Once the ground between Brazil and India was prepared, the Brazilian negotiators immediately invited Argentina into the process. The involvement of Argentina was considered so crucial that the negotiations with India for the development of the alternative framework began with a proposal developed by Argentina. Once it was worked out, India brought China into the group. With such a critical mass the Brazilian negotiators swayed a string of fresh Latin American participants to join the group (15).

In consultation with other developing countries, the coalition of the G20 issued its joint proposal on the eve of the Cancun ministerial, which opened on 11 September 2003 (WTO 2003a).[7] The proposal sought considerably greater reduction in all the three pillars of agricultural protection on the part of the EU and the U.S.[8] Whilst the EU-U.S. draft had proposed the so-called blended formula on market access for all countries, the G20 framework presented a counter-proposal with a more far-reaching cuts targeted specifically at developed countries. To provide meaningful cuts in domestic support subsidies, the G20 draft called for a complete elimination of the Blue Box.[9] Supporting the G33, it also called for the identification of special products (SPs), which would be exempt from tariff cuts, and an SSM, indicating all in all that their main goal was to unravel the protectionism in developed countries and the considerable concern for the provisions for special and differential treatment (SDT).[10]

[7] This document was first circulated as JOB(03)162/Rev.1 on 20 August 2003, and then submitted on 4 September as a formal proposal for the Cancun ministerial (see WTO 2008). It was co-sponsored by Argentina, Bolivia, Brazil, Chile, China, Colombia, Costa Rica, Cuba, Ecuador, El Salvador, Guatemala, India, Mexico, Pakistan, Paraguay, Peru, Philippines, South Africa, Thailand, and Venezuela.

[8] For a comparison of the proposals of the EU-U.S. positions versus the G20, see Clapp (2006) and Delgado and Campolino de O. Soares (2005).

[9] The WTO jargon compares the 'boxes' it uses for classifying trade subsidies to traffic lights, so the 'green box' translates into a 'go' signal and amber could be considered a cautionary light. However, there is no red box. Instead, there is a 'blue box', which is used for production-limiting programmes. It groups policies that are exempted from the general rule that all subsidies linked to production must be reduced or kept within defined minimal levels. It covers payments directly linked to acreage or animal numbers, but under schemes that also limit production by imposing production quotas or requiring farmers to set aside part of their land.

[10] SDT refers to preferential provisions that apply only to two groups of members: developing countries and the LDCs. Historically, the cases for and against SDT have been couched in developmental terms, a key argument being whether lower levels of

The Cancun ministerial ended in deadlock. The immediate cause for the stalemate was the differences that arose over the Singapore issues on the final day of the conference. However, simmering below this disagreement was the dispute on agriculture. Developing countries had been unhappy with the initial text issued by Carlos Perez del Castillo as the chair of the General Council for the start of the ministerial. The Derbez text, issued on 13 September, exacerbated the dissatisfaction and anger of developing countries (WTO 2003b; 2003c). Whilst these issues remained unresolved at Cancun, the G20 stood together despite the breakaway of Colombia, Costa Rica, Ecuador, El Salvador, Guatemala, and Peru under pressure from the U.S.[11] Interestingly, however, the group resisted fissure along the most obvious fault lines—between its agricultural exporters (led by Argentina and Brazil) and countries with a more defensive agenda in agriculture (led by India, and further backed by China).[12] The coalition continued to meet in the aftermath of Cancun at the ministerial and technical levels.

Negotiations were resumed in Geneva in March 2004, after considerable preparatory work, and the July package finally agreed upon on 1 August (WTO 2004). The G20 ended up making some concessions regarding the Blue Box. But in return, the group was able to gain some concessions from the EU and the U.S. through the acceptance of a tiered formula on market access (instead of the blended formula), retention of *de minimis* payments for subsistence farmers, and the recognition of SPs and an SSM for developing countries.[13] The G20 had successfully managed to develop its own negotiating agenda, and had gained further concessions in the July package.

---

development justify special treatment or, by contrast, make the adoption of standard rules even more desirable (Narlikar 2005; Tussie 1987).

[11] Some of these countries subsequently returned to the fold, either because of a change in government or because U.S. pressure came to a stop after a bilateral deal was closed. At the time of writing the membership of the G20 has risen to 23: Argentina, Bolivia, Brazil, Chile, China, Cuba, Ecuador, Egypt, Guatemala, India, Indonesia, Mexico, Nigeria, Pakistan, Paraguay, Peru, Philippines, South Africa, Tanzania, Thailand, Uruguay, Venezuela, and Zimbabwe (G20 2008b).

[12] To learn more on the shift from across border obstructionist defensiveness to a more nuanced position issue by issue on trade policy implementation in India, see Chapter 6.

[13] The tiered tariff reduction formula implies that the highest bound tariffs face the steepest cuts, allowing developing countries smaller reductions than developed ones receive. The tariff resulting from the formula will be the maximum duty permitted for a particular product and a particular country (Rebizo and Ibañez 2007).

Following the July package, however, much work still remained to be done, including the negotiation of modalities for the three pillars. This chapter does not discuss the details of these negotiations.[14] Suffice it to note here that G20 analysis found both the submissions of both the EU and the U.S. inadequate. The G20 argued that the U.S. proposal on domestic support would only result in more box shifting, and it was particularly unhappy about the attempt to reintroduce a peace clause, which might restrict members after the successful legal challenges of the cotton subsidies in the U.S. and sugar in the EU.[15] The G20 also expressed dissatisfaction with the EU's offer of tariff cuts as too low and 10 percent tariff lines to be designated as SPs too high. The G20's proposal provided a detailed alternative framework that included a developed version of the tiered formula on market access through four bands, mechanisms of limiting the Blue Box through product specific caps, and further cuts in domestic subsidies by the EU and the U.S.

The declaration that was agreed upon at the Hong Kong ministerial on 13 to 18 December 2005 did not go far (WTO 2005). Its principal achievement was the EU agreement to end export subsidies by 2013. To its credit, the 'four bands for structuring tariff cuts' referred to in paragraph 7 were a result of G20 research efforts and proposals. Other than that, the declaration reiterated the issues contained in the July package. An important point, which some developing countries would pick up subsequently, was the inclusion of paragraph 24 in the declaration, which states:

> We recognize that it is important to advance the development objectives of this Round through enhanced market access for developing countries in both Agriculture and NAMA [non-agricultural market access]. To that end, we instruct our negotiators to ensure that there is a comparably high level of ambition in market access for Agriculture and NAMA. This ambition is to be achieved in a balanced and proportionate manner consistent with the principle of special and differential treatment.

---

[14] For details of the agricultural negotiations, see Clapp (2006), as well as the WTO website <www.wto.org> for the latest proposals.

[15] The so-called peace clause had been a product of the Blair House accord, whereby countries had committed to exercise 'due moderation' when facing (illegal) subsidies that could be challenged under the dispute resolution mechanism. The clause expired in 2001, and several disputes were subsequently opened and won, having challenged the policies of the EU and the U.S.

The Doha round was supposed to have been concluded by January 2005. Admittedly, given the fact that the G20 has always been more than a blocking coalition, the recurrence of deadlock does not truly represent a success of the group. However, some of its members have emerged as 'veto players' in the WTO.[16] Moreover, the G20 has collectively demonstrated its ability to maintain its unity and further hold up the negotiations if needed, and its proposals have contributed significantly to the limited agreement that does exist on a deal in agriculture. These are no small achievements.

How Research Mattered: The G20 Experience

This section examines the specific ways in which research influenced the G20 position. It reviews three cases in which the G20 produced major, innovative ideas, and that would likely have been backed by research initiatives by member governments. Those cases are a proposal for a tired formula on market access, a proposal regarding an SSM, and a proposal for a product-specific cap.

These three cases are assessed against the two sets of hypotheses presented in the first section. Before launching into this discussion, however, one caveat is in order. The primary set of individuals interviewed for this study come from the core group of the G20: Argentina, Brazil, India, and South Africa.[17] As leading members of the G20, and as among the economically strongest members of the coalition, these countries in particular could be expected to invest in research to enhance their negotiating positions. Interestingly, however, interviews with negotiators, government officials, researchers in think tanks and other institutes, and NGOs directly or indirectly pointed at the limitations of research inputs. For instance, two interviewees from Argentina—one of them working in a leading think tank, the other a senior diplomat—stated:

---

[16] Veto players are individual or collective actors whose agreement is required for a change of the status quo (Tsebelis 1995). See Narlikar 2007 for an application of George Tsebelis's concept of 'veto player' to emerging powers in international institutions.

[17] China is the fifth member of this core group, which is sometimes referred to as the BASIC (Brazil, Argentina, South Africa, India, and China). However, despite being a founding member of the G20, its participation has been limited. In general, China's involvement fits well with the general caution it seems to exercise in its negotiations in the WTO ever since it became a member in 2001. This stance is partly just a function of the significant concessions that were part and parcel of the accession negotiations and partly a product of its strategy of 'accommodating and hedging' (see Foot 2006).

> My perception is that G20 positions are very general. I do not think there are vast amounts of research supporting position taking. Negotiators got together in Geneva and built their positions according to a common minimum denominator.[18]
>
> In the Doha round in general, research has been important, not necessarily critical or determining... Research is just an aspect of any negotiation. It is important to possess 'qualified' information but it is only one aspect of many others. Other variables are much more critical than research at the negotiation table.[19]

Another interviewee, this time a government official from Brazil, offered a more nuanced position, but still highlighted the limited value of research for the G20: 'Obviously, there is a connection between technical inputs and political control. I tell you, the political control is ours.'[20]

This link between political mandates and the research agenda was also emphasised by the Indians. To take one example, a researcher in a prestigious Indian think tank stated that ultimately any policy or negotiating position boils down to the 'political sense of the bureaucrats, who pick and choose the opinions that suit them'.[21]

> Most government officials interviewed pointed out that research inputs had not contradicted the positions taken by the G20. This finding reinforces the point that political agendas have been the major driving force behind research that might be used for negotiating purposes later on. That said, interviewees went on to give examples on how certain types of research had helped the G20 to develop a particular position. Some of these positions in fact subsequently provided the basis of a particular agreement or compromise (for instance in the July package or the Hong Kong declaration). In this regard, the above-mentioned researcher from India said: 'I knew the government's position was: the G20 needs to be backed—an understanding that I shared... our job was to provide practical leads to the government.[22]

Within the coalition, Brazil taken the lead in developing a well-trained staff of researchers and lawyers specialised in WTO negotiations who can provide such practical guides. Brazilian authorities noted the process of increasing legalisation and judicialisation of international trade relations after the Uruguay round and the establishment of the

---

[18] Interview with a researcher in an Argentinian think tank, 6 February 2007.

[19] Inteview with a senior Argentinian negotiator, 31 January 2007.

[20] Interview with a Brazilian foreign affairs official, 13 March 2007.

[21] Interview with a researcher in an Indian think tank, 20 March 2007.

[22] Interview with a researcher in an Indian think tank, 20 March 2007.

dispute settlement mechanism. Such awareness led the government to articulate a new public-private partnership for trade policy and trade litigation (Shaffer *et al.* 2006). Step by step, Brazil has developed a tripartite structure for WTO dispute settlement. The first component of the structure is the specialised WTO dispute settlement division located in Brasilia, and the coordination between this unit and Brazil's WTO mission in Geneva constitutes the second component. The third component is the coordination between both of these entities with Brazil's private sector and law firms hired by it (Shaffer *et al.* 2006). As an integral part of this third component, in 2003 Brazil's mission started a programme to facilitate training in WTO law and dispute settlement of young attorneys in law firms. Supported financially by the law firms, the internship programme aimed at creating a critical mass of legal experts capable of understanding the technicalities of agreements and the opportunities to challenge violations, thus moving Brazil from being at the receiving end to taking an active role in litigation.

The critical mass of legal expertise that emerged from the in-country cooperation between the public and private sector became an extremely valuable asset not only for defending individual business interests, but also for the Doha negotiations overall. The public-private partnership had multiplying external effects as Brazil shared its newly acquired knowledge with peer countries in intra-coalition cooperation. Brazil's acquisition of expertise on the ground and grasp of technical knowledge were thus transferred to the construction of knowledge-driven, applicable negotiating proposals. Of course, this also reinforced Brazil's position within the coalition and further contributed to the consolidation of its leadership.

The cases of all these countries within the G20 suggest that research and knowledge have made a difference within political constraints. Even if research and analysis do not actively set the grand agenda, they can determine the substantive nitty-gritty of the bargaining process that underlies multilateral trade negotiations. The following examples illustrate how this might be the case, and further suggest the ends that such research and analysis might aim at as well as the different degrees of success they can generate. Table 11–2 shows the various domestic organisations and groups within the four core member countries, which contributed in the production of research and also contributed to the legitimisation process.

Table 11–1: Research Players in the G20 Game

	Argentina	Brazil	India	South Africa
Ministries	• Foreign Affairs • Secretary of Agriculture	• Agriculture • Agrarian Development • Development, Industry and Commerce • Foreign Affairs	• Ministry of Commerce and Industry • Foreign Affairs	• Department of Trade and Industry • Department of Agriculture
Research institutes/ think tanks	• INAI (various funding sources: Buenos Aires Grain Exchange, Rosario Board of Trade, Bahia Blanca Grain Exchange, Chamber of the Oil Industry—CIARA) • CEI (part of the Ministry of Foreign Affairs: governmental founding)	• ICONE (funds provided by agribusiness associations; some projects supported by international organizations WB, IDB)	• National Council of Applied Economic Research (NCAER) (grants from the Indian Ministry of Finance; self-funding; funding from State Governments and the International Government Organisation) • Indian Council for Research on International Economic Relations (ICRIER) (self-funding) • Indian Institute of Foreign Trade (IIFT) (governmentally financed) • UNCTAD India Programme • National Law School University of India	• Trade Law Centre for South Africa (TRALAC) (financed by international agencies: Australian AID (AusAID), DANIDA (Denmark), Dutch Foreign Ministry, SIDA (Sweden) • University of Victoria • University of Stellenbosch • University of Durban Orange Free State
Business and other lobby groups	• Argentina Agriculture Association (*Federación Agraria Argentina*) • Argentine Rural Association (*Sociedad Rural Argentina*) • Buenos Aires Grain Exchange • Rosario Board of Trade • Bahia Blanca Grain Exchange • Chamber of the Oil Industry Confederaciones Rurales Argentinas	• National Confederation of Agriculture (*Confederaçao de Agricultura e Pecuaria do Brasil, CNA*) • National Confederation of rural peasant and workers (*Confederaçao Nacional dos Trabalhadores na Agricultura, CONTAG*)	• Federation of Indian Chambers of Commerce (FICCI) • Confederation of Indian Industry (CII)	• Agri South Africa

Table 11–1 (*cont.*)

	Argentina	Brazil	India	South Africa
Forums		• Working group at Itamaraty (CNA, CONTAG, ICONE, and Ministries) • Permanent Forum on International Agricultural Negotiations	• The Ministry of Commerce holds occasional seminars to keep contact with civil society	Agricultural Trade Forum (farmers organisations, government, labour, and consumer groups)

Tariff-Cutting Formulae

One of the major contributions of the G20 to the negotiation process was the critique of the blended formula proposal offered by the EU and the U.S. in the run-up to Cancun in August 2003. This critique was able to grasp the implications of the technical issues and come up with an alternative version. In several interviews, trade negotiators said this contribution of the G20 would not have been possible without the research taken on initially by India and subsequently by Brazil. For example,

> the blended formula was severely criticised by the G20, but it was not until India came up with a study that the group had strong arguments against the formula. The study demonstrated that the U.S. and EU proposal only benefited developed countries (in particular those with tariff peaks such as the U.S.). The research by India and the resulting paper allowed the G20 to be the first coalition to have frontally opposed the 'blended formula'.[23]

There were also references, in addition to the Indian paper, to the roles played by Argentina and Brazil in contributing to challenge the blended formula.[24] In particular, the Instituto de Estudos do Comércio e Negociações Internacionais (ICONE), a Brazilian agribusiness think tank, is reputed to have played a very important role in contributing

[23] Interview with Argentinian negotiator, 6 February 2007.

[24] Interviews with Argentinian negotiator, 6 February 2007, and with a researcher in a Brazilian think tank, 27 April 2007.

to this alternative approach to market access.[25] Unfortunately, despite repeated attempts, it was not possible to find the paper trail of the critique of the blended formula in May 2004. As a result, it is not possible to confirm which countries (and groups or organisations within them) took the lead on this initiative. However, a simple examination of the proposal strongly suggests that such a detailed proposal could not have been developed without a good deal of research into the area.

The Permanent Mission of Brazil (2004) issued a communication on behalf of the G20 on 7 May 2004, which analysed the blended formula in terms of 'a fundamentally flawed approach to agricultural market access'. Apart from taking the issue of the blended formula on the grounds of SDT, the draft claimed the following:

> There is a shared feeling that 'the Blended formula' is biased in favour of the tariff structures of its proponents, enabling them to maintain the protectionist *status quo*, since the highest tariffs would be subject to the lowest tariff reduction. In view of the difference between the tariff structures of developed and developing countries, 'the Blended formula' would impose an overly onerous burden of tariff reduction on developing countries. At the same time, it would enable developed countries to protect their tariff peaks on products of export interest to several Members, while the application of the Swiss- and duty-free components on their cluster of already low tariffs would result in minimal tariff reductions (2).

This critique provided the basis for the compromise that was struck as part of the July package. As a result, the so-called tiered formula emerged and appears in paragraphs 28–30 of the July package (WTO 2004). The G20 continued to hone the tiered formula and presented several papers on this (G20 2005a; 2005b). These were substantive proposals in terms of innovative ideas as well as technical detail. For instance, the G20 (2005a, para. 4) argued that

> overall proportionality of commitments between developed and developing countries should be achieved through lower tariff reductions and higher thresholds for the bands. Developing country Members will cut less than 2/3 of the cut to be undertaken by developed country Members.

Furthermore,

[25] ICONE's mission is the understanding of the global dynamics of agribusiness, bioenergy, and international trade through applied research.

> The G20 stresses that its proposal of the linear cut within the bands constitutes the real middle ground in market access negotiations and expects Members to converge to that proposal (G20 2005a, para. 7).

All these efforts were not expended in vain. Even though the detailed cuts still have to be agreed upon, elements of these proposals were incorporated into the Hong Kong declaration, which adopted four bands for structuring tariff cuts,

> recognizing that we need now to agree on the relevant thresholds—including those applicable for developing country Members (WTO 2005, para. 7).

Special Safeguard Mechanism

A second initiative that reveals evidence of some detailed research is on the SSM. The SSM forms the core of the G33 proposal, and is an area on which the G20 is divided. Anecdotal evidence refers to studies conducted by Argentina and Brazil on the impact of SPs and the SSM.[26] These studies suggested an adverse impact of the SP and SSM, as these provisions would nullify any market access concessions from developing countries. A proposal that would circumscribe the scope of SP-SSM was necessary.

The central drive for research in this area came from Argentina. The ministry of agriculture led work on this area, and then sent the initial proposal to the Instituto para las Negociaciones Agrícolas Internacionales (Institute of International Negotiations on Agriculture [INAI]) around the middle of 2005. In November 2005, INAI came up with a detailed proposal on the implementation of paragraph 42 of the July package. While accepting the SSM in principle, the draft came up with a set of rules within which it could be applied, including a time limit for how long the safeguard would be valid, along with provisions for the monitoring and surveillance of its use, as well as the monitoring and surveillance of its use. Continuing to work on this agenda, with Paraguay and Uruguay as co-sponsors, Argentina (2006) presented a draft to the WTO on this issue. This proposal went beyond the general principle of SSM to address issues on its implementation, including

[26] Interview with researchers in a leading Argentinian think tank, 6 February 2007; written communiqué from a lawyer working in an Argentinian think tank, 15 August 2007.

types of data to be used, and identified some very detailed specific triggers that should be used to activate the SSM.

The SSM proposal is particularly interesting as it shows the interaction between the technical and political components of research. Despite claims of evidence of the substantial costs that would result from the SSM, Argentina, Paraguay, and Uruguay have been cautious, avoiding an outright opposition to the mechanism. This is a consequence of the efforts of various coalitions of developing countries to maintain 'alliances of sympathy' among themselves. Given especially that 13 of the 23 members of the G20 are also members of the G33, overt opposition against the SSM by Argentina, Paraguay, and Uruguay could seriously jeopardise the long-term goals of the G20. Research on the implications of the SSM, and on ways to limit it in time and coverage, thus works within these political constraints.

Product-Specific Caps

The idea of product-specific caps is significant for two reasons. First, the emergence and step-by-step construction of the proposal shows the considerable learning that occurs as countries understand the jurisprudence and use it to their advantage to negotiate with increasingly clear and focused proposals and armed with the full range of technical insights that they acquire as they develop analytical skills when they litigate. Second, it shows the interaction that takes place between the legislative and the juridical sides of the WTO.

The initial statements of the G20 on the issue were presented at the informal Special Session of the Committee of Agriculture, on 11 November 2004. Brazil is reputed to have taken the lead in early 2005. The feasibility of applying ceilings to specific products to keep the aggregate measure of support in check gained ground after its successful experience with the cotton and sugar panels in 2004. The panels that Brazil won against cotton subsidies in the U.S. and sugar subsidies in the EU introduced the possibility of applying product-specific caps on domestic subsidies, a commitment that the U.S. had been reluctant to accept. Ceilings on specific products are meant to control the pro-cyclical effect of over-subsidisation in global markets when prices fall, which puts non-subsidising countries in a particularly fragile spot when the scramble to retain market shares breaks out. This is an option the U.S. has tried to retain in order to retain leverage precisely at such junctures.

Armed with the successful learning experience of litigation, Brazil took the lead on this issue. There is some evidence of this, some of it anecdotal, but there were also papers presented on this issue that were subsequently taken up by the G20 (G20 2005c, 74; 2007; Jales and Tachinardi 2006). Requests to the relevant organisations and ministries in Brazil for the papers that were written prior to the G20 statements on product-specific caps (before March 2005) unfortunately did not generate a favourable response. However, there is published evidence that detailed mechanisms for implementing product-specific caps were developed using significant research from ICONE. Based on the precedent set by the cotton case, ICONE researchers proposed a criterion for setting product-specific caps in terms of the adverse effects on other countries' exports: 'The definition of the tolerance level [to trade distortion] is crucial in the establishment of disciplines by product' (Costa *et al.* 2007, 2).

Thus legal precedent setting and subsequent additional research were fundamental contributions to the ability to propose reasonable goals, appropriate benchmarking, and policy instruments. Such an empirical approach suggests that the research will continue to perform a significant function as the coalition nurtures cooperation and continues to mature.

What Do These Cases Say?

The first section of this chapter presented two sets of hypotheses regarding the role of research: the first related to the dealings of the coalition with external parties and the second referred to the role of research in intra-coalition dynamics. What do these cases discussed here tell us about these hypotheses?

The first finding that emerges from the three cases is that the G20 did engage in the production of research that led to procedurally relevant knowledge. Nonetheless, the coalition has not endowed itself with a collective research capacity. Particular member countries of the coalition take the lead on specific issues, which are then incorporated as part of the G20 agenda. Consequently a division of labour emerges along the way. Importantly, however, this division is *de facto* rather than pre-planned and it is configured and reconfigured as issues appear on the agenda affecting specific interests.

A second finding of this study is that the three cases suggest that research initiatives of the G20 have made detailed contributions to the substance of the negotiations. However, these are neither first-mover initiatives nor grand agenda-setting visions. Rather, the coalition had arisen first and foremost as a political alliance against the EU-U.S. draft prior to the Cancun ministerial. Once this rather general agenda of agricultural reform was identified, research began to matter. All three instances examined in this chapter as illustrations of the ability of G20 research to influence the substance of negotiations also reinforce the importance of the political hooks (both as constraints and opportunities) on which research initiatives hang. The hypothesis regarding the influence of research for agenda setting is hence only partially confirmed.

The hypothesis on the distributive ends of research is confirmed. All of the statements, position papers, and formal proposals put forward show how the G20 has moved with counterproposals to those of the EU and the U.S. There have been no attempts to expand the zone of agreement. Rather, each of these cases has begun with a process of an elaborate critique of the proposals of the North, and only then the G20 has proceeded to suggest alternative approaches. All these proposals claim value from the North and defend the G20 against such declarations.

Finally, the legitimisation purposes of research emerge rather clearly in this chapter. Research taken on by member countries (or various institutions or actors within them) is not open-ended, but is directed toward the elaboration of the general mandate of the group, the legitimisation of it, or both. When used for legitimisation, an outside audience seems to be targeted—for instance the product-specific cap proposals, available on the websites of ICONE and the International Centre for Trade and Sustainable Development (ICTSD). The G20 statements and press releases further reflect the concern of the group to communicate its findings to an external audience. In terms of intra-coalition dynamics, the G20 certainly seems to have used available research to cement the group.

That said, not all the hypotheses were fully corroborated by the evidence examined in this chapter. For instance, this study has not been able to confirm the role of research as a cohesive element from the perspective of a club good, whereby the coalition can attract members and exclude non-members (thereby providing a greater incentive for countries to join the coalition). Instead, the G20 seems to have had the ability to keep members of other coalitions happy. This was reflected in the 'alliances of sympathy' that arose at the Cancun ministerial (Narlikar and Tussie 2004); it was further reflected in the joint press statement that was issued by the G110 at the Hong Kong ministerial, where Brazil and India played a major role. Far from excluding countries not belonging to the coalition, the G20 (2008a) website states:

> In the upcoming negotiations on modalities, the G20 will maintain its engagement in the negotiations, its internal coordination and its efforts to interact with other groups with a view to promoting developing countries interests in agricultural negotiations.

This attempt to engage constructively with other coalitions may be a product of some learning—the Brazil and India-led G10 coalition in the Uruguay round had refused to discuss and share findings with other developing countries and had ended up isolated in the endgame at Punta del Este. The full motivations of the G20 behind its willingness to work with other coalitions of developing countries, and the sustainability of such efforts however, lie beyond the scope of this chapter.

In addition, the G20 has attempted to logroll different issues onto its agenda to prevent defection. This is reflected most clearly in the Argentine proposal on SSM, which, although throwing light on the risks, stays well within the group's overall commitment to supporting other coalitions of developing countries including the G33. This tendency can be seen in all the efforts of the group to include detailed SDT provisions into its agenda that have the greatest relevance for tropical exporters within it. For instance, one interviewee from Brazil stated:

> Unity is vital for the coalition. Demands of small countries are taken into account... Some things that affect only two or three G20 members—such as preference erosion in tropical products—are taken into account because the G20 is concerned with defending all the interests of developing countries. A by-product of this is that it reinforces the unity of the coalition.[27]

Finally, the importance of research was confirmed in terms of its impact on domestic legitimisation. After the group had been created, considerable effort was expended in consulting with various in-country interest groups Admittedly, this process of 'consultation' was heavily

[27] Interview with a diplomat in the Permanent Mission of Brazil, Geneva, 23 March 2007.

state-driven (Hurrell and Narlikar 2006; Priyadarshi 2004). But nonetheless, it served an important function of legitimisation—this time to the domestic audience. This process also produced some reverse loops: once consulted, particular groups came up with some specific proposals, which in turn were fed back into the government of the member country. This idea is nicely captured by one interviewee in describing an informal technical group that unites three parties involved in the negotiations within Brazil, namely government, agriculture and agribusiness, and ICONE:

> The group meets several times during the week... All interests must be taken into account, not only the offensive interests. Otherwise, the balance within the group would be broken. This informal technical group works just like a small G20.[28]

Research, taken on by individual members and subsequently shared with other members of the coalition, mattered in the case of the G20. This chapter has highlighted the mechanisms whereby research came to make a difference in the negotiating agenda of the G20 and has also assessed the impact of this research in terms of outcomes. Admittedly, the political constraints are high, so the set-up of research is determined in a significant way by the interests of individual members as well as intra-coalition dynamics. But working with these constraints, research can go a long way in influencing the negotiating agenda of the coalition and providing an important source of its legitimacy.

Conclusion

This chapter has shown the increasing importance and participation of developing countries in the trade rule-making process at the WTO. The G20 has been able to increase its strength and bargaining power by building coalitions that have introduced proposals in the WTO negotiating agenda aiming at offsetting the proposals previously presented by the developed countries and perceived as unfair by developing countries. Specifically, three of the proposals introduced by the G20 have been analysed and the degree to which such proposals were backed by research was examined. In addition, the role played

[28] Interview with a diplomat in the Permanent Mission of Brazil, Geneva, 23 March 2007.

by research in influencing coalition politics both internally and with non-members has been studied. Thus, this chapter has attempted to establish the extent to which the empowered position of the South is related to intra-coalition research.

The coalition strategy implemented by the G20 was found to be effective in increasing the bargaining power of developing countries as well as in enhancing their ability to defend their interests without building collective research capacity to back the proposals. Instead, particular sources (in the cases analysed in this chapter, namely India, Brazil, and Argentina) took the lead on specific issues, which were then incorporated as part of the G20 agenda, in a spontaneous division of labour. In contrast to the G33, the G20 has tapped on a variety of sources as well as the hands-on expertise acquired in litigation.

The direct use of research for submitting proposals (a tiered formula on market access, limits to a SSM, and product-specific caps) played a significant role. Internally it provided cohesion to the coalition, discouraged defection and allowed the domestic legitimisation to negotiations where exporter interests were at stake. Paradoxically, so did the fact that such research was discarded when findings were considered inconvenient to the deployment of a particular political strategy (such as research on the costs of the SSM for some member countries). However, this study has not found evidence that research played a cohesive role from the perspective of a club good. On the contrary, the strategy of the coalition rested on some members' sharing their research with non-members in order to garner sympathy from other developing countries.

Finally, because the proposals introduced by the G20 arose as a response to the proposals of the EU and the U.S., research that indeed contributed to the substance of the negotiations was anchored in policy from the outset and subject to political constraints: once governments had committed to the alliance, research was commissioned and directed step by step following the needs and opportunities of the agenda. Governments remain at the helm and research is produced on demand. It is rarely arm's length. However, even within this 'direction', research plays an important role in the shape of the proposals that were put forward, first by individual governments and subsequently by the coalition. Research might not matter much in the initial agenda-setting phase, but the nitty-gritty of negotiations would be impossible without it. The G20 has managed to produce a series of small operational papers that may appear to routinely follow precedent, but they tap on a variety of in-country sources and are used politically at strategic points of the negotiations.

Bibliography

Amorim, Celso. 2003/04. 'The Lesson of Cancun.' *Politica Externa* 12(3):27–36.

——. 2004. 'Speech by the Foreign Minister of Brazil at the G20 Meeting.' 12 June. Sao Paolo. <www.brazil.org.uk/newsandmedia/speeches_files/20040612.html> [Accessed: February 2008].

Argentina, Paraguay, and Uruguay. 2006. *Revised Consolidated Reference Paper on Possible Modalities on Market Access—SSM: Some Unanswered Technical Issues.* JOB(06)/197/Rev.1. Committee on Agriculture Special Session, 21 June. Geneva: World Trade Organization. <www.agtradepolicy.org/output/resource/APU%20paper.pdf> [Accessed: February 2008].

Clapp, Jennifer. 2006. *Developing Countries and the WTO Agriculture Negotiations.* CIGI Working Paper No. 6. Centre for International Governance Innovation. <www.cigionline.org/cigi/download-nocache/Publications/document/workingp/develop_> [Accessed:

Costa, Cinthia, André Nassar, and Marcos Jank. 2007. *Trade-Distorting Domestic Support: Alternatives for Product-Specific Disciplines.* Sao Paolo: Institute for International Economics. <www.iconebrasil.com.br/arquivos/noticia/1384.pdf> [Accessed: February 2008].

Delgado, Nelson Giordano, and Adriano Campolina de O. Soares. 2005. *The G20: Its Origin, Evolution, Meaning, and Prospects.* Global Issue Paper No. 25. Heinrich Böll Foundation. <www.boell.de/alt/downloads/global/GIP_25_Engl_G-20.pdf> [Accessed: February 2008].

Faizel, Ismail. 2007. 'One Year Since the WTO Hong Kong Ministerial Conference: Developing Countries Re-claim the Development Content of the WTO Doha Round.' In Yong-Shik Lee, ed., *Economic Development Through World Trade: A Developing World Perspective.* The Hague: Kluwer Law International.

Foot, Rosemary. 2006. 'Chinese Strategies in a U.S.-Hegemonic Global Order: Accommodating and Hedging.' *International Affairs* 82(1):77–94.

G20. 2005a. 'G20 Proposal on Market Access.' 12 October. <www.agtradepolicy.org/output/resource/G20MarketaccessproposalOct05.pdf> [Accessed: February 2008].

——. 2005b. 'G20 Proposal: Elements for Discussion on Market Access.' 8 July. <www.agtradepolicy.org/output/resource/G20_Dalian_MarketAccess.pdf> [Accessed: February 2008].

——. 2005c. *G20 Statement: Blue Box.* Room D Consultations, March. <www.g-20.mre.gov.br/conteudo/19082005_Breviario.pdf> [Accessed: February 2008].

——. 2005d. *Two Years of Activities of the G20: Moving Forward the Doha Round.* <www.g-20.mre.gov.br/conteudo/19082005_Breviario.pdf> [Accessed: February 2008].

——. 2007. 'G20 Proposal for the Establishment of Product-Specific Caps in AMS.' <www.g-20.mre.gov.br/conteudo/proposals_caps.pdf> [Accessed: February 2008].

——. 2008a. *History.* <www.g-20.mre.gov.br/history.asp> [Accessed: February 2008].

——. 2008b. *Members.* <www.g-20.mre.gov.br/members.asp> [Accessed: February 2008].

Glover, David, and Diana Tussie, eds. 1993. *The Developing Countries in World Trade: Policies and Bargaining Strategies.* Boulder: Lynne Rienner.

Hurrell, Andrew, and Amrita Narlikar. 2006. 'A New Politics of Confrontation? Developing Countries at Cancun and Beyond.' *Global Society* 20(4):415–433.

Jales, Mário, and Maria H. Tachinardi. 2006. *Devising a Comprehensive IBSA Strategy on WTO Agriculture Negotiations: The Case of Brazil.* Sao Paolo: Institute for International Trade Negotiations. <www.iconebrasil.com.br/en/?actA=8&areaID=8&secaoID=73&artigoID=1277> [Accessed: February 2008].

Narlikar, Amrita. 2005. *The World Trade Organization: A Very Short Introduction*. New York: Oxford University Press.

Narlikar, Amrita, and John S. Odell. 2006. 'The Strict Distributive Strategy for a Bargaining Coalition: The Like-Minded Group and the World Trade Organization.' In John S. Odell, ed., *Negotiating Trade: Developing Countries in the WTO and NAFTA*. Cambridge: Cambridge University Press.

Narlikar, Amrita, and Diana Tussie. 2004. 'The G20 at the Cancun Ministerial: Developing Countries and Their Evolving Coalitions in the WTO.' *World Economy* 27(7):947–966.

Permanent Mission of Brazil. 2004. *The Blended Formula: A Fundamentally Flawed Approach to Agricultural Market Access*. TN/AG/GEN/9, 7 May. Geneva: World Trade Organization. <docsonline.wto.org:80/DDFDocuments/t/tn/ag/GEN9.doc> [Accessed: February 2008].

Priyadarshi, Shishir. 2004. *Decision-Making Processes in India: The Case of the Agriculture Negotiations*. Case Study 15. Geneva: World Trade Organization. <www.wto.org/english/res_e/booksp_e/casestudies_e/case15_e.htm> [Accessed: February 2008].

Rebizo, Maria Marta, and Ariel R. Ibañez. 2007. 'Sensitive Products: The July Modalities Text Made Plain.' *Bridges* 11(6):5–6. <www.ictsd.org/monthly/bridges/BRIDGES11-6.pdf> [Accessed: February 2008].

Shaffer, Gregory, Michelle Ratton Sanchez, and Barbara Rosenberg. 2006. *Brazil's Response to the Judicialized WTO Regime: Strengthening the State through Diffusing Expertise*. Working draft prepared for the ICTSD South America Dialogue on WTO Dispute Settlement and Sustainable Development, 22–23 June, Sao Paolo. Geneva: International Centre for Trade and Sustainable Development. <www.ictsd.org/issarea/dsu/resources/Brazil_paper.pdf> [Accessed: February 2008].

Tsebelis, George. 1995. 'Decision Making in Political Systems: Veto Players in Presidentialism, Parliamentarism, Multicameralism, and Multipartyism.' *British Journal of Political Science* 25:289–325.

Tussie, Diana. 1987. *The Less Developed Countries and the World Trading System: A Challenge to the GATT*. London: Frances Pinter.

World Trade Organization. 2001. 'Ministerial Declaration.' WT/MIN(01)/Dec/01. 14 November. Doha. <www.wto.org/english/thewto_e/minist_e/min01_e/mindecl_e.htm> [Accessed: February 2008].

——. 2003a. *Agriculture: Framework Proposal*. WT/MIN(03)/W/6, 4 September. Cancun. <docsonline.wto.org/imrd/directdoc.asp?DDFDocuments/t/WT/MIN03/W6.doc> [Accessed: February 2008].

——. 2003b. *Annexes to the Draft Cancun Ministerial Text*. Second revision, 13 September. Cancun. <www.wto.org/english/thewto_e/minist_e/min03_e/draft_decl_annex_rev2_e.htm> [Accessed: February 2008].

——. 2003c. *Draft Cancun Ministerial Text*. Derbez text. Second revision, 13 September. Cancun. <www.wto.org/english/thewto_e/minist_e/min03_e/draft_decl_rev2_e.htm> [Accessed: February 2008].

——. 2004. *Text of the 'July Package': The General Council's Post-Cancun Decision*. WT/L/579, 1 August. <www.wto.org/english/tratop_e/dda_e/draft_text_gc_dg_31july04_e.htm> [Accessed: February 2008].

——. 2005. *Ministerial Declaration*. WT/MIN(05)/Dec, 18 December. Hong Kong. <www.wto.org/English/thewto_e/minist_e/min05_e/final_text_e.htm> [Accessed: February 2008].

——. 2008. *The Cancun Draft 'Frameworks'*. Geneva. <www.wto.org/english/tratop_e/agric_e/frameworks_e.htm> [Accessed: February 2008].

CHAPTER NINE

CENTRALIZED PRODUCTION: THE GROUP OF 33

Paul Mably[1]

This chapter examines how the Group of 33 (G33) coalition of developing countries uses research produced or guided by an international non-governmental organisation (NGO) to advance their development objectives at World Trade Organization (WTO) negotiations. The G33's instruments of choice are special products (SP) and a special safeguard mechanism (SSM) under the market access pillar of talks on trade in agriculture.

Current international rules are seen by many developing countries as inadequate, if not inimical, to their pursuit of the three development objectives of food security, livelihood security, and rural development. Trade rules do not respond to the needs of countries where small-scale agriculture continues to be the dominant economic activity among their large rural populations, and where poverty alleviation and rural development depend to a large extent on the health of rural agriculture.[2] According to G33 negotiators consulted for the study described in this chapter, research—their own and that of other entities such as NGOs—has helped them to develop better negotiating positions to pursue these development needs.

Food security, livelihood security, and rural development are interrelated concepts (Stevens 2004, 4). Originally food security meant self-sufficiency in basic foodstuffs. More recently the emphasis has shifted to the importance of access to food by households, whether through production or employment. Herein lies the connection to livelihoods

---

[1] Paul Mably is a Canada-based independent consultant on international trade and development policy. The author gratefully acknowledges the generous contributions of the individuals interviewed for this chapter in addition to Diana Tussie and Ricardo Meléndez Ortiz.

[2] Agriculture still accounts for a large portion of the gross national product (GNP) of developing countries, as well as 70% of employment in low-income countries and 30% in middle-income countries. (This information and many of the other arguments reviewed below are referenced by Luisa Bernal (2004, 9–15) and the International Centre for Trade and Sustainable Development ([ICTSD] 2005b, ix, 4–11).

and rural development. Individual families unable to produce their own food must generate earnings to buy food. Similarly, countries that are not self-sufficient in food production must generate earnings from other economic activities to pay for commercial imports of food, or they must have access to concessionary food aid. Dependence on trade or aid for basic food requirements makes countries vulnerable under current global rules. Most poor countries depend for their earnings on one or two export commodities, whose prices on world markets are volatile and in long-term decline. Food aid supply is also unreliable, especially when food prices increase, and it sometimes comes with political strings attached. Therefore the risks of relying only or largely on food imports and food aid for stable access to food are high.

Current rules of trade permit huge subsidies for food production in developed countries. Small-scale producers in developing countries are unable to compete when this subsidised food is imported into their countries. These producers lose market share domestically, and are unable to compete abroad. Their situation, and therefore rural livelihoods and rural development, become ever more precarious.

Developing countries have formed coalitions in the WTO to fight for rules that reduce or eliminate food production subsidies in developed countries, that open developed country markets to agricultural exports from developing countries, and that protect food security, livelihood security, and rural development from the effects of subsidised food imports and import surges. The G33 was established specifically to fight for these three interrelated public policy objectives.

A coalition such as G33 must develop the capacity to generate new, policy-relevant knowledge through the commissioning of studies and the creation of working groups to draft proposals and innovative approaches to these complex policy problems. Little work has been done to understand the role that research has played within trade policy coalitions. There is also little understanding of the role of NGO research in nurturing trade policy processes within developing countries, or those of developing country coalitions. Preliminary work on NGO action in international trade forums indicates that NGOs are having increasing impact in support of developing countries (Mably 2006).

The present study considers what influence knowledge generation may be having at the G33 and the WTO, and specifically knowledge generated by the International Centre for Trade and Sustainable Development (ICTSD), a Geneva-based NGO. The study tests the hypothesis that coalitions use research for both external and internal purposes, and that both categories aim to build consensus during the process of negotiation. External purposes include both ensuring that the coalition's issue is placed on the agenda and receives serious consideration in the relevant decision-making forum (the WTO in this case) and legitimising the coalition position to the point where it is accepted as policy. Internal coalition purposes include attracting and holding new members to the coalition, and also preventing their defection from it. The study shows that the hypotheses are only partially valid. To support the conclusions it presents, the study relies on the literature on policy uptake (see the introduction to this volume), on telephone interviews with G33 negotiators and ICTSD staff, on research pieces produced by ICTSD and other sources, and on the coalition's public statements and proposals to the WTO.[3]

This chapter examines two specific interrelated policy change 'episodes'. The first is the generation of internal consensus among G33 member countries in defining the meaning and scope of SPs and the SSM. The second is the generation of consensus at the WTO on the articulation of SPs and the SSM on the negotiating agenda.

SPs and SSM are components of special and differential treatment (SDT), which developing countries have sought as a way to adapt WTO trade rules to supporting development goals. Each instrument has its own distinct purpose: SPs should provide targeted protection for specific products that would not survive under competitive conditions but are crucial to food security, livelihood security, and rural development. The SSM would allow countries to protect sectors that must compete against imports, either in times of import surges or of price depression.

Until the Doha round of trade negotiations is concluded, it is impossible to say whether research has led to policy change in the sense of changes to WTO rules. However, this chapter considers that the evolution and refinement of the G33's position on SPs and the SSM and the agreement of WTO members to put both issues on their negotiating agenda both represent shifts in policy, and thus it is meaningful to examine NGO research influence in relation to these shifts.

The second section of this chapter reviews the context and history of the two policy episodes, looking both inside the WTO and G33

[3] The individuals interviewed were Maria Fe Alberto-Chau Huu (Philippines), Christophe Bellmann (ICTSD), Emalene Marcus-Burnett (Barbados), Ahmad Mukhtar (Pakistan), and Edi Yusup (Indonesia).

and at the external influences upon them. The third section examines evidence gathering and link building—that is, research processes and research itself in the G33 coalition and the ICTSD. The fourth section provides evidence of the uptake of the research of ICTSD and other organisations by G33 and WTO policy makers. The fifth section sets out some concluding observations.

Context and History

Internal Context

When agriculture was brought under multilateral trade rules for the first time, in the Uruguay round, WTO members recognised that developing countries require special consideration. The SDT measures for developing countries in the Agreement on Agriculture (AoA) that were implemented in 1995 include, among others:

- lower reduction levels for tariffs (24% for developing countries versus 36% for developed countries), domestic support (20% versus 15%), and export subsidies (36% versus 24%);
- more time to implement these reductions (10 years);
- minimum reduction of tariffs by 10% (versus 15% for developed countries);
- relaxed provisions related to the accumulation and disposal of buffer stocks for food security purposes and for food aid; and
- exemption from conversion to tariffs of those non-tariff barriers applied to predominant staple foods in the local traditional diet.

While a group of developing countries welcomed these SDT provisions, many considered them to be insufficient to protect their food security and rural livelihoods under Uruguay round rules, and that these rules led to increasing poverty and inequality (Bernal 2004, 10). Even the emergency measures agreed in that round have proven inadequate. The AoA provides for special safeguards (SSG) that would allow all members to impose a temporary tariff above their bound rate in the case of a surge in imports beyond certain volumes (volume trigger) or when product prices fall below a certain threshold (price trigger). The SSG have been of little use to developing countries due to the stringent technical conditions attached to them and the fact that they are available only to countries that engage in tariffication, converting their non-tariff restrictions (NTBs) into tariffs—a total of just 22 developing countries. Most opted for ceiling tariff rates, therefore disqualifying them from use of the SSG.

Difficulties in using these defence mechanisms led developing countries to form the Like-Minded Group in 2000 during the renewed negotiations of the AoA.[4] The Like-Minded Group proposed a 'development box' of measures for flexible use of rules on trade in agriculture. The notions of the SP and SSM emerged in that context as specific development box mechanisms:

- The creation of a special safeguard mechanism available only to developing countries to mitigate damage from import surges of crops competing with domestic staples.
- The ability to raise tariffs on food security crops where tariff bindings were too low, without having to 'pay' with concessions in other trade areas.
- Exemptions from spending limits for crops that meet food security criteria.

Developing countries then honed these concepts in further submissions to the WTO. In early 2001, Korea proposed special consideration for key staple crops as border protection measures are reduced, and India proposed a food security box. It is the Africa Group that first raised the idea, in 2002, of allowing lower tariff reductions for strategic or special products to ensure food security, livelihood security, and rural development (Mamaty 2003). The Africa Group, Indonesia, and the Philippines also called for an agricultural safeguard mechanism for developing countries. By July 2003, on the eve of the WTO ministerial meeting in Cancún, a broader coalition of countries had formed to refine and push forward these ideas. Initially called the Alliance for SP and SSM, led by the Philippines, it presented a first statement to the WTO Special Session of the Committee on Agriculture on 18 July.[5]

[4] The Like-Minded Group consisted of Cuba, the Dominican Republic, El Salvador, Haiti, Honduras, Kenya, Nicaragua, Pakistan, Sri Lanka, Uganda, and Zimbabwe—mostly net food importers, dependent on one or a few crops for export revenues.

[5] The Alliance for SP and SSM comprised Cuba, the Dominican Republic, Honduras, India, Indonesia, Kenya, Mauritius, Nigeria, Pakistan, Panama, Peru, the Philippines, Turkey, Uganda, Venezuela, and Zimbabwe.

In September 2003 it became known as the Group of 33 developing countries.[6]

The G33 was established in Indonesia on 9 September 2003, a few days before the creation of the Group of 20 (G20) developing countries, and just prior to the WTO ministerial in Cancún. Its stated purpose is 'to ensure that the issue of food security, rural livelihood and rural development becomes an integral part of the agricultural negotiations...by vigorously promoting Special and Differential Treatment through the concept of Special Products (SP) and Special Safeguard Mechanism for all developing countries' (G33 2005b, 3). The G33 outlines its development aims in a letter to the World Bank: 'The Group has endeavoured to raise the concerns of the millions of subsistence and poor farmers in the developing world whose livelihood and food security will be threatened by an across-the-board substantial trade liberalization in agriculture, especially in an environment of highly distorted agricultural markets, and therefore the Group's mandate and concern is precisely poverty prevention and alleviation' (Bustami 2006, 2).

The WTO Committee on Agriculture responded slowly to these initiatives. By December 2002, an overview paper on agriculture negotiations referred to an 'exemption from reduction commitments for certain agricultural products which are of strategic importance in pursuing food security, product diversification, rural development and employment, and poverty alleviation' (WTO 2002, 4). In early 2003 two drafts of modalities for the further commitments were put forward, and one mentioned 'special products with respect to food security, rural development and/or livelihood security concerns' that could be subject to minimum tariff reductions (see also WTO 2003a; WTO 2003b, 4). The SSM was also contemplated. It took another year and a half before the WTO membership as a whole reached the consensus that constituted one of the policy episodes of this chapter: the endorsement of SPs and the SSM as a subject for WTO negotiation. This occurred when the General Council agreed to the July framework (for negotia-

[6] The G33 consists of 46 countries: Antigua and Barbuda, Barbados, Belize, Benin, Bolivia, Botswana, China, Congo, Côte d'Ivoire, Cuba, Dominica, the Dominican Republic, El Salvador, Grenada, Guatemala, Guyana, Haiti, Honduras, India, Indonesia, Jamaica, Kenya, Korea, Madagascar, Mauritius, Mongolia, Mozambique, Nicaragua, Nigeria, Pakistan, Panama, Peru, the Philippines, St. Kitts and Nevis, St. Lucia, St. Vincent and the Grenadines, Senegal, Sri Lanka, Suriname, Tanzania, Trinidad and Tobago, Turkey, Uganda, Venezuela, Zambia, and Zimbabwe. Bolivia, Indonesia, Pakistan, and Philippines are also members of the Cairns Group.

tions on trade in agriculture) on 1 August 2004. The July framework was a milestone because the WTO went beyond simply recognising commercial objectives to incorporating the protection of food security, livelihood security, and rural development as criteria for the selection of SPs and indeed for all SDT. There is also agreement on the establishment of an SSM to counteract sudden price fluctuations or import surges (Hoda 2005, 3–; ICTSD 2005b, 42).

The G33 submitted more technically elaborated proposals just prior to the meeting of WTO ministers in Hong Kong in December 2005. At that meeting, the ministers agreed that developing countries were entitled to designate an appropriate number of tariff lines as SPs, guided by indicators based on the three criteria, and that the new SSM may be triggered by either import price or volume fluctuations. Since Hong Kong, the G33 has produced proposals that use the criteria to define and operationalise SPs and the SSM. In March 2007 the G33 presented a tighter list of a dozen indicators that countries agreed may guide their identification of products for protection under SPs and the SSM (ICTSD 2007).

There are both opposition and support from other WTO members. Some—the United States, the European Union, and the Cairns Group of agricultural exporting countries—have been obstructive, although EU opposition is less intense due to the fact that it is courting support for its position on the designation of sensitive products.[7] Among the objections advanced are that there should be agreement on overall tariff reduction formulae before exceptions are discussed, that SPs would reduce the benefits of market access openings, and that they would negatively affect South–South trade. One proposal was a time-limited SSM (rather than a permanent SP mechanism), or the application of SPs and an SSM to certain products only or to those covered by low tariffs. The U.S. proposed limiting SPs to just five tariff lines and wants to see the SSM eliminated by the end of the Doha implementation period. There is opposition to exempting SPs from tariff reductions. In the meantime, developed countries continually pressure developing

[7] The idea of sensitive products was introduced into negotiations in order to provide flexibility for sensitive agricultural sectors in the developed countries, protected behind tariff peaks. The EU and the Group of 10 (G10) countries are pressing for 8% and 10% of tariff lines respectively to be designated as sensitive products. Although there is no formal link between sensitive products and special products, there will likely be relationships made between them in negotiations on overall tariff reduction formulas.

countries to lower their tariffs on industrial products and to open their services markets.

The G20 and the Group of 10 (G10) have generally been supportive of the G33 proposals, as have the African Group, the Asia, Caribbean, and Pacific (ACP) countries, and the group of least-developed countries (LDCs). But in May 2006, the chair of the Committee on Agriculture (Crawford Falconer) issued a reference paper that effectively profiled the differences among developing countries, specifically between the G33 position and that of farm-product exporting countries seeking greater market access for their products (WTO 2006a). Some Latin American countries have suggested that exported products are not crucial for food security and that commercial products should be excluded from SPs. Chile, Costa Rica, Paraguay, Uruguay, Malaysia, and Thailand have reiterated their concern about the effects on South–South trade. Malaysia and Thailand have presented a more restricted view on the eligibility of products for SPs by excluding products in which developing countries are dominant in world trade.[8] Pakistan has attempted to play a bridging role between the G33 and Cairns Group members, so far with little success (ICTSD 2007). More controversial still, the reference paper contained figures, produced by the WTO Secretariat, calculated according to the G33's proposal that 'at least twenty percent' of developing country tariff lines be eligible for designation as SPs (3). The secretariat found that when applied to two unnamed countries, this 20% would allow these countries to shield as much as 98.4% and 94% respectively of the total value of their farm imports from Doha round tariff cuts (3). The chair concluded that this level of designation would effectively exclude developing countries from the obligation to cut tariffs, and therefore that this level of trade could hardly be described as 'special' (4). The level of exclusion, said the chair, would have to come down from 20 percent of tariff lines.

Such arguments shift the focus away from the importance of the three development objectives, and back to purely commercial considerations, away from a focus on the reduction of subsidies to food production (where the U.S. and EU are sensitive), and back to the quest for market access (the priority goals for the U.S. and EU). They have put the G33

[8] See South Centre (South Centre 2006, 13–19) for tables comparing the positions of major blocs of WTO member countries. As major exporters of rice and palm oil respectively, Thailand and Malaysia are fearful that designation of these products as SPs will restrict their export potential for these products.

under tremendous pressure to make further concessions in order to propel renewed negotiations in agriculture, to refine and prioritise their indicators for food security, livelihood security, and rural development, and to demonstrate that the application of these indicators is not an undue blockage to farm trade.

The World Bank added to the pressure with a paper attempting to show that the application of SPs will actually increase poverty in low-income countries (Ivanic and Martin 2006). Studies by the ICTSD and other organisations have found that 'while some countries have expressed concern that SP flexibilities will exempt a large percentage of agricultural trade from reform, available empirical evidence suggests that these fears are unfounded' (Bellmann et al. 2006, 7) and that if indicators for food security, livelihood security, and rural development are used to designate SPs, the amount of affected agricultural trade is significantly less than the WTO Secretariat estimate (7). WTO negotiations on these issues continue.

The G33 emerges from a bottom-up understanding among civil society actors—small-scale farmers, NGOs, academics—that economic liberalisation has been negative for food security and rural communities. Like the G20 (see Chapter 11), which came together in reaction to U.S. and EU proposals on domestic support and export subsidies going into Cancun, the G33 understood that these proposals could only exacerbate the difficulties of their farmers and rural communities. While G33 countries enjoy a broad base of popular support for their WTO proposals, the high level of expectation from their base allows them less flexibility in negotiations than that enjoyed by the G20, which was created and functions in a more top-down fashion.

G33 membership is diverse, including large countries, small island states, and LDCs. The group's coordinator is Indonesia, but leadership in pulling the group together and giving impetus to its thinking came also from the Philippines and India. Barbados, China, Cuba, the Dominican Republic, Jamaica, Honduras, Kenya, Turkey, and Venezuela are among the most active members. African members have become more frequent contributors of late. The G33 meets as a technical group (negotiators) or as heads of delegation (ambassadors), monthly or more frequently, depending on the intensity of negotiations.

There are different levels of commitment and different interests among the countries of the G33. Countries such as Sri Lanka and India are very serious about SPs and are willing to make compromises to obtain them. Others, having more room to move between their bound and applied tariffs, or those with less research capacity to generate the information required to substantiate which tariff lines need to be covered by SPs, make much more far-reaching demands. Pakistan plays a bridging role among the various positions at the WTO. As in any coalition, in seeking to attract and hold its membership the G33 has had to make allowances for these differences. For example, the group accommodated the demand by African countries for a 20% minimum coverage of tariff lines by SPs, even though other countries would likely have settled for 10% or 15%. Since the U.S. has put forth a position for just five tariff lines to be covered by SPs, there exists a considerable gap.

G33 positions have evolved significantly from the days of the development box. There has been movement from a large number of idealistic demands to a small number that have a more realistic chance of being accepted for WTO negotiation. The many demands of the development box have mostly been whittled down to the proposals on SPs and SSM. G33 positions on these items have also changed. For example, the G33 first said that SPs should be subject to no tariff reductions; now the proposal is that some SPs may undergo tariff reductions of up to 10%, others 5%, with a substantial proportion still at no reduction. At first the G33 maintained that the three criteria by themselves were sufficient guidance for countries to define their SPs, that is, that there should be no indicators to guide the definition of these criteria; now the G33 has advanced an illustrative list of indicators to help apply the criteria, and continues to refine and prioritise these indicators. Another G33 opening position was that a country could select as many SPs as it felt necessary; now its position has evolved to a stance that up to 20% of tariff lines may be covered by SPs. On SSM, the G33 has dropped its insistence on the application of quantitative restrictions to safeguard food production.

According to Indonesia, the coordinator of the G33, these shifts are more a reaction to demands advanced by opponents at the table than the result of particular research inputs. But as G33 positions have narrowed, research has played a greater role. More rigorous research, some from outside sources, has gone into producing the shorter list of indicators. Australia, Thailand, and the U.S. say that the list has not diminished their fears that SPs will signify reduced market access (ICTSD 2007). The G33 is confronting these pressures with the determination that SPs and SSM are essential to any new agreement on agriculture: 'The Group should not be expected to join any consensus on modalities or any elements thereof, which do not incorporate the modalities on SPs and SSM' (G33 2006, 2).

External Influences

Beyond the WTO, other influences have an impact on the policy shifts under study. Some of these influences can help the G33 make its case at the WTO, while at least one constitutes a further obstacle.

Influences that nurture the G33 perspective include a more contemporary perspective on food security and its relationship to livelihoods, and the pressure from civil society groups and regionally based groups within the G33 countries. Christopher Stevens (2004) notes a clash between the perspective on food security developed by food security analysts and developing countries on the one hand and, on the other, the outmoded perspective of WTO texts and many trade negotiators. The WTO seems stuck in a 'much narrower [notion of food security] relating only to availability of imported food' (3). Furthermore, what provisions exist in WTO texts to deal with food security are merely toothless 'best endeavours' addressing the national level only. Food security analysts and developing countries with food and livelihood security deficits see the problem through a much wider lens that encompasses 'the production, trade, labour and transfer routes to food security' and poverty. This leads them to address the interrelated concepts of food security, sustainable livelihood, and rural development, including the effects of trade rules on the sub-national and household levels. This community of analysts nourishes the broader food security perspective in the G33 initiative on SPs and SSM and the G33 endeavour to update WTO thinking.

Civil society in the G33 countries continues to be a driver pushing the G33 to obtain rules to advance the three development criteria. Examples of such organisations are the Federation of Free Farmers of the Philippines or Global Justice in Indonesia. Among the means they use to press their demands are papers containing policy recommendations, petitions, meetings with ministers, and newsletters based on research from Third World Network, ICTSD, the Institute for Agriculture and Trade Policy (IATP), and Oxfam International. This body of knowledge also allows them to cultivate an informed, activist constituency in their countries. Sometimes it is the NGOs that mobilise the grassroots groups of farmers and other sectors. In the Philippines, Indonesia, and Pakistan, civil society groups participate in a national multi-stakeholder committee or taskforce that influences the countries' trade policy and positions. One G33 negotiator (Barbados) mentioned that many of her colleagues understand the importance of SPs and SSM simply because they have had experience and contacts at the grassroots level and see the effect of trade policies on small-scale agriculture. G33 representatives have also mentioned the role of international organisations such as ActionAid, the Carnegie Endowment, and Oxfam International as active and supportive advocacy players on the issues of food and livelihood security and SP/SSM issues. Their work has increased public understanding of the G33's rationale and positions, and put a face on those who will benefit directly, that is, small-scale agricultural producers and rural families in developing countries.

In some countries, producer and political interests in specific regions are pressing for SP and SSM protection for products likely to be vulnerable to imports and surges of imports. Those interviewed for this study reported very little pressure on G33 positions coming from the business sector.

Certain precedent-setting provisions in bilateral or regional free trade agreements (FTAs) constitute one external influence considered an obstacle to the G33 initiative. Many FTAs include provisions on sensitive products and the need to safeguard them from the effects of import surges. But there are concerns that such clauses might limit the flexibilities currently being sought at the WTO, particularly with respect to the SSM. For example, the U.S. is seeking the same sort of limitation in the WTO that it has successfully incorporated into bilateral agreements: namely, that safeguards may only be used during an FTA's transition period. This means that once tariff liberalisation has occurred, the developing country partner has no further recourse to a safeguard protection against import surges. This limitation has implications at the WTO, at least for trade covered by such FTAs, which is considerable for some developing country signatories.

Given the context and contradictory trends sketched briefly here, it is evident that to be useful, NGOs need to provide research inputs to the G33 that help the coalition keep the focus on the development aspects of negotiations (as opposed to the commercial ones), that expand on the outmoded and incomplete conceptualisation of food security and rural development prevalent at the WTO, that respond to a range of stakeholders, and, most importantly, that successfully counter the opposition to SP/SSM from countries with greater research capacity and political weight.

Gathering Evidence and Building Links

This section looks at the research methodology of the G33 and the ICTSD, specifically the gathering of evidence and the building of links among researchers, policy makers, and stakeholders.

The G33 and Research

The G33 has never developed its own research capacity. Rather, it has focussed on the content and timing of negotiating positions, tactics, and public statements. When asked to describe its policy-making process, the G33 coordinator cited the example of the way the G33 developed its indicators for the three development criteria. The G33 Technical Group held brainstorming seminars with the Food and Agriculture Organization (FAO), the South Centre, and ICTSD, using the FAO's (unpublished) list of indicators as a starting point. Member countries were asked to submit other indicators of importance to them. From these consultations emerged a list of 24 indicators upon which the Technical Group built its proposal, which it submitted first to the heads of delegation meeting, and then to the capitals. Finally, the delegation heads met to assess reactions from their capitals and to approve the proposal by consensus.

According to the coordinator, research plays a role at two points in this process: in the brainstorming sessions with the outside entities and in the process used by member countries to formulate the positions they bring to the coalition. Because coalition positions are based on member proposals, and not on those of outside entities, the coalition relies largely on research provided by its member countries. The Philippines, Indonesia, India, China, Jamaica, and Turkey play a major role here. The research by sources outside the G33, such as the FAO, the South Centre, ICTSD, Oxfam International, ActionAid, the Catholic Agency for Overseas Development (CAFOD), and a few academics, exerts its influence primarily on the thinking of member countries, rather than on the G33 directly.[9] Countries also occasionally ask the coordinator of the Technical Group to request research support from an outside source if the information is unavailable through the

---

[9] Many of these papers, as well as papers and statements from the G33 itself and ICTSD-commissioned research, are available at the ICTSD-run internet portal Agtradepolicy.org <www.agtradepolicy.org/page/resource/marketaccess.htm#safe>.

countries themselves. The South Centre, an intergovernmental organisation, appears to have a special role in that its comments are sought on concept development, negotiating positions, and document drafts. G33 representatives expressed appreciation also for FAO research on import surges and the SSM and for Oxfam's work in disseminating the G33 position and building public awareness.

On a day-to-day basis G33 negotiators in Geneva have the ability to do some research and formulation of positions, but they may turn to outside institutions and researchers for help with specific technical questions or to reinforce their confidence in the strength of their formulations. For example, ICTSD was asked to help the G33 build the concept of how to operationalise the three development criteria through the use of indicators. And when they set out to reduce the indicators from 24 to 18, G33 negotiators sought assistance from other research institutions in Geneva to validate their thinking.

Research Related to the International Centre for Trade and Sustainable Development

ICTSD is a Geneva-based NGO set up in 1996 by five founding NGOs 'to contribute to a better understanding of development and environment concerns in the context of international trade' (ICTSD 2006). It has provided research and analysis to assist certain G33 countries in substantiating their positions within the G33 coalition and at the WTO. These countries have had an influence on the positions taken by the G33.

ICTSD realises that the activity of researching and the research itself—which is its primary role—is insufficient to assure the uptake of that research by policy makers and stakeholders. Good research methodology involves building links among researchers, policy makers, and stakeholders. ICTSD plays what it calls the 'role of knowledge broker', a connector among these groups that identifies the required expertise, shepherds the research methodology that has been decided upon, makes sure that the research is adequate to policy maker and stakeholder needs, and facilitates a dialogue among the groups. The ICTSD role is not to influence the outcome of policy discussions directly. That, it says, is the job of the policy makers.

It was the experience with the issue of SP/SSM that ICTSD says helped it define its four-stage policy facilitation approach. The approach consists in identifying the knowledge gaps and 'policy windows', consulting with experts and country negotiators in Geneva to develop a research methodology, field testing the methodology in-country with local researchers and national stakeholders, and disseminating the findings of the national process. G33 countries use the findings to support their policy proposals.

Identification of the Knowledge Gaps and Policy Windows

ICTSD's entry point in working with some of the G33 countries was provided by the July framework of 1 August 2004. A policy window had opened. ICTSD saw the moment as a rare and 'strategic opportunity to inject public policy concerns into the WTO negotiations' (ICTSD 2005a, 6). Negotiating SPs and the SSM based on self-designation using indicators relating to the three development criteria suddenly seemed a realistic possibility. In response to representatives of some of the G33 countries, ICTSD recognised this as an opportunity to contribute, and—as acknowledged by G33 negotiators in interviews—to help define the type of analysis and information that was needed to make a case for SPs and SSM.

Consultations to Develop a Research Methodology

Accepting the invitation of key G33 members, in July 2004 ICTSD began consultations with many actors to set out a research methodology. A group of experts and some G33 negotiators convened in September 2004 for a first meeting, organised by ICTSD and the FAO, to discuss this methodology and how it could be presented in the WTO context. The results were then brought to a broader meeting of G33 negotiators. It became clear that the optimum point for intervention was at the national level, by guiding countries through a national, multi-stakeholder discussion on how to define their lists of SPs. It was decided that this definitional process could best be facilitated by determining indicators for food security, livelihood security, and rural development that would be meaningful to the situation of the rural poor and food insecure. Luisa Bernal (2004) of the South Centre was asked to write a first orienting paper on a methodology for designating SPs and SSM products according to these parameters.

ICTSD considers that these two meetings helped the G33 and the experts to get a clear grasp on how the discussion on SP/SSM could evolve to their benefit at the WTO, and how to move the issue forward in the negotiations—in other words, to establish a strategic path and a research methodology looking one or two years ahead. Once this

Table 10–1: Expert Studies on Special Products and the Special Safeguard Mechanism

- Special Products and the Special Safeguard Mechanism: An Introduction to the Debate and Key Issues in the Context of WTO Agricultural Negotiations (International Centre for Trade and Sustainable Development 2004)
- Guidelines for Approaching the Designation of Special Products and SSM Products in Developing Countries (Luisa Bernal, 2004)
- The Need for Special Products and Special Safeguard Mechanisms for Agriculture in the WTO: A Situational Analysis (Christopher Stevens, 2004)
- The New SSM: A Price Floor Mechanism for Developing Countries (Alberto Valdés and William Foster, 2005)
- Tariff Reduction, Special Products, and Special Safeguards: An Analysis of the Agricultural Tariff Structures of G33 Countries (Mario Jales, 2005)
- Special Products: Options for Negotiating Modalities (Anwarul Hoda, 2005)
- Methodology for the Identification of Special Products (SP) and Products for Eligibility Under Special Safeguard Mechanism for Developing Countries (Luisa Bernal, 2005)
- Lessons from the Experience with Special Products and Safeguard Mechanisms in Bilateral Trade Agreements (Carlos Pomareda, 2005)

pathway was visualised, it was easier to come up with the research methodology. Because negotiators were involved early on in the process of building a strategy to advance the discussion of SP/SSM in WTO negotiations, according to one negotiator, a feeling of ownership of the process developed.

On the basis of this understanding, and the commitment to supporting a domestic-level process in countries, ICTSD contracted a group of thinkers in 2005 to produce five more studies to help flesh out the strategy (see Table 10–1). Using these inputs, ICTSD developed 'a conceptual framework for how developing country Members of the WTO could operationalise the SP/SSM concepts in order to promote sustainable development' (ICTSD 2005b, x).

The framework is a methodology whereby individual developing countries use indicators for food security, livelihood security, and rural development at the national level to involve all relevant stakeholders in a conversation to identify where import vulnerabilities lie and which products should be protected by SPs and the SSM (ICTSD 2005b, xvi). This process is framed within a country's broader national strategy for agricultural development and poverty alleviation. The indicators are used to identify the intended beneficiaries of SP/SSM flexibilities. The methodology provides guidelines for assessing the potential direct and indirect impacts of further liberalisation of the selected products on the economy and on specific populations. According to ICTSD, it gives countries a tool to formulate their positions at WTO negotiations, based on the effects on real people at local and sub-national levels.

In-Country Field Testing and Application of the Methodology

Once the framework was formulated, ICTSD engaged negotiators and ambassadors of leading G33 countries to determine where the framework could be field tested. Six G33 countries—Barbados, Honduras, Kenya, Pakistan, Peru, and Sri Lanka—were selected, based on criteria of geography, food security status (for example, food-importing country, low-income food deficit country), local research capacity, and government support for the process. Local researchers were selected on the basis of advice from G33 officials. According to ICTSD observers, these consultations and the researchers' visits to Geneva to become familiar with the WTO and SP/SSM debates enhanced the G33 confidence in the research process. Some of the researchers were even included in national delegations to the WTO.[10]

ICTSD then worked with national governments and local researchers to apply the research methodology in the field test studies. Research methods were combined with national dialogues that served to build links among and involve the local researchers, officials in capitals, and local stakeholder groups from the private sector, academia, and civil society organisations. These latter had played a key role in propelling the issues of food security, livelihood security, and rural development onto the national and international agenda in the first place. They are the intended future beneficiaries of trade rules that include both SPs and the SSM. The dialogues allowed these groups to be heard. They strengthened the evidential base and relevance of the research, according to participants.

ICTSD sees another benefit from the multi-stakeholder dialogues at the national level. The research methodology is useful for identifying the special products that a country may put forward at the WTO, but it does not include a way of giving priority weightings to the products that are chosen—which depends on the idiosyncrasies of each country's political or socioeconomic situation. The dialogues were able to accomplish

[10] For a list of the 2005 studies, see ICTSD (2005b, 65).

this ranking such that countries would know which products to put at the top of their list, and which to put further down. According to ICTSD, this is extremely useful information for participating country negotiators in Geneva.

Dissemination of the Findings

The G33 has kept the country studies confidential because they form the basis for country lists of SPs at WTO negotiations. ICTSD (2005b) produced a summary document entitled *Strategic Options for Developing Countries*, which captures some of the lessons of the country studies, refines the methodology, and expands the non-exhaustive list of possible indicators for the selection of SPs and products for SSM protection. In November and December 2005, ICTSD convened several consultations to discuss the findings with the G33 and other developing country groupings. These meetings also involved developed country representatives and non-state actors. Finally, ICTSD used its publication *Bridges* to disseminate the findings (for example, see Bellmann 2006). One of the G33 representatives consulted for this chapter observed that these publications and forums aided in building relationships between the NGO and G33 negotiators.

The country studies were also found to be useful. A second group of five countries undertook them in 2006: Ecuador, Fiji Islands, Papua New Guinea, the Philippines, Vietnam (however, only the Philippines is a member of the G33). A third group, which included China, the Eastern Caribbean states, Indonesia, Mali, Tanzania, Uganda, and Nigeria, followed in 2007.

The primary research objective of all of these studies is to contribute to the internal discussion at national level, as defined in the conceptual framework, in order to assist participating countries in identifying their lists for SPs and SSM protection for use in WTO negotiations. The extent to which the studies have been effective in influencing domestic policy will only be measurable at the end of negotiations, when participating countries will present their lists of SPs to be included in their national schedule of commitments. But there have also been several important by-products of the national-level research process:

- The G33 picked up on the indicators elaborated through these studies for members' submissions to the WTO.
- Some of the findings of the country studies have proved useful as input to defend G33 positions at the WTO. An example is the infor-

mation used to refute the above-mentioned assertions of the chair of the Committee on Agriculture that the G33 proposal for a minimum 20% coverage of developing country tariff lines by SPs would result in excessive protectionism.
- The locally engaged researchers, ministry officials, and civil society participants improved their research skills and their conceptual and data analysis abilities in the area of trade policy. Some of the researchers have gone on to do other work using these new capacities (for example, the author of the Barbados study became that country's negotiator on agriculture at the WTO).

Feedback from G33 Representatives

G33 representatives interviewed for this chapter were asked for their comments on the ICTSD approach and research. These are some of their more pertinent observations:

- ICTSD 'plays an important role in developing a methodology that can help developing countries designate special products based on the indicators', said the coordinator of the G33 Technical Group (Indonesia), '...particularly [for] small countries without technical capacity'. The research methodology and research parameters are valuable because they provide a way of developing policy that is useable in WTO negotiations, said another representative (Pakistan).
- The process of involving local actors and stakeholders and stimulating exchange between them and policy makers was commended by another representative (Barbados). This research enjoys greater acceptance because it is produced locally, based on local experience, as opposed to research that is produced by outside consultants. These factors enhance the buy-in and ownership of the process, and the likelihood that research results will be used 'all the way up the chain'.
- Research on SP/SSM carried out by ICTSD or with ICTSD help is useful in helping developing countries determine if they need to designate SPs, and how many, since many countries do not have the research capacity to generate proposals on their own (Pakistan).
- The research has been useful in defining indicators that can actually be used by countries in spite of a lack of data-gathering capacities, and has helped create greater public awareness of the SP/SSM issue (Indonesia).

• ICTSD research papers were a valuable source not only for individual countries but also for the G33 coalition's proposals and statements on indicators. This has enhanced the credibility of the coalition on the SP/SSM issue. Those countries where ICTSD country studies are carried out are better prepared to discuss and lead the discussion on indicators within the coalition (Barbados).

These statements from G33 representatives support the notion that ICTSD research has had an influence on G33 and WTO policy.

The Evidence: Uptake by Policy Makers

In light of these testimonies, it is now possible to examine in more detail to what degree the research, whether by ICTSD or other sources, has been taken up in building a consensus on the meaning of SPs and the SSM within the G33 coalition, and to what degree this research is reflected in the deliberations and decisions of the WTO (where consensus has not yet been reached). Consensus building is not a one-time event, but a process—sometimes repeated several times as policy evolves. Research is one source of the meaning of SP/SSM, to the degree that it is assimilated or taken up by policy makers. But as the G33 negotiators who were consulted cautioned, research is only one of many factors in any given decision-making process. Tactical, strategic, and political factors also play a very large role. These may lead to decisions not indicated by research results. It is therefore not advisable to speak of direct causal relationships between given pieces of research and certain policy statements. 'Correlation' is an inadequate term for describing the relationship. The term 'influence' is used here instead, being stronger than 'correlation' but not implying causality.[11]

It is also worth remembering that the primary purpose of ICTSD's research on SP/SSM was to feed policy processes at the national level by helping selected countries establish their lists of SPs and defend their interests at WTO negotiations on this basis. Thus the most important effect of the research can most likely be assessed only once the Doha round has concluded, when developing countries will have presented their SP-SSM lists and the results of the negotiations will be known.

---

[11] *Collins English Dictionary* defines correlation as 'a mutual relationship between two or more things'. For 'influence', it says 'an effect of one person or thing on another'.

This question of uptake can be approached by relating it to the G33's goals and dynamics. The hypothesis to be tested posits that coalitions use research for two purposes, external and internal, both having the objective of building consensus during the process of negotiation. This hypothesis turns out to be only partially valid.

External Purpose

Coalitions can use research to facilitate negotiations with outside parties for two purposes: setting the policy agenda and legitimising their policy positions.

Agenda setting refers to the coalition's capacity to bring previously neglected policy issues to the attention of policy makers, in order to ensure that these issues will receive serious consideration and to generate significant public exposure on them.

This chapter considers two agenda-setting moments: the insertion of SP/SSM on the agenda of the countries forming the G33 coalition and the G33's insertion of SP/SSM on the WTO negotiating agenda. Were these insertions in some way fed by the research provided by ICTSD or other sources?

Given the timing, it is unlikely that ICTSD research influenced the G33's determination to focus attention on SP/SSM. ICTSD began producing research on this issue only in mid 2004, with a paper reviewing the debate surrounding SP/SSM to that time (see ICTSD 2004). The G33—at that time still referred to as the Alliance for SP and SSM—had already set its agenda on SP/SSM in July 2003. This group of countries may have been influenced by the research of other groups, such as the FAO and Oxford Policy Management (2003a; FAO 2003b; Hathaway 2001; Ruffer 2003; Ruffer and Vergano 2002).

Similarly, it is unlikely that ICTSD research influenced the WTO decision to put SP/SSM on its negotiating agenda. Developing countries began raising these concepts at the Committee on Agriculture as far back as 2002, with the first reference in the chair's report in December of that year. On 1 August 2004, at the General Council, all WTO members decided to include SP/SSM in the July framework for negotiations. Ministers of trade confirmed this decision in December 2005 at the Hong Kong ministerial. For the G33, the July framework indicated its success in getting SP/SSM onto the WTO agenda. The G33 coordinator stated in an interview that this was a political rather than a technical decision, meaning that research inputs played little role in it. ICTSD officials do not believe its mid-2004 review paper had any influence on the July framework.

With regard to research as a way to legitimise positions, once the policy issue has found a place on the agenda, it must be supported and defended vigorously with evidence-based arguments in order that a policy consensus may be achieved. Influential coalitions must have the resources to create, exchange, and disseminate knowledge within and outside their own networks, through meetings, conferences, publications, workshops, and websites. The knowledge is used to win new adherents to the desired policy position.[12]

Even if it is impossible to know what elements from the ICTSD studies will emerge in an eventual agreement on agriculture or in country schedules of products designated as SPs or for the SSM (because Doha talks have not concluded), it is nonetheless possible to trace the influence of ICTSD research in publicly available G33 and WTO documents, backed up by testimonies of the G33 and ICTSD interviewees. Five examples of this influence are offered herein.

The first three examples emerge from an analysis of ICTSD research in relation to key G33 proposals and statements legitimising their position and reflecting their internal consensus, as well as relevant WTO pronouncements and reports by ministers, the General Council, or the chair of the Committee on Agriculture during the 29 months from the decision of 1 August 2004 to the end of 2006 (see Table 10–2). The G33 coordinator (Indonesia) indicated that he took pains to make sure that all countries receive the research produced from all sources, including ICTSD. His opinion is that research is most influential in determining individual country positions and therefore what certain countries bring to the G33 table, and that it is country positions that form the basis for coalition discussion.

First, certain similarities are observable between Bernal (2004) and the G33 proposal on SP and SSM to the Committee on Agriculture on 3 June 2005 in the analysis of food security and in building the case for flexibility in the selection and use of SPs (G33 2005d). In synthesis, both refer to the need to define food security not only at the level of a country as a whole but also in relation to access to food by individual households, vulnerable population groups, and specific regions in each

[12] 'The chances of [the policy issues] surviving in the political stream depend upon the "technical feasibility and value acceptability" of the solution' (Mably 2006, 9).

Table 10–2: Relevant Documents, August 2004 to December 2006

G33 Proposals to the World Trade Organization
- G33 Proposal to Committee on Agriculture on Special Products and the Special Safeguard Mechanism, 3 June 2005
- G33 Proposal on the Special Safeguard Mechanism, October 2005
- G33 Proposal on the Modalities for the Designation and Treatment of any Agricultural Product as a Special Product by any Developing Country Member, 22 November 2005
- G33 Revised Proposal on the Special Safeguard Mechanism, 23 March 2006

G33 Statements
- G33 Ministerial Communiqué, Jakarta, 12 June 2005
- G33 Ministerial Statement, 11 October 2005
- G33 Press Statement, 20 April 2006
- Statement by the Delegation of the Philippines [to the Committee on Agriculture] on Special Products, 1 May 2006
- G33, the African Group, the Africa, Caribbean and Pacific Countries, and Least-Developed Countries Joint Communication on Special Products and the Special Safeguard Mechanism, 11 May 2006
- G33 Response to the World Bank Publication Dated 10 September 2006, 1 December 2006

World Trade Organization Documents
- Decision Adopted by the General Council on 1 August 2004 (July Framework), Annex A, Framework for Establishing Modalities in Agriculture, paragraphs 41 and 42
- Ministerial Declaration, Hong Kong, 18 December 18, 2005, paragraph 7
- Draft Possible Modalities on Agriculture, Chair Crawford Falconer, Committee of Agriculture, 12 July 2006, paragraphs 21–28 and Annex D on Special Products, and paragraphs 29–30 and Annex E on the Special Safeguard Mechanism

Studies Organized by the International Centre for Trade and Sustainable Development
- Eight expert studies on special products and the special safeguard mechanism, 2004 and 2005
- Special Products and Special Safeguard Mechanism: Strategic Options for Developing Countries, December 2005
- 11 country studies from 2005 and 2006 (unavailable to the public)

country, and the livelihood strategies of all these populations. Different groups will be affected by liberalisation differently, depending on their circumstances. Selection of SPs also must take into account the domestic context and circumstances of each country. Therefore no single indicator will succeed in capturing this diversity, nor will a common set of indicators be effective for all developing countries. Both documents also list several of the same indicators, such as the contribution of a given product to the country's gross domestic product (GDP) and employment, or its contribution to the diet of the poor and other vulnerable groups. Both argue that SPs should have access to the SSM as well.

The G33 (2005a) ministerial statement issued in Jakarta on 12 June 2005 goes into much less detail than the proposal of 5 June, but it does reiterate some ideas from both the proposal and the Bernal (2004) paper: 'Ministers emphasized that the complex nature of these concepts does not render feasible the establishment of a universal criteria [*sic*] for SPs. They strongly stressed that the selection and designation of an appropriate number of SPs must be made with a full appreciation of the domestic policy context and circumstances of individual developing countries concerned [and] be supportive of the overall development policy established by the said Member' (2). SPs should have 'guaranteed access to the SSM' (2).

It is the opinion of two country officials (Indonesia and Barbados) that there is a link between the Bernal 2004 research piece and these two G33 documents. Bernal's work would have been taken into consideration by one or more G33 countries, and been a factor in the fashioning of the G33 proposal and ministerial statement.

Second, at a later stage, one can observe many parallels between the lists of indicators for the three criteria, moving from the ICTSD studies by Anwarul Hoda (2005) and Luisa Bernal (2005) to the G33 Proposal on the Modalities for the Designation and Treatment of Any Agricultural Product as a Special Product (SP) by any Developing Country Member, dated 22 November 2005 (G33 2005e), and then to the Draft Possible Modalities on Agriculture, dated 12 July 2006, put forward by the Committee on Agriculture chair Crawford Falconer (WTO 2006b).[13]

[13] See Mably (2007, Appendix 2) for a comparative look at the indicators presented in the four documents.

The G33 appears to have built upon Hoda's half dozen indicators and a more elaborate set of some two dozen by Bernal to produce a similar number of fleshed-out indicators for consideration by ministers at the 2005 Hong Kong ministerial. Falconer includes the G33 list word for word in his draft, submitted just prior to the breakdown in WTO negotiations in July 2006.

There is not a one-to-one correspondence between the Bernal and G33 lists, however. Some of Bernal's suggestions were not taken up by the G33. The G33 in turn sometimes combines two ideas present in the Bernal list into a single indicator, or makes the indicator more specific and detailed. The group also includes many indicators that do not appear in the Hoda or Bernal lists.

Again, two of the G33 negotiators consulted in this study (Indonesia and Barbados) acknowledged the influence of these ICTSD papers on the thinking of certain G33 members with which ICTSD had been working. The G33 coordinator asked member countries to submit their ideas for indicators to the G33 Technical Group. The group's discussion to decide on the G33 list of indicators was based on these country submissions and did not refer to specific research pieces, according to the coordinator.

But ICTSD confirms that several of the countries are using indicators from its papers in their country-level studies. And according to the Barbados negotiator, most of the indicators used in the Barbados country study were included in those proposed by the G33 (sometimes with minor amendments). The indicators used in the other five country studies done in 2005 overlap considerably with those finally proposed by the G33.

It seems reasonable therefore to conclude that these six countries, and probably others, relied on ICTSD and other research when they made their submissions to the Technical Group, and for the suggestions and amendments they made at G33 meetings where the coalition's list of indicators was decided. Thus it can be said that the G33 proposal and the Falconer document to some extent reflect ICTSD research. The Barbados negotiator affirms that 'the G33 papers on indicators incorporate some of the indicators that appear in ICTSD's earlier papers'. Furthermore, 'the countries that had these [ICTSD] studies done were in a better position to lead the group in [the discussion on] indicators'.

Third, the statement on SPs by the delegation of the Philippines (2006), dated 29 April 2006, refers directly to ICTSD research on indicators, saying that ICTSD has 'undertaken objective and thorough analysis on possible methodologies of arriving at appropriate indicators, and they have arrived at the same conclusion as those of the G33' (para. 7). The statement mentions that research by the FAO and the Carnegie Endowment also corroborated the G33 position.

Paragraphs 2, 5, 8, and 10 of the Philippines statement appear to reiterate the arguments contained in *Strategic Options for Developing Countries*, the ICTSD December 2005 (45–46), for self-designation of SPs on the basis of an illustrative list of indicators, as opposed to a narrow set of indicators with set thresholds as proposed by some WTO members. According to the Philippines statement (2006, para. 10), a narrow set of indicators 'would fail to capture the size and diversity of agriculture sector in these countries'. An illustrative list 'would allow WTO Members to maintain the necessary flexibility to set their own thresholds and critical levels for each indicator' (ICTSD 2005b, 46). One G33 representative (Indonesia) confirms that the ICTSD paper was used to sustain the coalition argumentation against the use of set thresholds in the application of SPs.

Fourth, another example of the influence of ICTSD research on G33 documents emerged in the course of interviews with G33 negotiators. According to the representative from Barbados, FAO and ICTSD research on the SSM was instrumental in the G33's (2005c) decision to include both volume and price triggers in its SSM proposal to the WTO. Not all delegations were certain that the two triggers were required. These documents also helped the G33 legitimate the dual-trigger position among sceptical WTO members outside the coalition. The Indonesia negotiator recalled using South Centre research on the SSM to prepare the G33 arguments supporting both price and volume triggers for the Hong Kong ministerial in December 2005 (FAO 2003a; 2003b; 2005; ICTSD 2005b; Sharma 2006; South Centre 2003; Valdés and Foster 2005).

Fifth, there is the example of a document presented by Pakistan (2007) to the Committee on Agriculture in January 2007, along with a follow-up proposal in March (ICTSD 2007). These are both attempts by Pakistan to present a compromise on the selection and treatment of SPs, given the deadlock in negotiations between developing and developed countries. According to the ICTSD person interviewed, the January document uses elements from the Pakistan country-level study carried out with ICTSD in 2005 (not publicly available). For example, a table that demonstrates the relevance and application of the indicators

Pakistan proposes has been lifted straight from the country study. While this example does not show a direct influence of ICTSD research on consensus policy decisions at the G33 or the WTO, it does demonstrate in this instance at least that ICTSD research is used by national policy makers and has informed national policy and negotiating positions.

These five examples build a reasonable case that ICTSD research has assisted some G33 members in legitimising their positions in the coalition and at the WTO.

Internal Purpose

Research can be used—explicitly or covertly—to facilitate consensus building within a coalition and thereby cement its membership base. Coalitions can generate and apply research to influence internal coalition politics in two ways: by using research as a good to attract members to the coalition and by using research to prevent members from defecting.

First, with regard to attracting members to the coalition, at least some of the research that coalitions conduct may be regarded as a good; if countries do not invest in becoming members, they can be denied the benefit of shared research and representation in WTO meetings. This creates an incentive for countries to become members of the coalition and continue their allegiance to it.

Representatives consulted for this study could see no basis for thinking that research not publicly available (such as the ICTSD's country studies) either attracted new members to the coalition or prevented their defection. Rather, the G33 representatives consulted mentioned that countries tend to join the coalition because of their commitment to the issues of SPs and SSM and for political reasons, such as in order to gain from the greater clout of a coalition vis-à-vis some of the more powerful WTO players.

Second, with regard to research as a way to prevent defection, a coalition may expand its agenda or its position on an issue as a way to incorporate the concerns of smaller countries, based on research carried out by or made possible by a think tank or NGO. The technical character of WTO negotiations renders any such research assistance invaluable for smaller members.

Again, country representatives did not see the availability of research as a motivating factor for either joining or remaining in the coalition. Although the G33 has modified its stance to achieve consensus and accommodate the concerns of certain members (for example, regarding the Africa Group position that 20% of tariff lines should be covered by SPs), there is no evidence that outside research played a role in this accommodation. Tactical and strategic considerations play a much bigger role.

Given the response of those interviewed, the hypothesis on the role of outside research in internal coalition cohesion is a failed hypothesis at least with regard to the two policy episodes under discussion.

Conclusion

The G33 relies primarily on research produced by key member countries (e.g., India, Indonesia, Philippines), the FAO (a multilateral institution), the South Centre (an intergovernmental institution), and a handful of NGOs. Following on previous work, this chapter is interested particularly in the NGO role, specifically that of ICTSD. It focusses on ICTSD's contribution to two related policy changes: the generation of a consensus among G33 countries and, at the WTO, on SPs and SSM. Several conclusions can be drawn from this examination.

Research has played a positive and essential role in the drive of G33 countries to ensure their food security, livelihood security, and rural development through new WTO rules on SPs and SSM. Research has helped G33 members give increased meaning and applicability to the three development criteria and the two WTO mechanisms, within their own countries, within the G33, and with regard to other members of the WTO. As G33 positions have focussed and narrowed, research has played a greater role. It has aided the coalition in making broad development concepts usable for trade negotiations. All those interviewed concurred on this aspect of the value of research and believe that the G33 and its proposals are now taken more seriously by their negotiation opponents.

The success of the country studies has shown that ICTSD did indeed identify and fill a gap in research capacity that was available neither within G33 countries nor at the level of the coalition. G33 negotiators have vouched for the usefulness of this research and it has shown up in some countries' trade policy.

However, ICTSD research does not appear to have played a role in the effort to put SP/SSM on the agenda of either the G33 or the WTO, since these events occurred prior to ICTSD involvement.

Nor is it instrumental in attracting or retaining members of the G33 coalition.

Yet both ICTSD's research and its approach and methodology have nonetheless influenced two policy change episodes by helping countries legitimise the SP and SSM concepts and strengthen their positions. Country representatives involved in or informed by the country-level studies have brought to the coalition and the WTO elements that originated in that research, according to an examination of documents and interviews with G33 negotiators.

ICTSD research methods have facilitated a sense of ownership by countries of the research and research products at the national level, and their ability to take the results of this research forward to the G33 with greater confidence. Through research, countries understand their own situations better and therefore negotiate from a more informed position. Countries understand that indicators for which supporting data are available have more credibility. Better-documented positions have, in turn, lent policy makers in agriculture a higher level of credibility at the local level and in policy circles, at the G33, at the WTO, and with the public.

Furthermore, the ICTSD approach addresses one of the difficult problems for NGOs: how to link the reality of poor people on the ground with the reality of WTO negotiations and how to connect the material conditions of small-scale farmers and consumers with the abstract language of trade agreements. NGOs are under pressure from their funders on this point, and the G33 is under pressure from its political constituency to produce results for food security, livelihood security, and rural development. It is too early to see results in terms of new trade law, but ICTSD work appears to have successfully established an identifiable link between grassroots concerns and international trade policy.

References

Bellmann, Christophe, Constantine Bartel, and Jonathan Hepburn. 2006. 'Special Products in Agriculture: Some Empirical Evidence.' *Bridges* 10(3):5–7. <www.ictsd.org/monthly/bridges/BRIDGES10-3.pdf> [Accessed: December 2007].

Bernal, Luisa E. 2004. "Guidelines for Approaching the Designation of Special Products and SSM Products in Developing Countries." Paper presented for International Centre for Trade and Sustainable Development informal consultation on 'Special Products and Special Safeguard Mechanism after the July Framework: How Do

We Move Forward?' Geneva, 30 September. <www.agtradepolicy.org/output/ictsd/dialogues/2004-09-30/Bernal_paper.pdf> [Accessed: December 2007].

——. 2005. *Methodology for the Identification of Special Products (SP) and Products for Eligibility under the Special Safeguard Mechanism (SSM) by Developing Countries.* Geneva: International Centre for Trade and Sustainable Development. <www.agtradepolicy.org/output/resource/2005-L.Bernal.pdf> [Accessed: December 2007].

Bustami, Gusmardi. 2006. *Letter to World Bank President Paul Wolfowitz from the Ambassador to the WTO of the Republic of Indonesia.* 2 October.

Food and Agriculture Organization. 2003a. 'Fact Sheet: The Need for Special Safeguards for Developing Countries.' Rome. <www.fao.org/docrep/005/y4852e/y4852e05.htm> [Accessed: December 2007].

——. 2003b. 'Some Trade Policy Issues Relating to Trends in Agricultural Imports in the Context of Food Security.' 18–21 March. Rome. <www.fao.org/docrep/MEETING/005/Y8319e/Y8319e00.HTM> [Accessed: December 2007].

——. 2005. *No. 9: A Special Safeguard Mechanism for Developing Countries.* FAO Trade Policy Technical Notes on Issues Related to the WTO Negotiations on Agriculture. Rome. <ftp.fao.org/docrep/fao/008/j5425e/j5425e00.pdf> [Accessed: December 2007].

G33. 2005a. *G33 Ministerial Communiqué.* 12 June. Jakarta. <www.crnm.org/documents/press_releases_2005/Adopted%20Communique-12June05.pdf> [Accessed: December 2007].

——. 2005b. 'G33 Press Statement.' 11 October. Geneva. <www.agtradepolicy.org/output/resource/G33StatementOct05.pdf> [Accessed: December 2007].

——. 2005c. *G33 Proposal on Article [...] Special Safeguard Mechanism for Developing Countries.* October. <www.ictsd.org/ministerial/hongkong/docs/G33_Proposal_on_SSM_final1.pdf> [Accessed: December 2007].

——. 2005d. *G33 Proposal on Spacial Safeguard Measures.* JOB(05)/92, 3 June. Geneva.

——. 2005e. *G33 Proposal on the Modalities for the Designation and Treatment of Any Agricultural Product as a Special Product (SP) by Any Developing Country Member.* JOB(05)/304, 22 November. Geneva. <www.agtradepolicy.org/output/resource/G33_proposal_SPs_22Nov05.pdf> [Accessed: December 2007].

——. 2006. 'G33 Press Statement.' 20 April. Geneva. <www.tradeobservatory.org/library.cfm?refID=80711> [Accessed: December 2007].

Hathaway, Dale. 2001. 'A Special Agricultural Safeguard (SAS): Buttressing the Market Access Reforms of Developing Countries.' 21 March. Rome. <www.fao.org/docrep/005/Y3733E/y3733e05.htm> [Accessed: December 2007].

Hoda, Anwarul. 2005. *Special Products: Options for Negotiating Modalities.* Geneva: International Centre for Trade and Sustainable Development. <www.ictsd.org/dlogue/2005-06-16/Hoda.pdf> [Accessed: December 2007].

International Centre for Trade and Sustainable Development. 2004. *Special Products and the Special Safeguard Mechanism: An Introduction to the Debate and Key Issues in the Context of WTO Agricultural Negotiations.* ICTSD Background Paper. Geneva. <www.agtradepolicy.org/output/ictsd/dialogues/2004-09-30/ICTSD_paper.pdf> [Accessed: December 2007].

——. 2005a. *Special Products and the Special Safeguard Mechanism: Strategic Options for Developing Countries.* Geneva. <www.ictsd.org/dlogue/2005-11-25/SPs%20and%20the%20SSM%20Strategic%20Options%20Paper.pdf> [Accessed: December 2007].

——. 2005b. *Strategic Options for Developing Countries.* Issue Paper No. 6, December. Geneva. <www.agtradepolicy.org/output/ictsd/dialogues/2006-04-01/SP-SSM.pdf> [Accessed: December 2007].

——. 2006. 'Welcome to ICTSD.' Geneva. <www.ictsd.org/about> [Accessed: December 2007].

——. 2007. 'Ag Talks Set to Pick Up as Negotiators Await Falconer's "Hard-Talk" Questions.' *Bridges* 11(13). <www.ictsd.org/weekly/07-04-18/story2.htm> [Accessed: December 2007].

Ivanic, Maros, and Will Martin. 2006. *Potential Implications of Agricultural Special Products for Poverty in Low-Income Countries.* Draft of 16 October. Minneapolis: Institute for Agriculture and Trade Policy. <www.tradeobservatory.org/library.cfm?refID=89834> [Accessed: December 2007].

Jales, Mario. 2005. *Tariff Reduction, Special Products, and Special Safeguards: An Analysis of the Agricultural Tariffs Structures of G33 Countries.* July. Geneva: International Centre for Trade and Sustainable Development. <www.agtradepolicy.org/output/resource/Jalesfinal.pdf> [Accessed: December 2007].

Mably, Paul. 2006. *Evidence Based Advocacy: NGO Research Capacities and Policy Influence in the Field of International Trade.* IDRC Working Papers on Globalization, Growth, and Poverty No. 4. Ottawa: International Development Research Centre. <www.idrc.ca/uploads/user-S/11727031851GGPWP4-NGO.pdf> [Accessed: December 2007].

——. 2007. *The Role of Research on Trade Policy Changes Affecting the Developing World: Group of 33 Influence at the World Trade Organization.* Working Paper No. 77. Buenos Aires: Facultad Latinoamericana de Ciencias Sociales. <www.latn.org.ar/archivos/documentacion/PAPER_DOC77%20WP_%20Mably_%20G33-ICTSD%20trade%20policy%20change%20episodes%20study.pdf> (January 2008).

Mamaty, Isabelle. 2003. "Study on the Strategic Products for African Countries." November. African Union.

Pakistan, Delegation of. 2007. *Special Products: Possible Elements for Discussion.* 19 January. International Centre for Trade and Sustainable Development. <www.agtradepolicy.org/output/resource/PakSPJan07.pdf> [Accessed: December 2007].

Philippines, Permanent Mission of the. 2006. *Statement by the Delegation of the Philippines on Special Products.* 1 May, JOB(06)/131. Geneva. <www.philippineswto.org/Phi_Stat/phi_stat_on_sp.htm> [Accessed: December 2007].

Pomareda, Carlos. 2005. *Lessons from the Experience with Special Products and Safeguard Mechanisms in Bilateral Trade Agreements.* June. Geneva: International Centre for Trade and Sustainable Development. <www.ictsd.org/dlogue/2005-06-16/Pomareda.pdf> [Accessed: December 2007].

Ruffer, Tim. 2003. *Special Products: Thinking Through the Details.* June. Oxford: Oxford Policy Management. <www.opml.co.uk/document.rm?id=416> [Accessed: December 2007].

Ruffer, Tim, and Paolo Vergano. 2002. *An Agricultural Safeguard Mechanism for Developing Countries.* Oxford and Brussels: Oxford Policy Management and O'Connor and Company. <www.agtradepolicy.org/output/resource/Ruffer_SSM.pdf> [Accessed: December 2007].

Sharma, Ramesh. 2006. *Triggers and Remedy for Special Safeguard Mechanism.* Rome: Food and Agriculture Organization. <www.agtradepolicy.org/output/resource/Sharma_SSM_Dec06.pdf> [Accessed: December 2007].

South Centre. 2003. *Proposals on a Special Safeguard for Developing Countries in Agriculture.* SC/TADP/AN/AG/5, July. Geneva. <www.southcentre.org/publications/AnalyticalNotes/Agriculture/2003Jul_Special_Agriculture_Safeguards_Proposals.pdf> [Accessed: December 2007].

——. 2006. *State of Play in Agricultural Negotiations: Country Groupings' Positions.* SC/AN/TDP/AG/1-1, November. Geneva. <www.southcentre.org/publications/AnalyticalNotes/Agriculture/Stateofplay_October2006_FINAL_MA.pdf> [Accessed: December 2007].

Stevens, Christopher. 2004. *The Need for Special Products and Special Safeguard Mechanisms for Agriculture in the WTO: A Situational Analysis.* 30 September. Geneva: Institute of Development Studies. <www.agtradepolicy.org/output/ictsd/dialogues/2004-09-30/Stevens_paper.pdf> [Accessed: December 2007].

Valdés, Alberto, and William Foster. 2005. *The New SSM: A Price Floor Mechanism for Developing Countries.* April. Geneva: International Centre for Trade and Sustainable

Development. <www.ictsd.org/dlogue/2005-06-16/Valdes.pdf> [Accessed: December 2007].
World Trade Organization. 2002. *Negotiations on Agriculture: Overview.* TN/AG/6, 18 December. Geneva. <docsonline.wto.org/DDFDocuments/t/tn/ag/6.doc> [Accessed: December 2007].
——. 2003a. *Negotiations on Agriculture: First Drat of Modalities for the Further Commitments.* TN/AG/W/1, 17 February. Geneva. <docsonline.wto.org/DDFDocuments/t/tn/ag/W1.doc> [Accessed: December 2007].
——. 2003b. *Negotiations on Agriculture: First Drat of Modalities for the Further Commitments, Revision.* TN/AG/W/1/Rev.1, 18 March. Geneva. <docsonline.wto.org/DDFDocuments/t/tn/ag/W1R1.doc> [Accessed: December 2007].
——. 2006a. *Chairman's Reference Paper: Special Products.* 4 May. Geneva. <www.wto.org/english/tratop_e/agric_e/ref_paper_sp_e.pdf> [Accessed: December 2007].
——. 2006b. *Draft Possible Modalities on Agriculture.* Crawford Falconer, Chair, Committee on Agriculture. TN/AG/W/3, 12 July. Geneva. <www.wto.org/english/tratop_e/agric_e/mod_ag_12jul_e.pdf> [Accessed: December 2007].

PART FIVE

UNDERSTANDING EPISODES: IS THIS A NEW WORLD OF POST-ACADEMIC RESEARCH?

CHAPTER TEN

UNDERSTANDING INFLUENCE: THE EPISODE STUDIES APPROACH[1]

Fred Carden[2]

In spite of many years of research and a large number of studies, the influence of research on policy is much debated and poorly understood. Progress in understanding has certainly been made but much remains to be done. The communication of approaches to policy influence in communities of researchers is critically important. It is also not easy. The links between research and policy are indirect; the relationship is often emergent over very long periods of time; the role of research frequently goes unacknowledged; it is not easy to disentangle the influence of research from other factors; and research findings and recommendations may be overtaken by sudden political, economic or social transitions in a society that make them more or less relevant. These effects are all compounded in a community that commands a relatively weak position in its field—as is the case for many developing countries in regional and international trade negotiation where (rightly or wrongly) the institutions in Washington and Brussels play a central and powerful role. As Joekes and Medhora (2001) note, institutions matter in this field, and "*the global system remains biased towards addressing the imperatives of rich and powerful countries, and because capacities to take advantage of opportunities in the trade arena are weak in developing countries*." Two of the studies in this volume focus especially on this issue: Mably's review of the ICTSD support to the G33 and Narlikar & Tussie's episode study on the G20 both focus on challenges in strengthening the position of developing countries in the global trading system. That, in sum, is what makes these episode studies important and potentially useful if they can

[1] The views expressed are those of the author and do not necessarily reflect the views of the centers with which he is affiliated.

[2] Director of Evaluation, International Development Research Centre (Canada) & Research Fellow in Sustainability Science, Center for International Development, Harvard University.

contribute to strengthening ability and capacity in developing countries to take advantage of opportunities in the trade arena.

Most recent studies of policy influence (Court *et al.* 2005; Livny *et al.* 2006; Carden 2008) have covered a broad spectrum of issues in the cases of policy influence they have looked at, or have used singular cases to illustrate an approach (Pawson 2006). This is the first study of a number of episodes focused on a single issue. It therefore contributes to our understanding by giving much more depth and texture to the many elements of that issue, a depth single cases can almost never achieve. Understanding how research can influence policy is fraught with uncertainty, tentative conclusions and a certain amount of speculation. And, as Tussie notes in the opening chapter, a good deal of the explanation lies in the power politics of knowledge rather than in the mere strength of evidence. The choice, then, is whether or not to try to understand. One could take the view that it is an incremental process and that we have to learn as we go. Further, one could say that given all the uncertainties, there is no point in focusing on this, but rather to focus on solid research, well conducted and carefully formulated. This is the view of some researchers. They view their remit as the conduct of high quality research; its use is for others to determine, those who have a "policy bent" or a skill at building relationship and influencing important decision makers. This is a legitimate view and one that plays out in research of all kinds.

The researchers who prepared the episode studies presented here have taken a different view of research, what Tussie (this volume) refers to as post academic research. While they are concerned with basic understanding of how economies interact, they are also deeply concerned with the use of research to help improve trade indicator and positioning—and importantly with a longer-term view to improvements in the quality of life of their fellow citizens. They are conducting what Stokes (1997) calls "use-inspired basic research" and what the International Development Research Centre calls "development research" (Parliament of Canada 1970).[3] Development research, or use-inspired basic research, should address actual problems extant in developing countries, but the

[3] *The International Development Research Centre Act* specifies as the first object of the Centre that it will, 'initiate, encourage, support and conduct research into the problems of the developing regions of the world and into the means for applying and adapting scientific, technical and other knowledge to the economic and social advancement of those regions.'

solutions should be considered not only for their merits in dealing with that issue, but in relation to their potential for contribution to the long-term welfare and growth of societies. These researchers hold the view that the lack of clarity in how research can influence policy makes it even more important to make an effort to understand, not only so that they can affect the trade regime in their own setting, but so that they might identify some ideas, tools and frameworks that will help them in improving overall understanding of the trade process. They want to understand how and where a role can be played, what the mitigating factors might be, and to build frameworks for thinking about policy influence that they can use into the future. Thus, they are interested first in their own problem—most of the cases focus on local manifestations of a global or regional trade issue—that needs to be solved, and second in a longer term contribution to helping others understand the research-to-policy processes in the trade field. Here, researchers want to move beyond the academy to application of research to real world problems. This is the essence of use-inspired basic research, the essence of post academic research.[4]

In this chapter I will introduce the reader to the episode studies approach, the methodology behind these studies and, through proposing a framework, tease out the consequences of the issues raised above for the episode studies that follow. Here, we will follow on Tussie's definition of policy in the introduction to this book, where she defined policy as more than the products of policy change to encompass the processes of negotiation and influence.

Episode Studies

In diverse sectors—education, psychoanalysis, business studies, among others—authors talk about 'episodes' that can be addressed through research. **Episode studies**, so called by Simon Maxwell and colleagues at the Overseas Development Institute[5] (ODI, website) in their effort to figure out how to look at the influence of research on policy, takes

---

[4] I have deliberately presented a range of descriptors for this phenomenon to illustrate the point that in many research communities, researchers are grappling with how their research can contribute to real problems, but still contribute to broader understanding.

[5] As nearly as I can determine, the term was first used by the Overseas Development Institute as they began to do their own research on the influence of research

the idea a step further and identifies the episode of policy change as the starting point for a case study. The term is simply defined (ODI, Website) as a study '*that focuses on a clear policy change and tracks back to assess what impact research had among the variety of issues that led to the policy change. They could be focusing on a single episode or comparative episodes.*' This approach can be distinguished from other approaches to case studies that might start with the intervention (the research in this case) and look forward to telling the story of the influence that intervention had on the policy canvas.

George & Bennett (2005) describe a case study as 'a well-defined aspect of a historical episode that the investigator sets for analysis, rather than a historical event itself.' The episode study is therefore a particular approach to a case study. Its distinctiveness lies not so much in the nature of the question that is being asked (viz., how does research influence policy) but in the starting point. That is, it starts from the episode of policy change and looks back, rather than starting with the research episode and looking out. Like any case study it is meant to answer a particularly challenging and difficult question: how has one factor—research—influenced a change in policy? It is challenging because research is likely only one of several factors of influence and, coming from the perspective of the policy change, it may be less than clear, even to those directly involved what the factors were that resulted in a new (or revised) policy, and what role each played. It is difficult because we are usually talking about changes over long periods of time so memories about details fade. Further it is not uncommon that research may remain unacknowledged, deliberately or accidentally. What further complicates is the starting point. By the time the policy change happens a wide range of actors and factors have likely come into play. Teasing out the role of research is thus more difficult.

By the same token an episode study presents a clear picture that some change (at least at the policy level) has taken place. It does not suffer from the daunting challenge of investigating from the research event forward when it is often difficult to say whether or not a change has taken place. So, while it might miss some of the subtle changes that could in future be identified as a research contribution to policy change, it does start from a clear point of reference to a policy change.

---

on policy. (See http://www.odi.org.uk/rapid/Tools/Toolkits/Policy_Impact/docs/episode_studies.pdf)

Consistent with Tussie's definition of policy in this volume, in my own research I have taken the position that the influence of research on policy is multi-faceted and that the research contributions to improving policy capacities of researchers and policy makers, and broadening policy horizons are equally as important as actual changes in policy (Carden 2007, 2008). This is important in an episode study because it is a study at a point in time. Thus it can only take account of what has happened to that point, which could be capacity building or broadening of perspectives and horizons, with actual policy changes still in the future. From this perspective, much research has an influence on the policy process well before any policy change actually takes place. The contribution research has made to informing or influencing decision makers may well be lost to memory by the time a policy change takes place. This in no way reduces the merits or importance of the research influence—but it does make it harder to track.

These challenges do not negate the importance of a focus on actual policy change. They simply note that policy change is not the whole canvas. So what we are looking at here is a part of the picture, albeit a central one if we are concerned about the ultimate objectives of improving the lives and conditions of people. It does not imply that research that has not yet made a clear policy contribution is not good research or that it will not contribute in the future. Nor does it imply that all research that has influence is good research. Episode studies are always a snap shot: what is good today may not be viable in tomorrow's world and conversely, what is not viable today may well suit new conditions as societies and economies evolve and change.

Flyvberg (2001) notes that, '*(p)roof is hard to come by in social science because of the absence of 'hard' theory, whereas learning is certainly possible.*' Flyvberg makes the point that social science is not about generalizable predictive knowledge; rather he advances the proposition that, '*Predictive theories and universals cannot be found in the study of human affairs. Concrete, context-dependent knowledge is therefore more valuable than the vain search for predictive theories and universals.*' The case study is an ideal method for investigating what has actually happened, in what context (and for what purpose). I would add to this hypothesis. While we cannot generalize we can identify the contexts and relationships within which an event is more likely to occur. That is critical to the learning that emerges from the case study because it permits us to frame that learning in ways that allow us to adapt experiences to future activities. As Flyverg goes on to note, cases, even a single case, are also useful scientifically because they permit us to falsify hypotheses: a single experience demonstrated in a case that contradicts an hypothesis renders the hypothesis invalid and may also suggest its revision. Beyond falsification[6] of existing ideas, a series of cases may also result in a new hypothesis (essentially a generalization from experience) that could be further tested and modified. A single case may also result in a useful hypothesis, but we are more likely to accept the relevance and potential in hypotheses that emerge from multiple cases.

As Yin (1994) notes, case studies are especially useful when we want to understand the *how* and the *why*—the *what* can be better investigated in other ways. But when we are focusing on how things happened and the way in which they happened, then the case study opens us up to the relationships involved in the change, the context surrounding that change and the roles played by a wide range of actors, factors not easily captured in many other methods. The case study as a research method has gone from being seen as the weak reed to holding a legitimate place in the realm of social science, with all the important characteristics (when done well) of rigour, hypothesis generation, and falsification, extant in any well delivered research method.

So how definitive can we be with a set of such studies? How much can we say and how reliable are the findings? Can we merely confirm what we thought or can case studies falsify our notions of policy influence as well? Can a case study, or an episode study more specifically, say anything beyond the particular conditions and context within which it took place? I have put a number of caveats on these episode studies, perhaps more than they should reasonably be asked to bear. My task and intention is not to discount them but to be realistic about what we can say and what we cannot, and to highlight for the reader some ways to read the cases that might help in interpretation of the findings. I conclude this section noting that the case method has been significantly developed over the past two decades, and highlighting its potential as a method that permits both generation and testing of hypotheses about human systems, with a focus on learning and adaptation. This permits

[6] Here I refer to Karl Popper's notion of falsification, presented in Conjectures and Refutations (1963). He makes the point that if we look for confirmation of an idea or a theory, it is always possible to find it. In order to consider an idea or a theory as scientific it must be testable and possibly falsified in the process (in a way that crisis-based explanations of trade reform are not); further, we must be able to conceive of the possibility that the theory could be refuted at some time, even if we do not today have the tools to do so.

us to generate hypotheses based on experience that we can test in future and can revise and adjust over time. This testing and application to real world settings is the essence of post academic research. Interpretation of the cases is the subject of the next part of this chapter.

What to Look For in the Chapters

The beauty of an episode study is in the narrative. It presents a rich story, a history of events surrounding the policy change. As you read each of these narratives, you should be left with the feeling that you were there, the most important characteristic of a good story. You can make connections to your own experience and find ideas that you might use "next time". In that sense, each episode can be read on its own and each has its own protagonists, its own crises and resolutions and its own ending. One can draw elements from each case and put together a useful personal profile to help think through policy influence. But a set of episode studies presents a further opportunity for cross-case learning. This calls for some comparability among the cases, and some consideration of the possibility that learning across cases could help us to generalize to other work in a similar field. While there are limits to generalizability in the social sciences, we can argue the merits that a set of case studies, building on previous work and experience in this field, can provide a textured framework that serves as a starting point for design of new initiatives. They help articulate the theory that guides the interventions. That design will inevitably evolve as context and events unfold. But as use-inspired basic research, the merit of these studies is not solely in their own history but in what they tell us of value to expanding our knowledge and capacities and for application to other settings. This approach "forces us to contemplate programmes in their true and awesome complexity".[7]

Learning across case studies calls for some sort of framework for sorting and making sense of the data and information. A framework is sometimes the starting point and sometimes emerges in the reading of case material. A framework is never fully complete and should never be taken as a final answer. Over time and the application to new cases, it adjusts, changes, adds new elements and sometimes drops elements

[7] Pawson, Ray. 2006b. Simple Principles for the Evaluation of Complex Programmes, in A Killoran *et al.*, eds., Public Health Evidence: 224.

that are demonstrated as weak or incorrect. So while it may change over time, a framework creates a common language and way to debate our learning from the cases. Frameworks therefore do not give evidence that influence happened; rather they sort the factors and provide an opportunity to learn from the cases and in future, apply to learning from other cases. Frameworks can best be further developed through application. In this way, data can be collected throughout the development of efforts at policy influence, whether advocacy, research or application of research. This will permit adjustments to the framework, providing supporting evidence for its merits, adding new elements and refuting some aspects. This approach to a framework is consonant with Weick's concept of sensemaking, that "[s]ensemaking is not about truth and getting it right. Instead it is about continued redrafting of an emerging story so that it becomes more comprehensive, incorporates more of the observed data, and is more resilient in the face of criticism."[8]

Three sets of learning have gone into the framework proposed for probing these cases. Reviews of the literature and other frameworks produces some preliminary perspectives based on the work of others (Neilson 2001; Vibe, Hovland & Young 2002; Court & Young 2005; Weiss 1977a, 1977b, 1982, 2003). Second, a study conducted on the influence of IDRC-supported research on public policy examined a relatively large set of rich case studies and found a significant commonality of policy influence that informs this framework (Carden 2007, 2008). Third, and most importantly, the cases produced for this study provide a rich source of ideas and evidence about the role of research in trade policy.

From the IDRC-supported study cited above, two things are very clear. Intent matters; and, second, policy relevant research that directly affects important economic issues is much easier to insert into the policy process than is research not clearly tied to economic conditions. Neither point is surprising. And both are central in trade policy research, creating excellent opportunities for influence. Intent indicates a clarity in objectives and purpose, that the researchers know why they are engaging in the research and are also clear about who should be influenced in the process—sometimes it is other researchers, sometimes it is politicians, sometimes bureaucrats, sometimes the community. Intent becomes an element to consider then: is the team clear on why it is doing the

[8] Weick, Karl E., *et al.* "Organizing and the Processes of Sensemaking," Organization Science. 16 (4):415.

research and who it intends to influence? Lack of clarity on these points will weaken (but not eliminate) the opportunities for influence.

On the second point, where the economy is concerned governments are attentive. Particularly when an economic crisis emerges, decision makers seek out assistance in overcoming the crisis. But they are not limited to crisis management; therefore focus on trade policy has more opportunities to gain the attention of policy makers than does research not clearly or directly tied to economic betterment.

Where do we see evidence of influence in these episode studies? Assessing influence of research is a difficult challenge. Working back from a policy episode, we can know that a policy change has occurred. Evidence of the research role, as discussed earlier, is neither clear cut, nor is it always remembered. Sometimes it is deliberately masked. We are therefore reduced to two things. This first is opinion about influence: do the researchers think they had influence and why; and do the policy makers think the research influenced them (and why). But this is fraught. We know that memory is selective and that the human mind rewrites history on an ongoing basis. Further, we know that the views people espouse consciously do not necessarily reflect how they act and what they do (Banaji *et al.* 2003). So, where the opinions weave a logical story (in our view), we tend to accept them and where they do not, we tend to reject them. This is not a very solid base of evidence; further, going this route we are always left with doubt and are subject to countervailing arguments. However, sometimes this is the best we can do.

Secondly, as an alternative, is to look at how people act and try to determine changes in action over time. The benefit of this approach is that it is tied to the concrete behaviours, actions and activities that people undertake. It permits us to falsify based on the evidence in outcomes. These behaviours and outcomes can be documented and demonstrated: for example, that a trade researcher presented findings to a decision maker in advance of the decision. Das, (Ch. 7), presents evidence of requests from policy makers for research on trade facilitation, for example; by contrast, in George & Kirkpatrick, (Ch. 3), the researchers could not influence the departments that actually had policy making influence in ensuring sustainability.[9] While this may still

[9] This approach which entails establishing in some detail what changes you will expect to see happen as a result of the intervention has a strong basis in several approaches to evaluation, notably in Outcome Mapping (Earl, Carden & Smutylo, 2001; Theory

in some cases be subject to memory and its faults, it has the benefit of concreteness and the ability to identify the specific changes that have or have not occurred. In terms of future application it will also permit the development of a profile of changes in behaviour and action that is sought. These can then be tracked over the course of the research and its presentation (and application) to demonstrate solid evidence in outcomes, such as in the approach outlined in Outcome Mapping (Earl *et al.*, 2001). The findings on outcomes can thus be used as a design tool when intent for influence is present in the research design. Until we begin to document over time, it will continue to be difficult to link outcomes to research, advocacy, politics or anything else too tightly.

If we think in terms of questions such as, What change was expected? What are the markers that tell us we are moving towards that change? What change has happened? What's the evidence that change has happened (who is doing what differently and what if any change in status do we see (*inter alia*, health, education, welfare status)? The issue becomes an inquiry into the evidence of whether or not the changes in action, behaviour and activity that the research intended to influence show evidence of taking place. The assessment of impact then is against the intent, assumptions and expectations that are at play. This takes us back and forth between the change in policy—the episode—and the intent of the research when it was conducted. In this sense, studies that look both forwards and back are easier to investigate than studies that look only either back or forwards. The reality of course is often quite different. The evaluator usually finds that the attention to detail on data gathering over the life of a program loses out to the urgency of the work that needs to be done. And so the evaluator must move forward with what data is available and put forward the information s/he has and propose implications that can be tested in future. In this sense if we think of evaluation as future oriented, what we have in front of us in any evaluation is as rigorous as possible a look back to assist in making hypotheses for how we move forward. These hypotheses can be tested, verified or falsified, or modified in some way for the next activities.

Taking this view, the next section of the chapter will look at what has emerged from the cases and place this in a framework which is proposed

Based Evaluation (Weiss, 2002); Pawson (2005, 2006a) and the many representations of Theory of Change (for example, Keystone accountability (2006)).

as a useful tool for trade researchers and policy makers to think about how they build relationships and influence policy in future.

Three key elements emerge from the cases:

Context: All the cases reflect extensively on the environment within which the policy decision was made. This is an overriding feature in the literature (Patton, 1997; Weiss, 2003, to name only two) as well as other recent studies of the influence of research on policy processes (Carden 2007, 2008; Court, Hovland & Young 2005; Livny *et al.* 2006). What is going on in the environment is not only important in the terms noted above (economic pertinence), but particularly in terms of openness and alignment. I will return to these features in a moment because they appear central in many of these cases.

The Research Approach: The approach taken to the research and the roles played by researchers and decision makers seem important. Not all the research took the same starting point. What various researchers and decision makers saw as important varied over time. Three factors seem particularly important:

- the nature of the relationships between researchers, decision makers and interested publics;
- the approach taken in delivery of the research; and
- the factors that play into the ability and willingness of decision makers to use research findings appear to be relatively consistent across the cases.

The Research Itself: What is actually done in the policy episodes presented in the cases varies enormously. What seems most important here is the *why*, the intent behind the research. Sometimes it is research carried out to provide information; sometimes it is in response to a query from a decision maker or another actor in the policy process; sometimes it is research carried out to advocate a position, either by decision makers or by a group hoping to influence them (in this context research that does not support the position is unlikely to see the light of day); and sometimes the focus is primarily on research to provide advice on implementation: how can the new ideas or approaches be operationalized?.

The next section will return to each of these in more detail.

Context

Context is important because it identifies government receptivity to research findings. The IDRC study (Carden 2007, 2008) noted five different policy contexts, from clear government demand for research through to complete indifference.[10] What we also see in this framework

[10] These five contexts emerged from the analysis of 23 case studies in which we found a range of contexts surrounding the relative success or failure of the influence of research on public policy. These are described in Carden 2008 as: i) *Clear government demand for policy support*—where researchers have direct access to introduce ideas and findings into an ongoing policy process; ii) *Government interest in research, but leadership is absent*—where the issue is on the policy makers agenda but they do not have a grasp on how to implement, requiring that the researchers take account not only of research findings but also of implementation issues such as institutionalization, clear communication of results and potentially some advocacy efforts; iii) *Government interest in research, but with a capacity shortfall*—where researchers must consider the nature of capacity and resource gaps that limit response, taking implementation considerations to a significantly deeper level; iv) *an emergent issue activates research but leaves policy makers uninterested*—where research is "ahead of the curve" in building understanding of a problem that will likely emerge in future; here—the domain of much research—researchers must think of a range of strategies to bring the issue to the policy table including advocacy with interested publics, the nature of communications they undertake and the relationships they maintain with the relevant policy community; and v) *Government treats the research with disinterest or hostility*—where the researcher has almost no chance of influence without a shift in thinking at the decision making level; researchers may bide their time for an opening, they may engage in advocacy with groups interested in the problem (if they can identify any), or they may move on to other issues.

Table 1: Framework for Case Analysis

Element Case	**Context (where)**	**Approach**	**Research**
	Openness – receptive → adversarial Alignment – conforming to pre-held views → exploring a question – → leveling the playing field	Relationships – Knowledge broker – Research Entrepreneur – Networking & exchange Approach – expert – who's engaged – Issue identification (defined problem or research anticipation)	Research to create new knowledge on an issue Advocacy to support a position Advice for implementation (knowledge to action)
Core questions	What is the evidence that the policy community was seeking inputs into the decision process? – such as data, research, advocacy, community, business sector, international), timing of requests/fora/invitations/participation in event To what extent did the research support a previously held position? – timing; political or methodological affiliation; nature of the question;	What role did the researcher play in interacting with the decision community? – such as bridging ideas to real world implications; selling ideas to decision makers; networking and exchange among key researchers and decision makers.	What is the focus of the research that influenced the episode? – creating new knowledge – focus on the policy implications of knowledge; – focus on how to translate knowledge to action

is that much research is started well before there is any public interest in the issue—this is the nature of research, to be ahead of the curve and prepared with findings when the information is needed. The skilled research teams are those that have good skills at anticipation and can have findings available when these are needed. They also have the skills to bring issues to the table either directly or through various interest groups. In the context of trade policy episodes, this framework is less directly relevant as we are seeing examples that all fall, to some extent at the demand end of this spectrum. What we do see though is that there are two factors in context that seem particularly important in trade research: **openness** and **alignment**.

By openness, we refer to the receptivity of the policy environment. One may think of it on a five-point scale as outlined in the IDRC study or on a range from receptive to indifferent. Clearly where the policy environment is most open, the opportunities for research to influence are much greater. This is borne out in the studies; for example, in India (Das. Ch. 7), the Ministry of Commerce and Trade was concerned about the trade facilitation problems faced by Indian exporters and sought research support to preparing their arguments for the WTO (World Trade Organization) negotiations. At the other end of the spectrum (George & Kirkpatrick, Ch. 3), the Sustainability Impact Assessment (SIA) process had a difficult time influencing sustainability in the trade arena, in part because the departments responsible for trade negotiations were usually not in a position to fulfill any commitments on sustainability because this normally falls under a different department (often environment). They treated the sustainability requirements largely with indifference because they knew they could play no role in enforcement. This created clear challenges for SIA, which was often in conflict with decision processes—as George & Kirkpatrick note, politics trumps research.

Alignment has two dimensions. One is the obvious alignment of research interests and findings with views held in the decision making community. Not unexpectedly, where alignment is strongest, opportunities for influence are greatest—of course influence even in this ideal setting is not a given; it depends as well on the other factors I will come to in a moment. Research to support the development of the North American Free Trade Area (NAFTA) is an excellent example of strong alignment (Gomez & Gunderson, Ch. 2). In this example, a difficult economic environment in Canada was leading to change. When work began on the free trade agreement research in the 1980s, the Canadian economy was in the worst shape it had been in since the Great Depression, with inflation and unemployment both at double digit levels; efforts to that point had revolved around significant government intervention in the economy with nationalization and nationalism both very strong. But as the Macdonald Commission began its research in support of developing a regional trading bloc in North America, the mood was shifting to increased relevance for a more open economic growth in the country. A second important influence was the presence of external pressures from other trading blocs on North America to engage on this basis. So the research that largely (almost exclusively) came out in support of the free trade area and identified key policies that needed to be implemented was timely and strongly supported not only by Government but also by large parts of the Canadian public (though objections in some quarters on nationalist grounds continue even today). In the early days of the case presented from Egypt (Ghoneim, Ch. 6), trade policy processes in the country were opaque; and the institutional set-up was incomplete. So, while the principle of trade liberalization was in place, there was not the institutional capacity within the government to make use of research to support liberalization. Alignment was therefore weak at this stage, although over time, alignment improved as government interest in trade liberalization increased. In Botto and Bianculli's chapter (Ch. 4), we see the reassertion of the political agenda in both incidents they investigate. Research came into play once the major policy decisions around regional cooperation on trade had been made with the creation of the trading zone known as Mercosur. Initially the research was of interest and merit. But as experience grew, and as political interests reasserted themselves, research influence faded.

In a slightly different perspective on alignment, the alignment may be with one group that is operating in opposition to a powerful interest. Two cases present this way (Narlikar & Tussie, Ch. 8; and Mably, Ch. 9). In both of these cases, an organization representing the weak partner in a trade regime, made effective use of research in its efforts to fight against control by Brussels and Washington (EU and US) of the global trade rules and agenda. The research was aimed at leveling the playing field and was effective in helping a group that needed to coalesce against an adversary. Narlikar & Tussie tell the story of the G-20 efforts to influence agricultural policy reform and bring the views of countries in the South to a table dominated by the EU and the US. Even where some of the G-20 members might suffer setbacks in some of the individual policies advocated, the group remained united around the larger goals of ensuring more equitable treatment for its members. In this case we can see that alignment with the G-20 (Group of 20 countries), in opposition to the EU and US, was strong. Mably describes the work of the ICTSD (International Centre for Trade and Sustainable Development) in support of the G-33 (Group of 33 Countries), again to support G-33 efforts to negotiate with the WTO on behalf of its members, who are all developing countries. The membership holds a wide range of interests and perspectives, from some with a strong felt need for protection to others with products they want to move to international markets so are much more willing to compromise. But across the membership a common focus on "food security and livelihoods" helped maintain their unity in the face of the more traditional focus of the WTO on "food provision".

Thus, the degree of openness in the decision community, and alignment (whether it was to work with decision makers, or fight against a strong opposition in a policy making struggle) play central roles. Openness provides an audience with a stake in the research. Alignment provides the common space for dialogue and opens up the opportunity for influence. What neither does is guarantee influence. As we will examine in the following sections, understanding what research is key, how to communicate findings, how to engage, not only with decision makers but with interested publics, and being able to respond to dilemmas in implementation, all play crucial roles in ensuring that influence is achieved.

Approach

The second element of the framework refers to the approach taken to the research. As noted above, the key question is the relationship between the researchers and the decision community; in some cases, interested publics also play a role. Following a discussion of the nature of relationships we found in the cases, we will briefly discuss the key factors that were at play.

The relationships between researchers and decision makers were significantly affected by the skill levels of the negotiators and the researchers. Where skill levels were low, there was limited use of research and it was much more difficult to build trust between the two groups (Das, Ch. 7), and of course, politics continues to play a role in the relationships. As Das also noted, however, as skill levels increased, the research teams collaborated with decision makers to finalize proposals, resulting in a stronger potential for influence of the research as it was framed in terms the policy makers could understand. As George & Kirkpatrick note (Ch. 3), the more complex the question at hand, the more the door seemed to be open for political influence to play an important role. A third important factor noted was not so much skill level, but what research was seen as legitimate. In Argentina, it appears that the research served as a bridge for the policy makers until they developed their own confidence on the key issues. Once they established their own confidence and some experience on the issues, the research influence faded and was replaced by the political issues and decisions based on the experience of the negotiators (Botto & Bianculli, Ch. 4) In Nigeria, trade research was often not seen as legitimate unless it was conducted by the Central Bank (Ajayi & Osafo-Kwaako, Ch. 5). Further, the distance of the two premiere research institutes from the capital decreased their legitimacy and influence in the eyes of the decision makers. They were simply too far away from the decision makers to be easily called on. In cases where relationships were stronger (Ghoneim, Ch. 6), it is still difficult to identify whether or not the research was used, or how much could be attributed to various research undertakings. Nevertheless it seems clear in his study of trade liberalization in Egypt that as relationships strengthened over time, the openness to research increased and the number of opportunities for doing research increased. The other aspect of research relationships that emerges in several cases, is relationships among the advocates of a particular position: research served in some cases to strengthen the alliance and its case. Mably (Ch. 8) notes that the research conducted by the ICTSD was used by the G-33 to reinforce the coalition of countries by giving it knowledge and ideas with which to work in their trade negotiations and proposals. The same held with research conducted for the G-20 as described by Narlikar & Tussie (Ch. 8), where research was one of the political assets of the G-20, but the skills were held in individual members who contributed research to the coalition, not so much by the coalition as a whole. For example, India took the lead on research on the blended formula that lead to the coalition strongly opposing the blending as advocated by the US and EU. The early research findings were taken up by Brazil which led the communications strategies for the G-20's opposition. The G-20 used the same approach to build its relationships outside the coalition, for example in its alliances with the G-110 at the Hong Kong Ministerial.

These factors set the tone. Two types of relationships can be identified:

- **Knowledge broker**
  - The knowledge broker role seems the most important to emerge in these cases. This may have to do with the complicated nature of trade research, hence the challenges in its effective presentation to policy makers and interested publics. And it likely has to do with importance of trade to an economy, hence the increased likelihood of contestation over any decision in this arena. In Das' case in India (Ch. 7), the researchers knew that the range of interests they had to deal with would certainly clash over time. It was therefore important that they manage the relationships and broker the needs of each important group so none would feel they were being ignored. The ICTSD (Mably, Ch. 9) presents a classic knowledge broker case. ICTSD was not the principal actor; rather it was carrying out research in support of the G-33, bringing ideas and information to that coalition so that it could act more effectively in its negotiations with the EU and US. The G-33 focused on the politics and tactics while the ICTSD gave it ammunition to work with. Sustainability Impact Assessment as described by George & Kirkpatrick (Ch. 3) attempted this role but given the anticipatory nature of impact assessment and the highly politicized nature of the context it seemed to play little more than an enlightenment role. In discussion over free trade in Canada, the Macdonald Commission played an important knowledge broker role (Gomez & Gunderson, Ch. 2). The policy makers had a poor understanding of the research they were exposed to and many of the researchers were not good at communicating their findings. The Commission played a key role in bridging this gap. In an equally important development, the Commission was also able to translate the research into language suitable for public consumption, increasing the public understanding of the research and thereby mitigating the public opposition to a shift from a strongly nationalistic approach to a regional approach to trade and economic development more generally.

- **Networker**
  - Within coalitions such as the G-20 and G-33, networking was important for coalition building. But it was also important for

building relationships outside coalitions. In Nigeria (Ajayi & Osafo-Kwaako, Ch. 5), the policy makers played a key networking role, with heavy use of consultative processes. In the G-20 research process, the researchers played strong networking roles (Narlikar & Tussie, Ch. 8), not only within the coalition but in building coalitions with other groups on specific issues, such as the 'Alliance of Sympathy' at Cancun and the alliance with the G-110 mentioned earlier. The importance of networking is reinforced when we look at some of the weaker cases of influence. In Egypt for example, where influence was initially quite weak, it was only once the researchers starting building strong networks with policy makers that they began to have some hope and opportunity for influence (Ghoneim, Ch. 6).

A third type of relationship, that of **research entrepreneur**, often shows quite strongly in cases of policy influence. While it does not manifest strongly in these cases (though we do see an example of *policy* entrepreneurs in the Nigeria example, with three key individuals acting as entrepreneurs to move towards decision (Ajayi & Osafo-Kwaako, Ch. 5), it is nevertheless a role that should be considered as key. A research entrepreneur is one who usually builds strong relationships with core policy and decisions makers, establishing trust over time and focusing research efforts on issues known to be of concern to policy makers.

Research/Action

The third element of the framework has to do with what was actually done. In some cases, the foundation of the work was the research that was conducted. In other cases, advocacy was the key. And in three cases (Mably, Narlikar & Tussie, George & Kirkpatrick), we see a primary concern with translating knowledge to action.

Not surprisingly, in many cases (Das, Ajayi & Osafo-Kwaako, Ghoneim, George & Kirkpatrick, Gomez & Gunderson, Botto & Bianculli) the starting point was the research itself. In Das, there was cooperation in the research especially when it touched on issues of economic interest and where the economic advantage was clear (for example, in supra regional cumulation, the advantage was not clear so the research was not of general interest). In Osafo-Kwaako, while research was the starting point, the research was conducted largely by groups with known biases and with a lack of participation from other interests. Combined with poor communication of the research results, this dramatically limited the influence the research had on the policy processes. In Ghoneim, we see the research on trade liberalization growing in influence as the topic gained more traction. In George & Kirkpatrick, we see that the modeling of trade services is fraught with uncertainty, but the research appeared to play a role over time in influencing national studies on the effects of trade services even where the research conducted within the program itself might not have been used. We see in Gomez and Gunderson the importance of independent, high quality research in influencing both decision makers and interested publics. In Argentina (Botto & Bianculli) it would appear that the researchers never successfully established their legitimacy as key players in building the trade relationships on these issues in Mercosur. The research was considered at early stages but soon appears to fade.

ICTSD focused on advocacy first and the conduct of research within the framework of the needs of one party, the G-33. ICTSD focused on leveling the playing field (between developed and developing countries); it acted to keep issues important to its members—from the developing world—on the trade agenda in the face of strong opposition from the EU and US. They found that narrowing the research agenda increased their influence, perhaps because of the strategic effort and action needed on man fronts to keep each issue alive. Stronger focus meant more concentrated attention to the issues it was championing. The same holds for the case presented by Narlikar & Tussie where again, a developing country group, the G-20, was attempting to strengthen its negotiating position with the EU and US. But as this case illustrates so well, seldom is any case purely research, advocacy or focused on knowledge to action.

The G-20 case maintains elements of all three. Not only did the G-20 use research to support a position, it also used research to explore new ideas and issues before they were on the negotiating table. The G-20 also focused extensively on translating knowledge to action. For example, because of the importance of product specific caps, research was key to underlining the positive and negative impacts of caps on trade distortion, and to help set reasonable levels of tolerance. This focus on the implementation of research was an important negotiating point. In a similar vein, as reported by Das, in India, recognizing the highly conflicted nature of the field and the strongly held positions of key interest groups, the researchers developed mechanisms for conflict resolution to ensure that the research could move to action. In developing the NAFTA policy episodes, the Macdonald Commission (Gomez & Gunderson) was also strongly oriented to action and used strategies of negotiation and communication to help move the research findings through to practice as a central part of their work.

Success Factors

In looking at the cases against this framework, we see a number of success factors emerging over and over again. These are enumerated here with particular acknowledgement of Das who, in developing his case in India, identified many of these. These factors enrich the framework as a strategic planning device by identifying what has to be considered in using research to influence policy. There is no order of priority to these. Each is important and comes into play to varying degrees in each case of policy influence.

Trust

Trust between researchers and policy makers is key. Without it, the ability to advocate regardless of the quality of the research is severely constrained. The trust needs to go both ways, but given the highly politicized nature of trade policy making, clearly the researchers have the greatest challenge in building a trusting relationship with policy makers. Such relationships tend to be built over long periods of time, not within the context of a single policy incident. Enduring interest and focus on trade issues gives researchers a much greater legitimacy and increases the potential for trust.

Research quality

Research must be recognized to be of good quality. Policy makers may not themselves be qualified to assess the quality of research but they rely on their advisors to ensure that research they do use is of good quality. Reputation of the researchers over time for high quality research is an important factor. As Weiss (2003) notes, it is not so much that policy makers can assess the research quality themselves, but that they want to know it is highly regarded by those who can—hence reputation becomes a proxy for quality.

Communication with people

The ability of researchers to relate effectively to decisionmakers plays an important role. Understanding who to influence (whether it is the bureaucrats, the decisionmakers themselves or interested publics) is key and the ability to communicate effectively with them should not be underestimated.

Communication of ideas

The production of good ideas is what research is striving to achieve. But beyond the production of ideas, their communication is important. The language of decision makers and researchers is not the same. Many researchers argue that their responsibility is to produce findings and it is up to others to make use of them. But in the rapidly moving field of trade research, researchers must find ways to translate their ideas into language that policy makers understand and must relate their research directly to the trade agenda if they hope to have influence.

Representativeness

The degree to which research focuses on issues of prime concern to the community reflects its ability to influence. If the decision community does not see its issues represented in the research problem and findings it is far less likely to be able to make use of the research.

Timeliness

A critical challenge for researchers is to be able to anticipate issues far enough in advance to be able to present findings in a timely way. Research is usually not conducted quickly; therefore researchers need to be ahead of policymakers in determining what issues will emerge and carrying out research that can then be applied to the problems presented by policy makers.

Conclusions

Post academic research as presented in these chapters, seeks to see active use of research findings to inform decisions. It is carried out by those researchers who see direct relevance of the research enterprise to social and economic improvement. They do not reject or neglect the importance of quality of the research, but focus especially on issues of critical performance in a society or economy. As with the concept of use-inspired basic research, post academic research seeks to make sense of what is happening and create hypotheses about what works and what does not, hypotheses that can be tested, re-tested and refined over time as new cases emerge. It is about sensemaking and the effort here is to suggest a common language to help trade researchers with that process. Post academic research recognizes that context is central to both the findings and their use and that, rather than the simple application of global rules of practice, post academic research requires ongoing reflection and adjustment as conditions—political, social and economic—evolve. This chapter has proposed a framework for understanding these episodes of policy influence. It does not pretend to be definitive; in fact it takes the opposite tack, noting that influence in highly context dependent and requires constant navigation of difficult and highly political waters. It implies a number of questions that can be asked in designing the research as well as strategies for influence and highlights arenas where debate will be strong and can derail the process.

As Tussie notes two main types of policy change dominate these cases, instrumental change and conceptual change. Conceptual changes such as that illustrated in the NAFTA case can also lead to instrumental changes when the policy regime is radically altered. Both these types of change are illustrated in the framework. What is most important is having an understanding what type of change you are engaged with: whether conceptual change or instrumental change, openness and alignment are key; what changes is which alignments are the most important and where the openness needs to reside—in the leadership for conceptual change or in the administration for instrumental change. Clearly these are ideal types so one can seldom focus solely on leadership or administration, but they do play different roles in each type of change. This typology adds a further dimension to the framework, asking the researchers to think about the type of policy change in developing their strategy for action.

To return to the hypotheses posed by Tussie at the start of this volume, we see ample evidence of the first hypothesis, that changes are opaque, take place over long periods of time and are caused by a side range of factors. This emerges clearly in the preceding framework based on the episode studies. We can expand this hypothesis slightly to add that the factors act differently in each case so no clear single formula for success can ever emerge.

The second hypothesis, that the relationships between research and policy are two-way, dynamic and complex is amply illustrated with some episodes demonstrating the role of research in building the capacity and confidence of policy makers to proceed on their own (Botto & Bianculli), and some illustrating inputs from research rather more directly into the policy process (Gomez & Gunderson). The complexity is further reinforced in a way by the inability of the policy process to move easily into complex settings and often retreating to a political response without seeking evidence. This hypothesis suggests limits to the potential for research to influence policy in fast-moving, highly politicized contexts as these appear unable to absorb and build on the inherent complexity of the relationships.

On the third hypothesis, that an empirical study of an episode of policy change can allow us to clarify the complexity of the causal relationships between research and policy change, the jury is still out. While the hypothesis is not falsified, neither is it strongly supported, in its call for identification of causal relationships through empirical research. It does not rule out the possibility, for example, that a theoretical approach based on an understanding and exploration from the perspective of the theory of the change inherent in the research might not give us a better grasp of the causal (or contributory) role played by research. Without going into the history and place of theory-driven approaches, as Pawson (2006b) suggests, "[t]he core axiom of the theory-driven approach is to make explicit the underlying assumptions about how an intervention is supposed to work—the 'programme theory'—and then to use this theory to guide evaluation... Thus the success of the intervention is a matter of the integrity of the sequence of programme theories and, in particular, how different stakeholders choose to respond to them."[11] Such an approach could be instructive in building our understanding of

[11] Pawson, R. ibid.: 223.

the relationship between research and policy, particularly where there is intent in the research process to influence policy.

The fourth issue raised by Tussie in her introduction is not so much an hypothesis but an important query into the additionality of research in the policy process. The studies illuminate many aspects of the query, noting all the while the central importance of politics in trade negotiations and policy making. The episodes suggest the hypothesis that (high quality) research adds value where there is openness to change in the policy context, good alignment with key interests, relevance to an economic problem and where researchers develop the necessary skills that intent to influence policy would suggest: communications, relationships and a sense of timing.

Influence does not happen easily, nor can it be guaranteed, even if all the "right" factors seem to be in place. In the trade arena we see potential for influence of research because of the importance of trade to an economy: it is incumbent on policy makers to at least consider the implications of trade research—once they understand them. But we also see challenge: as several cases note, research does not trump politics. Thus the influence of research is often once a major policy decision has been taken, in the elaboration and adjustment of that decision to address certain specific needs. And even here, success is not guaranteed, and requires active engagement by the researchers in building effective trusting relationships with decision makers. These cases and the framework provide signposts to help other trade researchers to do what they can to achieve maximum influence, by identifying what to watch for, what advantage to seize, and the importance of relationships to success.

References

Banaji, Mahzarin R., Max H. Bazerman & Dolly Chugh. 2003. *How (Un)ethical Are You?* in, Harvard Business Review, December: 3–11.

Carden, Fred. 2008. Knowledge to Policy: Making the most of research for development. London, India, Singapore & Ottawa. Sage Publications & IDRC. Forthcoming.

——. 2007. *"Context Matters: The influence of IDRC-supported research on policy processes"*, in, The Policy Paradox in Africa: Strengthening links between economic research and policymaking, Elias T. Ayuk and Mohamed Ali Marouani, editors. Trenton, NJ & Ottawa, CA: Africa World Press and International Development Research Centre.

Court, Julius, Ingie Hovland, and John Young, eds. 2005. Bridging Research and Policy in Development: Evidence and the change process. Warwickshire, UK: ITDG Publishing.

Earl, Sarah, Fred Carden and Terry Smutylo. 2001. Outcome Mapping: Building learning and reflection into development programs. Ottawa: IDRC.

Flyvbeg, B. 2001. Making Social Science Matter. Cambridge University Press: 73.
George, A.L. and A. Bennett. 2005. Case Studies and Theory Development in the Social Sciences. Cambridge, MA: MIT Press.
Joekes, Susan and Rohinton Medhora. 2001. Trade Policies in Developing Countries: What role for capacity building and research? IDRC, Ottawa: 5.
Keystone accountability. 2006. Developing a Theory of Change: A framework for accountability and learning for social change. London: Keystone accountability.
Killoran, Amanda, Catherine Swann, Michael P. Kelly, eds. 2006. Public Health Evidence: Tackling health inequalities. Oxford, New York: Oxford University Press.
Livny, Eric, Archana Mehendale and Alf Vanags. 2006. Bridging the Research Policy Gaps in Developing and Transition Countries: Analytical lessons and proposals for action. Global Development Network. http://www.gdnet.org/middle.php?oid=1283
Neilson, Stephanie. 2001. Knowledge Utilization and Public Policy Processes: A literature review. Evaluation Unit, IDRC.
Overseas Development Institute. nd. Website. http://www.odi.org.uk/rapid/Tools/Toolkits/Policy_Impact/docs/episode_studies.pdf)
Parliament of Canada. 1970. *The International Development Research Centre Act.*
Patton, Michael Quinn. 1997. Utilization Focused Evaluation: The new century text. Third edition. NY: Sage Publications.
Pawson, Ray. 2005. Method Mix, Technical Hex, Theory Fix. Presentation to the International Conference on Mixed Methods Research Design.
——. 2006a. Evidence-based Policy: A realist perspective. London, Thousand Oaks, New Delhi: Sage.
——. 2006b. Simple Principles for the Evaluation of Complex Programmes, in Killoran, Amanda, Catherine Swann, Michael P. Kelly, eds. 2006. Public Health Evidence: Tackling health inequalities. Oxford, New York: Oxford University Press: 223–238.
Popper, Karl. 1963. Conjectures and Refutations. NY: Routledge.
Stokes, D.E. 1997. Pasteur's Quadrant: Basic science and technological innovation. Washington, DC: Brookings Institution Press.
Vibe, Maja de, Ingie Hovland and John Young. 2002. Bridging Research and Policy: An annotated bibliography. ODI Working Paper 174. London: Overseas Development Institute.
Weick, Karl E., Kathleen M. Sutcliffe and David Obsstfeld. 2005. "Organizing and the Processes of Sensemaking," in Organization Science. 16 (4): 409–421.
Weiss, Carol H. 1977a. Using Social Research in Public Policy Making. Lexington, MA: Lexington Books., DC heath and Co.
——. 1977b. "*Research for Policy's Sake: the enlightenment function of social research*", Policy Analysis 3(4): 531–45.
——. 1982. *Knowledge Utilization in Decision Making: Reflections on the terms of the discussion*, in, Research in Sociology of Education and Socialization. 3: 21.
——. 2002. *What to Do Until the Random Assigner Comes.* in, Evidence Matters: Randomized trials in education research. Frederick Mosteller and Robert Boruch, eds. Washington, DC: Brookings Institution Press. 198–224.
——. 2003. *Studying Research Utilization.* A speech at IDRC, 24 March. Ottawa: IDRC Evaluation Unit.
Yin, Robert K. Case Study Research: Design and methods. 2nd edition. NY: Sage.

CHAPTER ELEVEN

THE OTHER SIDE OF THE EQUATION: HOW POLICY INFLUENCES RESEARCH IN THE TRADE POLICY DOMAIN

Susan Joekes

> *Literature on the research-policy link is now moving towards a more dynamic and complex view that emphasises a two-way process between research and policy, shaped by multiple relations and reservoirs of knowledge.*
>
> —Overseas Development Institute

This chapter discusses the 'instrumentality' of research, that is, the influence of policy making on research. It examines the conditions under which research is produced and the types of research products that are prepared. These activities take place at the interface of research and policy. Understanding them enriches our comprehension of 'post-academic' work as described by Diana Tussie elsewhere in this volume.

The case studies in this volume indicate that the use of research in the trade policy process is strongly instrumental. Policy makers rarely make use of pure, unbiased, research-based evidence. They seek knowledge that is useful to them for the occasion at hand. The interaction between the conditions of the production of research and the uses for which that research is sought can explain the cloistered nature of research as data and the unreliable nature of research as ideas (to use the categories set out by Carol Weiss 1979, and discussed by Tussie in Chapter 1).

The instrumentality of research is fairly straightforward in the case of two of the three categories of research that Weiss (1979) proposes are used in the trade policy process. In the cases of 'data' and 'arguments' research products, the raw material and presentation of the research are both more or less selectively tailored to the needs of the commissioning party. Paradoxically, the third type of research, which deals in ideas, can also sometimes—but not always—be instrumental, but in a different way. Although some ideas work can be fundamentally innovatory or drive forward 'blue sky' thinking, in the trade field, mainstream economics (the world view of the epistemic community that prevails in the study of international trade) is ideologically wedded to certain propositions and its products are biased toward them at all levels. Ideas research on trade associated with the episteme can often shift the paradigm, as in the types of policy change that Tussie refers to as 'conceptual' in Chapter 1. Nevertheless, it is biased research, which embodies a conceptual paradigm that—in this case—is not as proven and unassailable as presented by its advocates. This claim is explained here, with a proposal that the bias and instrumentality in some ideas research relating to trade policy making has arisen and persists in part because of the conditions of production in economic policy research.

This chapter concludes by drawing out the implications of this situation for policy development and research capacity building. It may enhance the capacity of policy makers' to demand and make use of research-based evidence and it can stimulate high-quality and technically advanced outputs. But there are also negative consequences, especially for the accumulation of knowledge, policy debate, and research capacity building. Some recommendations are made for donors, designed to counteract those negative outcomes.

Methodology of the Case Studies

The use of episode studies, the analytical method employed for the cases in this book, promotes an unusual degree of focus in studying the role of research as a factor in policy making. As discussed in chapters 1 and 10, episode studies facilitate a focus on two main issues not usually addressed in an examination of influences on the policy process. A third characteristic of episode studies can also be identified. All three factors invite a deconstruction of the notion of research, not only distinguishing different types of research outputs (as already advanced by Tussie) but also examining variations in the context and circumstances under which researchers carry out their work.

First, by dealing with readily identifiable, discrete policy changes, episode studies makes it possible to explore the relative importance of research compared to other inputs to policy making at a particular point in time. By contrast, most work on the policy influence of research traces how some given body of research or set of research findings is taken up, examining its influence throughout a diffuse policy process drawn out over time. Episode studies therefore highlight the fact that multiple research outputs may be brought to bear on a particular episode. Several of the case studies in this volume bear out this point, notably Ahmed Farouk Ghoneim in Chapter 6, Rafael Gomez and Morley Gunderson in Chapter 2, Clive George and Colin Kirkpatrick in Chapter 3, and Diana Tussie and Amrita Narlikar in Chapter 8.

Second, episode studies in trade policy often relate to situations in which a discrete policy decision needs to be made, with the need for policy decision being more or less acute and pressing. However intense or protracted the decision process, such situations are assumed to bring an unusual degree of openness on the part of policy makers to research, because comparative assessments of different potential outcomes are needed to guide decisions. Openness to comparative analysis of this kind may translate into active demands from policy makers for research input. As Tussie argues, the existence of a crisis may provoke the need for policy change but it does not explain the nature of the changes that ensue. Political factors may be determinants, but there are also patterns in type of research inputs sought by policy makers.

The case studies also plainly show that in trade policy making the demand for research is not limited to front-line decision makers. Whether in open or closed decision-making systems, other stakeholders find opportunities in such situations to use research-based evidence to support their positions.

Finally, studying episodes of trade policy making has one further merit in relation to analysis of the research-policy interface. The focus strictly on the policy-making stage within the policy process as a whole may not always be legitimate. However, in this volume, it is a viable methodological approach. Trade policy is a domain in which policy decisions are easily converted into the instruments by which policy change is realised. (Of course, as Ghoneim notes, the impact of trade policies is another matter altogether; that is not at issue here.) Trade policy decisions are largely put into effect through the imposition of tariffs and other border measures and changes in policy take the form of alterations to the tariff schedule and intensity or type of border controls and other measures. Decisions are converted into executive directives or legislative provisions and enforced more or less mechanistically thereafter by bureaucratic actions of the customs service. Trade policy decisions sometimes focus on the simplification and enhancement of these enforcement efforts or have this as an intended secondary effect (as with moves toward tariff unification). But the general point holds that, when compared with health or social policies for instance, policy enforcement is relatively simple in this field.

In other settings, taking decision-making episodes out of context may be misconceived and misleading. Material changes are usually the consequence of a complex, drawn-out process starting with an initial policy change decision and continuing with the subsequent implementation of that change. Consideration of the role of research in later stages of the policy process, notably in monitoring and evaluation and the iterative adjustment of policy and practice, has shaped the studies of the role of research in policy in health systems that were among the earliest contributions to this whole field of inquiry (e.g., the work of Sandra Nutley 2003, and her colleagues in the United Kingdom). Where study of the dynamics of interaction of research and implementation is involved, use of the alternative 'tracer' approach may be necessary. In the trade field, however, analysts can proceed without consideration of the impediments to implementation posed by a poor policy environment (Ayuk and Marouani 2007).

The Research and Information Needs of Decision Makers

The circumstances in which trade policy change can take place can be organized into a four-way categorisation of circumstances. The first category comprises negotiated trade policy changes that are the product of trade negotiations with two or more other countries. These constitute the large majority of episodes studied in this volume. The other three situations all concern unilateral trade policy changes. These are sometimes made unilaterally in response to external pressures, sometimes as part of a strategic redesign of trade and other economic management policies, and sometimes as part of an effort to improve the coherence of national policies. There are distinct research and information needs in each situation.

Trade Negotiations

The information needs of government in negotiating situations are extremely complex. Tussie notes that during periods of active negotiation of international trade agreements, government policy makers are engaged in two types of interaction. The first is with the other party or parties to the negotiation and the second is with domestic interests. There is an iterative process between the two types of interaction. Interaction with the external negotiating party depends on and is informed by the outcomes of interaction with domestic interests. The case studies suggest that an iterative process of some kind does take place, whether the policy-making system is relatively open (as in India) or relatively closed (as in Egypt). For India, in Chapter 7 Abhijit Das suggests that the consultative process helps make relationships among domestic interests less conflictual by virtue of the sharing of the knowledge base generated by research. The fact that the research was explicitly geared to coming up with policy recommendations addressing producers' articulation of the problems they were facing also facilitated this outcome. By the same token, the consultative process and the producers' acceptance of the evidence presented to them also validated the research findings.

In principle, the negotiating team has to critically examine and then synthesise the arguments and convictions of domestic interest groups to produce the set of requests and offers to the other party that constitutes the negotiating package. This may be done from scratch by compiling options on the basis of interest group representations, or may be accomplished through adjustments to a pre-existing internally generated working package. Ghoneim points out in Chapter 6 that in Egypt, where consultations with interested parties are informal and not open to public scrutiny, it is not known to what extent government research findings are shared, and whether and to what extent the domestic interest groups that hold discussions with government elaborate their case with research findings, as opposed to, for example, issuing offers or warnings.

The complexity of the exercise relates directly to the openness of the policy process. Information needs are simpler where there is no systematic representation of interest groups and consultations, when the interests of the most economically or politically powerful groups automatically hold sway, or when particular international alliances are pursued for security or opaque, non-public interest reasons. Alternatively, the complexity of policy making and high level of uncertainty may lead the government to adopt decision rules of a different order, such as favouring downstream processing industries with export potential over producers of intermediate goods (Kheir El-Din 2008).

More than one such negotiating package will be needed, however it may be formed. Indeed, ideally at least three are required: a 'best aspirations', a fallback or reserve position, and a BATNA (best alternative to a negotiated agreement). Moreover, repeated rounds of domestic consultations take place as the situation evolves, producing a series of modifications to the official stance in the negotiations or a sequential refinement. In the end, multiple packages will have been under consideration at one time or another.

The specification of each package should rest on a comprehensive, long-term assessment of the impact on development, according to whatever development goals and objectives prevail in the country. But it is impossible to achieve a rigorous, comprehensive assessment of a full negotiating package. Although some analytical tools have been developed, there is no agreed methodology for full assessment, either ex post or, in the face of uncertainty, ex ante. Where data limitations are severe and research capacity is weak, the potential for even approximate estimations is very limited. Trade policy is a prime case in which some of the questions that concern policy makers cannot be answered on the basis of existing evidence (Schmitz 2007). Assessment exercises are always partial and incomplete, leaving scope for discretion on the part of the government in playing its hand.

In practice, research is brought to bear to describe the probable first round effects of negotiating packages. But even providing this information constitutes a complex technical exercise. The case studies show that such research can be carried out inside government, by a special technical unit (as in Argentina) or by commissioned researchers in publicly funded universities (Argentina), think tanks (Nigeria, India), or business organisations such as ICONE in Brazil (see Chapter 8). Researchers or organisations may wish to offer recommendations independently, or they may try to anticipate policy makers' requirements and supply assessments and impact calculations on their own initiative from either a supportive or a critical stance. In some cases, perhaps, propositions generated by researchers may strike a chord and be useful to the negotiators. But in general the research demands are too specific and (as Tussie notes) too path dependent to be anticipated by outsiders. Whoever the provider, research findings are most likely to be the results of work that originates at the interface of research and policy making because this is where the history of the negotiating path is located.

Another type of research information needed by negotiators relates to the effects of different bargaining package options on the domestic interests of the negotiating partner. Negotiations are a two-sided game and information about the other party's position and constraints is vital to the outcome. Information is needed as an aid to understanding the other party's reaction or to suggesting new concessions or issue linkages that will take the wind out of the sails of the other party's bid. The negotiating team will try to understand what gains and costs to its interests are associated with its position, the strength of the lobbies and interest groups it faces, and the history of its past negotiating positions.

Much of this kind of research—fleshing out scenarios and assessing the others party's real interests and likely moves—goes on in rich countries during negotiations. In developing countries it relies more on publicly available information. The amount of such information has greatly increased in the recent past. Information brokerage organisations such as the International Centre for Trade and Sustainable Development (ICTSD) and the Institute for Agriculture and Trade Policy (IATP) have been established and advocacy organisations such as Oxfam, the Third World Network, Consumers International, and the Consumer Unity and Trust Society (CUTS) have turned to publicising information and reports on the internet that, in varying proportions, provide information to observers about the trade policies of industrialised countries. Despite the charges of lack of transparency in its procedures, the website of the World Trade Organization (WTO) is a repository of detailed information about individual countries' interests and approaches to negotiations. The Organisation for Economic Co-operation and Development (OECD) has a similar website. The United Nations Conference on Trade and Development (UNCTAD) also devoted considerable resources in the 1990s to providing public information about the negotiating interests in and positions taken by the main industrialised countries in the Uruguay Round negotiations for the benefit of its developing country members. Where parliamentary and congressional records exist, they also of course provide material on the domestic interests and arguments over trade policy making in the country concerned. Embassy staff in the countries concerned can supply additional intelligence if they have the resources to do so.

George and Kirkpatrick explore an unusual case in Chapter 3. In its Sustainability Impact Assessment project, the European Union sponsored studies designed to give the developing countries that are in trade negotiations with the EU information about the likely domestic effects of their own negotiating options. That activity uses a particular methodological framework, but the EU's aid and cooperation program extends more conventional trade technical assistance on a large scale, which has the same general aim. Other donors, notably the United States Agency for International Development (USAID), provide similar support on a case-by-case basis, but not usually to its counterpart in negotiations. Indeed, USAID (2005) is expressly forbidden to support technical assistance that acts counter to the interests of U.S. corporations. In part, the EU exercise is a methodological experiment. The assessment template includes sustainability considerations in order to illustrate how a development metric could include not only economic but also social and environmental costs and benefits.

Demand for another type of research—horizontal information, as opposed to vertical inputs to policy—may also emerge in the context of negotiations. Governments may find it necessary to persuade domestic groups—and perhaps themselves—that negotiated outcomes have fulfilled the public interest. Advocacy materials, quintessentially built on research arguments, are needed to justify the policy position after the fact. These research products are not inputs to policy decisions, but they are part of the policy process broadly defined. In an open political system such communication is a routine obligation of the government. In settings with strong local research capacity, a culture of policy debate, and good information availabilities, the factual accuracy of such materials will be open to challenge. But in any case these research products have a very different status from that assumed in the literature on policy influence. They are weapons deployed by policy makers to give credence to decisions. The link to research rests in the fact that the more pure and impartial such advocacy materials appear to be, the more plausible they may be.

Horizontal communication is used in some other situations that are the subject of several of the case studies in the book: when governments seek alliances with other parties to multilateral (WTO) or plurilateral (EU partnership) negotiations, or when stakeholders seek alliances with other interest private sector or civil society representational groups. Research is similarly used with political intent in all such situations.

Non-Negotiating Situations

Trade policy changes are also undertaken outside the context of international negotiations or away from the negotiating table. Five of the case studies in this book address such situations (India, Hong Kong ministerial meeting, and consensus building among the G33 and on special products [SPs] and the special safeguard mechanism [SSM]). At least three other types of circumstances exist. Policy makers do not have such time-critical research requirements on these occasions but their information needs are still considerable.

First, trade policy changes have often been introduced unilaterally to meet conditionalities attached to sovereign lending by the international financial institutions (IFIs). These constituted debt-led trade openings, as discussed by Tussie. The information and analysis basis for such policies, essentially adopted under duress, has mostly emanated from the IFIs themselves or from commissioned researchers belonging to the epistemic community anchored in the IFIs. However, as Tussie notes, there is a paradox here. The policy mix advocated by the economic orthodoxy of neo-liberalism does not, in fact, require that trade liberalisation be undertaken simultaneously with macroeconomic stabilisation. As discussed below, and Tussie herself suggests, its uptake under these conditions is explained by the power politics of knowledge, specifically the doctrinal force of trade liberalisation regardless of the niceties of the timing and contextual conditions of implementation. The EU's SIA project discussed by George and Kirkpatrick is a peculiar variant of this scenario, at the crossroads of aid and trade policy.

Trade policy changes can also be the result of strategic initiatives by the government. Domestic pressures to seek out new strategies for growth or poverty reduction may be strong, and trade policy changes may be seen as part of the means to address such pressures. After a regime change, new governments may decide that full acceptance by the international policy-making community is necessary for financial stability, economic integration, and technological innovation. As trade liberalisation has been a central part of this agenda for the past 20 or 30 years, changes in trade policy in a liberalising direction may be seen as key to such acceptance. South Africa is a prime example of such a case and Egypt could be put in the same category (concerning the early part of the period discussed by Ghoneim in Chapter 6).

When strategic changes are contemplated outside a negotiations framework—or to push the conceptual envelope of such negotiations (including the consensus building efforts by the G33 and on SPs and SSMs as discussed in the case studies)—the research needs are broader. There is a place for wide-open, provocative thinking, with paradigmatic discussions if large changes in orientation are under consideration. The drivers of such change may be newly appointed policy makers, perhaps in a newly formed government, or researchers, in their role as public intellectuals. There may also be recourse to technical expertise to understand the potential impact of possible trade policy changes and to specify precise policy instruments. The information requirement is less urgent and less constrained by the exigencies of negotiations, but research must still be technically well informed and must yield operationally useful findings. Thus, as the case studies show, the information needs in this situation are a hybrid of ideas and argumentation, and in the operationalisation phase, data-based analysis.

Finally, trade policy changes may result from the pursuit of policy coherence—the search for consistency and cross-reinforcement within policy instruments. A good example is the current assessment of the development impact of OECD countries' foreign economic policies taken in aggregate as opposed to having each line ministry's actions considered separately. The evident inconsistencies between aid, trade, and agricultural support policies are a case in point. The case studies of the SIA project in the EU and perhaps also of India in this volume also fit into this category.

Trade Policy as a Driver of Research

Finally, it is a mistake to credit researchers as prophets, always the intellectual innovators at the leading edge of analysis. Policy developments in negotiations have sometimes opened windows for new analysis and pushed out the research boundary. Being driven primarily by commercial and political interests, some trade negotiations are concluded with little or no prior analytical work. Researchers scramble after the event to develop useful conceptual approaches, tools, and data that will make it possible to track the impact of the new policies and inform the design and modification of new policies. Work on trade in services as promoted by the General Agreement on Trade in Services (GATS) is a prime example. The classification of four modes of delivery that was institutionalised with the conclusion of the GATS provoked a stream of work to elaborate and operationalise the definition of the modes, to explore their relevance for sectors and activities previously regarded as non-traded, e.g., health and education, and to consider the development impacts and policy options. Another example is the OECD and work on measuring and categorising subsidies, primarily but not only with regard to agriculture, which was clearly stimulated by intergovernmental discussions at the WTO. Work in these areas is lively and continuing worldwide.

In summary, trade negotiations give rise to a particularly acute form of demand for substantial and timely research inputs. But episodes of non-negotiating trade policy change also generate research needs. The case studies in this volume show that research inputs to the full range of policy-making situations cover all the types of research that are covered by Weiss's (1979) classification. Although the mapping is not exact, research as ideas—normative research—is most used to inform locally initiated, unilaterally designed changes to trade policy and used in the launch of negotiations of new types of trade agreements. This form of research is also helpful in building alliances in the context of multilateral trade negotiations. Research as argumentation is deployed in knowledge intermediation and in advocacy work by both government and stakeholders. The most common type of research in the thick of negotiations is data-heavy research, which is needed for the operationalisation of policy options. The emergence of post-academic research at the interface between the policy and research communities is a professional-institutional response to meet information needs of this last kind.

Policy makers often need knowledge intermediation by way of the synthesis (and, if possible, by adding of value to) publicly available information. A number of research providers can deliver such material. But as information needs become more detailed, whether preliminary to or part of negotiations, confidentiality becomes essential to the research process, echoing the practice in the trade negotiations. Whether the research demands relate to domestic interests and impacts, or to the situation in other countries, the research process and its products become more cloistered. Only technicians employed in the public service, researchers with very close relations with the policy-making community, or consultants contractually bound not to divulge their results to any other party can participate in this kind of work. The need for confidentiality binds researchers ever more tightly into the professional world of the research-policy interface.[1]

Characteristics of Research Production in Trade Policy

The production of economic research or knowledge products has some peculiar features compared to other knowledge-based activities (or, in

[1] This characterisation of trade policy research as cloistered and path dependent is borne out by a recent evaluation of the Mercosur Network funded by the International Development Research Centre (IDRC). The evaluators investigated the impact of the project research outputs that cover three thematic areas: trade, macroeconomic coordination, and foreign direct investment. Work in all three areas was judged to be of 'excellent' scientific quality. However, the work on trade did poorly in terms of academic citations, receiving far fewer citations than work in the other two areas. Nevertheless, in terms of policy relevance, the reverse held: the work on trade was considered by respondents to be the most 'useful', 'involving the highest level of commitment and detail' (McMahon and Porta 2007, s. 4, p. 38).

trade terminology, services). Moreover, in the specific subset of economics analysis relating to international trade, the production conditions for research interact with the particular needs of policy makers and generate some distinctive outcomes.

As discussed, most of the knowledge products used in trade policy making rest on high levels of technical expertise. But unlike most other knowledge-based service providers, economists in general and trade researchers in particular are not subject to supplier certification or quality control of their outputs in any strict sense.

In fields such as engineering, accountancy, architecture, and medicine, practitioners must generally be members of recognised professional bodies that set entry standards and monitor members' performance. When performance falls short, members can be sanctioned and penalised by exclusion from the professional body. In WTO/GATS terms, these are accredited professions. Economics has much looser forms of validation of technical qualification and no comprehensive system of quality control of practitioners' work.

With regard to individuals' professional standing, educational qualifications are the primary validation of personal competence. Academic or other institutional affiliation is another screening device for professional standing. Affiliation to policy research networks, such as the United Kingdom's Centre for Economic Policy Research (CEPR), South Africa's Trade and Industrial Policy Secretariat (TIPS), and the Middle East's Economic Research Forum (ERF), provides researchers with another label. Network membership is most meaningful when membership is not fully open but subject to peer acceptance. In that case, the network serves as a filter or validation screen. By contrast, consulting companies put forward teams of staff members to work on particular projects, rather than high-profile researchers. The corporate reputation of the company rests on the performance of these teams, and there may be only light scrutiny of individuals' professional standing in that case. Consulting companies may also supply the services of consultant experts to round out the qualifications of such a team; they usually have similar technical qualifications to academic researchers, with the addition of experience in policy advisory work.

There are few regular standards for assessing experts' performance, that is, for verifying the quality of their research products. In the accredited professions, checklists and templates are applied to products to verify internal coherence, consistency with industry standards, factual accuracy, and comprehensive treatment. Second opinions are sought as checks on services supplied. (For the past few years, investment analysts in the United States have become legally required to provide an independent second opinion on the recommendations they submit to clients.) Time and gravity are the ultimate tests of whether architectural and civil engineering products meet performance standards, but catastrophic outcomes are rare because construction specifications are subject to rigorous double checks prior to the realisation of the design. In accountancy, although product standards are in some respects regionally specific (e.g., American versus European accounting standards), they are also subject to periodic review through transparent consultative processes. Most notably, accounting standards are significantly revised when corporate scandals reveal deficiencies (as happened in the U.S. with Enron). In medicine, similarly, the standards for care and treatment that apply to the work of all practitioners are the reference point for performance evaluations; these standards are also subject to revision over time. In the health sciences, performance standards also rest on an edifice of scientific testing, replication of research results, and secondary reviews and assessments of multiple trials.

The thinness of expert qualifications and the lack of performance standards in economics are especially problematic in the field of international economics and trade policy. Although rarely acknowledged as such, it is a field driven by one near-hegemonic idea and, by extension, by fierce disputes over arguments and data analysis.

The contribution of trade expansion—the international integration of markets—to growth and incomes is a foundational proposition of economics as an intellectual discipline, to the point that it is often taken as axiomatic. Different variants of the proposition have been developed from the times of the classical economists onwards—from Smith and Ricardo, followed by Heckscher and Ohlin's derivation of testable propositions about the factor price consequences of trade, followed by attempts to explain the rapid growth of intra-industrialised country trade and the prevalence of intra-industry trade within the same framework. The intellectual power of trade liberalisation as an idea—moreover, one easily put into practice—allowed it to become the central tenet of the neo-liberal economic reform agenda that has been put into effect worldwide since the 1980s. By extension—and despite technical advice suggesting that it should not always have precedence in policy implementation, as noted by Tussie in Chapter 1—the proposition that trade expansion through liberalisation necessarily benefits all countries has come to have the status of doctrine to the epistemic community composed of mainstream economists.

The scope for attachment to any doctrine is heightened when the methodology for testing theories and claims is inadequate. For orthodox economists, much more is at stake in trade liberalisation than is normally recognised. Its doctrinal status means that attempts to test its claims rigorously are threatening to its proponents. The vehemence with which technical analyses disputing the gains from trade liberalisation are dismissed can only be understood in this connection. For instance, a quite remarkable and disproportionate number of public attacks was mounted by senior economists in 2007 based on a dissenting background report on trade commissioned by Christian Aid, a British-Irish non-governmental organisation (NGO). In such a case, there is little place for economists as intellectual sanitation workers (to use Robert Solow's phrase). Dissenting voices are quickly branded as renegades rather than quality controllers when an entire world view is being challenged.

In fact, the contribution of trade liberalisation to growth and development under current conditions is unproven (Winters *et al.* 2004; Cockburn *et al.* 2007; Conway 2004). Heterodox economists have put forward a number of arguments challenging the validity of the proposition. The main challenges have been that the direction of causality is doubtful, namely that export capacity may follow rather than precede economic growth and capacity development and that trade liberalisation is responsible for such reversals as deindustrialisation in many African and Latin American countries. t has also been pointed out that many markets are volatile and distorted and that exemptions and supports to weaker trading partners need to be in place if poor economies are to realise gains from globalisation sufficient to outweigh the negative shocks and costs of adjustment to new market conditions. In practice, the world trading regime embodies many such exemptions, which have been arrived at through negotiation, as well as many anomalies and distortions that continue to be part of the trade regime despite the supposed merits of multilateral trade negotiations as a mechanism for removing such distortions.

Trade liberalisation retains its simple doctrinal status because, in marked contrast to the relative simplicity of the proposition itself, there are no agreed criteria for assessing the developmental value of trade liberalisation or for predicting the impact of episodes of trade opening. The methodological challenge is undoubtedly considerable. There is a wide range of possible development-related metrics for measuring the impact of changes in trade policy, including growth in national income, productivity growth, export performance, the trade balance, factor incomes (wages and profits), personal incomes, income inequality, and so on. An extremely fine level of detail is needed to predict shocks and problems for specific socioeconomic groups and locations, even in the short term, and, by extension, to give practical guidance on compensating or support measures. The time scale for prediction and the degrees of indirect effect to be computed are indeterminate. Attribution of causality is complicated by the presence of compounding factors. In addition, the whole exercise is constrained by more or less severe data limitations. In the face of all these problems, it is perhaps unsurprising that the economic evaluation and prediction methodologies that are used are not well established.

The most developed methodological tool for predicting effects is an economic simulation based on a model of the production and financial interrelationships among sectors, deployment of and returns to capital and labour, and consequences for different groups (e.g., consumers, poor households, wage workers, small farmers). But the contribution of modelling to knowledge of the impacts and interpretation of the results of modelling exercises in trade policy is very contentious. The construction of the tool is open to challenge, particularly in the way that welfare is conceptualised and measured, and the assumptions in the specification of the most widely used models are often implausible, especially with respect to elasticities, the exchange rate, and causality (Taylor and Von Arnim 2006). In recent years there have been many empirical tests of hypotheses about the effects of trade policy on particular socioeconomic groups in different countries. Authoritative summaries of this work indicate that no general conclusion about the impact of trade-liberalising measures is possible and that all depends on context, initial conditions, and flanking policies (Cockburn *et al.* 2007). Such specificities undermine not only the general case but also the ability to make robust ex-ante assessments of trade policy changes.

In 2006 an external evaluation was carried out of the World Bank's research (Banerjee *et al.* 2006). The work on trade was singled out for strong criticism. World Bank staff researchers claimed, for example, that countries that used large tariff cuts to open their trade to the beneficial effects of globalisation had seen more poverty reduction than those that have not. Several of the trade research products are castigated as being of inferior technical quality. Accordingly, the evaluators allege that the World Bank 'proselytized the new work without appropriate caveats on its reliability...it is becoming clear that the Bank seriously over-reached in prematurely putting its globalization, aid and poverty publications on a pedestal' (53). Civil society's critique of the operations of the World Bank (e.g., Oxfam's Make Trade Fair campaign) alleges that the research agenda and dissemination of research results were also influenced by power politics and the flawed governance of the international financial institutions. Economists' ideological imperative to declare the trade liberalisation thesis proven was another factor, at the very least by holding staff researchers back from objecting to strong general inferences being made in official publications on the basis of tenuous and selective evidence. The external evaluation of World Bank research notes 'a serious failure of the checks and balances that should separate advocacy and research' (6).

Tussie suggests that one defining characteristic of post-academic research is that it draws on 'evidence for a cause that weighs more than academic or professional validation'. The lack of routine independent review of World Bank research outputs suggests that attachment to the cause of liberalisation is certainly relevant to individuals' retention in that organisation.

Given the lack of knowledge about trade policy impacts, demonstration of 'attachment to the cause' is used as a selection criterion by all actors in the trade field who seek research-based information for policy making (or by those providing unsolicited inputs to, or who contest, such policy making). The nature of the cause takes different forms along the spectrum from critical research to advocacy. At one end is the cause of trade liberalisation. Next could be a predisposition to trade liberalisation, subject to a hard-headed assessment of value of trade-negotiating packages to national welfare. Next after that, the cause could be an assessment weighted in favour of particular interest groups; or the cause could be the maintenance in power of the government itself, when horizontal information, by way of ostensibly neutral arguments for decisions taken non-transparently, is needed; or finally, in a mirror image of the epistemic doctrine, the cause could be an absolute antipathy to trade liberalisation. The case studies show that post-academic researchers have been playing a range of roles across this divide. They are perhaps closest to acting as authentic intellectual sanitation workers when they test out the specifications of potential negotiating packages against the touchstone of the public interest, but they serve more like knowledge brokers and advocates, presenting a selective view of the evidence, when their work is used to assuage interest groups or public opinion.

In some of these situations, researchers are judged by an additional criterion: their ability to read 'intentionality' on the part of the commissioning body. This aptitude is highly prized when research activity is commercialised and provided by consulting firms (whether involving people whose primary identity is as academic researchers, or incorporated enterprises, large or small, local or international). The commissioning body can be either the government, or an interested party to a trade negotiation, or a civil society stakeholder, or a donor.

Commissions from donors (bilateral, regional and multilateral development agencies, including the World Bank) are extremely important in value terms in most developing countries, both as regards the fee rates paid and the quantum of work on offer. In some cases, donor funds also fund government commissioned research through budgetary or direct sector support. In many countries, injection of aid funds by donors is the monetary basis for the development sector in trade as in other fields, sustaining a new industrial knowledge-based service industry. No less than in the World Bank, the bulk of donor funding is ideological in character. It is doubly predisposed to support the production of evidence in favour of trade liberalisation. First, donors' intellectual world view and intellectual and research agenda are largely those of orthodox mainstream economics. Second, it is influenced to some degree by donor agencies' home country commercial interests. The current round of WTO negotiations and all regional and bilateral trade agreements have been initiated by richer countries seeking commercial opportunities for their exporters through negotiated opening of other markets. The condition, noted above, that USAID funds cannot be used for work that threatens the interests of U.S. corporations is the most egregious example of this bias.

Private sector clients have a simpler motivation, which can be partly offensive and partly defensive of their interests in, respectively, market opening elsewhere or continued tariff protection of the home market. Most such analyses of markets and production capabilities and threats remain confidential either to the businesses themselves or to the negotiating process. Where there is a tight relationship between business interests and government (as in the Middle East and North Africa, for example), private sector appraisals can weigh heavily in the official negotiating position. This type of research is rarely in the public domain or open to research scrutiny.

Finally, civil society organisations can also be considered as clients for trade research. Several international NGOs spend significant amounts of resources on research and advocacy. In the larger organisations the work is mostly done in-house but in others by commission from outsiders. Consumer organisations are a special case, representing a well-defined functional group with interests in trade policy. Consumer organisations play a special role, serving the public good by speaking for a group (consumers) whose gains are highly diffuse—although often claimed to be significant. Their low level of political organisation undermines their ability to publicise the benefits they are likely to receive from trade liberalisation. In consequence, an inappropriate weight is given in the trade policy process to producer and other groups that are threatened by opening of the domestic market. Moreover, the articulation of consumer benefits is a challenge. Consumer protection instruments have merit in their own right, and in developing countries consumer organisations undoubtedly help to bring product safety, quality, and process standards closer to those enjoyed by consumers in richer countries. But identification of the consumer interest in trade policy is complicated by the fact that individual members are income earners as well as consumers, and thus are concerned with employment as well as product price outcomes. Although there have been some notable advocacy efforts, consumer organisations have had some difficulty moving the consumer protection agenda to the global level. Advocacy work by other international NGOs active in the trade policy field is limited by the lack of clear assessment methodology for trade agreements. This makes for some imbalance in the campaign materials produced. The well-resourced Make Trade Fair campaign, for example, is selective in its promotional work, focussing on concerns for small producers in developing countries hit by premature and ill-considered market opening (Oxfam International 2008). The state of the evidence does not provide a sound basis for focussing on this group in particular. Researchers working for these organisations are certainly primarily accountable to the cause rather than to comprehensive, independent, and rigorous analysis of the evidence.

Conclusion

The standard conception of research is coloured by the notion of research as a public good, that is, of publicly funded research produced in publicly funded institutions (such as universities) or directly commissioned by government acting as the embodiment of the public interest. In this ideal picture, research results are fed immediately into the public domain to be tested by other analysts and to improve the information base on which public opinion is shaped in a process of debate and knowledge contestation.

In fact, as has been discussed, there are multiple sources of research funding. In most countries, only a small part of it, if any, is produced publicly in this sense, and the bulk of trade policy research is produced on commission. There is no necessary reason for commissioned work (whether with private or public funds) to fall short of objective scientific standards. But the practice of economics, especially in the field of trade, is characterised by inadequate producer certification, product quality, and testing standards. These production conditions for research make objective, scientific research very scarce. Where much of the commissioning is ideologically driven, research is mostly not scientifically robust. It is primarily instrumental rather than scientifically objective, and research is commissioned and used by actors with political or ideological agendas. Researchers must be skilled at reading intentionality to be effective in their work as agents and producers of research on commission. The path-dependent nature of the agenda for post-academic research, politically embedded and determined during a continuing process of discussions with policy makers, clearly requires this aptitude.

Where argumentation is concerned, researchers and research are inherently unreliable, in the sense that they position themselves (not necessarily consciously) as impartial and objective but in their choice of narratives, analysis, and selection of data, they are biased toward the interests of the commissioning party. The analogy is with unreliable narrators in literary works, where unreliability can be due to a powerful bias, a lack of knowledge, or even a deliberate attempt to deceive the reader or audience. By contrast, data-based research in trade is usually carried out in the close context of trade negotiations. When the work is required as part of the preparations for coming to the negotiating table, or when it is requested on a commercial basis, the contractual conditions for the research require the researcher to maintain strict confidentiality of the research results. The findings are not put into the public domain and do not serve to augment the knowledge base on which public debate over policy options depends. This failure impedes the cumulation of inputs into public debate about policy options, undermines transparency, disenfranchises and disempowers stakeholders, and leads to a lack of accountability of researchers, exacerbating the producer certification problem.

There is thus a symbiotic and circular reinforcement relationship between the work of principals and agents in these circumstances. The justificatory purpose of commissioned research gives rise to reverse causality in the research to policy relationship. Interested principals commission research that will set out an explanation that can be transformed into a rationalisation that entrenches a particular trade policy position. Knowledge brokers (whether or not they operate on commission to another party) may package narratives for specific purposes and identify key messages for consistency with a particular ideological stance. Thus instrumentalism characterises vertical research that supports negotiating positions biased toward particular interests or is dictated by non-economic factors as well as horizontal research that explains the outcome of negotiations after the fact to legitimise acceptance or to seek public support in pursuit of a formal consensus. However, the status of such work changes if it is subject to a consultative process with real debate about the substance of the findings. In that case the process builds shared understanding of a potential policy and reduces friction, and as a result the findings may move closer to becoming received or socially validated knowledge.

There are a number of lessons in this situation for donors such as International Development Research Centre (IDRC) that seek to generate new knowledge, support research capacity building, and stimulate the use of evidence in policy making. More specifically, support should have two aims: to enhance the cumulation of knowledge in the public domain and to seek to enhance the quality of research outputs, by promoting professional practices in international economics enabling practitioners to approach the validation processes used in other knowledge-based services. Measures to achieve these objectives could include:

- support for multiple knowledge providers in any one situation, in order to stimulate replication tests and to facilitate the production of second opinions;
- support for strong research infrastructure, in the form of research institutions and independent research capacity building;
- strengthening of policy makers' demand for research and support for the creation or consolidation of policy research networks open to newcomers; and

- seeking to ensure that research findings are widely disseminated and research results are routinely put into the public domain, with lags if necessary for policy-sensitive outputs.

References

Ayuk, Elias and Mohamed Ali Marouani, eds. 2007. *The Policy Paradox in Africa: Strengthening Links Between Economic Research and Policymaking.* Trenton NJ and Ottawa: Africa World Press and International Development Research Centre.

Banerjee, Abhijit, Angus Deaton, Nora Lustig, *et al.* 2006. *Tariff Reduction, Special Products, and Special Safeguards: An Analysis of the Agricultural Tariffs Structures of G33 Countries.* World Bank, Washington DC.

Cockburn, John, Bernard Decaluwé, and Véronique Robichaud. 2007. 'Trade Liberalization and Poverty: Lessons from Africa and Asia'. In, *Future Trade Research Areas that Matter to Developing County Policy Makers: A Regional Perspective on the Doha Development Agenda and Beyond*, United Nations Economic and Social Commission for Asia and the Pacific <www.unescap.org/publications/detail.asp?id=1254> [Accessed: May 2008].

Conway, Kevin. 2004. 'Trade Liberalization: Poverty's Friend or Foe'. International Development Research Centre, Ottawa. <www.idrc.ca/en/ev-62673-201-1-DO_TOPIC.html> [Accessed: May 2008].

Kheir El-Din, Hanaa. 2008. *The Political Economy of Trade Policy in the Middle East and North Africa: A Study of Selected Sectors in Egypt and Morocco.* Research Report. Economic Research Forum for the Arab Countries, Iran, and Turkey. <www.erf.org.eg/CMS/getFile.php?id=1184> [Accessed: May 2008].

McMahon, Gary and Fernando Porta. 2007. *Evaluating the MERCUSUR Network: Research, Outreach, and Organization.* MercoNet and International Development Research Centre.

Nutley, Sandra, Isabel Walter, and Huw Davies. 2003. 'From Knowing to Doing: A Framework for Understanding the Evidence-into-Practice Agenda'. *Evaluation*, 9(2):125–148.

Oxfam International. 2008. 'Make Trade Fair'. <www.maketradefair.com> [Accessed: May 2008].

Schmitz, Hubert. 2007. 'Reducing Complexity in the Industrial Policy Debate'. *Development Policy Review*, 25(4):417–428.

Taylor, Lance and Rudiger Von Arnim. 2006. *Modelling the Impact of Trade Liberalisation: A Critique of Computable General Equilibrium Models.* Oxfam Research Report. Oxfam, Oxford.

United States Agency for International Development. 2005. *FY 2005 Statutory Checklists.* Washington DC. <www.usaid.gov/policy/ads/200/202saa.pdf> [Accessed: May 2008].

Weiss, Carol. 1979. 'The Many Meanings of Research Utilization'. *Public Administration Review*, 39(5):426–431.

Winters, L. Alan, Neil McCulloch, and Andrew McKay. 2004. 'Trade Liberalization and Poverty: The Evidence So Far'. *Journal of Economic Literature*, 42(1):72–115.

BIBLIOGRAPHY

Achike, Ifeyinwa, Chukwuma Agu, and Moses Oduh. 2005. *Impact of Common External Tariff and Economic Partnership Agreements on Agriculture in Nigeria.* Enugu: African Institute for Applied Economics.

Adams, Roy, and Lowell Turner. 1994. 'The Social Dimension of Freer Trade.' In Maria Cook, and Harry Katz, eds., *Regional Integration and Industrial Relations in North America.* Ithaca: ILR Press, 82–104.

Adegbite, Oyeyemi. 2005. *Impact of Proposed New Tariff Regime on the Revenue of the Federal Government of Nigeria: Summary of Findings.* Report prepared for the Federal Ministry of Finance, Nigeria.

Adjovi, Epiphane, Basile Awassi, Aboubakrine Beye, and Murray Smith. 2002. *Final Report: Study of the Implications of the Common External Tariff in ECOWAS.* Report prepared for the ECOWAS Secretariat and the European Commission.

Agu, Chukwuma, Okey G. Oji, and Charles C. Soludo. 2003. *Potential Impacts of Extension of UEMOA Tariffs to All ECOWAS Member States: A Case Study of Impacts on Revenue and Trade Balance in Nigeria.* Enugu: African Institute for Applied Economics.

Ajakaiye, Olu. 2005. "Utilization of Economic Research Findings in Policy Making in Sub-Saharan Africa: Challenges and Opportunities." Paper prepared for 'African Economic Research Institutions and Policy Development: Opportunities and Challenges', Dakar, 28–29 January. <www.idrc.ca/uploads/user-S/11085715181Utilization_Economic_Research_Finding.pdf> [Accessed: January 2008].

Ajakaiye, Olu, and Adedoyin Soyibo. 1999. "Trade Liberalization in Nigeria, 1970–93: Episodes, Credibility, and Impact." In Ademola Oyejide, Benno Ndulu, and Jan Willem Gunning, eds., *Regional Integration and Trade Liberalization in Sub-Saharan Africa*, vol. 2. London: Macmillan, 147–177.

Akinlo, Enisan. 1995. "Improving the Performance of the Nigerian Manufacturing Subsector after Adjustment: Selected Issues and Proposals." *Nigerian Journal of Economic and Social Sciences* 38(2):91–110.

Amorim, Celso. 2004. 'Speech by the Foreign Minister of Brazil at the G20 Meeting.' 12 June. Sao Paolo. <www.brazil.org.uk/newsandmedia/speeches_files/20040612.html> [Accessed: February 2008].

——. 2003/04. 'The Lesson of Cancun.' *Politica Externa* 12(3):27–36.

Aninat del Solar, Augusto, and Mercedes Botto. 2006. *Trade Negotiations and Policy Design in Latin America: Is There Any Scope for Research Impact?* Bridging Brief Series. Moscow: Global Development Network. <www.eerc.ru/details/download.aspx?file_id=10016> [Accessed: January 2008].

Aninat del Solar, Augusto. 1982. *A Study of Basic Aspects of a Common External Tariff for ECOWAS.* Geneva: United Nations Conference on Trade and Development.

Aprodev, Begegnungszentrum für Aktive Gewaltlosigkeit, Berne Declaration, Campagna per la Riforma della Banka Mondiale, Centre for International Environmental Law, Center for Environmental Public Advocacy, Eurostep, Fern, Friends of the Earth Europe, Green Alternative, ICDA, International Confederation of Free Trade Unions, KULU Women and Development, Solidar, Solidaridad International, Weltladen-Dachverband, Women in Development Europe, Weltladen-Dachverband, Werkgroep Globalisering, World Development Movement, and WWF European Policy Office. 2002. *Joint NGO statement on Sustainability Impact Assessments of EU Trade Policy.* July. Brussels. <trade.ec.europa.eu/doclib/html/122192.htm> [Accessed: January 2008].

Aremu, Issa. 2005. *End of (Textile) Industry? A Critical Study of the Collapse of Textile Industry in Nigeria and the Implications for Employment and Poverty Eradication.* Lagos: Friedrich Ebert Stiftung.

Argentina, Paraguay, and Uruguay. 2006. *Revised Consolidated Reference Paper on Possible Modalities on Market Access—SSM: Some Unanswered Technical Issues.* JOB(06)/197/Rev.1. Committee on Agriculture Special Session, 21 June. Geneva: World Trade Organization. <www.agtradepolicy.org/output/resource/APU%20paper.pdf> [Accessed: February 2008].

Author. 1999. "WTO Negotiations: Invest in Research." *Economic Times*, 20 October, <www.bsos.umd.edu/econ/panagariya/apecon/ET/et-05-oct99.htm> [Accessed: 6 November 2007].

Ayuk, Elias and Mohamed Ali Marouani, eds. 2007. *The Policy Paradox in Africa: Strengthening Links Between Economic Research and Policymaking.* Trenton NJ and Ottawa: Africa World Press and International Development Research Centre.

Baldwin, Robert E. 1989. *Measuring Nontariff Trade Policies.* NBER Working Paper No. 2978. National Bureau of Economic Research. <ideas.repec.org/p/nbr/nberwo/2978.html> [Accessed: January 2008].

Banaji, Mahzarin R., Max H. Bazerman & Dolly Chugh. 2003. *How (Un)ethical Are You?* in, Harvard Business Review, December: 3–11.

Banerjee, Abhijit, Angus Deaton, Nora Lustig, *et al.* 2006. *Tariff Reduction, Special Products, and Special Safeguards: An Analysis of the Agricultural Tariffs Structures of G33 Countries.* World Bank, Washington DC.

Bankole, Abiodun, Olawale Ogunkola, and Ademola Oyejide. 2005. "Import Prohibition as a Trade Policy Instrument: The Nigerian Experience." In Peter Gallagher, Patrick Low, and Andrew Stoler, eds., *Managing the Challenges of WTO Participation.* Geneva: World Trade Organization.

Banting, Keith. 2004. 'Economic Union and Development Prospects for Canada.' *Canadian Encyclopedia.* <canadianencyclopedia.ca/index.cfm?PgNm=TCE&Params=A1ARTA0002515> [Accessed: December 2007].

Banting, Keith, George Hoberg, and Richard Simeon. 1997. 'Introduction.' In Keith Banting, George Hoberg, and Richard Simeon, eds., *Degrees of Freedom: Canada and the United States in a Changing World.* Montreal and Kingston: McGill-Queen's University Press.

Bates, Robert H. 1998. "The Political Framework of Agricultural Policy Decisions." In Carl Eicher, and John Staats, eds., *International Agricultural Development.* Baltimore: Johns Hopkins University Press, 234–239.

Bates, Robert H. and Anne O. Krueger, eds. 1993. *Political and Economic Interactions in Economic Policy Reform: Evidence from Eight Countries.* Oxford: Blackwell.

Bellmann, Christophe, Constantine Bartel, and Jonathan Hepburn. 2006. 'Special Products in Agriculture: Some Empirical Evidence.' *Bridges* 10(3):5–7. <www.ictsd.org/monthly/bridges/BRIDGES10-3.pdf> [Accessed: December 2007].

Bernal, Luisa E. 2005. *Methodology for the Identification of Special Products (SP) and Products for Eligibility under the Special Safeguard Mechanism (SSM) by Developing Countries.* Geneva: International Centre for Trade and Sustainable Development. <www.agtradepolicy.org/output/resource/2005-L.Bernal.pdf> [Accessed: December 2007].

——. 2004. "Guidelines for Approaching the Designation of Special Products and SSM Products in Developing Countries." Paper presented for International Centre for Trade and Sustainable Development informal consultation on 'Special Products and Special Safeguard Mechanism after the July Framework: How Do We Move Forward?' Geneva, 30 September. <www.agtradepolicy.org/output/ictsd/dialogues/2004-09-30/Bernal_paper.pdf> [Accessed: December 2007].

Bhattacharya, Debapriya. 2005. "Least Developed Countries in Trade Negotiations: Planning Process and Information Needs." *Asia-Pacific Trade and Investment Review* 1(1).

Bouzas, Roberto, Pedro da Motta Veiga, and Ramón Torrent. 2002. *In-Depth Analysis of MERCOSUR Integration, Its Prospects, and the Effects.* Report presented to the Commission of the European Communities, Observatory of Globalization, November. Barcelona.

Boychuk, Gerard, and Keith Banting. 2003. 'The Paradox of Convergence: National Versus Sub-National Patterns of Convergence in Canadian and U.S. Income Maintenance Policy.' In Richard Harris, ed., *North American Linkages: Opportunities and Challenges for Canada*. Calgary: University of Calgary Press.

Braun, Dietmar and Andreas Busch, eds. 1999. *Public Policy and Political Ideas*. Cheltenham: Edward Elgar.

Brooks, Stephen, and Alain Gagnon. 1988. *Social Scientists and Politics in Canada: Between Clerisy and Vanguard*. Kingston: McGill-Queen's University Press.

Brown, Drusilla, and Robert Stern. 1987. 'A Modeling Perspective.' In Robert Stern, Philip Trezise, and John Whalley, eds., *Perspectives on a U.S.-Canadian Free Trade Agreement*. Washington DC: Brookings Institution Press, 155–190.

——. 1989. 'Computable General Equilibrium Estimates of the Gains from U.S.-Canadian Trade Liberalisation.' In David Greenaway, Thomas Hyclak, and Robert Thornton, eds., *Economic Aspects of Regional Trading Arrangements*. London: Harvester Wheatsheaf.

Brunner, Jose Joaquin, and Guillermo Sunkel. 1993. *Conocimiento, sociedad y politica*. Santiago de Chile: FLACSO-Chile.

Bruno, Michael. 1993. *Crisis, Stabilization, and Economic Reform: Therapy by Consensus*. Oxford: Oxford University Press.

Bustami, Gusmardi. 2006. *Letter to World Bank President Paul Wolfowitz from the Ambassador to the WTO of the Republic of Indonesia*. 2 October.

Cameron, Duncan, and Janice Gross Stein. 2000. 'Globalization, Culture, and Society: The State as a Place amidst Shifting Spaces.' *Canadian Public Policy* 26 (Supplement): S15–S34.

Campaign to Reform the World Bank, Friends of the Earth Europe, Greenpeace International, and Women in Development Europe. 2006. *Learning Lessons from Sustainability Impact Assessments: The Responsibility of the European Union to Exclude Natural Resources—Forestry, Fisheries, and Minerals—from the WTO NAMA Negotiations*. 21–22 March. Brussels. <www.foeeurope.org/publications/2006/NGO_Statement_natural_resources_SIAs_March06.pdf> [Accessed: January 2008].

Campbell, Jorge, ed. 1999. *Mercosur. Entre la realidad y la utopía*. Buenos Aires: CEI-Editorial Nuevo Hacer, Grupo Editor Latinoamericano.

Canada. Department of Finance. 1988. *Canada-United States Free Trade Agreement: An Economic Assessment*. Ottawa: Canadian Government Publishing Centre.

Caplan, Nathan. 1979. 'The Two-Communities Theory and Knowledge Utilization.' *American Behavioral Scientist* 22(3):459–470.

——. 1979. "The Two-Communities Theory and Knowledge Utilization." *American Behavioral Scientist* 22(3):459–470.

Carden, Fred. 2008. *Knowledge to Policy: Making the most of research for development*. London, India, Singapore & Ottawa. Sage Publications & IDRC. Forthcoming.

——. 2007. 'Context Matters'. In E. Ayuk and M.A. Marouani, eds., *The Policy Paradox in Africa: Strengthening Links Between Economic Research and Policymaking*. Trenton NJ and Ottawa: Africa World Press and International Development Research Centre.

——. 2004. 'Issues in Assessing the Policy Influence of Research'. *International Social Science Journal*, 56(1):135–151.

Carden, Fred, Stephanie Neilson, Terry Smutylo, *et al.* 2002. *IDRC-Supported Research in the Public Policy Process: A Strategic Evaluation of the Influence of Research on Public Policy*. Working paper. International Development Research Centre, Ottawa.

Chant, John. 2005. 'Macro Stability and Economic Growth: What the Macdonald Commission Said.' In David Laidler, and William Robson, eds., *Prospects for Canada: Progress and Challenges Twenty Years after the Macdonald Commission*. Toronto: C.D. Howe Institute, 13–24.

Chudnovsky, Daniel, and Fabio Erber. 1999. 'MERCOSUR's Impact on the Development of the Machine Tools Sector.' *Integration and Trade* 7/8. <www.iadb.org/intal/aplicaciones/uploads/publicaciones/i_INTAL_IYT_7-8_1999_Chudnovsky-Erber.Pdf> [Accessed: March 2008].

Chudnovsky, Daniel, Masafumi Nagao, and Staffan Jacobsson. 1987. *Bienes de Capital y Tecnología en el Tercer Mundo*. Buenos Aires: Centro Editor de América Latina.

Clapp, Jennifer. 2006. *Developing Countries and the WTO Agriculture Negotiations.* CIGI Working Paper No. 6. Centre for International Governance Innovation. <www.cigionline.org/cigi/download-nocache/Publications/document/workingp/develop_> [Accessed:

Clay, E.J. and B.B. Schaffer eds. 1984. *Room for Manoeuvre: An Explanation of Public Policy in Agriculture and Rural Development*. London: Heinemann Educational Books.

Cline, William. 1997. *Trade and Wage Inequality*. Washington DC: Institute for International Economics.

Cockburn, John, Bernard Decaluwé, and Véronique Robichaud. 2007. 'Trade Liberalization and Poverty: Lessons from Africa and Asia'. In, *Future Trade Research Areas that Matter to Developing County Policy Makers: A Regional Perspective on the Doha Development Agenda and Beyond*, United Nations Economic and Social Commission for Asia and the Pacific <www.unescap.org/publications/detail.asp?id=1254> [Accessed: May 2008].

Collins, Susan, ed. 1998. *Imports, Exports, and the American Worker*. Washington DC: Brookings Institution Press.

Commission for Environmental Cooperation. 1999. *Analytic Framework for Assessing the Environmental Effects of the North American Free Trade Agreement.* Montreal: Commission for Environmental Cooperation. <www.cec.org/programs_projects/trade_environ_econ/pdfs/frmwrk-e.pdf> [Accessed: January 2008].

Conway, Kevin. 2004. 'Trade Liberalization: Poverty's Friend or Foe'. International Development Research Centre, Ottawa. <www.idrc.ca/en/ev-62673-201-1-DO_TOPIC.html> [Accessed: May 2008].

Corbo, Vittorio and Stanley Fischer. 1995. 'Structural Adjustment, Stabilization, and Policy Reform: Domestic and International Finance'. In H. Chenery, ed., *Handbook of Development Economics*, 1 edition. Santiago: Pontificia Universidad Católica de Chile, Instituto de Economía.

Costa, Cinthia, André Nassar, and Marcos Jank. 2007. *Trade-Distorting Domestic Support: Alternatives for Product-Specific Disciplines.* Sao Paolo: Institute for International Economics. <www.iconebrasil.com.br/arquivos/noticia/1384.pdf> [Accessed: February 2008].

Court, Julius, Ingie Hovland, and John Young, eds. 2005. *Bridging Research and Policy in Development: Evidence and the Change Process*. London: Overseas Development Institute.

Court, Julius, and John Young. 2004. 'Bridging Research and Policy.' *Forum: Newsletter of the Economic Research Forum* 11(1).

——. 2003. *Bridging Research and Policy in Development: Insights from 50 Case Studies.* Workign Paper 213. London: Overseas Development Institute. <www.odi.org.uk/publications/working_papers/wp213.pdf> [Accessed: January 2008].

Cox, David, and Richard Harris. 1992. 'North American Free Trade and Its Implications for Canada: Results from a CGE Model of North American Trade.' *Economy-wide Modeling of the Economic Implications of a Free Trade Agreement with Mexico and a NAFTA with Canada and Mexico*. Washington DC: United States international Trade Commission.

——. 1986. 'A Quantitative Assessment of the Economic Impact on Canada of Sectoral Free Trade with the United States.' *Canadian Journal of Economics* 19(3):377–394.

——. 1985. 'Trade Liberalization and industrial Organization: Some Estimates for Canada.' *Journal of Political Economy* 93(1):115–145.

Crandall, Robert. 1987. 'A Sectoral Perspective: Steel.' In Robert Stern, Philip Trezise, and John Whalley, eds., *Perspectives on a U.S.-Canadian Free Trade Agreement*. Washington DC: Brookings Institution Press, 241–243.

Crewe, Emma, and John Young. 2002. *Bridging Research and Policy: Context, Evidence, and Links*. Working Paper 173. London: Overseas Development Institute. <www.odi.org.uk/Publications/working_papers/wp173.pdf> [Accessed: 14 November 2007].

Cypher, James. 1992. "Labor Market Implications of the Mexico-U.S. Free Trade Agreement." Paper presented at the Allied Social Science Association meeting, New Orleans, January.

Das, Tarun. 2006. "The Impact of Research on Policymaking: The Case of Labor Market and External Sector Reforms in India." Bridging Brief Series, Moscow: Global Development Network. <gdn.eerc.ru/Details/PolicyBrief.aspx?id=508> [Accessed: 6 November 2007].

Davies, Huw, Sandra Nutley, and Isabel Walter. 2005. "Assessing the Impact of Social Science Research: Conceptual, Methodological, and Practical Issues." Background discussion paper for the ESCR Symposium on Assessing the Non-Academic Impact of Research, University of St. Andrews, 12–13 May.

de Vibe, Maja, Ingeborg Hovland, and John Young. 2002. *Bridging Research and Policy: An Annotated Bibliography*. Working Paper 174. London: Overseas Development Institute. <www.odi.org.uk/publications/working_papers/wp174.pdf> [Accessed: January 2008].

Delgado, Nelson Giordano, and Adriano Campolina de O. Soares. 2005. *The G20: Its Origin, Evolution, Meaning, and Prospects*. Global Issue Paper No. 25. Heinrich Böll Foundation. <www.boell.de/alt/downloads/global/GIP_25_Engl_G-20.pdf> [Accessed: February 2008].

Devarajan, Shantayanan and Sherman Robinson. 2002. "The Influence of Computable General Equilibrium Models on Policy." TMD Discussion Paper No. 98, Washington DC: International Food Policy Research Institute. <www.ifpri.org/divs/tmd/dp/papers/tmdp98.pdf> [Accessed: 7 November 2007].

Diamond, Larry Jay and Marc F. Plattner. 1995. *Economic Reform and Democracy*. Baltimore: Johns Hopkins University Press.

Diaz-Alejandro, Carlos. 1975. 'Trade Policies and Economic Development'. In P.B. Kenen, ed., *International Trade and Finance: Frontiers for Research*. Cambridge: Cambridge University Press.

Dollar, David, and Aart Kraay. 2001. "Trade, Growth, and Poverty." World Bank. <papers.ssrn.com/sol3/papers.cfm?abstract_id=632684> [Accessed: 13 November, 2007].

Dollar, David and Jakob Svensson. 1998. *What Explains the Success or Failure of Stuctural Adjustment Programs?* World Bank Policy Research Working Paper No. 1938. World Bank, Washington DC.

Dolowitz, David, and David Marsh. 1996. "Who Learns What from Whom: A Review of the Policy Transfer Literature." *Political Studies* 44(2):343–357.

Drache, Daniel, and Duncan Cameron, eds. 1985. *The Other Macdonald Report: The Consensus on Canada's Future that the Macdonald Commission Left Out*. Toronto: Lorimer.

Drazen, Allen and William Easterly. 2001. 'Do Crises Induce Reform? Simple Empirical Tests of Conventional Wisdom'. *Economics and politics*, 13(2):129–157.

Drazen, Allen and Vittorio Grilli. 1990. *The Benefits of Crises for Economic Reforms*. NBER Working Paper No. W3527. National Bureau of Economic Research.

Dungan, Peter. 1985. *The Macroeconomic Impacts of Free Trade with the United States: Lessons from the FOCUS-PRISM Models*. Working Paper DP85-6. Toronto: University of Toronto.

Earl, Sarah, Fred Carden and Terry Smutylo. 2001. *Outcome Mapping: Building learning and reflection into development programs*. Ottawa: IDRC.

Economic Intelligence Unit. 2006. *Nigeria: Country Forecast*. London: Economist.

Edwards, Meredith. 2004. *Social Science Research and Public Policy: Narrowing the Divide.* Policy Paper No. 2. Canberra: Academy of the Social Sciences in Australia. <www .assa.edu.au/Publications/OP/op22004a.pdf> [Accessed: January 2008].

Edwards, Sebastian. 1997. 'Trade, Liberalization Reforms, and the World Bank'. *American Economic Review*, 87(2):43–48.

——. 1989. *Openness, Outward Orientation, Trade Liberalization, and Economic Performance in Developing Countries.* NBER Working Paper No. W2908. National Bureau of Economic Research, Washington DC.

Egypt. Ministry of Foreign Trade. 2003. *Export Promotion Strategy.* Second year. Cairo.

Eremenko, Igor, and Katerina Lisenkova. 2004. *Financial Sector Reforms in Ukraine: Role of Local Research and Foreign Advisors.* Bridging Brief Series. Moscow: Global Development Network. <www.eerc.ru/details/download.aspx?file_id=10009> [Accessed: January 2008].

Euro-Mediterranean Parliamentary Assembly. 2005. *Resolution of the Euro-Mediterranean Parliamentary Assembly on Economic and Financial Issues, Social Affairs, and Education.* 21 November. Rabat. <libr.sejm.gov.pl/oide/empa/2_rabat_en.pdf> [Accessed: January 2008].

European Commission. 2002. *Communication from the Commission on Impact Assessment.* COM(2002) 276 final, 5 June. Brussels. <eur-lex.europa.eu/LexUriServ/LexUriServ .do?uri=CELEX:52002DC0276:EN:NOT> [Accessed: January 2008].

——. 2007. 'List of Impact Assessments Planned and Carried Out.' Brussels. <ec.europa.eu/governance/impact/practice_en.htm> [Accessed: January 2008].

——. 2006a. 'EU Trade SIA Stocktaking Conference: Agenda and Speeches.' Brussels. <ec.europa.eu/trade/issues/global/sia/sem0306_prog.htm> [Accessed: January 2008].

——. 2006b. *Handbook for Trade Sustainability Impact Assessment.* Brussels. <trade.ec.europa .eu/doclib/html/127974.htm> [Accessed: January 2008].

——. 2005a. *Impact Assessment Guidelines.* SEC(2005) 791. Brussels. <ec.europa.eu/ governance/impact/docs/SEC2005_791_IA%20guidelines_annexes.pdf> [Accessed: January 2008].

——. 2005b. 'Sustainability Impact Assessment: FAQs.' Brussels. <ec.europa.eu/trade/ issues/global/sia/faqs.htm> [Accessed: January 2008].

——. 2003a. 'SIA of Trade Agreements: Making Trade Sustainable?' Brussels. <ec.europa.eu/comm/trade/issues/global/sia/seminar.htm> [Accessed: January 2008].

——. 2003b. *SIA of Trade Agreements: Making Trade Sustainable?* Proceedings of the DG Trade Seminar, 6–7 February. Brussels. <trade.ec.europa.eu/doclib/docs/2006/ september/tradoc_130035.11.pdf> [Accessed: January 2008].

European Commission. Directorate General Trade. 2003. *Challenges Identified at the Seminar and Replies from the Commission.* Following the DG Trade Seminar, 6–7 February. Brussels. <trade.ec.europa.eu/doclib/html/130036.htm> [Accessed: January 2008].

Evans, Peter B., Harold Karan Jacobson, and Robert D. Putnam, eds. 1993. *Double-Edged Diplomacy: International Bargaining and Domestic Politics.* Berkeley: University of California Press.

Faizel, Ismail. 2007. 'One Year Since the WTO Hong Kong Ministerial Conference: Developing Countries Re-claim the Development Content of the WTO Doha Round.' In Yong-Shik Lee, ed., *Economic Development Through World Trade: A Developing World Perspective.* The Hague: Kluwer Law International.

Feenstra, Robert, and Gordon Hanson. 1997. 'Foreign Direct Investment and Relative Wages: Evidence from Mexico's Maquiladoras.' *Journal of International Economics* 42(3–4):371–383.

Flyvbeg, B. 2001. Making Social Science Matter. Cambridge University Press: 73.

Food and Agriculture Organization. 2005. *No. 9: A Special Safeguard Mechanism for Developing Countries.* FAO Trade Policy Technical Notes on Issues Related to the WTO

Negotiations on Agriculture. Rome. <ftp.fao.org/docrep/fao/008/j5425e/j5425e00.pdf> [Accessed: December 2007].
——. 2003a. 'Fact Sheet: The Need for Special Safeguards for Developing Countries.' Rome. <www.fao.org/docrep/005/y4852e/y4852e05.htm> [Accessed: December 2007].
——. 2003b. 'Some Trade Policy Issues Relating to Trends in Agricultural Imports in the Context of Food Security.' 18–21 March. Rome. <www.fao.org/docrep/MEETING/005/Y8319e/Y8319e00.HTM> [Accessed: December 2007].
Foot, Rosemary. 2006. 'Chinese Strategies in a U.S.-Hegemonic Global Order: Accommodating and Hedging.' *International Affairs* 82(1):77–94.
Fundación de Investigaciones Económicas Latinoamericanos. 1993. *El comercio administrado de los '90: Argentina y sus socios*. Buenos Aires: Editorial Manantial.
G20. 2008a. *History*. <www.g-20.mre.gov.br/history.asp> [Accessed: February 2008].
——. 2008b. *Members*. <www.g-20.mre.gov.br/members.asp> [Accessed: February 2008].
——. 2007. 'G20 Proposal for the Establishment of Product-Specific Caps in AMS.' <www.g-20.mre.gov.br/conteudo/proposals_caps.pdf> [Accessed: February 2008].
——. 2005a. 'G20 Proposal on Market Access.' 12 October. <www.agtradepolicy.org/output/resource/G20MarketaccessproposalOct05.pdf> [Accessed: February 2008].
——. 2005b. 'G20 Proposal: Elements for Discussion on Market Access.' 8 July. <www.agtradepolicy.org/output/resource/G20_Dalian_MarketAccess.pdf> [Accessed: February 2008].
——. 2005c. *G20 Statement: Blue Box*. Room D Consultations, March. <www.g-20.mre.gov.br/conteudo/19082005_Breviario.pdf> [Accessed: February 2008].
——. 2005d. *Two Years of Activities of the G20: Moving Forward the Doha Round*. <www.g-20.mre.gov.br/conteudo/19082005_Breviario.pdf> [Accessed: February 2008].
G33. 2006. 'G33 Press Statement.' 20 April. Geneva. <www.tradeobservatory.org/library.cfm?refID=80711> [Accessed: December 2007].
——. 2005a. *G33 Ministerial Communiqué*. 12 June. Jakarta. <www.crnm.org/documents/press_releases_2005/Adopted%20Communique-12June05.pdf> [Accessed: December 2007].
——. 2005b. 'G33 Press Statement.' 11 October. Geneva. <www.agtradepolicy.org/output/resource/G33StatementOct05.pdf> [Accessed: December 2007].
——. 2005c. *G33 Proposal on Article [...] Special Safeguard Mechanism for Developing Countries*. October. <www.ictsd.org/ministerial/hongkong/docs/G33_Proposal_on_SSM_final1.pdf> [Accessed: December 2007].
——. 2005d. *G33 Proposal on Spacial Safeguard Measures*. JOB(05)/92, 3 June. Geneva.
——. 2005e. *G33 Proposal on the Modalities for the Designation and Treatment of Any Agricultural Product as a Special Product (SP) by Any Developing Country Member*. JOB(05)/304, 22 November. Geneva. <www.agtradepolicy.org/output/resource/G33_proposal_SPs_22Nov05.pdf> [Accessed: December 2007].
Garrett, Geoffrey. 1998. *Partisan Politics in a Global Economy*. Cambridge: Cambridge University Press.
Garrett, James L. and Yassir Islam. 1998. *Policy Research and the Policy Process: Do the Twain Ever Meet?* Gatekeeper Series no. 74. International Institute for Environment and Development, London. <www.iied.org/pubs/pdfs/6138IIED.pdf> [Accessed: March 2008].
Gaston, Noel, and Daniel Trefler. 1997. 'The Labour Market Consequences of the Canada-U.S. Free Trade Agreement.' *Canadian Journal of Economics* 30(1):18–41.
——. 1994. 'The Role of International Trade and Trade Policy in the Labour Markets of Canada and the United States.' *World Economy* 17(1):45–62.
George, A.L. and A. Bennett. 2005. *Case Studies and Theory Development in the Social Sciences*. Cambridge, MA: MIT Press.

George, Clive, and Bernice Goldsmith. 2006. 'Impact Assessment of Trade-Related Policies and Agreements: Experience and Challenges.' *Impact Assessment and Project Appraisal* 24(4):254–258.

George, Henry. 1886. *Protection or Free Trade: An Examination of the Tariff Question with Especial Regard for the Interests of Labor*. New York: Robert Schalkenbach Foundation, 1980.

Ghoneim, Ahmed Farouk. 2006. 'Law Making for Trade Liberalization and Investment Promotion in Egypt.' In Noha El-Mikawy, ed., *The Imperative of Good Governance: Economic Reform, Political Will, Incentives, and Capacities for Meaningful Participation*. Cairo: Economic Research Forum for the Arab Countries, Iran, and Turkey.

Ghoneim, Ahmed Farouk, and Noha El-Mikawy. 2003. 'Political Economy Aspects of Trade Reform in Egypt.' In Heba Nassar, and Ahmad Ghunaym, eds., *Institutional and Policy Challenges Facing the Egyptian Economy*. Cairo: Center for Economic and Financial Research and Studies.

Giorgi, Débora. 2003. *Mercosur. El Arancel externo común. Propuestas para su reforma*. Paper commissioned by the Ministry of Foreign Affairs, Argentina.

Globerman, Steve. 2000. *Trade Liberalisation and the Migration of Skilled Professionals and Managers: The North American Experience*. London: Blackwell Publishing.

Glover, David, and Diana Tussie, eds. 1993. *The Developing Countries in World Trade: Policies and Bargaining Strategies*. Boulder: Lynne Rienner.

Goldstein, Judith and Robert O. Keohane, eds. 1993. *Ideas and Foreign Policy: Beliefs, Institutions, and Political Change*. Ithaca: Cornell University Press.

Gomez, Rafael, and Morley Gunderson. 2005. 'Does Economic Integration Lead to Social Policy Convergence? An Analysis of North American Linkages and Social Policy.' In Richard Harris, and Thomas Lemieux, eds., *Social and Labour Market Aspects of North American Linkages*. Calgary: University of Calgary Press, 309–356.

——. 2002. 'The Integration of Labour Markets in North America.' In George Hoberg, ed., *Capacity for Choice: Canada in a New North America*. Toronto: University of Toronto, 309–356.

Gourevitch, Peter. 2005. 'Economic Ideas, International Influences, and Domestic Politics: A Comparative Perspective'. In V. Fitzgerald and R. Thorp, eds., *Economic Doctrines in Latin America: Origins, Embedding, and Evolution*. Basingstoke: Palgrave Macmillan.

Grindle, Merilee, and John W. Thomas. 1991. *Public Choices and Policy Change: The Political Economy of Reform in Developing Countries*. Baltimore: Johns Hopkins University Press.

——. 1990. "After the Decision: Implementing Policy Reforms in Developing Countries." *World Development* 18(8):1163–1181.

Grinspun, Ricardo. 1991. "Are Economic Models Reliable Policy Tools? Forecasting Canadian Gains from Free Trade." Paper presented at the conference on 'Critical Perspectives on North American Integration', York University, 6–8 December.

Gunderson, Morley. 2007. 'How Academic Research Shapes Labor and Social Policy.' *Journal of Labor Research* 28(4):573–590.

——. 1999. 'Labour Standards, Income Distribution, and Trade.' *Integration and Trade* 3 (January–February):24–52.

——. 1998. 'Harmonization of Labour Policies under Trade Liberalization.' *Relations industrielles/Industrial Relations* 53(1):24–52.

——. 1993. 'Labour Adjustment Under NAFTA: Canadian Issues.' *North American Outlook* 4(1–2):3–21.

Haas, Peter. 1992. 'Introduction: Epistemic Communities and International Policy Coordination'. *International Organization*, 46(1):1–35.

Haggard, Stephan, Steven Benjamin Webb, and World Bank. 1994. *Voting for Reform: Democracy, Political Liberalization, and Economic Adjustment*. New York: Oxford University Press.

Hall, Peter A., ed. 1989. *The Political Power of Economic Ideas: Keynesianism Across Nations.* Princeton NJ: Princeton University Press.
Hamilton, Robert, and John Whalley. 1985. 'Geographically Discriminatory Trade Arrangements.' *Review of Economics and Statistics* 57(3):446–455.
Harris, Richard, and David Cox. 1985. 'Summary of a Project on the General Equilibrium Evaluation of Canadian Trade Policy.' In John Whalley, ed., *Canada-United States Free Trade.* Toronto: University of Toronto Press.
Harris, Richard. 1985. 'Jobs and Free Trade.' In David Conklin, and Thomas Courchene, eds., *Canadian Trade at a Crossroads: Options for New International Agreements.* Toronto: Ontario Economic Council 188–203.
Harris, Richard, and David Cox. 1984. *Trade, Industrial Policy, and Canadian Manufacturing.* Toronto: Ontario Economic Council.
Hart, Michael. 2005. 'International Trade: Tinker or Transform to Re-energize the Canada-U.S. Economic Relationship.' In David Laidler, and William Robson, eds., *Prospects for Canada: Progress and Challenges Twenty Years after the Macdonald Commission.* Toronto: C.D. Howe Institute, 121–133.
——. 1994. *Decision at Midnight: Inside the Canada-U.S. Free-Trade Negotiations.* Vancouver: University of British Columbia Press.
Hathaway, Dale. 2001. 'A Special Agricultural Safeguard (SAS): Buttressing the Market Access Reforms of Developing Countries.' 21 March. Rome. <www.fao.org/docrep/005/Y3733E/y3733e05.htm> [Accessed: December 2007].
Head, Keith, and John Ries. 1998. 'Immigration and Trade Creation: Econometric Evidence from Canada.' *Canadian Journal of Economics* 31(1):47–62.
Helliwell, John. 2001. 'Canada: Life Beyond the Looking Glass.' *Journal of Economic Perspectives* 15(1):107–124.
Helmy, Omneia. 2005. *The Impact of Trade Liberalization on Government Revenues in Egypt.* ECES Working Paper No. 101. Available in Arabic. Cairo: Egyptian Center for Economic Studies. <www.eces.org.eg/Publications/Index3.asp?l1=4&l2=1&l3=115> [Accessed: April 2007].
Herbst, Jeffrey. 1993. *The Politics of Reform in Ghana, 1982–1991.* Berkeley: University of Califorinia Press.
Hirschman, Albert O. 1976. 'Some Uses of the Exit-Voice Approach: Discussion.' *American Economic Review* 66(2):386–389.
——. 1970. *Exit, Voice, and Loyalty: Responses to Decline in Firms, Organizations, and States.* Cambridge MA: Harvard University Press.
Hoda, Anwarul. 2005. *Special Products: Options for Negotiating Modalities.* Geneva: International Centre for Trade and Sustainable Development. <www.ictsd.org/dlogue/2005-06-16/Hoda.pdf> [Accessed: December 2007].
Hurrell, Andrew, and Amrita Narlikar. 2006. 'A New Politics of Confrontation? Developing Countries at Cancun and Beyond.' *Global Society* 20(4):415–433.
Iglesias, Valeria. 2004. "The Influence of Research in Foreign Trade Policymaking: The Argentine Case." Paper presented at regional workshop on "The Influence of Research in Foreign Trade Policies: The Case of Argentina, Brazil and Chile," FLACSO, Buenos Aires, 18 November.
Informetrica. 1985. *Economic Impacts of Enhanced Trade: National and Provincial Results.* Ottawa: Department of External Affairs.
International Centre for Trade and Sustainable Development. 2007. 'Ag Talks Set to Pick Up as Negotiators Await Falconer's "Hard-Talk" Questions.' *Bridges* 11(13). <www.ictsd.org/weekly/07-04-18/story2.htm> [Accessed: December 2007].
——. 2006. 'Welcome to ICTSD.' Geneva. <www.ictsd.org/about> [Accessed: December 2007].
——. 2005a. *Special Products and the Special Safeguard Mechanism: Strategic Options for Developing Countries.* Geneva. <www.ictsd.org/dlogue/2005-11-25/SPs%20and%20the%20SSM%20Strategic%20Options%20Paper.pdf> [Accessed: December 2007].

—— 2005b. *Strategic Options for Developing Countries.* Issue Paper No. 6, December. Geneva. <www.agtradepolicy.org/output/ictsd/dialogues/2006-04-01/SP-SSM.pdf> [Accessed: December 2007].

——. 2004. *Special Products and the Special Safeguard Mechanism: An Introduction to the Debate and Key Issues in the Context of WTO Agricultural Negotiations.* ICTSD Background Paper. Geneva. <www.agtradepolicy.org/output/ictsd/dialogues/2004-09-30/ICTSD_paper.pdf> [Accessed: December 2007].

——. <www.agtradepolicy.org/output/resource/PakSPJan07.pdf> [Accessed: December 2007].

International Monetary Fund. 2005. *Nigeria: Request for a Two-Year Policy Support Instrument.* IMF Country Report No. 05/432. Washington DC: International Monetary Fund. <www.imf.org/external/pubs/ft/scr/2005/cr05432.pdf> [Accessed: 13 November 2007].

Inwood, Gregory. 2005. *Continentalizing Canada: The Politics and Legacy of the Macdonald Commission.* Toronto: University of Toronto Press.

——. 1998. "The Universe Is in Trouble: Please Advise—Social Science Research and Knowledge Utilization in the Research Program of the Macdonald Commission." Paper presented at the annual general meeting of the Canadian Political Science Association, Ottawa, 31 May.

Ivanic, Maros, and Will Martin. 2006. *Potential Implications of Agricultural Special Products for Poverty in Low-Income Countries.* Draft of 16 October. Minneapolis: Institute for Agriculture and Trade Policy. <www.tradeobservatory.org/library.cfm?refID=89834> [Accessed: December 2007].

Jacobsen, John. 1995. 'Much Ado about Ideas: The Cognitive Factor in Economic Policy'. *World Politics*, 47(2):283–310.

Jaitley, Arun. 2003. "Statement by H.E. Mr. Arun Jaitley, Minister of Commerce and Industry and Law and Justice." WT/MIN(03)/ST/7, Cancun, 10 September 2003. Geneva: World Trade Organization.

Jales, Mário, and Maria H. Tachinardi. 2006. *Devising a Comprehensive IBSA Strategy on WTO Agriculture Negotiations: The Case of Brazil.* Sao Paolo: Institute for International Trade Negotiations. <www.iconebrasil.com.br/en/?actA=8&areaID=8&secaoID=73&artigoID=1277> [Accessed: February 2008].

Jales, Mario. 2005. *Tariff Reduction, Special Products, and Special Safeguards: An Analysis of the Agricultural Tariffs Structures of G33 Countries.* July. Geneva: International Centre for Trade and Sustainable Development. <www.agtradepolicy.org/output/resource/Jalesfinal.pdf> [Accessed: December 2007].

Jenkins, Rob. 1999. *Democratic Politics and Economic Reform in India.* Cambridge: Cambridge University Press.

Jenson, Jane. 1994. 'Commissioning Ideas: Representation and Royal Commissions.' In Susan Phillips, ed., *How Ottawa Spends 1994–95.* Ottawa: Carleton University Press.

Joekes, Susan and Rohinton Medhora. 2001. *Trade Policies in Developing Countries: What role for capacity building and research?* IDRC, Ottawa: 5.

Jordana, Jacint and Carles Ramió. 2002. *Diseños institucionales y gestión de la política comercial exterior en América Latina.* Institution for the Integration of Latin America and the Caribbean, Buenos Aires.

Kahler, Miles. 1992. 'External Influence, Conditionality, and the Politics of Adjustment'. In S. Haggard and R.R. Kaufman, eds., *The Politics of Economic Adjustment: International Constraints, Distributive Conflicts, and the State.* Princeton NJ: Princeton University Press.

Keeler, John T.S. 1993. 'Opening the Window for Reform: Mandates, Crises, and Extraordinary Policy Making'. *Comparative Political Studies*, 25(4):433–486.

Kesselman, Jonathan. 2005. 'Labour Markets and Social Policy: Impacts of the Macdonald Commission Report.' In David Laidler, and William Robson, eds., *Prospects for Canada: Progress and Challenges Twenty Years after the Macdonald Commission.* Toronto: C.D. Howe Institute, 67–82.

Keystone accountability. 2006. Developing a Theory of Change: A framework for accountability and learning for social change. London: Keystone accountability.

Kheir El-Din, Hanaa. 2008. *The Political Economy of Trade Policy in the Middle East and North Africa: A Study of Selected Sectors in Egypt and Morocco.* Research Report. Economic Research Forum for the Arab Countries, Iran, and Turkey. <www.erf.org.eg/CMS/getFile.php?id=1184> [Accessed: May 2008]

Kheir El-Dinn, Hanaa, and Ahmed El-Dersh. 1992. 'Foreign Trade Policy in Egypt: 1986–1991.' In Said El-Naggar, ed., *Foreign and Intra-Regional Trade Policies of Arab Countries*. Kuwait: Arab Monetary Fund.

Killoran, Amanda, Catherine Swann, Michael P. Kelly, eds. 2006. *Public Health Evidence: Tackling health inequalities*. Oxford, New York: Oxford University Press.

Kingdon, John W. 1984. *Agendas, Alternatives, and Public Policies*. Boston: Little, Brown.

Kirkpatrick, Colin, and Clive George. 2006. 'Methodological Issues in the Impact Assessment of Trade Policy: Experience from the European Commission's Sustainability Impact Assessment (SIA) Programme.' *Impact Assessment and Project Appraisal* 24(4):325–334.

Kirkpatrick, Colin, and Norman Lee. 2002. *Further Development of the Methodology for a Sustainability Impact Assessment of Proposed WTO Negotiations.* Institute for Development Policy and Management and Environmental Impact Assessment Centre, University of Manchester. <www.sia-gcc.org/gcc/download/new_method_april_2002_civil.pdf> [Accessed: January 2008].

Kirkpatrick, Colin, Norman Lee, and Oliver Morrissey. 1999. *WTO New Round: Sustainability Impact Assessment Study, Phase One Report.* Institute for Development Policy and Management and Environmental Impact Assessment Centre, University of Manchester, and Centre for Research on Economic Development and International Trade, University of Nottingham. <www.sia-trade.org/wto/Phase1/frontpage1.htm> [Accessed: January 2008].

Krueger, Anne O. 1993. *Political Economy of Policy Reform in Developing Countries.* Cambridge: Cambridge University Press.

Laird, Sam and Patrick Messerlin. 1990. 'Institutional Reform for Trade Liberalization'. *World Economy*, 13(2):230–249.

Lall, Sanjaya. 2000. *Selective Industrial and Trade Policies in Developing Countries: Theoretical and Empirical Issues.* Working Paper No. QEHWPS48. Oxford: Queen Elizabeth House, University of Oxford. <ideas.repec.org/p/qeh/qehwps/qehwps48.html> [Accessed: 13 November 2007].

Lamy, Pascal. 2005. *Trade Can Be a Friend, and Not a Foe, of Conservation.* Speech at the WTO Symposium on Trade and Sustainable Development, 10–11 October. Geneva: World Trade Organization. <www.wto.org/english/news_e/sppl_e/sppl07_e.htm> [Accessed: January 2008].

Langille, Brian. 1996. 'General Reflections on the Relationship of Trade and Labor (Or Fair Trade Is free Trade's Destiny.' In Jagdish Bhagwati, and Robert Hudec, eds., *Fair Trade and Harmonization*, vol. 2, Legal Analysis. Cambridge MA: Harvard University Press, 231–266.

Lavagna, Roberto. 2001. 'Los desafíos del Mercosur.' In Daniel Chudnovsky, and J.M. Fanelli, eds., *El disafío de integrarse para crecer: balance y perspectivas del Mercosur en su primera década*. Buenos Aires: Signo XXI de Argentina Editores.

Lindquist, Evert A. 2001. *Discerning Policy Influence: Framework for a Strategic Evaluation of IDRC-Supported Research.* Background paper. International Development Research Centre, Ottawa.

Livny, Eric, Archana Mehendale and Alf Vanags. 2006. Bridging the Research Policy Gaps in Developing and Transition Countries: Analytical lessons and proposals for action. Global Development Network. http://www.gdnet.org/middle.php?oid=1283.

Mably, Paul. 2007. *The Role of Research on Trade Policy Changes Affecting the Developing World: Group of 33 Influence at the World Trade Organization.* Working Paper No. 77. Buenos Aires: Facultad Latinoamericana de Ciencias Sociales. <www.latn.org.ar/archivos/documentacion/PAPER_DOC77%20WP_%20Mably_%20G33-ICTSD%20trade%20policy%20change%20episodes%20study.pdf> (January 2008).

——. 2006. *Evidence Based Advocacy: NGO Research Capacities and Policy Influence in the Field of International Trade.* IDRC Working Papers on Globalization, Growth, and Poverty No. 4. Ottawa: International Development Research Centre. <www.idrc.ca/uploads/user-S/11727031851GGPWP4-NGO.pdf> [Accessed: December 2007].

Macdonald, Donald. 2005. 'The Commission's Work and Report: A Personal Perspective.' In David Laidler, and William Robson, eds., *Prospects for Canada: Progress and Challenges Twenty Years after the Macdonald Commission.* Toronto: C.D. Howe Institute, 5–12.

Magun, Sunder, Someshwar Rao, Bimal Lodh, Laval Lavallée, and Jonathan Pierce. 1988. *Open Borders: An Assessment of the Canada-U.S. Free Trade Agreement.* Discussion Paper No. 331. Ottawa: Economic Council of Canada.

Mamaty, Isabelle. 2003. "Study on the Strategic Products for African Countries." November. African Union.

Marchat, Jean Michel, and Taoufik Rajhi. 2004. *Estimates of the Impact of a Common External Tariff on the Nigerian Manufacturing Sector: Some Simulation Results Based on Firm-Level Data.* Working paper. Washington DC: World Bank.

Mbekeani, Kennedy, Taimoon Stewart and Nguyen Thang. 2003. "Viewpoint: WTO—The Knowledge Deficit in Trade Negotiations." International Development Research Centre. <www.idrc.ca/en/ev-44739-201-1-DO_TOPIC.html> [Accessed: 6 November, 2007].

McBride, Stephen, and Russell Williams. 2001. 'Globalization, the Restructuring of Labour Markets, and Policy Convergence.' *Global Social Policy* 1(3):281–309.

McMahon, Gary and Fernando Porta. 2007. *Evaluating the MERCUSUR Network: Research, Outreach, and Organization.* MercoNet and International Development Research Centre.

Milner, Helen and Keiko Kubota. 2001. *Why the Rush to Free Trade? Democracy and Trade Policy in the Developing Countries.* Paper prepared for the annual meeting of the American Political Science Association. San Francisco.

Milner, Helen, Edward Mansfield, and Peter Rosendorff. 2000. 'Free to Trade? Democracies, Autocracies, and International Trade Negotiations'. *American Political Science Review,* 94(2):305–322.

Minogue, Martin. 1997. 'Theory and Practice in Public Policy and Administration'. In M.J. Hill, ed., *The Policy Process: A Reader*, 2nd edition. New York: Harvester-Wheatsheaf.

NAFTA Environmental Review Committee (Canada). 1992. *North American Free Trade Agreement: Canadian Environmental Review.* October. Ottawa: Government of Canada.

Narlikar, Amrita, and John S. Odell. 2006. 'The Strict Distributive Strategy for a Bargaining Coalition: The Like-Minded Group and the World Trade Organization.' In John S. Odell, ed., *Negotiating Trade: Developing Countries in the WTO and NAFTA.* Cambridge: Cambridge University Press.

Narlikar, Amrita. 2005. *Bargaining over the Doha Development Agenda: Coalitions in the World Trade Organization.* Working Paper No. 36. Latin American Trade Network.

Narlikar, Amrita. 2005. *The World Trade Organization: A Very Short Introduction.* New York: Oxford University Press.

Narlikar, Amrita, and Diana Tussie. 2004. 'The G20 at the Cancun Ministerial: Developing Countries and Their Evolving Coalitions in the WTO.' *World Economy* 27(7):947–966.

Nash, John and Wendy Takacs. 1998. *Trade Policy Reform: Lessons and Implications*. World Bank, Washington DC.

Neilson, Stephanie. 2001. *Knowledge Utilization and Public Policy Processes: A Literature Review*. Evaluation Unit, International Development Research Centre, Ottawa.

Nigeria. Federal Ministry of Commerce. 2006. *Minutes of Tariff Technical Meeting* BD.12237/S.403T, 17 October. Abuja: Federal Ministry of Commerce.

——. Federal Ministry of Finance. 2003. *Comprehensive Review of Nigeria's Customs and Excise Tariffs: Framework Paper and Summary of Reports*. Abuja: Federal Ministry of Finance.

Niño, Jaime. 2004. *What Determines Trade Regimes and Reforms? The Role of Ideas and Democracy*. Paper presented at the annual meeting of the American Political Science Association. Chicago.

Nutley, Sandra, Isabel Walter, and Huw Davies. 2003. 'From Knowing to Doing: A Framework for Understanding the Evidence-into-Practice Agenda'. *Evaluation*, 9(2):125–148.

Odell, John S., ed. 2006. *Negotiating Trade: Developing Countries in the WTO and NAFTA*. Cambridge: Cambridge University Press.

Olympio, John. 2006. *Needs Assessment of the Trade Department of ECOWAS for EPA Negotiations*. Report prepared for the ECOWAS Secretariat.

Organisation for Economic Co-operation and Development. 1994. *Methodologies for Environmental and Trade Reviews*. OCDE/GD(94)103. Paris: Organisation for Economic Co-operation and Development. <www.olis.oecd.org/olis/1994doc.nsf/linkto/ocde-gd(94)103> [Accessed: January 2008].

Oxfam International. 2008. 'Make Trade Fair'. <www.maketradefair.com> [Accessed: May 2008].

Overseas Development Institute. nd. Website. http://www.odi.org.uk/rapid/Tools/Toolkits/Policy_Impact/docs/episode_studies.pdf

Pakistan, Delegation of. 2007. *Special Products: Possible Elements for Discussion*. 19 January.

Papageorgiou, Demetris, Armeane M. Choksi, and Michael Michaely. 1990. *Liberalizing Foreign Trade in Developing Countries: The Lessons of Experience*. Washington DC: World Bank.

Parliament of Canada. 1970. The International Development Research Centre Act.

Patton, Michael Quinn. 1997. *Utilization Focused Evaluation: The new century text*. Third edition. NY: Sage Publications.

Pawson, Ray. 2006a. *Evidence-based Policy: A realist perspective*. London, Thousand Oaks, New Delhi: Sage.

——. 2006b. "Simple Principles for the Evaluation of Complex Programmes," in Killoran, Amanda, Catherine Swann, Michael P. Kelly, eds. 2006. *Public Health Evidence: Tackling health inequalities*. Oxford, New York: Oxford University Press: 223–238.

——. 2005. Method Mix, Technical Hex, Theory Fix. Presentation to the International Conference on Mixed Methods Research Design.

Permanent Mission of Brazil. 2004. *The Blended Formula: A Fundamentally Flawed Approach to Agricultural Market Access*. TN/AG/GEN/9, 7 May. Geneva: World Trade Organization. <docsonline.wto.org:80/DDFDocuments/t/tn/ag/GEN9.doc> [Accessed: February 2008].

Philippines, Permanent Mission of the. 2006. *Statement by the Delegation of the Philippines on Special Products*. 1 May, JOB(06)/131. Geneva. <www.philippineswto.org/Phi_Stat/phi_stat_on_sp.htm> [Accessed: December 2007].

Pomareda, Carlos. 2005. *Lessons from the Experience with Special Products and Safeguard Mechanisms in Bilateral Trade Agreements*. June. Geneva: International Centre for Trade and Sustainable Development. <www.ictsd.org/dlogue/2005-06-16/Pomareda.pdf> [Accessed: December 2007].

Popper, Karl. 1963. *Conjectures and Refutations*. NY: Routledge.

Porta, Fernando, and Jorge Fontanals. 1989. 'La integratión intraindustrial: el caso del Acuerdo Argentino Brasileño en el sector de bienes de capital.' *Integracíon Latinoamericana* 152:14–15.

Priyadarshi, Shishir. 2004. *Decision-Making Processes in India: The Case of the Agriculture Negotiations.* Case Study 15. Geneva: World Trade Organization. <www.wto.org/english/res_e/booksp_e/casestudies_e/case15_e.htm> [Accessed: February 2008].

Przeworski, Adam. 1991. *Democracy and the Market: Political and Economic Reforms in Eastern Europe and Latin America.* Cambridge: Cambridge University Press.

Rebizo, Maria Marta, and Ariel R. Ibañez. 2007. 'Sensitive Products: The July Modalities Text Made Plain.' *Bridges* 11(6):5–6. <www.ictsd.org/monthly/bridges/BRIDGES11-6.pdf> [Accessed: February 2008].

Refaat, Amal. 2003. *Trade-Induced Protection for Egypt's Manufacturing Sector.* ECES Working Paper No. 85. Cairo: Egyptian Center for Economic Studies. <www.eces.org.eg/Publications/Index3.asp?l1=4&l2=1&l3=98> [Accessed: April 2007].

——. 1999. *New Trends in Egypt's Trade Policy and Future Challenges.* ECES Working Paper No. 36. Cairo: Egyptian Center for Economic Studies. <www.eces.org.eg/Publications/Index3.asp?l1=4&l2=1&l3=36> [Accessed: April 2007].

Reich, Robert. 1991. *The Work of Nations: Preparing Ourselves for Twenty-First Century Capitalism.* London: Simon and Schuster.

Remmer, Karen. 1990. 'Democracy and Economic Crisis: The Latin American Experience'. *World Politics,* 42(3):315–335.

Restier-Melleray, Christiane. 1990. 'Experts et expertise scientifique: le cas de la France.' *Revue française de sciences politiques* 40(4):546–585.

Richardson, J. David. 1995. 'Income Inequality and Trade: How to Think, What to Conclude.' *Journal of Economic Perspectives* 9(3):33–55.

Riddell, W. Craig. 2005. 'Labour Markets and Social Policy: What the Macdonald Commission Said.' In David Laidler, and William Robson, eds., *Prospects for Canada: Progress and Challenges Twenty Years after the Macdonald Commission.* Toronto: C.D. Howe Institute, 53–66.

Rius, Andrés. 2003. *The Knowledge Systems Implications of Building Institutions for High-Quality Growth.* Working paper. International Development Research Centre, Ottawa.

Robinson, Ian. 1998. 'NAFTA, Social Unionism, and Labour Movement Power in Canada and the United States.' *Relations industrielles/Industrial Relations* 49(4):657–693.

Rodriguez, Francisco, and Dani Rodrik. 1999. *Trade Policy and Economic Growth: A Skeptic's Guide to Cross-National Evidence.* WBER Working Paper No. 7081. Cambridge MA: National Bureau of Economic Research.

Rodrik, Dani. 1997. *Has Globalization Gone Too Far?* Washington DC: Institute for International Economics.

——. 1995. 'Political Economy of Trade Policy'. In G.M. Grossman and K. Rogoff, eds., *Handbook of International Economics.* New York: Elsevier.

Royal Commission on the Economic Union and Development Prospects for Canada. 1985. *Report of the Royal Commission on the Economic Union and Development Prospects for Canada.* Donald Macdonald, chair. Ottawa: Minister of Supply and Services Canada.

Royal Society for the Protection of Birds, and Birdlife International. 2003. *Trade and Environment: Sustainable Development (and Sustainability Impact Assessments).* Sandy, Bedfordshire, and Cambridge. <www.birdlife.org/action/change/trade/sdsia.pdf> [Accessed: January 2008].

Ruffer, Tim, Val Imber, and Jibrin Ibrahim. 2004. *The Political Economy of Trade Policy in Nigeria.* Prepared for the Department for International Development (Nigeria), mimeo.

Ruffer, Tim. 2004. *An Assessment of Nigeria's Import Prohibitions Policy.* Study prepared for the United Kingdom Department for International Development. Oxford: Oxford Policy Management.

——. 2003. *Special Products: Thinking Through the Details.* June. Oxford: Oxford Policy Management. <www.opml.co.uk/document.rm?id=416> [Accessed: December 2007].

Ruffer, Tim, and Paolo Vergano. 2002. *An Agricultural Safeguard Mechanism for Developing Countries.* Oxford and Brussels: Oxford Policy Management and O'Connor and Company. <www.agtradepolicy.org/output/resource/Ruffer_SSM.pdf> [Accessed: December 2007].

Sabatier, Paul A. and Hank C. Jenkins-Smith, eds. 1993. *Policy Change and Learning: An Advocacy Coalition Approach.* Boulder: Westview Press.

Sachs, Jeffrey, and Andrew Warner. 1995. "Economic Reform and the Process of Global Integration." In George L. Perry, and William C. Brainard, eds., *Brookings Papers on Economic Activity 1995.* Washington DC: Brookings Institution Press, 1–118.

Saner, Raymond. 2001. 'WTO versus Regional Trade Agreements'. In R. Saner and I. Maidana, eds., *Trade Negotiation Cases, Analyses, Strategies at Bilateral, Regional, and Multilateral Levels, Bolivia, 2000.* Bolivia: Editorial "Los Amigos del Libro".

Sassen, Saskia. 1988. *The Mobility of Labor and Capital: A Study in International Investment and Labor Flow.* Cambridge: Cambridge University Press.

Schmitz, Hubert. 2007. 'Reducing Complexity in the Industrial Policy Debate'. *Development Policy Review,* 25(4):417–428.

Shaffer, Gregory, Michelle Ratton Sanchez, and Barbara Rosenberg. 2006. *Brazil's Response to the Judicialized WTO Regime: Strengthening the State through Diffusing Expertise.* Working draft prepared for the ICTSD South America Dialogue on WTO Dispute Settlement and Sustainable Development, 22–23 June, Sao Paolo. Geneva: International Centre for Trade and Sustainable Development. <www.ictsd.org/issarea/dsu/resources/Brazil_paper.pdf> [Accessed: February 2008].

Sharma, Ramesh. 2006. *Triggers and Remedy for Special Safeguard Mechanism.* Rome: Food and Agriculture Organization. <www.agtradepolicy.org/output/resource/Sharma_SSM_Dec06.pdf> [Accessed: December 2007].

Shepsle, Kenneth. 1985. 'A Comment on Derthick and Quirk'. In R.G. Noll, ed., *Regulatory Policy and the Social Sciences.* Berkeley: University of California Press.

SIA-EMFTA Consortium. 2006. *Sustainability Impacts of the Euro-Mediterranean Free Trade Agreement: Final Report on Phase 2 of the SIA-EMFTA Project.* Impact Assessment Research Centre, University of Manchester. <www.sia-trade.org/emfta/en/Reports/Phase2FinalreportMar06.pdf> [Accessed: January 2008].

Simeon, Richard, George Hoberg, and Keith Banting. 1997. 'Globalization, Fragmentation, and the Social Contract.' In Keith Banting, George Hoberg, and Richard Simeon, eds., *Degrees of Freedom: Canada and the United States in a Changing World.* Montreal and Kingston: McGill-Queen's University Press.

Simeon, Richard. 1987. 'Inside the Macdonald Commission.' *Studies in Political Economy* 22(Spring):167–179.

Smith, William, Carlos Acuña, and Eduardo Gamarra. 1994. *Democracy, Markets, and Structural Reform in Contemporary Latin America: Argentina, Bolivia, Brazil, Chile, and Mexico.* Transaction Publishers, New Brunswick NJ.

Solidar. 2005. *Trade for Decent Work, Decent Life: Assessment before Agreement.* Statement for the 6th World Trade Organization ministerial, Hong Kong.

Sonnen, Carl, and Mike McCracken. 1985. 'Free Trade: The Economic Case Is Positive.' *Monthly Economic Review* 4(11).

South Centre. 2006. *State of Play in Agricultural Negotiations: Country Groupings' Positions.* SC/AN/TDP/AG/1-1, November. Geneva. <www.southcentre.org/publications/AnalyticalNotes/Agriculture/Stateofplay_October2006_FINAL_MA.pdf> [Accessed: December 2007].

——. 2003. *Proposals on a Special Safeguard for Developing Countries in Agriculture.* SC/TADP/AN/AG/5, July. Geneva. <www.southcentre.org/publications/AnalyticalNotes/

Agriculture/2003Jul_Special_Agriculture_Safeguards_Proposals.pdf> [Accessed: December 2007].

Squire, Lyn. 2002. "Bridging Research and Policy: An Overview." Paper prepared for ABCDE, Oslo, June. <wbln0018.worldbank.org/eurvp/web.nsf/Pages/Paper+by+Lyn+Squire/$File/SQUIRE.PDF> [Accessed: January 2008].

Stallings, Barbara. 1992. 'International influence on Economic Policy: Debt, Stabilization, and Structural Reform'. In S. Haggard and R.R. Kaufman, eds., *The Politics of Economic Adjustment: International Constraints, Distributive Conflicts, and the State.* Princeton NJ: Princeton University Press.

Stevens, Christopher. 2004. *The Need for Special Products and Special Safeguard Mechanisms for Agriculture in the WTO: A Situational Analysis.* 30 September. Geneva: Institute of Development Studies. <www.agtradepolicy.org/output/ictsd/dialogues/2004-09-30/Stevens_paper.pdf> [Accessed: December 2007].

Stokes, D.E. 1997. *Pasteur's Quadrant: Basic science and technological innovation.* Washington, DC: Brookings Institution Press.

Stokes, Ernie. 1989. 'Macroeconomic Impact of the Canada-U.S. Free Trade Agreement.' *Journal of Policy Modeling* 11(2):225–245.

Stolper, Wolfgang, and Paul Samuelson. 1941. 'Protection and Real Wages.' *Review of Economic Studies* 9(1):58–73.

Stone, Diane and Andrew Denham, eds. 2004. *Think Tank Traditions: Policy Research and the Politics of Ideas.* Manchester: Manchester University Press.

Stone, Diane. 2002. 'Using Knowledge: The Dilemmas of Bridging Research and Policy'. *Compare,* 32(3):285–296.

Stone, Diane, Simon Maxwell, and Michael Keating. 2001. "Bridging Research and Policy." Paper prepared for an international workshop funded by the United Kingdom Department for International Development, Warwick University, 16–17 July. <www.gdnet.org/pdf/Bridging.pdf> [Accessed: January 2008].

Stone, Diane. 2000. 'Knowledge, Power, and Policy'. In D. Stone, ed., *Banking on Knowledge: The Genesis of the Global Development Network.* London: Routledge.

SUSTRA. 2003. *Sustainability Impact Assessment: Policy Brief Paper.* Based on the SUSTRA seminar on "Sustainability Impact Assessment, 26–27 April 2003, Center for Philosophy of Law (CPDR), Université catholique de Louvain, Louvain-la-Neuve. Montellier. <www.agro-montpellier.fr/sustra/publications/policy_briefs/policy-brief-sia-eng.pdf> [Accessed: January 2008].

Taylor, Lance and Rudiger Von Arnim. 2006. *Modelling the Impact of Trade Liberalisation: A Critique of Computable General Equilibrium Models.* Oxfam Research Report. Oxfam, Oxford.

Trefler, Daniel. 2005. 'International Trade: 20 Years of Failed Economics and Successful Economies.' In David Laidler, and William Robson, eds., *Prospects for Canada: Progress and Challenges Twenty Years after the Macdonald Commission.* Toronto: C.D. Howe Institute, 111–121.

——. 2004. 'The Long and the Short of the Canada-U.S. Trade Agreement.' *American Economic Review* 94(4):870–895.

Trudeau, Gilles, and Guylaine Vallée. 1994. 'Economic Integration and Labour Law and Policy in Canada.' In Maria Cook, and Harry Katz, eds., *Regional Integration and Industrial Relations in North America.* Ithaca: ILR Press, 66–81.

Tsebelis, George. 1995. 'Decision Making in Political Systems: Veto Players in Presidentialism, Parliamentarism, Multicameralism, and Multipartyism.' *British Journal of Political Science* 25:289–325.

Tussie, Diana. 2006. *Understanding the Use of Research in Trade Policy.* Document prepared after "The Use of Research in Trade Policy: Workshop to Understand the Contributions from Episodic Studies. Buenos Aires.

——. 1987. *The Less Developed Countries and the World Trading System: A Challenge to the GATT.* London: Frances Pinter.

United States Agency for International Development. 2005. *FY 2005 Statutory Checklists*. Washington DC. <www.usaid.gov/policy/ads/200/202saa.pdf> [Accessed: May 2008]

——. 2005. *ECOWAS Common External Tariff (ECOTrade) Recommendations Regarding Changes in Tariff Rates*. van de Walle, Nicolas. 2001. *African Economies and the Politics of Permanent Crisis, 1979–1999*. Cambridge: Cambridge University Press.

United States Trade Representative. 1993. *The NAFTA: Report on Environmental Issues*. Washington DC: Office of the United States Trade Representative.

Valdés, Alberto, and William Foster. 2005. *The New SSM: A Price Floor Mechanism for Developing Countries*. April. Geneva: International Centre for Trade and Sustainable Development. <www.ictsd.org/dlogue/2005-06-16/Valdes.pdf> [Accessed: December 2007].

Vibe, Maja de, Ingie Hovland and John Young. 2002. Bridging Research and Policy: An annotated bibliography. ODI Working Paper 174. London: Overseas Development Institute.

Webber, David J. 1991. 'The Distribution and Use of Policy Knowledge in the Policy Process'. *Knowledge and Policy*, 4(4):6–36.

Weick, Karl E., Kathleen M. Sutcliffe and David Obsstfeld. 2005. "Organizing and the Processes of Sensemaking," in *Organization Science*. 16(4):409–421.

Weiss, Carol H. 2003. *Studying Research Utilization*. A speech at IDRC, 24 March. Ottawa: IDRC Evaluation Unit.

——. 2002. *What to Do Until the Random Assigner Comes*. in, *Evidence Matters: Randomized trials in education research*. Frederick Mosteller and Robert Boruch, eds. Washington, DC: Brookings Institution Press. 198–224.

——. 1991. 'Policy Research as Advocacy: Pro and Con'. *Knowledge and Policy*, 4(1/2):37–56.

——. 1982. 'Knowledge Utilization in Decision Making: Reflections on the terms of the discussion,' in, *Research in Sociology of Education and Socialization*. 3:21.

——. 1979. 'The Many Meanings of Research Utilization.' *Public Administration Review* 39(5):426–431.

——. 1977. *Using Social Research in Public Policy Making*. Lexington, MA: Lexington Books., DC heath and Co.

——. 1977. 'Research for Policy's Sake: The Enlightenment Function of Social Research.' *Policy Analysis* 3(4):531–545.

Winham, Gil. 2005. 'International Trade: What the Macdonald Commission Said.' In David Laidler, and William Robson, eds., *Prospects for Canada: Progress and Challenges Twenty Years after the Macdonald Commission*. Toronto: C.D. Howe Institute, 99–110.

Winters, L. Alan, Neil McCulloch, and Andrew McKay. 2004. 'Trade Liberalization and Poverty: The Evidence So Far'. *Journal of Economic Literature*, 42(1):72–115

Wonnacott, Ronald, and Paul Wonnacott. 1967. *Free Trade between the United States and Canada: The Potential Economic Effects*. Cambridge MA: Harvard University Press.

Wood, Adrian. 1995. 'How Trade Hurt Unskilled Workers.' *Journal of Economic Perspectives* 9(3):57–80.

World Bank. 2005. *World Development Report 2005: A Better Investment Climate for Everyone*. Washington DC: World Bank and Oxford University Press. <siteresources.worldbank.org/INTWDR2005/Resources/complete_report.pdf> [Accessed: January 2008].

——. 2006. *Nigeria: Country Economic Memorandum*. Draft. Washington DC: World Bank.

World Trade Organization. 2008. *The Cancun Draft 'Frameworks'*. Geneva. <www.wto.org/english/tratop_e/agric_e/frameworks_e.htm> [Accessed: February 2008].

WWF. 2002. *Changing the Balance of Trade: A Seminar on Sustainability Assessments of EU Trade Policy*. 9–10 July. Brussels. <www.panda.org/downloads/policy/july2002 balancedtradeproceedings_mt0n.doc> [Accessed: January 2008].

World Trade Organization. 2007. *Statistics Database.* Trade Profile for Egypt, October. <stat.wto.org> [Accessed: January 2008].
——. 2006. "Communication from India: Proposal on GATT Article VIII." TN/TF/W/77, 10 February. Geneva: World Trade Organization.
——. 2006. *Chairman's Reference Paper: Special Products.* 4 May. Geneva. <www.wto.org/english/tratop_e/agric_e/ref_paper_sp_e.pdf> [Accessed: December 2007].
——. 2006. "Communication from India: Proposals on GATT Article X." TN/TF/W/78, 13 February. Geneva: World Trade Organization.
——. 2006. *Draft Possible Modalities on Agriculture.* Crawford Falconer, Chair, Committee on Agriculture. TN/AG/W/3, 12 July. Geneva. <www.wto.org/english/tratop_e/agric_e/mod_ag_12jul_e.pdf> [Accessed: December 2007].
——. 2005. *Ministerial Declaration.* WT/MIN(05)/Dec, 18 December. Hong Kong. <www.wto.org/English/thewto_e/minist_e/min05_e/final_text_e.htm> [Accessed: February 2008].
——. 2005. *Trade Policy Review: Nigeria.* Geneva: World Trade Organization.
——. 2005. *Trade Policy Review: Report by Egypt.* WT/TPR/G/150/Rev.1. Geneva: World Trade Organization. <docsonline.wto.org:80/DDFDocuments/t/WT/TPR/S150R1-0.doc> [Accessed: January 2008].
——. 2004. *Text of the 'July Package': The General Council's Post-Cancun Decision.* WT/L/579, 1 August. <www.wto.org/english/tratop_e/dda_e/draft_text_gc_dg_31july04_e.htm> [Accessed: February 2008].
——. 2003. "Minutes of the Meeting of the Council for Trade in Goods, 12–13 June 2003." G/C/M/70, 19 August 2003. Geneva: World Trade Organization.
——. 2003a. *Agriculture: Framework Proposal.* WT/MIN(03)/W/6, 4 September. Cancun. <docsonline.wto.org/imrd/directdoc.asp?DDFDocuments/t/WT/MIN03/W6.doc> [Accessed: February 2008].
——. 2003b. *Annexes to the Draft Cancun Ministerial Text.* Second revision, 13 September. Cancun. <www.wto.org/english/thewto_e/minist_e/min03_e/draft_decl_annex_rev2_e.htm> [Accessed: February 2008].
——. 2003b. *Negotiations on Agriculture: First Drat of Modalities for the Further Commitments, Revision.* TN/AG/W/1/Rev.1, 18 March. Geneva. <docsonline.wto.org/DDFDocuments/t/tn/ag/W1R1.doc> [Accessed: December 2007].
——. 2003c. *Draft Cancun Ministerial Text.* Derbez text. Second revision, 13 September. Cancun. <www.wto.org/english/thewto_e/minist_e/min03_e/draft_decl_rev2_e.htm> [Accessed: February 2008].
——. 2002. *Negotiations on Agriculture: Overview.* TN/AG/6, 18 December. Geneva. <docsonline.wto.org/DDFDocuments/t/tn/ag/6.doc> [Accessed: December 2007].
——. 2001. 'Ministerial Declaration.' WT/MIN(01)/Dec/01. 14 November. Doha. <www.wto.org/english/thewto_e/minist_e/min01_e/mindecl_e.htm> [Accessed: February 2008].
——. 1999. *Trade Policy Review: Report by the Secretariat.* WT/TPR/S/55. Geneva: World Trade Organization. <docsonline.wto.org:80/DDFDocuments/t/WT/TPR/S55-2.DOC> [Accessed: January 2008].
——. 1998. *Trade Policy Review: Nigeria.* Geneva: World Trade Organization.
Yin, Robert K. *Case Study Research: Design and methods.* 2nd edition. NY: Sage.

INDEX

LaVergne, TN USA
07 April 2010
178499LV00006B/53/P

9 789004 172784